BAROLO TO VALPOLICELLA
The Wines of Northern Italy

Nicolas Belfrage MW was born in Los Angeles and raised in New York and England. He studied in Paris, Siena and London, taking a degree at University College London in French and Italian. The author of the double award-winning *Life Beyond Lambrusco*, published in 1985, he has been working in and writing on Italian wines since the early 1970s. He is a regular contributor to *Decanter* magazine. In 1994 he sold his specialist Italian wine importing business and moved to Tuscany. Today he divides his working life between Florence and London, sloping off to his isolated house in the French department of the Lot when he can't stand the pace any more.

BAROLO TO VALPOLICELLA

The Wines of
Northern Italy

NICOLAS BELFRAGE

faber and faber
LONDON·NEW YORK

First published in 1999
by Faber and Faber Limited
3 Queen Square London WC1N 3AU
Published in the United States by Faber and Faber Inc.,
a division of Farrar, Straus and Giroux Inc., New York

Typeset by Faber and Faber Ltd
Printed in England by Clays Ltd, St Ives plc

Nicolas Belfrage is hereby identified as author of this
work in accordance with Section 77 of the Copyright,
Designs and Patents Act 1988

A CIP record for this book
is available from the British Library

ISBN 0–571–17851–0 (hbk)
0–571–17852–9 (pbk)

2 4 6 8 10 9 7 5 3 1

This first of two I dedicate to my first of two,
Beatriz

Contents

——

CONTENTS

List of profiled producers

Abrigo, Orlando; Treiso, Piemonte (tel. 0173 630232; fax 56120), p. 89

Accomasso, Lorenzo; La Morra, Piemonte (tel. 0173 50843), pp. 64–5

Accordini, Stefano; San Pietro in Cariano, Veneto (tel. 045 7701733), p. 171

Alessandria Gianfranco; Monforte d'Alba, Piemonte (tel. 0173 787222), p. 70

Allegrini; Fumane di Valpolicella, Veneto (tel. 045 7701138; fax 7701774), p. 170

Altare, Elio; La Morra, Piemonte (tel./fax 0173 50835), p. 65

Anselmi, Roberto; Monteforte d'Alpone, Veneto (tel. 045 7611488; fax 7611490), pp. 204–5

Araldica Vini Piemontesi; Castelboglione, Piemonte (tel. 0141 762576; fax 762433), pp. 104–5

Ascheri, Giacomo; Bra, Piemonte (tel. 0173 412394; fax 432021), p. 80

Azelia; Castiglione Falletto, Piemonte (tel./fax 0173 62859), p. 63

Barale, Fratelli; Barolo, Piemonte (tel. 0173 56127; fax 56350), pp. 59–60

Baltieri; Mizzole, Veneto (tel. 045 557616), p. 181

Batasiolo; La Morra, Piemonte (tel. 0173 50130; fax 509258), pp. 65–6

Begali, Lorenzo; San Pietro in Cariano, Veneto (tel. 045 7725148), p. 171

Bellavista; Erbusco, Lombardy (tel. 030 7760276; fax 7760386), pp. 317–18

Bellei, Francesco; Bomporto, Emilia (tel. 059 909117; fax 818100), p. 319

Berlucchi, Guido; Borgonato, Lombardy (tel. 030 984381; fax 984293), p. 314

Bertani; Negrar, Veneto (tel. 045 6020146; fax 6020138), p. 175

Bertini, Luigi; Monticello, Piemonte (tel. 0173 64628; fax 460406), p. 130

Boglietti, Enzo; La Morra, Piemonte (tel. 0173 50330), pp. 102–3

xi

Bolla, Fratelli; Verona, Veneto (tel. 045 8670911; fax 8670912), p. 180
Borgo del Tiglio; Cormons, Friuli-VG (tel. 0481 62166; fax 630845),
p. 252
Borgogno, Giacomo, & Figli; Barolo, Piemonte (tel. 0173 56108; fax
56344), p. 60
Boscaini, Paolo; Marano diValpolicella, Veneto (tel. 045 6800840; fax
6800837), p. 174
Bovio; La Morra, Piemonte (tel. 0173 50190; fax 509580), p. 66
Braida/Bologna; Rocchetta Tanara, Piemonte (tel. 0141 644113; fax
644584), pp. 101–2
Brezza, Giacomo, & Figli; Barolo, Piemonte (tel. 0173 56191; fax
56354), p. 60
Brigaldara/Stefano Cesari; San Pietro in Cariano, Veneto (tel. 045
7701055; fax 6800311), pp. 171–2
Brovia; Castiglione Falletto, Piemonte (tel./fax 0173 62852), p. 63
Brunelli, Giuseppe; San Pietro in Cariano, Veneto (tel. 045 7701118; fax
7702015), p. 172
Bussia Soprana; Monforte d'Alba, Piemonte (tel./fax 039 305182), p. 70
Bussola, Tommaso; Negrar, Veneto (tel./fax 045 7501740), pp. 176–7
Cà dei Frati/Dal Cero; Sirmione, Lombardy (tel./fax 030 919468),
pp. 209–10
Cà del Bosco/Zanella; Erbusco, Lombardy (tel. 030 7760600; fax
7268425), pp. 315–17
Campagnola, Giuseppe; Marano di Valpolicella, Veneto (tel. 045
7703900; fax 7701067), p. 174
Cantina del Castello; Soave, Veneto (tel. 045 7680093; fax 6190099),
pp. 201–2
Cà Rugate; Monteforte d'Alpone (tel. 045 6175082; fax 6175907),
p. 205
Casòn Hirschprunn; Magrè, Alto Adige (tel./fax 0471 817258), pp. 304–5
Castello di Verduno; Verduno, Piemonte (tel. 0172 470122; fax
470298), p. 82
Caudrina; Castiglione Tinella, Piemonte (tel. 0141 855126; fax 855008),
pp. 125–6
Cavallotto, Castiglione Falletto, Piemonte (tel. 0173 62814; fax 62914),
p. 63
Cavicchioli; San Prospero, Emilia (tel. 059 908828; fax 906163), p. 121
Ceretto; Alba, Piemonte (tel. 0173 282582; fax 282383), p. 78
Cesconi; Lavis, Trentino (tel. 0461 240355), pp. 281–2
Chiarlo, Michele; Calamandrana, Piemonte (tel. 0141 75231; fax
75284), p. 80
Ciabot Berton; La Morra, Piemonte (tel./fax 0173 50217), p. 66
Cigliuti, Fratelli; Neive, Piemonte (tel./fax 0173 677185), p. 87

Clerico, Domenico; Monforte d'Alba, Piemonte (tel./fax 0173 78171), pp. 70–71

Coffele; Soave, Veneto (tel. 045 7680007; fax 6198091), p. 202

Colla, Poderi; Alba, Piemonte (tel. 0173 290148; fax 441498), p. 79

Colterenzio, Cantina Sociale; Cornaiano, Alto Adige (tel. 0471 664246; fax 660633), p. 245

Conterno, Aldo; Monforte d'Alba, Piemonte (tel. 0173 78150; fax 787240), pp. 71–2

Conterno, Giacomo; Monforte d'Alba, Piemonte (tel. 0173 78221; fax 787190), pp. 72–3

Conterno Fantino; Monforte d'Alba, Piemonte (tel. 0173 78204; fax 787326), p. 74

Conterno, Paolo; Monforte d'Alba, Piemonte (tel./fax 0173 78415), p. 73

Contratto, Giuseppe; Canelli, Piemonte (tel. 0141 823349; fax 824650), pp. 80–81

Coos, Dario; Nimis, Friuli-VG (tel. 0432 790320), p. 222

Coppo, Luigi; Canelli, Piemonte (tel. 0141823146; fax 832563), p. 276

Corino, Giovanni; La Morra, Piemonte (tel./fax 0173 50219), pp. 66–7

Correggia, Matteo; Canale d'Alba, Piemonte (tel./fax 0173 978009), pp. 103–4

Corteforte; Fumane di Valpolicella, Veneto, p. 170

Corte Sant'Alda; Mezzane di Sotto, Veneto (tel. 045 8880006; fax 8880477), p. 182

Dal Forno, Romano; Cellore d'Illasi, Veneto (tel./fax 045 7834923), pp. 182–3

Degani, Fratelli; Marano di Valpolicella, Veneto (tel. 045 7701850; fax 7701163), p. 174

Dipoli, Peter; Laives, Alto Adige (tel. 0471 954227), pp. 258–9

Dorigo, Girolamo; Buttrio, Friuli-VG (tel. 0432 674268; fax 673373), p. 243

Fantino, Alessandro & Gian Natale; Monforte d'Alba, Piemonte (tel. 0173 787113), p. 74

Felluga, Livio; Cormons, Friuli-VG (tel. 0481 60203; fax 630126), pp. 302–3

Fenocchio, Giacomo; Monforte d'Alba, Piemonte (tel. 0173 78311; fax 787218), p. 74

Fenocchio, Riccardo; Monforte d'Alba, Piemonte (tel. 0173 78335; fax 78606), p. 74

Ferrari, Aleardo; Sant'Ambrogio diValpolicella, Veneto (tel. 045 7701379; fax 7701563), p. 169

Ferrari Fratelli Lunelli; Trento, Trentino (tel. 0461 972311; fax 913008), pp. 322–3

Rosso, Gigi; Castiglione Falletto, Piemonte (tel. 0173 262369; fax 262224), pp. 63–4

Ruggeri & C.; Valdobbiadene, Veneto (tel. 0423 975716; fax 973304), p. 212

Russiz Superiore, Marco Felluga; Capriva del Collio (tel. 0481 99164; fax 960270), pp. 243–4

Sandrone, Luciano; Barolo, Piemonte (tel./fax 0173 56239), pp. 61–2

San Leonardo; Borghetto, Trentino (tel./fax 0464 689004), pp. 248

San Michele Appiano, Cantina Sociale; Appiano, Alto Adige (tel. 0471 664466; fax 660764), pp. 272–4

San Rustico; Marano diValpolicella, Veneto (tel. 045 7703348; fax 6800682), p. 175

Santa Maddalena, Cantina Sociale; Bolzano, Alto Adige (tel. 0471 972944; fax 981624), p. 192

Santa Sofia; San Pietro in Cariano, Veneto (tel. 045 7701074), p. 172

Santi; Illasi, Veneto (tel. 045 6260600; fax 7235772), p. 183

Sartori, Casa Vinicola; Negrar, Veneto (045 6020133; fax 6020134), p. 179

Scarpa, Antica Casa Vinicola; Nizza Monferrato, Piemonte (tel. 0141 721331; fax 702872), pp. 115–16

Scarzello, Giorgio, & Figli; Barolo, Piemonte (tel. 0173 56170), p. 62

Scavino, Paolo; Castiglione Falletto, Piemonte (tel./fax 0173 62850), p. 64

Schiopetto, Mario; Capriva del Friuli, Friuli-VG (tel. 0481 80332; fax 808073), pp. 216–17

Sebaste, Mauro; Alba, Piemonte (tel. 0173 262148), p. 79

Seghesio, Aldo & Riccardo; Monforte d'Alba, Piemonte (tel. 0173 78269; fax 78202), p. 76

Serafini & Vidotto; Nervesa della Battaglia, Veneto (tel. 0422 773281; fax 0421 44314), pp. 242–3

Settimo, Aurelio; La Morra, Piemonte (tel. 0173 50803; fax 509318), p. 69

Soave, Cantina Sociale; Soave, Veneto (tel. 045 7680888; fax 7681203), pp. 203–4

Speri, Fratelli; San Pietro in Cariano, Veneto (tel. 045 7701154; fax 7704994), pp. 172–3

Suavia; Soave, Veneto (tel./fax 045 7675089), p. 204

Sylla Sebaste; Barolo, Piemonte (tel. 0173 56266; fax 56353), p. 62

Tedeschi, Fratelli; San Pietro in Cariano, Veneto (tel. 045 7701487; fax 7704239), p. 173

Tercic, Matijaz; San Floriano del Collio, Friuli-VG (tel. 0481 884193), p. 219

Termeno, Cantina Sociale; Termeno, Alto Adige (tel. 0471 860126; fax 860828), p. 288

Maps

Acknowledgements

The following have assisted in the writing of this book by generously giving time, information, guidance, or help of some sort: Matteo Ascheri, ex-President of the Union of Producers of Alba Wines; Thomas Augschöll of the Bolzano Chamber of Commerce; Roberto Bandinelli of the Department of Viticulture, University of Florence; Richard Baudains; Luigi Bertini; Emilio Fasoletti of the Valpolicella Consortium; Patrizia Felluga; Roberto Ferrarini; Nino Franceschetti; Gianpaolo Giacomelli of the Enoteca of Liguria; Aldo Lorenzoni of the Soave Consortium; Fausto Maculan; Massimo Martinelli, President of the Consortium for Barolo, Barbaresco, Alba, Langhe and Roero; Giovanni Minetti; Leonardo Montemiglio of ICE, Rome; Aldo Vacca; Mattia Vezzola; Maurizio Zanella.

Thanks are due also to my wife Candida and my business partner Colin Loxley for their understanding and support.

About this book

Just as parents of twins usually intend and expect to have one baby at a time, so this was originally conceived as a single opus. As research proceeded, however, it became increasingly apparent that the amount of material available in a work on the world's largest and most diverse wine-producing nation at a time of rapid expansion and diversification was going to produce a child either grossly overweight or with some of its essential characteristics pared away. It was therefore agreed that we would split the work in two, this first part covering the North, the second dealing with the Centre and South. Each book will cover essentially the same type of material, but some of the peripherals will be different. This volume, for example, includes in the Introduction a brief historical overview, touching only briefly on the aspect of wine law – in the second I shall say more on this constantly changing but essential subject, greatly relieved to have the extra time to bring it as fully up to date as possible.

At the end of this volume is, with a few alterations, an article of mine originally written for *Decanter* magazine, which gives what the title suggests: 'A Rapid Guide to the Wines of Italy'. This will be matched in the companion volume by an analytical list of the wines of Italy according to grape variety, similar to the one I produced for my first book, *Life Beyond Lambrusco*. A number of people have told me how useful they found this for purposes of quick reference, and I hope they will find the Rapid Guide equally useful.

Now to the meat of the matter: how is it laid out?

First, vinous Italy is divided into four zones, two for each volume: North West and North East in this book; Centre and South in the other. Each zone receives a general introduction, followed by a rapid tour of the principal wine-producing areas, region by region. The names of these areas will be in SMALL CAPITALS on first mention.

This is followed by a consideration of the major indigenous grape varieties of each zone, from three points of view: the grape itself, which on first mention will be printed in BOLD CAPITALS; the wines principally associated with that grape; and the producers which best represent those wines.

I have chosen this ampelographical, i.e., grape-based, approach – as I did in *Life Beyond Lambrusco* – because I feel that Italian wine's principal *patrimonio* (a favourite Italian word) resides in this wealth of grape types that have been preserved in a world where just a few varieties of French origin have taken over almost everywhere outside Europe, and to a considerable extent within Europe too.

Indeed, those French varieties, together with a few from Germany and Eastern Europe, have invaded Italy itself in a big way, and I therefore devote an entire section to them (and their wines and producers) under the heading 'International Varieties'. I do this in each volume, although the section in this book is much more substantial since it is in the North, and especially the North East, that the 'internationals' have achieved the greatest penetration. It is therefore here that I discuss the historical background to the phenomenon.

In dealing with grape varieties and their wines I have taken the somewhat subjective approach of considering them in order of importance, rather than in alphabetical order, although geographical-regional considerations have also affected the order where such an approach seems to make sense.

As to producers, I have necessarily given the widest coverage to those in the most important *denominazioni*, otherwise the book would never end. The order followed in these sections varies and is made clear in the relevant section. In dealing with producers I have used the following conventions in an attempt to make clear what's what:

When it first appears (except as a passing reference), the name of the producer will be printed in **bold**. Thereafter that producer's name will be printed normally except where he/she is subsequently profiled. (An appendix lists the selection of producers who are profiled, together with telephone and fax numbers, where available, to enable travellers to contact them should they so wish; if I were to do this for all producers the result would be voluminous and tedious.)

In lists of producers, the producer's name is followed by the name of his or her principal wine relevant to that section, in brackets; this may be a DOC name, but it is more often a *cru* name. This in turn is followed – at the first mention only – by the town or commune in which the winery is situated. When, on occasion, I have broken with this convention, I hope the nature of the information given is clear from the context. I should also mention that the location generally conforms to one or both of the major guides to Italian wines, *Vini d'Italia* from Gambero Rosso/Slow Food [now available in English under the title *Italian Wines*] and *I Vini di Veronelli*, this in order that those interested may be able to seek further information in those guides.

So if you want to know more about a producer whose name is not in bold, check the index for the first listing or the profiled producers list (p. xi). Producers are generally profiled in the section which relates to their best-known or most prestigious wines, but to avoid much repetition and a loss of focus, the profile usually includes details of *all* his or her wines of interest or note, not just those of a particular grape.

Here is a schematic presentation of the layout:

Overview

Zone	Production Areas	
THE NORTH WEST	Region	Area
	LOMBARDY	FRANCIACORTA

Grapes, Wines and Producers

Major indigenous grapes	Associated wines	Producers		
		Name	Principal wine(s)	Town/commune
DOLCETTO (bold capitals on first mention)	DOLCETTO D'ACQUI (small capitals on first mention)	**Banfi** (bold on first mention)	(Argusto) (in brackets)	Strevi (not given after first mention)

Introduction

Wine production in Italy goes back beyond the time of the Etruscans and the Greeks, but it was these two peoples who brought system to bear upon what was previously a rather haphazard affair. The Etruscans, coming probably from Asia Minor, settled in central Italy around the early years of the first millennium BC. Their civilization seems to have peaked roughly between 800 and 400 BC, and many artefacts found in necropolises and other sites of archeological interest attest to their respectful consideration for the product of the vine. They seem to have liked their wine in abundance, because they trained their vines up trees, with super-long cordons capable of bearing multiple bunches, the method serving as a model for the various high-trained systems still extant in Italy today.

The influence of the Greeks began a little later, mainly in the south, in those parts of Sicily, Calabria, Campania and Puglia known to the settlers and traders as Magna Grecia or, alternatively, as Oenotria: Winelandia. The Greek approach to viticulture was quite different, much nearer to the densely cultivated, low productivity-per-plant philosophy that reigns today among quality producers in France and, by extension, in Italy and round the world.

It is only fair that Italian wine producers should today be availing themselves of Gallic methods, since it was they, as Romans, who introduced the vine to Gaul in the first place. The Romans were canny enough to combine the best of the systems they inherited by absorption or conquest, and during the centuries of their dominion wine reached a high point economically and culturally. That the Romans were wine *appassionati*, indeed, is abundantly recorded by the likes of Virgil, Horace, Columella and Pliny the

Elder, even if they did have some curious drinking habits such as mixing their wine with resin, herbs and even sea-water for purposes, one presumes, of conservation rather than of flavouring.

After the fall of the Roman Empire the culture of vine and wine was carried forward by monks, whose main purpose (they would have us believe) was to make wine available for the Eucharist. The monks were, effectively, a link between two wine cultures. By the middle Middle Ages, as prosperity increased, there developed once again a thriving wine trade in what had become a political chessboard of a land where empire and papacy, Frenchman and German and Spaniard, not to mention local potentates such as the Medici, moved their rooks and pawns around the board in an unceasing if generally fruitless effort to secure lasting advantage. This is the historic background to the political patchwork that is Italy today: not one country, despite Garibaldi, but a bewildering collection of localities all fiercely clinging to their local traditions – cultural, linguistic, sartorial, culinary and especially (for our purposes) ampelographical – and impelled by the need to guard their constantly threatened identity.

Life, then, was a hazardous affair, and the antidote to crying all the time was to sing, laugh, perform. And what better accompaniment to those practices than wine? Dante and Petrarch, Boccaccio, Poliziano and Lorenzo de' Medici himself sang wine's praises in that Tuscan dialect which was to become the Italian language. Botticelli and numerous other painters used it as a motif, major or minor, in their works. Antinori, Frescobaldi, Ricasoli, Guicciardini Strozzi, Gherardesca – all names still in some way connected with wine – traded in it, through organizations like Florence's Vinattieri guild. And philosophers like Marsilio Ficino, said by some to be the 'Father of the Renaissance' for his bringing together of the Platonic and the Christian traditions, held wine as sacred to the 'convivium' (in Socratic terms 'symposium'), that meeting of hearts and minds out of which so much beauty was to flower in so short a time.

Following the glory years of the Rinascimento, culture in general and wine culture in particular underwent something of a dip out of which it only began to emerge in the nineteenth century. This was a period of intense activity on the part of writers and ampelographers which was rising to a crescendo just as the scourges of oidium and peronospera struck, followed by the *coup de grâce* in the form of phylloxera.

2

It has been suggested that these diseases were responsible for the subsequent decline of Italian wine in the first half of the twentieth century, but one gets the impression that the sinking fortunes of the economy generally and the catastrophe of two world wars fought on home soil had at least as much to do with it. The same could be said of France, of course, but there was a crucial difference in that the great French wines of Bordeaux, Burgundy, Champagne, etc. already had an established market for high quality wine at relatively elevated prices, so that they were in a much better position to ride the storms. For various reasons the Italians had largely failed to develop such a market, and now they took refuge in the hopelessly antiquated or the anonymously industrial, this being the situation and image of Italian wine at the time I began taking an interest in the 1970s.

In reality, the changes which were to propel Italian wines on to an altogether higher plane in a fairly short period of time had begun in the previous decade. In 1963 a law was passed which introduced the concept of Denominazione di Origine Controllata, the controlled denomination of origin, and by the end of the decade there were already several actual DOC wines, including some of today's best-known names – Barolo and Barbaresco, Valpolicella and Soave, Chianti and Vernaccia di San Gimignano (the first DOC, in 1966). While the rigour of some of the law's disciplines were later to create considerable friction between the regulators and the regulated, leading to a new law in 1992, at least the foundation was laid for a relatively systematic approach to wine production and commercialization, bringing a semblance of order into what had thitherto effectively been a state of anarchy.

It was in the 1960s that the first of the new wave wines began appearing. In Alba, Beppe Colla of Prunotto introduced the first single-vineyard Barolo, a phenomenon subsequently to be described by the French word *cru* (see page 24). In Friuli's Collio, Mario Schiopetto was devising the prototypes of the Friulian white wine revolution. In Bolgheri, Marchese Mario Incisa della Rocchetta, together with Giacomo Tachis of Antinori, backed by none other than Professor Emile Peynaud of Bordeaux, were nurturing that Sassicaia which was to show the world that Italy, too, is capable of producing great claret-style reds.

Another change occurred in the 1960s which was to have a profound effect on the agriculture and in particular on the viticulture of the peninsula. This was the ending of *mezzadria*, the share-cropping system by which a peasant who worked a patch of land gave half his produce to the owner of the land by way of rent. *Mezzadria* was based on the principle of self-sufficiency, so that, in your tiny plot, apart from your cow, your ox, your pig, your goat, your chickens and ducks, your dog and your cat, you would have a 'promiscuous' vineyard where the vines would bed down with olive, fruit and nut trees, tomatoes, cabbages, artichokes and other vegetables, grains and pulses, onions, garlic, herbs – everything necessary for the maintenance of your family with minimal recourse to that scarcest of commodities, money. Great in ecological terms, perhaps, and also for the aesthetic aspect of the countryside; one still today finds occasional examples of mixed-culture vineyards, and they are undeniably postcard-picturesque. But it's not the best of methods for growing quality grapes.

In the late 1960s and early 1970s there was a flurry of viticultural activity as, encouraged by the state, advised by regional 'experts' and subsidized by the Common Agricultural Policy, proprietors whose land had previously been under *mezzadria* rushed to plant specialized vineyards in conformity with the local DOC, actual or potential. Mistakes which have had a medium- to long-term negative effect on Italian viticulture were made in those heady days: in central Italy there was much planting of clones of Sangiovese (and one in particular: R10) which have since repeatedly been shown to be inappropriate for the making of high quality wine, acceptable as they may be for the volume production thought to represent the ideal for that time. Meanwhile there was in some areas definite official encouragement, not to say pressure, to adopt high-training methods like *tendone* and *pergola* for purposes of that volume production which seemed desirable at the time.

But there was more going right than going wrong, especially in producers' minds. It was from this time that the ethos of quality – as distinct from marketability or typicity – really began taking off, in some cases bringing producers into head-on collisions with the law; don't forget that the idea of wine-making according to officially imposed formula was very new to Italians, who are not at the best of times positively inclined towards teamwork and obedience. Antinori's famous Tignanello, first made in 1971 in the Chianti Classico zone but without the requisite grape mix, was an early maverick, later (from the second vintage, in 1975) compounding its crime by including Cabernet Sauvignon in the blend, not to mention the *barrique*-ageing which completely distorted its typicity in Ricasolian terms (see Glossary). Another renegade which followed shortly after was Le Pergole Torte of Sergio Manetti at Monte Vertine, a 100% Sangiovese at a time when such a phenomenon did not or was not supposed to exist under the strict letter of the law in the zone of Chianti Classico.

Others preferred to talk the law round to their way of thinking. An example is Count Ugo Contini Bonacossi of Villa di Capezzana in the Tuscan zone of Carmignano. Having brought cuttings of Cabernet Sauvignon back with him from a trip to Château Lafite, and having propagated and planted them with encouraging results, he succeeded in getting Cabernet written into the Carmignano DOC (1975) at up to 10%.

In some places the law's mistake was that it allowed for yields well in excess of the maxima for quality grape production. Elsewhere – or even in the same places – it allowed for 'improvement' by the blending in of wines from other provenances (read the South). These were clearly laws for and by industrialists, not for (and certainly not by) artists. This was and remains the case (in respect of production maxima, though no longer in respect of blending) for Valpolicella and Soave, wines of ancient pedigree betrayed by the very law-makers who were supposed to defend them. Quality producers, such as Giuseppe Quintarelli, who voluntarily limited their production, had no choice but to emphasize to the maximum their own identity on the label while playing down the name of their denomination.

In Piemonte, Angelo Gaja was doing the same, since even though his denomination was nothing to be ashamed of in terms of yields, blends or ageing requirements, the reality was that so much of what was called Barbaresco DOC (and, even more so, Barolo DOC) was over-extractive through excessive maceration or oxidized due to extended ageing without due care in old barrels, or indeed illicitly blended; not wines that Gaja and his ilk would wish to be associated with.

It was in the 1970s that the fashion really began to take hold, among the more forward-thinking producers, of visiting other regions of the wine world, mainly France – Bordeaux, Burgundy, Champagne and academic centres like Montpellier – but also California, at that time considered the repository of the most advanced ideas on the making of wine. These adventurers brought back with them what were then seen as the revolutionary techniques (ordinary as they may seem today) of induced malo-lactic fermentation, the use of cultured yeasts, the technology of refrigeration, and the mechanics and mystique of the small oak barrel or *barrique* which today has grown into something of a cult. But the main message the pioneers returned with was that tradition does not necessarily equal good and that experiment is the better part of experience.

My own introduction to Italian wines took place at around this time. I had been involved with wines professionally for about five years (though a drinker of them since my teens), and while my fairly frequent visits to Italy were not ostensibly to do with wine I had ample opportunity, or made it, to taste as widely as I could. I brought with me a reasonable knowledge of the Italian language and the prevailing prejudice that Italian wine was meant to be cheap and cheerful without, one hoped, too much banana skin and shoe polish involved in its making. But what I took away was quite different.

My strongest impression was that what Italy had to offer was something unique. Here was an amazing collection of grape types and wine styles at the existence of which I had scarcely guessed, and whose discovery fascinated me. In many cases the wines were an acquired taste or, all too frequently, faulty or stretched, so the fascination was not so much in the reality as in the potential, but that wasn't so important. The main thing was that they were *different*. They must, I reasoned, have something going for them or their makers wouldn't have stuck with them for all those decades or centuries, but would have switched to those same French varieties that everyone else in the expanding wine world was planting (as in fact had happened widely in Italy's own North East). With a bit of work and polish (speaking purely figuratively, you understand) they could be made to shine, I thought, like the stars of a hitherto undiscovered galaxy.

I did not realize it at the time, but I had been bitten by the same bug that was intoxicating producers up and down the land. There weren't so many of them then, but the 1980s saw them multiply, and during the 1990s they became a formidable army.

If the late 1960s and early 1970s was the decade of the law-makers, the late 1970s and early 1980s was that of the winemakers.

6

Grubby, mouldy, dank and dingy cellars were cleaned up or rebuilt and the concept of hygiene took hold. Huge old leaking barrels with rickety staves and microbes in their millions adhering to their unscraped interiors were dismantled and replaced with *botti* which were newer and smaller and made of oak, usually from Slavonia as was the custom, but increasingly from France, rather than the local chestnut or acacia. Concrete gave way to stainless steel, leave-it-to-nature to computer program, the human touch to the mechanical, the picturesque to the functional.

I am far from being a promoter of wine-by-formula; indeed I am a firm believer in what you might call the 'soul' of wine, insofar as the chemist's approach tends to reduce wine to a commodity, at which point I cease to be interested. So I am not by any means suggesting that all the above was positive; to be sure some of it was grossly exaggerated, throwing up abominations like the 'super-clean' white which, although being without defect, invariably tasted like every other white wine regardless of its varietal or its origin. But perhaps it was necessary to throw out all that old bathwater in order to have a fresh start, even if a few cherished babies had to go too.

Anyway, the upshot was that, by the mid-1980s, Italy's top producers were on a par with the best in the world in terms of technique and technology – indeed Italy had become a leading manufacturer of oenological equipment. The wines of 1985 were worlds away from those of 1965 and a vast improvement even on those of 1975. Yet there were still precious few which could stand comparison with the best from France, California and even Australia. For Italy to catch up with and even, possibly, overtake its rivals would require a great deal more work.

In my first book on Italian wines, *Life Beyond Lambrusco* (1985), I wrote that Italian wine had achieved perhaps thirty per cent of its potential. Today the figure would be perhaps sixty per cent – referring only to that small proportion which is attempting to improve, not to the mass. To go the next thirty per cent of the way (no one ever achieves one hundred per cent of their potential) it was becoming apparent by the mid-1980s that the next step would need to involve nothing less than a revolution in the vineyard. This is altogether different from the modernizing of the winery, the trial and error process taking a great deal longer in a situation where the raw material on which to base experiments only manifests once a year, while vineyard maturity takes literally decades to achieve.

It has been suggested, by some iconoclast wag, that what Italy needs now is to rip out all its vineyards and start again. This is clearly an exaggeration, yet in certain areas it is nearer to the truth than one might think. Following the large-scale *specializzazione* of vineyards of the post-*mezzadria* years, many areas are due around now and over the next ten or twenty years for large-scale replanting, and as this happens the results of numerous trials are being given practical application. In today's planting programmes all sorts of considerations ignored, consciously or unconsciously, at the time of the last surge, are entering into play: clonal selection, massal selection, new varieties, suitability of rootstocks, planting densities, seeding of leguminous plants between rows, new training systems, canopy management, the requirements of an updated mechanization, a disappearing labour force . . .

Field research into these various aspects has been going on, in some cases, for decades, but certainly since the mid-1980s, with ever increasing vigour. Some of these trials are being run by individual producers, perhaps with the help of notable agronomists like Professor Attilio Scienza. Some are conducted in conjunction with the viticultural departments of nearby universities. Some are undertaken under the auspices of producers' consortia – the best known of this type being Chianti Classico 2000, initiated in 1987. Indeed, the Consorzio Chianti Classico has taken to holding yearly seminars for selected journalists with wine samples to illustrate their findings – which include the identification of a superior clone of Sangiovese (R24) and the demonstration, to my satisfaction at least, that planting certain leguminous vegetables between rows can noticeably improve quality.

It is impossible to go into detail in a limited space on all the research being carried out. Suffice it to say that the next generation of vineyards will be very different from the last, and when those vineyards mature we will at last be able to verify to what extent Italy is capable of taking on the world with its own grape varieties, as well as those French ones which other producing nations have taken to referring to as 'international'.

Is it pretentious to suggest that Italy ever *could* surpass a wine nation of the stature of France? The very notion would have been unthinkable, even laughable, fifteen years ago, yet today it is just about possible to run it up the flagpole even if few would be willing to salute. Consider Italy's advantages: mean temperatures, without being so high as to over-ripen the fruit, are superior to those of France for purposes of ripening grapes, as is implicitly recognized by the law against the use of sugar to increase alcohol in Italy as compared with France's heavy dependency on the stuff. The topography and soil of ubiquitously hilly, yet green, Italy are proportionately more suitable for quality grape-growing than those of almost any nation on earth. And behind it all stands that millennial tradition – the fact that Italians, figuratively and literally, have wine flowing in their blood.

One must also recognize, however, that from a different perspective it is this very tradition that constitutes the greatest barrier to Italian wine's next great leap forward. The barrier here is psychological, imbedded so deeply, indeed, in the psyche of ordinary Italians that they don't even realize it exists. There is still a feeling, not among the modern movers and shakers but among their fathers, among their field-workers and, worst of all, among too many of the law-makers and bureaucrats (the latter being a plague upon the Italian body politic), that what we are doing is what we have always done, is what we ought to continue doing for ever (even if 'for ever' began just out of the reach of the memory of the current older generation).

Concurrently, there is a tendency on the part of the Italian people at large to take wine for granted, just as the British take whisky for granted, to the extent that your average consumer is quite likely to turn up his nose at a wine of complexity and strong character at meal-time (which is practically the only time the average Italian drinks wine) because it is '*troppo impegnativo*' (too demanding). Attitudes like this have worked against the development of a wine cult such as has grown up in predominantly non-producing nations like Britain, Belgium, Japan or the United States, where wine is seen as infinitely interesting by a small but significant sector of the population. I suspect that until such time as a cult of wine does develop (and I am not talking about the business of wine, nor the technology of wine, but about the sheer *love* of wine); until that air of excitement exuded by certain producers, some of the press, consumer organizations like the Slow Food movement, filters through fully to the grass roots, the potential will not be maximized.

It will not happen tomorrow, but it could develop over the

coming century. Change in technique and technology is fast; change in agriculture is a lot slower, but by 2050 Italy's vineyards could be mature examples of the best in the world; change in national attitudes are slower still, but even this is happening.

I would love to be able to check the scene out in the year 2100. Who knows what the scientists might come up with to make that possible?

Vineyard, winery and law

Italy is a unique entity in the world of wines. No other country, not even France, is so comprehensively dedicated to the vine and its products. However, like the human body, its one-ness is to some extent an illusion, being on examination made up of a vast complexity of parts, some of which appear at first view to have precious little connection with one another.

Like the body, the whole divides into sections (like arms, legs, torso, head) which then divide into smaller bits, and so on down to individual grapes which would correspond to the body's molecules – the building blocks from which the entire system is constructed and on which it depends.

The main sections, from the point of view of one who seeks a simple approach to this vinous anatomy, are viticulture and oenology, together, I suppose, with commercialization (although I do not intend to look at the latter aspect here). You could liken these, respectively, to the legs (since the whole operation stands on viticulture), the arms (which gather and manipulate the raw material) and the genitals (which allow the whole business to turn over and constantly renew itself); or, alternatively, to the feeding system (which takes in the raw material), the digestive system (which processes and redistributes it in various altered forms) and the reproductive system.

There is one important part remaining: the head. In our analogy with wine, this not inconsiderable organ, or group of organs, may stand for the laws governing the growing, processing and distributing of the grape and its products. Some may feel that in the case of Italy the law should rather be represented by a lower section of the anatomy, especially in its American pronunciation, but we would not wish to be unkind. Let us just say that, if the head stands for the law, then we may regrettably be obliged to recognize that its brains appear at times a little addled.

VITICULTURE

Italy lies roughly between the 47th and the 35th parallels, corresponding in the north with the vineyards of central France and in the south with those of southern Spain and north Africa. It is largely mountainous, with Alps in the north and the Apennine ridge running right through the land, like a huge backbone, from the French Mediterranean border to the tip of the Calabrian toe, and on, indeed, into Sicily.

These extremes of latitude and altitude allow for a rich tapestry of climates and micro-climates which, taken with a wide range of different soil types not to mention an enormous diversity of social, political, linguistic and culinary traditions built up over the many centuries that this land has been civilized, make for the kind of complexity referred to above.

A key feature of this complexity is the multiplicity of grape types, indigenous and imported, that have developed here since ancient times: from Greece, Asia Minor, Dalmatia, Illyria, Spain and, more recently, from France, Germany and eastern Europe. Well over a hundred are being seriously cultivated somewhere or other in the peninsula even today, while hundreds more fall into the category of 'authorized varieties' even if their commercial use is extremely limited. Add to that the hundreds which used to be planted but have virtually disappeared since the devastations of phylloxera and other diseases, plus the hybrids that were developed to deal with that situation at the lower end of the market, and you arrive at a total of something like a thousand.

Numerous cultivation methods have been developed over the centuries in various parts of the country, but, as has been mentioned, they can all be traced back to two main archetypes, Etruscan and Greek. Of the former, important modern manifestations include the *tendone,* which involves high trellising with a dense leaf canopy on top that keeps all grapes as well as all foliage underneath the canopy in permanent shade (against all the precepts of modern canopy management); and the *pergola* or *pergoletta,* high to medium-high with one or two arms, slanted or at right angles, or arched over in a so-called *doppio archetto capovolto* (little double arch with the head pointing down). The former, or variations on it, has been widely adopted in the plains of Emilia-Romagna and down the east coast, while the latter remains dominant in the central North (*pergola trentina* in Trentino-Alto Adige; *pergola veronese* in Valpolicella, Soave and Bardolino). Medium-height systems like *sylvoz* or *casarsa* have meanwhile caught on in eastern Veneto and Friuli.

All these are characterized by low to medium-low density (1,600 to 3,200 plants per hectare) and high production per plant (3 to 6 kilos or more) with relatively low concentration of extract per berry – in other words, they are good for the churning out of large volumes of inexpensive table wine, which is just what they were originally intended for in the 1950s when they began to replace higher density vineyards for ease of mechanization (previously farmers tended to use animals rather than ploughs and planted much tighter rows in order to maximize their limited space).

The low-trained style (as far as the fruiting branch or cane is concerned) is by now traditional in parts of the North West, in particular in the classic zones of Piemonte. As quality increasingly takes over from quantity as the guiding principle in the vineyard, so are growers throughout the north turning (or turning back) to such systems as *spalliera* (inverted L-shape, training along horizontal wires, usually with a cordon spur formation which means a mature arm with a greater or lesser number of nodes from each of which a fruiting cane sprouts) and *guyot*, single or double (again the inverted L, the horizontal part of which is a new cane with several buds, as distinct from an established branch with several canes kept short).

These systems involve considerably higher numbers of vines per hectare (4,000 to 10,000 plants per hectare) and less production per plant (0.5 to 2 kilos), generally resulting in significantly lower total yields. They are by now *de rigueur* for new plantings of international grapes destined for high quality bottles and are steadily encroaching on the area devoted to high-trained vineyards, to the extent that one pundit, looking out over a sea of vines in the Alto Adige recently, could say: 'In thirty years time there won't be a single *pergola* left.' Whether that is true for Alto Adige remains to be seen. It is true, however, that there are still plenty of new plantings which take more account of the tractor and the saving of labour (*per forza* – of necessity – an Italian might say, seeing as the youth of the species is vanishing from the countryside) than of the ultimate fruit quality.

I touched in the Introduction upon the type of experiments that are going on in viticultural circles in Italy, so I won't expand here. Suffice it to underline the awareness, on the part of quality-minded Italians, of the need for radical changes in the vineyard and the intense activity resulting from that awareness.

OENOLOGY

WINEMAKERS

In *Life Beyond Lambrusco* I quoted Luigi Veronelli, the guru of the early years of the Italian fine wine revolution, as saying that Italy had 'first-rate grapes and second-rate winemakers'. Funny how perceptions change – an observer today, noting the backward nature of so many of Italy's vineyards and the enthusiasm of so many winemakers to produce the best, might almost say the opposite.

The technique and technology of wine production has today become an international concern, so it is probably more appropriately considered in a book devoted to that subject alone, rather than in one about the wines of a given nation. What is unique to a country, more than machines or methods, is the type of person engaged in the process and the styles of wines produced, and in these respects Italy has its own peculiar mix. For these purposes I intend to borrow or at least paraphrase to some extent from *Life Beyond Lambrusco*, since the situation has not changed radically in the past fifteen years; except, perhaps, in a couple of respects.

At the most modest level there is the peasant farmer for whom grapes represent only a part of total agricultural production. Then there is the specialist grower who sells his crop regularly to a *commerciante* or to the local *cantina sociale*. Each of these may have some primitive equipment to enable him to satisfy the needs of the family or a small regular clientele, but the resultant wine is likely to be far from commercial, however wonderful he may think it is and however much he may turn up his nose at something vastly superior. (I have a friend who exactly fits the description; when he first pooh-poohed my SuperTuscans, claiming his piddle was better, I thought he must be joking; it took me years to realize he really meant it!)

Next up the scale come the peasant artisans, specialist vinegrowers of perhaps the second or third or fourth – or twelfth – generation who have taken the bold decision to withhold at least a part of their grapes from the usual merchant, raise a loan and invest in some proper equipment in order to have a real go at making quality wine. They are likely to be young and ambitious to break the mould of generations and board the bandwagon that they can see gathering speed around them. Their fathers will be horrified at their insistence on cutting away already formed bunches in order to reduce production and concentrate extract, and at the ridiculous experiments with strange low-yielding vines and expensive oaks, but after a few rows and an honourable mention in one of the guides, not to mention a bit of success at selling some of those fancy-priced bottles, the old boy is pacified and the younger generation, with luck, goes from strength to strength.

The winery of a peasant artisan would be classified as an *azienda agricola* or *azienda agraria*, that is to say an agricultural holding (sometimes called a *tenuta*) or farm (*podere, cascina, fattoria, maso* are all descriptives in this context). However, the fact that a property is described by one of these words does not necessarily signify that it is small or peasant-owned – the owner may be a *conte* or a *marchese* belonging to a family that goes back centuries, and the property may be, or may have been (before the government chewed away at it through taxation or appropriation), of considerable extension.

Then there are the new arrivals, those for whom owning an *azienda agricola* is the height of fashion or ambition. People from all walks and provenances continue to enter the world of upmarket agriculture, especially those who have earned a lot of money from other pursuits such as law, industry, commerce or the arts, or through inheritance. (Hence the adage: To make a small fortune in the wine business you need a large fortune from elsewhere.) The 'in' locations for the monied classes with a penchant for being seen as fine wine producers remain the gracious hills of up-country Veneto, with its well-groomed hills and towns, its Palladian villas and mountain backdrops; and central or coastal Tuscany, with, respectively, those magnificent Renaissance-painting hills or that quasi sub-tropical neo-Californian climate and feel.

Foreigners, too, drawn by the combined attractions of Italian landscape, architecture, gastronomy and lifestyle (if rather less so by the bureaucracy and the tax system), have maintained if not intensified the invasion which began in the 1960s, when magnificent properties were going for a modest song as distinct from the Wagnerian aria they command today. Britons, Americans, Germans and Swiss are all well represented in this respect.

Such *parvenus* to the land, be they Italian or no, generally arrive with little or no experience in viticulture or oenology, so they need to hire professionals. These will be of two types, resident or consultant, and will generally have a qualification in agrarian studies and/or oenology from one of Italy's main wine colleges – in the north this means Alba in Piemonte, San Michele all'Adige in Trentino or Conegliano in the Veneto; they may even teach in these and/or other institutions of higher learning. The residents one rarely hears about, although the most famous of them all, Giacomo Tachis, was for decades resident winemaker at Antinori, even if he did have interests elsewhere.

Certain of the roving consultants of today, however – Tachis included, despite being in semi-retirement – have become VIPs in their own right, being credited at least partially with some of Italy's greatest wines, and having multiple clients perhaps as far apart as Puglia and Piemonte, for whom they whiz up and down the *autostrade* in powerful motorcars to pop in on periodically, spending most of the rest of their time on the mobile phone or in front of the computer. The most famous of these, while rarely Tuscan, tend to operate largely in Tuscany: Niccolò d'Afflitto, Luca d'Attoma, Franco Bernabei, Maurizio Castelli, Roberto Cipresso, Carlo Ferrini, Vittorio Fiore, Giorgio Marone, Attilio Pagli, Paolo Vagaggini, not forgetting the daddy of them all, Giulio Gambelli. There are, however, several of superstar status whose centre is elsewhere in Italy, even though their work may carry them to far-flung parts: Donato Lanati and Giuliano Noe in Piemonte; Giorgio Grai in Alto Adige; Attilio Scienza, the ubiquitous viticulturist, in Trentino; Riccardo Cotarella and Lorenzo Peira in the Centre; Severino Garofano in the southern mainland.

A more recent phenomenon – somewhat detached from the mainstream reality of Italian viti-viniculture – is the foreign 'flying winemaker', the Antipodean who, being free at the time of the European harvest, having done his or her thing or things between February and May, has come north, or, more probably, has been called north by some group serving British supermarkets, to teach a few grandmothers how to suck eggs (as envious Italians tend to see it). The contribution of these antipodeans – the best-known of whom include Geoff Merrill and Martin Shaw of Australia (the latter having now retired from the Italian scene), Kim Milne and Matt Thompson of New Zealand and Gaetane Carron of Chile – has mainly been in the area of improving quality at the lower end of the price scale, not surprisingly considering the market at which their products are aimed, and in this they have done a creditable job, although I am not aware of them being behind any wine which could be described as outstanding. The proposition that these visitors have revolutionized Italian quality wine production, which certain journalists or spin doctors seem to wish to promote, seems to me indicative of a complete misunderstanding of what classic Italian wine is about, i.e. the people and the *terroir* – isn't that, indeed, what all classic wine is about?

But back to the Italians themselves. We have looked at the small proprietor – sophisticated peasant or countrified *nouveau-riche* – but we have not yet considered the large-scale private grower, for whom the making of wine exclusively from one's own grapes is neither a hobby nor a cottage industry but a business (the analogy in French terms would involve a comparison between the *viticulteur* of Burgundy and the proprietor of a *grande marque* champagne). Outside Tuscany there is no appreciable concentration of such people, but they can be found sporadically up and down the land: one thinks, in this context, of Gaja or Rocche dei Manzoni in Piemonte, Cà del Bosco or Bellavista in Lombardy, Armani or Guerrieri Rizzardi in Veneto, Hofstätter in Alto Adige, Livio Felluga or Livon in Friuli.

There are rather more medium- to large-scale producers of the type that make wine from grapes not only grown by themselves but also grown by others, often on a long-term contractual basis. This is technically an *azienda vitivinicola*, although it is not necessary to use this term unless the amount of grapes bought-in exceeds that of those estate-grown. Such operations include the likes of Ceretto, Fontanafredda, Bruno Giacosa, Marchesi di Barolo and Pio Cesare in Piemonte; Maculan, Masi and Zenato in Veneto; Lageder, Niedermayr and Tiefenbrunner in Alto Adige; Marco Felluga in Friuli.

Multiple operations of this type include Gruppo Italiano Vini, a group (as the name suggests) of producers in various parts of northern and central Italy including Cà Bianca in Piemonte, Nino

Negri in Valtellina, Lamberti and Santi in Verona and Conti Formentini in Collio; and Zonin, whose production is so enormous
that despite having 900 hectares of vineyard in various parts of the
centre and north – from Castello del Poggio in Piemonte to Cà
Bolani in Friuli via Lombardy and Veneto as well as Castello
d'Albola in Tuscany – they need to buy in hundreds of thousands
of quintals of grapes and wine.

Then there is the seriously large-scale private producer who may
own vineyards, even fairly extensive, high-quality vineyards, but
the majority if not the totality of whose production derives from
grapes or wines purchased. Well-known names would include
Bersano and Giordano in Piemonte and several in Verona: Bolla,
Montresor, Pasqua, Sartori. Finally in the private category, there is
the industrial producer who only uses bought-in wines and musts.
Such a one, in Veneto, is Santa Margherita of Pinot Grigio fame.
An example in Alto Adige is the colossus Schenk, who bottle a
quarter of a million hectolitres of wine annually.

The *cantina sociale* or growers' cooperative is a major force to
be reckoned with in the context of Italian wine. There are those,
especially in northern Italy, which are capable of outstanding quality and which can be numbered among the best producers in
absolute terms in a given zone, being extremely well equipped and
intelligently managed. Some critics object to the cooperatives'
practice of lowering the standard of their inexpensive wines by
reserving the grapes of their best vineyards, or highest selection, for
crus which they sell at elevated prices to frequently enthusiastic
applause from the pundits. But it is hard to fault this marketing
strategy from their point of view, since by winning medals and cita-
tions they move their overall image (if not their overall quality)
upmarket in the eyes of consumers, which is ultimately good for
the people they represent, namely those self-same peasant growers
with whom we began.

The area of northern Italy with the greatest wealth of quality
cooperatives is easily Alto Adige, where the *cantine sociali* vie with
the privates for supremacy. The following are all capable of good
to excellent wines: Andriano, Burggräfler, Caldaro, Colterenzio,
Cornaiano, Cortaccia, Gries, San Michele Appiano, Santa Maddalena, Terlano, Termeno and Viticoltori Alto Adige. Trentino,
too, is well off with Cavit, Lavis, MezzaCorona and Mezzolombardo, as well as the semi-cooperative Concilio Vini. Piemonte's

best are spread about and are hard put to match the best of the privates, but a worthy job is done by Araldica Vini Piemontese, Carema, Vinchio e Vaglio Serra and Viticoltori dell'Acquese, with a special mention going to Produttori del Barbaresco whose *crus* Barbarescos are among the finest wines of Italy. Veneto and Friuli are less well-off for really good *cantine sociali*, but C.S. Valpolicella at Negrar, C.S. Soave and Valdobbiadene in the former, and Cormons in the latter, turn out some pretty fair wines at the top of the range.

WINE STYLES

Northern Italy produces just about every style of wine known to man, and then some, at good to excellent quality level – the exception being fortified, though there are unfortified versions which perform a similar role.

Full red wines

These are perhaps the most important of the classic styles here, especially in Piemonte (Barolo, Barbaresco, Gattinara, Barbera d'Alba and Barbera d'Asti) and Valpolicella (Amarone, Superiore), indeed in the North East generally in relation to an increasing number of excellent bordeaux-style wines. Traditionally these wines, especially those of Alba, would receive a lengthy maceration on the skins followed by several years (six, eight, ten – more!) in *botte*. In the past twenty years or so younger producers less concerned with creating something unique than in turning out wines that people would want to drink without having to wait half a lifetime have reduced, sometimes drastically, both the period of maceration and that of wood maturation. They have also experimented with high initial fermentation temperatures and systems for mixing the skins and pulp during maceration to achieve more colour earlier, and of course with smaller and smaller oak, of French provenance in increasing preference to Slavonian. The name of the game, for these producers, is not to eliminate tannins and their ability to help the wine resist the ageing process over a protracted period, but to ensure that they are as soft and ripe as possible, not green, harsh and drying. There is more on this subject in the section on Barolo.

The *passito* styles of Valpolicella, Recioto and Amarone, are in fact considerably more 'classic', in the original sense, than are

Barolo and Co., although apart from the use of semi-dried grapes and the difficulty of getting a fermentation going in mid-winter there is not, in terms of debates raging, a great deal of difference between the two. As in Barolo, the new-wave producer here is aiming more and more at achieving primary fruit aromas and sheer drinkability, as distinct from the tertiary aromas of ageing with durability. The Valpolicella producer will, if anything, be a little more adventurous with wood, using local cherry and chestnut as well as Slavonian and French oak.

As for bordeaux-style wines, increasingly common in Lombardy, Alto Adige, Trentino, Veneto and Friuli, these are more and more following the Bordeaux lead in respect of how they are made. To repeat what has been said above, and to pre-empt what will be said later on international varieties, the challenge here is more in the vineyard than in the *cantina*.

Full-bodied, oaked reds also have a tradition, if limited, in Trentino (Teroldego) and Alto Adige (Lagrein).

Medium- and light-bodied red and rosé wines

Lighter wines are more to the taste of the average Italian than the full-bodied sort. Basically, all this person wants on an ordinary day is a wine to wash his meal down with, something that is not *impegnativo* (that doesn't make demands) – Italians don't generally imbibe wine for the effect but as an accompaniment to food. So in Piemonte, give him a modest Barbera Monferrato, or a Dolcetto, or even a Nebbiolo of the lighter ilk and he'll be happy. In Lombardy he'll prefer a little Valcalepio or a Terre di Franciacorta Rosso to some *barriqued* bordeaux-style job, or maybe a Barbera from Oltrepò Pavese, or a Chiaretto from eastern Garda. In Veneto it's Bardolino or Valpolicella *normale* he'll go for, or one of the lesser wines of Breganze, of Colli Berici, of Colli Euganei, of Piave or of Lison-Pramaggiore. In Friuli he'll want a nice little Merlot or a Cabernet Frank, and in Trentino and Alto Adige, although, as in Friuli, the more weighty wines of the bordeaux style are now catching on internationally, the average punter will gladly pass up such delights for an uncomplicated Schiava. Nor should we forget the rather tasty Rosatos or 'Kretzers', made from the Lagrein grape in South Tyrol, wines which slip down a damn sight more easily than those big black Lagrein Dunkels or those impenetrable Teroldegos.

Dry white wines

Italy's dry whites have come a long way in fifteen years. When I was writing *Life Beyond Lambrusco* it hadn't been all that long previously that Italians had 'discovered' cultured yeasts and long, slow fermentation at low temperatures. Unfortunately, too many of them had failed to discover the primary aromas of the grapes themselves, and while the wines were coming out clean, yes, without oxidation (certainly an improvement on certain past performances), they were almost entirely lacking in perfume or personality, smelling all too frequently of bubble gum and pear drops.

Today, various modifications have been made and techniques introduced to remedy this sorry situation. Again, such techniques are universal, and do not require a lengthy airing here. Suffice it to say that methods like crio-maceration (the freshly crushed pulp resting on the skins at a low temperature for a few hours to pick up aromas without, one hopes, tannins); a maximum of protection (of grapes as well as wine) from oxygen – apart from the deliberate process of hyper-oxygenation, that is; refinements in the use of enzymes and yeasts, not to mention *barrique*-fermentation (with or without *bâtonnage*) and maturation, have done much to bring Italian white wine into the twentieth, indeed the twenty-first, century.

One fairly recent innovation, now catching on as a means whereby one's wine might stand out in a densely crowded market, is the imaginative intermingling of white grapes of diverse origins, the art being to use the properties of each to the advantage of the whole rather than to lose all individual identity in a massive melting pot. This issue is discussed in the chapter on blends.

Sparkling wines

Dry sparkling wines have grown appreciably in number and in quality over the past fifteen years, and are becoming a significant aspect of wine production in northern Italy, so much so that I have devoted a chapter to *metodo classico* wines and need not further discuss them here. The other unique Italian dry sparkling wine, Prosecco di Conegliano/Valdobbiadene, is likewise discussed in its place, that's to say under the grape Prosecco (see page 211).

North West Italy is, of course, the world's centre for sweet white sparkling wines in the form of Asti and Moscato d'Asti, and they too are discussed in their place (see page 124). Another sweet white sparkling wine, obscure but not totally unknown, is the Recioto

Spumante of Soave, indeed of Gambellara; and there are other oddments belonging to this category scattered about, such as the sparkling Fior d'Arancio from Orange Muscat grapes, found in Veneto's Colli Euganei; and of course the sweeter versions of Franciacorta which, like sweet champagne, exist in extremely limited proportions.

Perhaps the oddest of all northern Italian oddities is the sparkling red Valpolicella Recioto, a wine comparable with only one other in all the world, Australian sparkling Shiraz, with which it shares several characteristics: the marriage of weight and lightness, of richness of extract and exuberance, as well as the potential for considerable longevity thanks to its reserves of alcohol, sugar, acidity, tannin and even carbon dioxide – in short every one of the natural intrinsic preservatives in the ambit of wine. Another sweet red wine with bubbles is, of course, Lambrusco, discussed under that grape, as are similar wines from the Freisa and Brachetto varieties. The dry sparkling reds from these grapes, as well as from Barbera and Croatina, are likewise discussed under their respective varieties. Recioto della Valpolicella is viewed under its main variety, Corvina.

Still sweet wines

These have their place here too, both in the red department (Recioto della Valpolicella) and in the white: there are also white Reciotos from Valpolicella, as well as sweet Moscato Passitos from Piemonte and Valle d'Aosta; not to mention the more normal non-sparkling Reciotos from Soave and Gambellara, nor the more esoteric, generally one-off stickies, blends or varietals, dotted about the place, *tipo* late-harvest Arneis.

The North also has its representative of the oxidized style of wine in the sweet sherry-like Vino Santo of Trentino. Production is tiny, reflecting the weakness of the market for such beverages; yet it still hangs in there. Finally, there is the distilled version of wine, grappa, for which Trentino, of all the regions of Italy, is most famous. I have not tackled this subject in the present book, considering grappa to be not wine, but a wine product, as is vinegar. Unlike vinegar, however, I'll happily drink a good one, although the rough stuff makes me feel like throwing up.

ITALIAN WINE LAW

All national wine laws in the European Union are necessarily based on the fundamental EU law which divides wines into two categories: Quality Wines and Table Wines.

The quality designation in Italy, based on the law of 1963 updated in 1992, is DOC (Denominazione di Origine Controllata), which guarantees a wine's geographical provenance, its varietal make-up and certain details of production such as yield of grapes per hectare, percentage of wine permitted per given weight of grapes, minimum sugar (grape) and alcohol (wine) levels, minimum acidity, length of ageing, type of recipient for ageing, etc.

DOC does not, however, necessarily guarantee the quality of a wine. Only the higher designation, DOCG (the G stands for Garantita) is supposed to guarantee quality (by tasting), and that is by no means reliable. People aiming to make top wines in Italy but not wishing to conform to the legal constraints applicable in their zone have in the past thirty years deliberately downgraded their denomination (to Vino da Tavola) in order to upgrade quality; hence the 'SuperTuscan' and its ilk.

The law is now pulling these wines back into the official fold, having introduced new broader DOCs and a higher grade of Vino da Tavola called IGT (Indicazione Geografica Tipica), comparable with the French Vin de Pays. Examples of the first type are the new Piemontese DOCs 'Piemonte', 'Langhe' and 'Monferrato', covering just about any wine which used to go under the rather vague description, now *passé*, Vino da Tavola con Indicazione Geografica. In other words Piemonte, exercising its prerogative as a regional authority, has decided that all quality wines within its ambit shall be DOC (or DOCG), the only other option being Vino da Tavola without any indication of provenance, grape variety or vintage.

Other regions have opted for a burgeoning of IGTs, which has suddenly brought countless new obscure names into a field which was already seriously overloaded with nomenclature. These *vini tipici*, as they are called, are subject to considerably tighter controls than their predecessors (even though the controls tend to be a lot looser than for DOC), principally in respect of the fact that the wine in the bottle now has to be traceable back by means of accompanying documentation to an actual vineyard, a sophistication not required of the old Vino da Tavola con Indicazione Geografica (heaven only knew where some of *those* came from).

One would think IGT to be a more satisfying bracket for a genuine quality producer. Yet there are those who would have preferred to retain their apparently lowly but paradoxically prestigious Vino da Tavola status, succumbing to the cunning pressure of the authorities only because the latter, as I have said, have outlawed on ordinary Vino da Tavola labels the naming of any grape variety, geographical provenance or, most crucially, vintage date. A fantasy name and a back-label description may get round the first two, but consumers spending their precious money on a high-class bottle want to know the year when the wine in it was produced. One ploy has been to use a lot number (referring supposedly to the date of bottling) which just happens to coincide with the vintage year. Ah yes, they are a people of infinite resource, are the Italians!

Other quality indications one might come across on the Italian wine label include the following:

Riserva: this ought to indicate higher quality, certainly extra ageing at the winery;

Superiore: despite the suggestion of higher quality, this generally means nothing much more than a higher alcoholic degree than the *normale* of the same type;

Classico: in the twentieth century a number of ancient wine-growing areas were extended so as to allow others, usually in less favoured parts adjacent, to exploit the name; in these cases the word Classico indicates the original area; the main examples are Valpolicella and Soave;

Cru has come to have in Italy a much wider sense than its original French meaning of the particular plot. *Cru* names may have actual geographical significance (and usually do in Barolo or Barbaresco), but elsewhere are all too often little more than brand names, although these may help to identify the best bottles provided you know where to check them out;

Imbottigliato all'origine . . . or *Imbottigliato dal viticoltore* . . . are formulas for expressing that the wine was bottled (and, presumably, made) at the place where the grapes were grown; in other words 'estate bottled'.

The only broadly applicable guarantee of quality, however, is the producer's name, together with the name of his wine or wines. That is exactly what this book attempts to present: the best producers in their context, and their best wines.

So, may I wish you happy reading . . . and tasting.

I
THE NORTH WEST
Piemonte, Valle d'Aosta, Lombardy, Liguria, Emilia

———

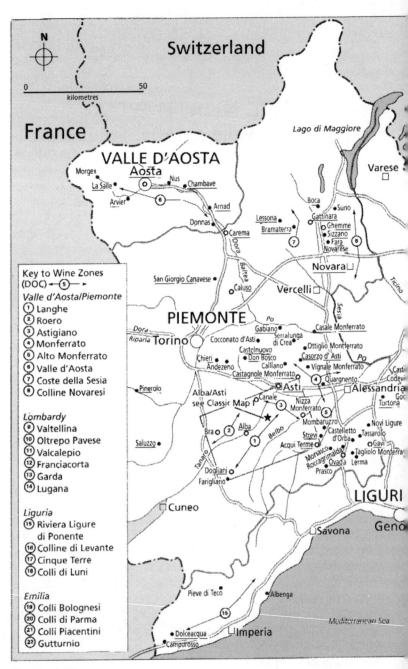

The North West.

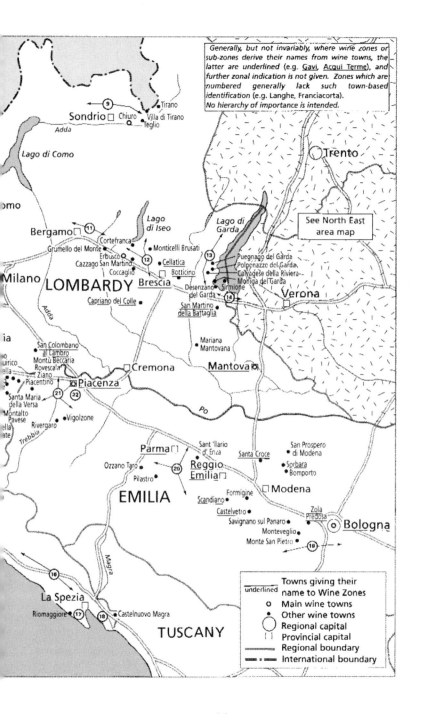

Generally, but not invariably, where wine zones or sub-zones derive their names from wine towns, the latter are underlined (e.g. Gavi, Acqui Terme), and further zonal indication is not given. Zones which are numbered generally lack such town-based identification (e.g. Langhe, Franciacorta).
No hierarchy of importance is intended.

(9) → Tirano

Sondrio □ Chiuro ○⋯ Villa di Tirano
Adda ⋯ Teglio

Trento ○

Lago di Como

omo

Lago di Iseo

Lago di Garda

See North East area map

Bergamo □ (11) ← Cortefranca
Grumello del Monte • Monticelli Brusati
Erbusco ○ (12) Cellatica
Cazzago San Martino • Coccaglio □ Botticino
(13)
Puegnago del Garda
Polpenazze del Garda
Calvagese della Riviera
Desenzano del Garda • Moniga del Garda
Sirmione
Milano LOMBARDY Brescia (14)
Capriano del Colle •
San Martino della Battaglia
Verona

Adda

Mariana Mantovana •

San Colombano al Lambro
urico Montù Beccaria
ella Rovescala •
Ziano Piacentino
Santa Maria della Versa
Montalto Pavese •
Rivergaro • Vigolzone •
Trebbia
(21) (22)
□ Cremona
Mantova ○

Po

Santa Croce
Sant'Ilario d'Enza
San Prospero di Modena
Sorbara •
Bomporto •

Parma □
Ozzano Taro •
Pilastro •
(20) Reggio Emilia □
□ Modena

EMILIA
Scandiano
Formigine •
Castelvetro •
Zola Predosa
Savignano sul Panaro •
Monteveglio •
Monte San Pietro •
(18)
Bologna ○

Magra

(18)

La Spezia
Riomaggiore • (17) (18) • Castelnuovo Magra

TUSCANY

underlined Towns giving their name to Wine Zones
○ Main wine towns
◯ Other wine towns
Regional capital
□ Provincial capital
Regional boundary
International boundary

29

There is a very good case for contending that north-western Italy is the most exciting wine zone in the world. Of course, I am aware that there is in this view a goodly measure of subjectivity. However, it is a subjectivity well supported by a number of people whose opinions I consider worthy.

I am also aware that, in making such a contention in relation to an arbitrary Italian wine zone, I might be treading on some very sensitive corns. What about the Gironde?, some will object. I didn't say 'best', I said 'most exciting'. Bordeaux may produce the greatest reds and sweet whites in the world (in some people's view; not mine) but I doubt whether anyone who has spent years in that atmosphere of arrogance and profound self-satisfaction would describe it as exciting.

So, what about Burgundy? On its own, too limited in terms of grape varieties and wine styles, though combine it with Champagne (for wine styles), or northern Rhône (for varieties) – which you would be entitled to do given my somewhat arbitrary declaration of the North West as a single zone – and I will admit you've probably got a winner. What about the Loire, Alsace, the Midi, not to mention all those other fascinating and/or developing zones dotted about the world, in Australia, New Zealand, South Africa, California, Chile, Argentina, Spain, Portugal, Hungary, etc.? Fine – I'm not saying there do not exist other exciting wine producing zones, only that Piemonte is (I think) the most exciting.

On what do I base my opinion? A certain dynamism in the approach of producers, a hunger for improvement, plus the old favourite, *terroir*, using the word in the broadest possible sense. It means the land – topography, geology, climate; it means the ambience, the people, their words and ways, their viticultural, oenological and culinary traditions – everything that comes together to form an overall picture. North West Italy, I would suggest, has it all in spades. Except maybe the weather.

The dominant feature of this zone, with the exception of Emilia, is mountains. Valle d'Aosta is just a mass of Alps, one higher than the other, it seems, as you drive through the main valley on your way from Turin towards Haute Savoie, including the world's most ambitious non-Himalayan upward thrust of rock, Monte Bianco, through which you drive very slowly behind the inevitable exhaust-belching truck for 13 kilometres at exorbitant cost. Beyond the northern border of Lombardy and Piemonte is Switzerland. The western flank of Piemonte, south of Valle d'Aosta, is solid Alps, and the southern flank consists of more modest mountains, but mountains none the less, here called Maritime Alps and, further east, Ligurian Apennines. Liguria is really nothing more than mountains with a narrow coastal strip called the Italian Riviera where people spend their summer sitting in endless rows of deckchairs on what bits of beach they can find (better the rocks, and the fishing ports).

Italy's longest river, the Po, rises just across the border in the French Maritime Alps, and flows through mountain and foothill to Turin and eastward until, a little way north-east of Alessandria in Piemonte, it picks up its principal tributary, the Tanaro (the one that flash-flooded in 1994, leaving thousands of hectares of land and thousands of bottles and massive overturned barrels of Barolo under mud). Here it begins to form that vast, fertile valley which bears its name, a valley which fans out triangularly to its widest point on the Adriatic coast south of Venice.

The most important area for quality wine production in Piemonte lies around the 45th parallel, just about level with Bordeaux. The quality growing zones of Lombardy are actually around the level of Beaujolais. There is a widespread idea that Italy, like Spain, lies to the south of France. As regards viticultural northern Italy this simply is not the case.

In terms of climate there are understandably considerable variations over such a sizeable area, although with the exception of the Ligurian coastal region one could call it generally 'continental' and not at all Mediterranean as one might expect. It has, then, rigorous winters, with frequent fogs rising out of the relative warmth of the alluvial valleys, and hot summers, often rainless for extended periods, with the warm weather capable of extending quite far into autumn, which is good news for late-ripeners like Nebbiolo and Barbera – except, of course, when autumn rains combine with warmth to favour moulds, a factor which can negatively affect, by dilution if not by rot, a potentially fine vintage.

While on vintages, it should be stressed that vintage variation is as great here as it is anywhere in the wine world, especially regarding the late-ripening black grapes. Again, the idea that Italy equals south equals dependably warm climate, does not apply here. Anyone coming to North West Italy in winter without clothing at least adequate for a London winter will quickly learn the error of their assumptions.

In fact, not only is there considerable variation from vintage to vintage, there can be major differences from sub-zone to sub-zone within a given vintage. There are vintages which are positively triumphal for the Nebbiolos of Alba, while being distinctly substandard not just in the rest of Italy but even in the rest of Piemonte. Reason? Because by the time the October sun comes out after September rains practically everyone else's grapes will have been picked; only Nebbiolo is left to benefit from the glorious Indian summer.

A climatic occurrence of some frequency and considerable impact, hail, is even more selective. This phenomenon only strikes in patches, so that one vineyard can be devastated while its neighbour is unaffected. This may happen anywhere in the north, but is particularly significant in intensely planted areas such as Barolo/Barbaresco or Valtellina.

Just as the zone's geology is divided between mountain, hill and plain, so is its viticulture. In Valle d'Aosta and the adjacent part of Piemonte, in northern Lombardy and in parts of Liguria, grapes have been grown for centuries in steep to quasi-perpendicular vineyards where terraces sometimes seem carved into the very mountain face. Needless to say, the soils in these sites are pretty low in fertility rating, the work is back-breaking, little mechanizable, and the return scarcely worth the labour, which is truly one of love. The situation is not aided by a tendency of youth Italy-wide (or rather Italy-long) to escape from what they see as the laborious life of a farmer to what they imagine to be the relatively cushy conditions of the city.

At the opposite end of the spectrum are the flatland wines,

mainly the Lambruscos of the extremely fertile plain of Emilia capable of being produced in industrial quantities on high trellising at very low cost. In case anyone is wondering how I can justify including the wines of Emilia in the North West zone, which as far as I know has not been done before, I answer (a) that the ampelographical association between Emilia and the North West is much closer than it is between Emilia and its political partner, Romagna: quite apart for the obvious link between Colli Piacentini and Oltrepò Pavese, there is a part of the Lambrusco growing area, near Mantua, which is actually in Lombardy; and (b) that effervescent light reds like Emilia's Lambrusco are a traditional feature of north-western viniculture, in the form of frothing dry Barberas and Dolcettos, not to mention semi-sparkling dry and sweet Freisas and Brachettos. This is true of no other part of Italy.

The hills in the middle, though, are where the quality wines come from. There are the clusters of the Langhe and Roero zones in the Alba area, of the Monferrato and around Asti further east, of Novara and Vercelli, of Torino and Ivrea, and around Acqui, Ovada and Gavi in the extreme south east of Piemonte. There are Alpine foothills north of the cities of Bergamo and Brescia in Lombardy – in the Franciacorta zone, and on the west bank of Lake Garda. And there are the hills of the Oltrepò Pavese, south of Milan, with the adjacent group of the Colli Piacentini just inside north-western Emilia, extending in an eastward direction to the Colli di Parma and the Colli Bolognesi, all effectively the northern foothills of the Apennine ridge.

The people of North West Italy tend to be of two types. Here are Italy's two most modern cities – Turin in Piemonte, Milan in Lombardy – and a major section of Italy's financial and industrial activity. Here, too, is Italy's greatest port, Genoa, as well as such wealthy cities of the plain as Parma and Modena. Thus you find the kind of sophisticated, internationally minded population one associates with such conurbations.

But in the rural areas the peasant remains a vital force, partly due to the Napoleonic inheritance laws which have carved the territory into ever-tinier pieces, partly due to a persistent demand, not yet annihilated by the supermarket culture, for the produce of small individual farmers, and in viticultural areas particularly to the steadily increasing price of grapes enabling growers to continue in their ways whilst making a moderate to good living. These are folk who prize their traditions, love their land, speak their local dialect and are largely impervious to outside influence.

The gastronomic art is strong here, too, which is always an aid to a strong viniculture. The great white truffle is at home here, as are various extraordinary *funghi*; cheeses like taleggio and gorgonzola and grana padana; and there are the cured hams not just of Parma but of various localities, fresh pasta, game, seafood from Liguria, fish from the sub-Alpine lakes, and on and on. Simple but wonderful *locande* and *trattorie* abound, and there is no shortage of top flight restaurants either, not just in the cities but in numerous towns and villages. There is nothing quite so satisfyingly indulgent as spending a day winding and weaving from winery to winery in the Langhe or Monferrato, or in Franciacorta or the Bergamo hills or Oltrepò Pavese or the Colli Piacentini, with nothing much to do but eat and drink – er, taste.

And the range of wine styles one *can* taste from the hill-growing areas of Italy's North West is amazingly diverse. The subject has been generally treated in the previous chapter, so I'll not repeat myself here. But if one had to credit just one feature for the 'exciting' nature of the North West Italian wine scene it would have to be the ampelographical strength in depth which stands behind the amazing range of styles. We shall look presently at the grape varieties and their wines. but first, a brief consideration of the regions and of their most significant place names and viticultural areas.

Production areas

PIEMONTE AND VALLE D'AOSTA

If the North West is one of the world's most exciting wine zones, it is largely thanks to Piemonte, and in particular to that central macro-*conca*, or protective shell, formed by the Alps to the north and west, the Apennines to the south. Indeed the visual impression, as you drive westward from Alessandria on a rare clear day, of these colossi rising on the horizon in the distance on three sides is one you never forget. Nearer at hand are the beautiful roller-coaster hills of Asti and the Monferrato, of the Langhe and Roero, on which the amazing array of Piemontese varieties is planted.

A feature of these hills is that they have exposures in all directions of the compass to suit the wide range of characterful grape varieties in production. Southern exposures tend to be reserved for the best grapes of a given area, which may be Nebbiolo, Barbera, Dolcetto, Moscato or Cortese. It is generally more important for late-ripening black varieties to get the best exposure, while earlier ripeners like Dolcetto or Cabernet can be relegated to east or west. Burgundian varieties such as Chardonnay or Pinot Noir, much on the increase (especially the former), may actually thrive better facing north, their problem being more in the area of premature ripening, with consequent lack of balance, generally in the form of low acidity.

In this way the hypothetical owner of a hypothetical hill in, say, the Alba area, can use all sides: Nebbiolo towards the south (also near the top, for best drainage); Barbera south but lower down, or round to the south-east or south-west; Dolcetto east or west; Chardonnay or Sauvignon Blanc to the north. The differing ripening times of these grapes also enables the small grower to use his expensive vinification equipment several times – all in all a very efficient system, at least in theory.

Soils in the hills of Piemonte obviously vary considerably, but taking as an example the Langhe and Roero zones of the province of Cuneo, there tends to be a fairly sharp dividing line between the calcareous clay, in which the fuller reds are born, and the sandy marl, which suits lighter reds and whites. In neither case, given the steep to precipitous slopes involved, is there much structure in the form of pebbles or stones. Erosion can therefore be a problem, especially where vineyards are planted down-slope, or *ritocchino*, as many are these days to enable tractors to pass between rows without toppling over, crushing their driver, which is a risk of the cross-hill planting (*giro a poggio*) that most producers tend to prefer.

LANGHE is a name often used to describe the hilly area in which the grapes for world-famous Barolo and Barbaresco, among others, are grown. More specifically, Langhe is the name of a multi-DOC created in the mid-1990s to cover divers varietals, mainly of indigenous origin, grown on both banks of the Tanaro: Nebbiolo, Dolcetto, Freisa (reds), Favorita, Chardonnay and Arneis (whites). Langhe Rosso and Langhe Bianco may be blends of any non-aromatic red or white variety recommended or authorized for the area.

Although the Langhe denomination overlaps into the Roero, on the left bank of the Tanaro River, the hills of that name are situated on the right bank with the super-prosperous little town of ALBA, famous for exotic chocolates and truffles as well as for wines, at their heart. This being arguably Italy's most prestigious wine town, Alba is as good a centre as any on which to base a few days' gastronomic tour to the area, even though hotel accommodation is not as plentiful as one might expect in the circumstances.

Driving south and west from Alba one might head for the lofty town of LA MORRA, from whose highest square, site of the famous Belvedere restaurant, one can get a comprehensive view of the other major villages of Italy's most celebrated denomination, Barolo. The vineyards, planted principally to Nebbiolo but with a certain admixture, in less favourable sites, of Barbera, Dolcetto and one or two others, fall away under one's feet and rise again in a virtually uninterrupted mass to the town of CASTIGLIONE FALLETTO on the next ridge facing east, from which they fall again only to rise up to SERRALUNGA on the succeeding ridge. To the right or south, lower down, is the village of BAROLO itself, and

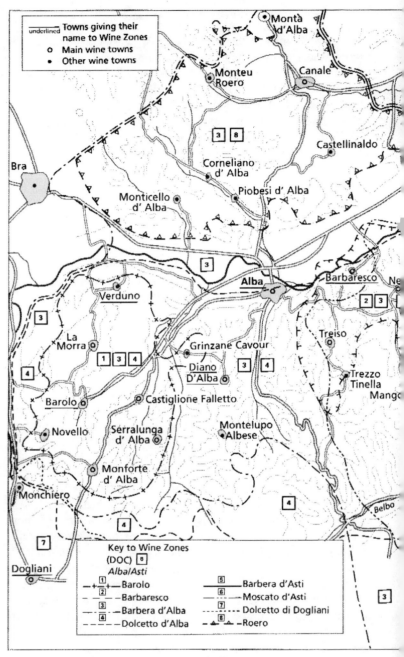

38

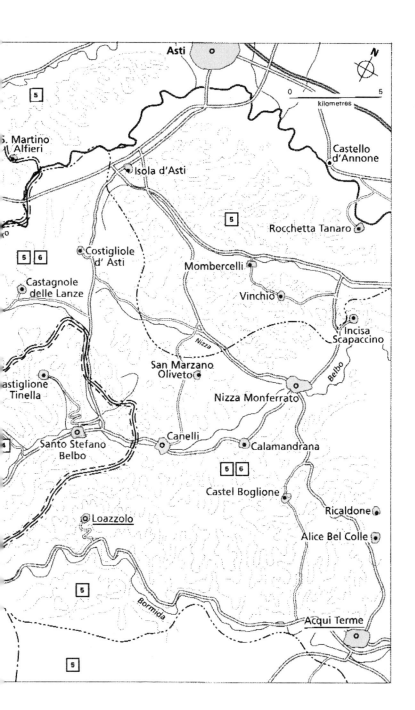

beyond that, right at the southern confine of the zone, high on the ridge, sits MONFORTE D'ALBA.

All this is overlapped by the larger DOC zones of Barbera d'Alba and Dolcetto d'Alba, which also stretch north and east of the town. There are a couple of lesser Dolcetto DOC zones here as well, that of DOGLIANI to the south of Barolo, and that of DIANO D'ALBA between Barolo and Alba itself. There is also the tiny zone of VERDUNO, one of the lesser Barolo communes, which boasts a separate DOC for the Pelaverga grape variety.

On the other side of Alba, still on the right bank of the Tanaro, taking the scenic route east out of the town, one comes to TREISO, first of the three principal villages of the relatively diminutive zone of the supposed 'queen' to Barolo's 'king': BARBARESCO. After Barbaresco, with its unmistakable tower, one arrives at NEIVE. Again the finest sites are dedicated to Nebbiolo, but with a mix similar to that of Barolo.

To the north of Alba flows the Tanaro River, on the opposite or left bank of which is the DOC zone called ROERO. Here the hills are lower, but steeper, than those of the Langhe, and there is the previously mentioned divide between two soil types: the lighter soils with a marked sand component, yielding perfumed whites and reds of distinctly less structure than is generally found on the right bank; and the heavier calcareous-clay sort, from which some of the great Nebbiolos and Barberas of the Langhe are derived. Barbera has traditionally been the principal red grape here, especially in the heavier soils, but there is mounting evidence today that Roero Nebbiolo (which, confusingly, may also come under the DOC Nebbiolo d'Alba) can rival the great Barolos, and many of the newer plantings are to that variety. In recent years there has been an increasing invasion, too, of international varieties, Roero, of lesser renown, being more open to invasion than the Langhe, although Barolo and Barbaresco have by no means escaped the odd incursion. The focal point of the Roero is undoubtedly CANALE, where both soil types are found.

Heading north and east from Alba, one enters the hill-rich DOC zone of ASTI, south of the town of Asti itself. The name on its own is used only for the well-known sweet *spumante*, although this word has now been deleted from the title for fear of downmarket connotations. However, the name Asti also combines with various varietal names to form what I shall frequently refer to as a 'multi-

DOC' (name of place preceded or followed by the name of any one of a range of grape names or wine styles). Thus for example Moscato d'Asti, a semi-sparkling wine of generally superior quality, some of the best of which in fact comes from the Alba side of the border to the west and from the province of Alessandria to the east. Thus, too, the potentially excellent Barbera d'Asti, not to mention Dolcetto, Freisa and Grignolino d'Asti.

LOAZZOLO is the name of a commune within the Asti area whose sweet Moscato from semi-dried grapes has its own DOC, unlike STREVI, a village near Acqui from which none the less come some of the greatest *passito* Moscatos of Italy.

Nomenclature and geography conspire in this zone to cause great confusion in the wine student's mind, because the zone of MONFERRATO, named after a group of hills and not a town, largely overlaps that of Asti. Barbera del Monferrato DOC may be produced throughout the Monferrato, whereas the DOC for Cortese confines itself to the ALTO (or Upper) MONFERRATO, while Grignolino del Monferrato Casalese, named after the town of CASALE MONFERRATO, is confined to the sector north of Asti on the Tanaro's left bank.

For good measure there is also a Ruchè di CASTAGNOLE MONFERRATO, named after the eponymous town in the Casalese, not to be confused with Castagnole delle Lanze (near Neive) nor yet with any of the Castigliones, Castelboglioes, Castellazzos or Casalborgones that abound in the area; still less with any of the too-numerous-to-be-counted Castelnuovos, one of which, CASTELNUOVO DON BOSCO, gives its name to a red Malvasia DOC, a wine almost as obscure as the Malvasia of CASORZO d'Asti in the Casalese.

Heading west from Casale, towards Turin, one may miss by blinking the DOC zones of Rubino di CANTAVENNA and GABIANO, names applied to blends of Barbera, Grignolino and Freisa of minimal production. Freisa, dry and still or semi-sweet and gassy, assumes more importance in an area east of Turin based on the town of CHIERI, said to be the variety's historical home.

In the south-eastern section of the province of Turin the commune of Pinerolo and thirty or so others make up a recently created and still utterly obscure multi-DOC called PINEROLESE with various sub-DOCs based on the better-known Piemontese red varieties plus a couple of weirdos called Doux d'Henry and Ramie, the former from the variety of the same name and the latter from the equally obscure Avana, Averengo and Neretto grapes.

Another recent creation, likewise obscure, is the small multi-DOC COLLINE SALUZZESI, in the province of Cuneo south of Pinerolese, where Pelaverga seems positively illustrious beside the bizarre wines of the Quagliano grape, featuring a sparkling sweet brew as well as a dry red table wine.

North of Turin is a more established area known as the CANAVESE, under which recently established DOC may be produced the varietals Barbera and Nebbiolo, or a red blended from either/or, or others, plus a white based on Erbaluce. Erbaluce, indeed, is the grape behind the wines of CALUSO – dry white, *passito* or *spumante*.

Further north in the same direction, technically in Piemonte but physically and spiritually in the Valle d'Aosta region, is the historic CAREMA zone, one of those mountainous terraced-vineyard areas mentioned above. One of the most classic Nebbiolo-based wines is made here, although in volumes ranging from small to minuscule.

VALLE D'AOSTA, in fact, is the umbrella name given to the wines of that region's sole multi-DOC, many of whose sub-DOCs, indeed grapes, betray a historic French, predominantly Burgundian, influence. The Pinot family is here in force, and there's even Gamay, while the so-called 'Malvoisie' turns out to be Pinot Grigio in disguise. Monte Bianco being the dominant feature of this small region, everything, including vineyards, is on mountainous terrain, and although there are over twenty sub-DOCs total production of quality wine rarely exceeds 4,000 hectolitres, with no single wine arriving even at 1,000 hectolitres. Most are destined for native or touristic consumption, so are of little interest in an international context; Blanc de MORGEX et de LA SALLE, from the grape of that name, being the only one with any pretensions at all.

Other place names of vinous significance (or not quite total insignificance) include ARVIER, TORRETTE, NUS and CHAMBAVE, all with red blends based on the Petit Rouge variety, the latter also producing what can be a tasty Moscato Passito; also ARNAD-MONJOVET and DONNAS, whose red blends are based on Nebbiolo, known locally as Picoutener.

Back in Piemonte and moving east, in the provinces of Novara and Vercelli, on either side of the Sesia river (which flows from the Alps southward into the Po just north of Alessandria), we come across yet another Nebbiolo zone. The king of Italian grapes, here called Spanna and supposedly – but not invariably – blended with Vespolina, Bonarda/Uva Rara or Croatina, is said to have a much longer tradition as a dry red table wine in this zone than in the Albese, GATTINARA at least having been held in high regard Europe-wide from the sixteenth century almost to the present day. Following persistent fraud – which Italians elegantly call *sofisticazione* – with twentieth-century producers wishing to cash in on the wine's good name, Gattinara slipped drastically in public esteem in the post-war period, a decline that recent elevation to DOCG status for both Gattinara and GHEMME has done little to correct, despite the efforts of a few dedicated producers.

Other Nebbiolo-based DOCs produced in the area include BOCA, SIZZANO and FARA on the left bank of the Sesia, with Ghemme (province of Novara), LESSONA and BRAMATERRA on the right with Gattinara (province of Vercelli). Actual production of these wines today is pitifully low, the response to which has been the recent creation of two multi-DOCs, COSTE DELLA SESIA (right bank) and COLLINE NOVARESI (left bank) in an attempt to revive interest with varietal wines or younger blends.

Descending in a great leap to the south-east corner of the region, in the province of Alessandria, we come upon a few areas of real import in international wine terms. Going from west to east, the first is ACQUI (full name Acqui Terme), a spa and market town, the first part of whose name is attached to three separate DOCs: Barbera, Dolcetto and Brachetto d'Acqui, the last being a DOCG. Next is OVADA, a town which seems, to the driver speeding southward on the *autostrada* towards Genoa, to be perched particularly precariously on its clifftop, and which gives its name to an especially rich and earthy Dolcetto; then to GAVI, famous for its dry white wines (usually still, sometimes sparkling) based on the Cortese grape; and finally to the COLLI TORTONESI on the Lombardy border, this being a relatively obscure multi-DOC embracing Cortese, Barbera and Dolcetto in various styles.

Which leaves PIEMONTE itself, a multi-DOC established in 1994 to cover a variety of cascades from higher denominations (which used to appear as *vino da tavola con indicazione geografica*) such as Piemonte Barbera, Piemonte Cortese, Chardonnay, Pinots Bianco, Grigio and Nero, Moscato (*frizzante* and *passito*), Brachetto, Bonarda and Spumante (dry). A major significance of the Piemonte DOC is that it has provided a model for other regions to follow in the effort to pull away from the *vino da tavola* scourge (as the authorities see it). The Piemonte denomination does not apply region-wide but only in established quality wine areas of the provinces of Alessandria, Asti and Cuneo, allowing producers to reserve their respective higher names for better wines while remaining within the DOC system with their lesser creations.

LOMBARDY

Lombardy, neighbouring Piemonte to the east, may be the richest and most populous region of Italy, featuring industries galore and the urban giant of Milan backed up by the cities of Brescia and Bergamo. But in quality wine production terms it is distinctly less wealthy than its rival – although it must be acknowledged that Piemonte is a hard act to follow. One reason for this is that Lombardy has very little in the way of autochthonous (i.e. indigenous) grape varieties. On the other hand, Lombardy has been quite adept at borrowing what's interesting from others, so you'll find Piemonte's Nebbiolo, Barbera and Cortese at good quality levels, Trentino's Marzemino and Schiava, the French contingent in force, some of the Germans (Riesling Renano, for example), the Lambrusco of Emilia, the Verdicchio of the Marche (Trebbiano di Lugana), Garganega, Moscato, Malvasia – all interesting but more associated with somewhere else.

Lombardy has also demonstrated enterprise in its borrowing of wine styles from other places. The bottle-fermented sparkling wines of Franciacorta are indisputably the best in Italy – some would say the best in the world outside Champagne. In Lombardy you can find wines attempting to emulate the best of Bordeaux and of Burgundy, not to mention respectable versions of the Barbera d'Asti style, of the Amarone della Valpolicella style, and of the frothy Emilian style.

The northernmost viticultural zone of Lombardy – indeed of Italy, barring the Alto Adige – is the VALTELLINA. This 30-odd kilometre stretch of vineyard due north of Bergamo (but almost inaccessible from that city, for lack of roads across the mountainous divide) is mainly planted on steep to precipitous slopes along the north bank of the Adda river, which flows east to west from the Swiss Alps past the city of Sondrio towards Lake Como. The often terraced vineyards are therefore south facing and have the benefit of the river before them and the mountains behind to temper the fierce Alpine weather. So it has been since ancient times, the earliest wines being based, probably, on the Rossola, Pignola and Brugnola grapes that still make up a minority part of the blended Valtellina *normale*, although today the partners of mainstay Nebbiolo (or Chiavennasca, as they call it in these parts) tend to be increasingly Merlot and/or Pinot Nero. Another indication of antiquity is the existence of the Amarone-like Sforzato (Sfursat), which may be made using a mix of the above-mentioned grapes, while Valtellina Superiore, with its four sub-denominations, must be 95% Nebbiolo.

In the south-western corner of the Lombardy region is OLTREPÒ PAVESE, so named because it is situated in the province of Pavia beyond the Po, from the standpoint of Milan. Milan manages to absorb most of the area's very considerable production – not far short of a million hectolitres – which accounts for the fact that one rarely sees Oltrepò Pavese wines outside the region. Perhaps the Milanese like the wines because they remind them of quiet Sundays spent in the rolling, wooded hills, far from the city's madness; and why not stock up while you're there?

The Oltrepò multi-DOC offers a wide variety of styles, some delightfully artisanal but unsuitable for export, ranging from still or frothing blended reds, mainly based on Barbera, to varietal French-style reds (Pinot Nero, Cabernet), to still or frothy dry or medium whites (both Rieslings, Cortese, Sauvignon, Chardonnay, Pinots Grigio and Nero vinified *in bianco*), to bottle-fermented sparklers, to Malvasia or Moscato medium-to-sweet semi-sparklers, right through to fully sweet Moscatos either *passito* or *liquoroso*.

Between north and south there is a central viticultural zone, or series of zones, stretching from Bergamo across to the western and southern shores of Lake Garda. The wine of Bergamo's hills is called VALCALEPIO, an area running from slightly north-west of the city over to the west shores of Lago d'Iseo. The red and white are blends of Cabernet plus Merlot and Pinot plus Chardonnay respectively, despite which promising start (for Francophiles) one rarely finds anything particularly exciting.

The FRANCIACORTA zone starts on the southern shores of Lago d'Iseo and runs to the west of the city of Brescia. This is another beautifully wooded, hilly area, studded with the elegant villas of the sort of super-wealthy people who find it amusing to try and produce top quality bordeaux, burgundy or (mainly) champagne look-alike wines. By their price ye shall know them. Despite the prevailing Francophilia, however, the most important red wine here, Terre di Franciacorta Rosso, is expected to throw some Nebbiolo and Barbera into the otherwise Cabernet/Merlot blend. The white, thank heavens, is free from any such native taint, being a blend of Chardonnay, Pinot Bianco and Pinot Nero vinified *in bianco* – that is, without the grapes' red skins used in the vinification process.

To the west and east of the city of Brescia, however, are two historic DOC zones, named after central villages, which do contain Italian, if not Lombard, grapes: respectively CELLATICA and BOTTICINO. Perhaps their lack of popularity has something to do with the strangeness of their blend, which in both cases includes Marzemino, Schiava and Barbera, plus others. A third zonelet, CAPRIANO DEL COLLE, boasting a similarly eclectic grape-mix, lies south of the city; there is also a Trebbiano under this name, supposedly principally of the Soave or Lugana clone. Lugana, indeed, is partially within the territory of Lombardy, but it is mainly a Veneto wine.

Continuing our odyssey among oddities in an eastward direction, we come upon RIVIERA DEL GARDA BRESCIANO on the western shores of Italy's largest lake in which Lombardy's sole indigenous grape of any significance, Groppello, displays itself either varietally or in a red mixed with Sangiovese, Marzemino and Barbera. The Chiaretto of the same denomination is one of northern Italy's better rosés. The white is supposedly a mix of Rieslings Renano and Italico, although producers here do not necessarily respect the law (but where do they?).

Within the boundaries of Garda Bresciano but of a different variety is the separate DOC SAN MARTINO DELLA BATTAGLIA where for some reason Tocai Friulano has found a home from home.

A recently established catch-all DOC for varietal wines from certain communes of the province of Mantua in close proximity to the lake is GARDA. The denomination mainly covers communes in the province of Verona, in Veneto, and will be examined more closely on page 148.

The city of Mantua, in the Po Valley plain and therefore seeming to have greater affinity with Emilia-Romagna, is none the less technically in Lombardy, and is associated with two wines which betray its schizoid tendencies: the earth-shattering COLLI MORENICI MANTOVANI DEL GARDA Rosso, which combines Merlot, Verona's Molinara and Negrara, and Romagna's Sangiovese; and the equivalent Bianco, based on Romagna's Trebbiano and Veneto's Garganega. The local Lambrusco MANTOVANO, on the other hand, is clearly of an Emilian persuasion.

LIGURIA

Arching like an inverted crescent moon along the Riviera from just north of the marble hills of Carrara to the French border, via the cities/provinces of La Spezia, Genoa, Savona and Imperia, Liguria is almost as long as Italy's heel, Puglia. Indeed it can take longer to drive through, so frequent are the bends in an *autrostrada* that, if it isn't curving through a tunnel, is arching round over a gorge cut by one of the many streams tumbling down through mountains which loom on one side and descend on the other precipitously to the Mediterranean, sometimes appearing, in a reversal of the perspective, actually to grow out of the sea.

This is tourist country, not wine country – certainly not modern wine country. Less than one two-hundredth of Italy's production comes from here, most of it being consumed locally at prices which export markets would refuse to pay for the quality. These days it may make sense to grow fruits and vegetables out of season under plastic, as increasingly seems to be happening; it makes little sense to work a vineyard which may be so steep as to require hauling equipment and even soil up from terrace to ancient dry-stone terrace, or taking harvested grapes out by mini-funicular. The old boys may still be slaving away up there as their forefathers have done for centuries, but the younger generation doesn't want to know.

Ligurians think of their geography, and their viticulture, as dividing into two sections, as seen from a Genovese perspective: the Ponente, or the land of the setting sun, and the Levanto, land of the rising sun. The vast majority of production is dry white table wine, to go with the plentiful seafood and/or to be sipped by tourists in seaside *caffè* on hot summer days. What reds there are tend to be concentrated at the two extremities, which are also the

47

points farthest south. The proximity of the sea makes the climate just that bit too cool for regular ripening of red grapes.

In terms of vines grown, Liguria's connection with the North West zone is tenuous. Piemonte's Favorita may be related to Liguria's dominant grape, Vermentino, but the latter is essentially a Mediterranean variety, associated with Sardinia and the Tuscan coast. The only firm connection is the Ponente's Ormeasco, a Ligurian form of Dolcetto, but the production is tiny. And there is Sangiovese, and Trebbiano, in the Levanto to balance that influence. Nevertheless, to take Liguria out of the North West and include it in Central Italy would be geographically anomalous, and I wouldn't want to upset anyone's habitual views . . .

At the Levanto, or Tuscan, end, in the province of La Spezia, the first quality viticultural zone of note is the relatively recently established COLLI DI LUNI, the hills on either side of the Magra Valley inland from La Spezia. Vermentino is the main white grape here, Sangiovese the main red, but as one producer put it: 'Here we have complete anarchy – no one follows the *disciplinare*, we simply use what we find in our vineyards.' In the white department, that is likely to mean Trebbiano Toscano, Albarola (a version of Trebbiano) and Bosco, while in the red it can mean Ciliegiolo, Canaiolo Nero, the local Pollera, as well as Cabernet Sauvignon. This is not only the most prolific production area in Liguria, but is rapidly establishing itself as the best. COLLINE DI LEVANTO is a much larger area with similar characteristics, though the recently established DOC is in its infancy.

The best-known of Liguria's wine zones historically, CINQUE TERRE, is on the seaward side of La Spezia, overlooking the coast. This must be a contender for the world's most intensely terraced vineyard, admirable for its aesthetic appeal if rather less so for its rather bizarre white wine based on the autochthonous Bosco grape, together with Albarola and Vermentino. The same grapes are used for a strange *passito* wine called Sciacchetrà, the name of which, I am expertly advised, has no etymological connection (except by clang association) with the Ponente's Sciac-trà, despite repeated journalistic efforts to establish a connection. The name is probably (I am told) derived from a town in Palestine named Shekar, there having been a Middle Eastern community here in the ninth century.

The RIVIERA LIGURE DI PONENTE has a considerably more

impressive track record for quality wine production than the Levanto, but the reality is distinctly less interesting in international terms. The multi-DOC covers white varietals Vermentino and Pigato and reds Rossese and Ormeasco, the latter also coming in *rosato* form under the above-mentioned Sciac-trà which means 'crush and rack' in dialect.

Best-known of the Ponente's wine zones is doubtless that surrounding the village of DOLCEACQUA, which makes a speciality of the indigenous Rossese grape.

You can go a lifetime without ever seeing or tasting a wine from Liguria – unless you go to Liguria, that is – so I've probably already covered too much space. Just to add, however, that for a comprehensive taste of the wines of Liguria you can visit the Enoteca Regionale at the delightful hilltop town of Castiglione Magra in the extreme east of the region, near La Spezia.

EMILIA

So what is an Emilian persuasion? It will not do to be simplistic about this and say that Emilia equals Lambrusco equals industrial wine in vast quantities from high-trained vineyards on land which is pancake flat as far as the eye can see. In fact the wines of Emilia are surprisingly diverse, and by no means all from *la pianura*, the plain. The most interesting ones, in fact, are produced in the Apennine foothills, from Piacenza eastward and slightly southward through the agricultural/industrial centres of Parma and Reggio Emilia to Bologna, the regional capital of Emilia-Romagna and the effective dividing line between its two parts.

Emilia connects up with Lombardy, wine-wise, in two quite separate sectors, that of plain-produced Lambruscos, overlapping the two regions between Modena and Mantua, and that of hill-grown vines of the Colli Piacentini which adjoins the Oltrepò Pavese. Apart from Lambrusco, Ancellotta and Pignoletto, and to a lesser extent Malvasia, all of which are Emilian specialities, the varieties grown relate either to the North West (the Piemontese group) or the North East (the internationals). On the other hand, the viticultural relationship with Central Italy, in particular with the other half of the political region, Romagna, is tenuous.

There is also a sharp contrast between the complexity and confusion of Emilian viniculture and the relative simplicity of that of

Romagna. One of the problems the wine student faces is the sheer number of different wines and styles that campanilistic bureaucrats – more than producers, one suspects – have managed to wangle on to the statute books. Even Lambrusco is geographically considerably less straightforward than at first meets the eye.

Coming from the north, the zone begins with Lambrusco Salamino di SANTA CROCE, named after a village just off the *autostrada* as you drive south from Mantua to Modena. East of Santa Croce is the town of SORBARA, these two being on the flat. From more hilly territory south of Modena comes a third DOC Lambrusco, Grasparossa di CASTELVETRO. DOC production of each of these is in the area of 60,000 hectolitres per annum, while production of Lambrusco REGGIANO, from around the city of Reggio Emilia, equals the other three put together. That said, non-DOC Lambrusco production, generally of the sweet, screw-cap stuff, far exceeds that of DOC wine.

Moving east to west, the first non-Lambrusco zone is the multi-DOC COLLI BOLOGNESI, a large area south of Bologna on either side of the *autostrada* as you drive into the foothills of the Apennines heading for Florence. Although the *disciplinare*, the regulation that 'disciplines' the content of named wines, provides for most of the French contingent as well as Barbera and Riesling Italico, the most produced wine is the local Pignoletto (from the white grape of that name), which may be still, semi- or fully sparkling, or *passito*. The litany of sub-DOCs under the name Colli Bolognesi is repeated with variations for divers sub-zones, of which ZOLA PREDOSA is the only one that consumers outside the immediate area are likely to have heard of, thanks to the producer Vallania (the others, for the record, are COLLINE DI RIOSTO, COLLINE MARCONIANE, MONTE SAN PIETRO, COLLINE DI OLIVETO, TERRE DI MONTEBUDELLO and SERRAVALLE). In all there are no fewer than fifty sub-DOCs of ever-decreasing international recognizability under the overall heading of Colli Bolognesi: a marketer's nightmare.

The village of SCANDIANO, just south of Reggio, boasts an eclectic multi-DOC including Malvasia, Marzemino and Lambrusco Montericco as well as some international varietals of which the most important is Sauvignon, a grape that enjoys a traditional association with the zone. However, only the blended white, based on Sauvignon, is produced in any volume among DOCs.

Moving slightly further west again, the COLLI DI PARMA DOC is limited to Sauvignon and Malvasia, and a Rosso whose main significance resides in the fact that it is made up of Barbera, Bonarda and Croatina; in other words, we are approaching Emilia's virtual extension of Lombardy's Oltrepò Pavese, the COLLI PIACENTINI.

This last, as the name suggests, is a hilly zone specializing in frothing semi- to fully aromatic whites from Malvasia, Moscato and others, white table wines from Sauvignon, Chardonnay and members of the Pinot family, and reds from Barbera and Bonarda (these may or may not be frothing) or Cabernet and Pinot Noir. In the white department there is a local hero called Ortrugo, not found elsewhere; there is also a so-called Trebbianino di Val Trebbia – which of course contains little or no Trebbiano. The best-known and most-produced red is Gutturnio from, among others, the commune of ZIANO PIACENTINO; it is a Barbera/Bonarda blend which may or may not be *frizzante*.

Grapes, wines and producers – red

NEBBIOLO

If it is true, as some including myself would claim, that Nebbiolo is one of the world's greatest red grape varieties, along with Cabernet Sauvignon, Merlot, Pinot Noir and Syrah, it is equally true that, unlike Cabernet and Merlot at least, it is a temperamental creature, not to say neurotic, multi-faceted perhaps, but full of contradictions.

If you don't give it the right site, a rootstock that inhibits vigour, a limestone-based soil, south to south-west exposure near to but generally not at the top of the slope, it won't perform. It buds earlier than any other variety around, so it is very susceptible to frost damage. It ripens later than any, so it is vulnerable to poor autumn weather. It is a bore to tend in the vineyard on account of excessive vigour. It is inclined both to uppish acidity and tough tannins, thus requiring very careful handling in the vinification. On the other hand it is capable in the right conditions of achieving high sugar levels, which manifest themselves not just in the form of alcohol but also in a wonderful, almost porty, sweetness on the back-palate even in a technically 'dry' wine.

While the vine was very probably cultivated in the Langhe before, perhaps indeed long before, the fourteenth century, it was not until the appearance in 1303 of Pier de' Crescenzi's *Ruralium Commodorum* that we find any documentary mention of it. De' Crescenzi calls 'Nubiola' a grape of great vinosity, making a wine 'for keeping, very potent' which 'is much praised in the city of Asti and those parts'; to be noted that de' Crescenzi spent many years as a judge at Asti, in which province Nebbiolo was much cultivated until relatively recently.

Actually it is only in the last couple of hundred years that mentions of the vine variety, as distinct from the excellent red wines of the Langhe, of the provinces of Aosta and Vercelli and of the Valtellina (major Nebbiolo production zones), have become at all frequent, although G.B. Croce in 1606 did briefly acknowledge its existence in its current spelling. Nineteenth-century references to Nebbiolo indicate that, prior to the coming of phylloxera, Nebbiolo was much more widely planted than it is today, having had, as we have seen, a major presence in the Asti-Monferrato area of eastern Piemonte, from which it has now effectively disappeared, as well as being well represented in the Saluzzese, Pinerolese and Canavese.

After the débâcle, when it came to replanting on American rootstock, growers in many places abandoned Nebbiolo wholesale in favour of such accommodating varieties as Barbera. Only in a few very restricted areas did producers keep faith with it, so that despite its qualitative eminence it still today occupies but a fraction of total vineyard area in the North West (about 6 per cent of total vineyard area in Piemonte and 7.5 per cent in Lombardy; 27 per cent in Valle d'Aosta, but that's still only 200 hectares or less).

Some forty different clones of Nebbiolo have been identified, Nebbiolo being a grape that mutates easily according to the *terroir* in which it is cultivated. Three clones dominate the scene in the classic vineyards of the Albese: Lampia, Michet and Rosé. Lampia, the one most widely distributed, is the most reliable producer, though some say that Michet (probably a genetic mutation of Lampia through viral infection) gives the higher quality. Rosé, while perhaps the most perfumed of the three, is easily the lightest in colour and body, and is rarely planted nowadays, indeed is more likely to be replaced; Barolo producers have enough trouble getting colour from their grapes. In the past few years the Piemonte region's Experimental Centre for Viticulture and Oenology, in conjunction with the University of Turin, has developed nineteen new clones, most of them derived from the three mentioned.

Nebbiolo appears to be capable of achieving consistent excellence only in the clay and limestone soil of the Albese, where fogs, floods and hail-damage are commonplace. In the sandier soils of Roero, in Vercelli and Novara, on the steep slopes of Carema, and in Lombardy's Valtellina, Nebbiolo performs creditably, just occasionally brilliantly. Elsewhere in the world, as elsewhere in Italy, it rarely quite makes it, and while pioneers like Jim Clendennen in California and Gary Crittenden in Australia have achieved something approaching its structure and its aroma, no one yet outside Alba seems to have succeeded in marrying structure and typicity with charm. As a 'holy grail' variety, Nebbiolo presents a challenge to the modern seeker-producer at least equal to that of Pinot Noir.

THE WINES IN PIEMONTE

BAROLO

The Nebbiolo wine *par excellence* is, of course, Barolo, named, as we have seen, after a village in the middle of the eponymous zone. It is a small zone in world terms, with an average annual production (of Nebbiolo for Barolo) of under 40,000 hectolitres, tiny in comparison even with Pinot Noir in the Côte d'Or. Now that Barolo has 'caught on' in world wine market terms this restricted production, or low supply, contributes significantly to an ever-increasing pressure on availability (downward) and price (upward).

Under new regulations, Barolo DOCG must be aged for three years (Riserva for 4¾ years) of which one (previously two) must be in wood, be it for *normale* or *riserva*. These are the legal minima which, traditionally, even under the old regulations, many producers conceived as inadequate, believing Barolo to be a wine needing even longer ageing in barrel in order to shed some of its famous astringency and to take on that complexity and noble decadence that characterize the greatest examples. Forty or more days on the skins during fermentation, and four years (often much more) in large Slavonian oak barrels, were commonplace procedures until twenty or so years ago.

Even today, maceration durations of twenty to thirty days and oak maturation of four years and beyond have not passed from favour. Giovanni Conterno's Monfortino, for example – a very expensive, limited production Barolo Riserva which its producer could sell several times over despite the high price – is aged seven to eight years in *botte*, in the barrel. Even so, Conterno's motto is that when a Barolo goes into bottle it should be *'imbevibile'* (undrinkable). It should, on the other hand, be a great bottle after twenty, thirty, forty years.

There is a tendency on the part of modernists to reduce drastically the traditional maceration and maturation in wood periods, to the point of racking the juice off the skins after three or four days' maceration (or less), using repeated punching down or roto-fermentors or tanks equipped with inner paddles, plus dangerously high fermentation temperatures, to get out colour and extract. By such practitioners wood-ageing is today reduced to the new statutory minimum of one year (or less), and it will take place mainly in French *barriques* or *tonneaux*.

The modernists aim at greater fruitiness and roundness and easier, earlier drinkability, less 'defects' in the form of oxidation or uppish volatile acidity, maintaining that softer tannins and easier acids do not prejudice ageing capability, especially as these wines will have more wood tannins from having been aged in newer, smaller oak than the traditional style. To my palate the modernists have yet to come up with anything as magical as an old Giacosa or Giacomo Conterno, and there is far too prevalent a tendency to drown the delicate and complex perfumes of Nebbiolo in wood aromas; but it is true that there are to date few if any 'old' Barolos of the modern style to judge from, and perhaps we should wait and see whether the perfumes return in a more rounded wine after several years' ageing.

The modernists' principal spokesman, Elio Altare of La Morra, is caustic in his dismissal of that *tipicità* which, for him, represents tradition. 'It's not the acids and the tannins that make a great wine; it's the balance. Today, if a wine isn't agreeable when you uncork it you (the consumer) won't buy it again. Perhaps,' he adds with a wink, 'perhaps I should add a bit of that *merdina* or *sporchezza* (shit, dirt) which makes a wine "typical".'

It is important in any case to note that the majority of producers today, including some of the greatest, tend to settle for a middle road between the two extremes. Beppe Colla, one of the most respected of old guard *barolisti*, puts it this way: 'You can have as much structure as you like (in the form of acids and tannins); the essential factor is that they should be covered by the fruit.' This means three things: pick the best fruit you can ('If you wouldn't eat it, don't pick it', Mauro Mascarello tells his harvesters); avoid oxidation at all stages of vinification (Altare goes so far as to keep his wine in a state of reduction); and, however long you age the wine in your barrels, make sure they are always properly topped up.

My personal inclination, for what it's worth, is to side with the traditionalists, by which I mean the good ones, like Bruno Giacosa,

Giovanni and Aldo Conterno, Mauro and Bartolo Mascarello. As Colla says, the first principle should be the dominance of the primary fruit (and floral, specifically rose) characteristics of the wine. All too often, one finds oak sticking out like a sore thumb, presumably in deference to the 'international market'. Small oak, preferably not too new and certainly not too 'high toast', can soften what might otherwise be a tough old buzzard, and there are those in Alba who are indeed capable of managing it remarkably well. But the old-timers in Alba would say, and I would agree, that any fool anywhere can achieve oak aromas in a wine, but only Nebbiolo producers in the Albese can achieve the wonderful and subtle, and therefore easily covered, aromas of which their own home-grown grape is capable and which make it unique in the world.

The question is: are we aiming to make great Barolo, or great wine? I would maintain that there are a number of the latter which would not qualify in the former category. I realize that the tide of opinion is against me among consumers, journalists and, increasingly, producers, but the proof of the pudding, to paraphrase while mixing metaphors, is in the drinking. Which means that the majority are right for them, but I'm right for me.

Another polemic which has caused a stir in recent years in Barolo/Barbaresco circles is that surrounding the introduction of other grape varieties into what, both by the old regulations and the new, is supposed to be a 100% varietal wine. Being strictly illegal, no one will admit to doing this, and opinions as to whether Cabernet (or Merlot, or Syrah, or Barbera) is being sneaked into the mix range from 'absolutely not' to 'up to 30%'. The main reason for doing it, one should explain, would be to improve Nebbiolo's colour which tends both towards lightness and an appearance of premature maturation (orangeing); and it is a fact that some remarkably purple-hued wines have popped up among the orangey ones in tastings recently, much to the amazement of all present. Another reason for such blending would be to improve 'fruitiness', that criterion which, some fetishists would say, is the only valid one for the judging of quality wine (whereas the great old-style Nebbiolos of maturity are full of mineral and animal aromas – goudron, leather – as well as flower and fruit, both fresh and dried). Purists would say, and the law has re-affirmed, that such a practice is no more acceptable in Barolo/Barbaresco than it would be in Burgundy with its wonderful varietal Pinot Noirs.

Come to think of it, maybe it is a good idea.

In any case, some of the very loftiest names have been associated with this sort of illicit blending. Say no more.

Until the 1970s Barolo was for the most part a non-*cru* wine, like non-vintage champagne (in the nineteenth century Barolo was often sweet – due, some say, to stuck fermentations – so tradition doesn't have that strong a grip). The story then was that the best wines came from a judicious blend comprising, say, a bit of La Morra, with its relative roundness and softness, a bit of Serralunga with its firm structure and classic lines, a bit of Monforte with its power cum elegance, a bit of Barolo with its earthy richness, a bit of Castiglione Falletto with its own intrinsic harmony. The story, indeed, had its convincing side, and I myself bought it when researching *Life Beyond Lambrusco*. I am not sure to this day that there isn't an element of truth to it, but the fact remains that virtually all top Barolo today is, or purports to be, from single vineyards or at least from delimited sub-zones. Indeed, the *crème de la crème* will come, as in Burgundy, from *crus* of quite diminutive dimensions. No one has got around yet to making a classification of the *grand cru*, *premier cru* type; indeed, such a classification would appear unlikely in view of the political battles that have arisen over the mere recognition of superior sub-zones, let alone their grading according to quality.

The best sites

In any case, in accordance with new regulations arising out of DOC law 164 of 1992, these superior sub-zones (the rather unpoetic word *sottozona* here takes on a very precise meaning – see Glossary) in each Barolo commune are in the process of being officially identified, although, as indicated, the definitive lists remain the subject of spirited intra-communal debates, which have been raging now for several years. Below is a list of the *sottozone* considered (at the time of writing) probable for the various communes:

BAROLO: Albarella, Bergeisa, Bricco, Bricco Viole or Bricco delle Viole, Brunate, Cannubi, Castellero, Cerequio, Coste di Rose, Crosia, Fossati, La Villa, La Volta, Le Coste, Liste, Monghisolfo or Cannubi Boschis, Monrobiolo, Muscatel or Cannubi Muscatel, Paiagallo, Preda, Ravera, Ruè, San Pietro, San Lorenzo or Cannubi

San Lorenzo, Sarmassa, Terlo, Valletta or Cannubi Valletta, Via Nuova, Vignane, Zonchetta, Zuncai.

CASTIGLIONE FALLETTO: Altenasso, Bricco Boschis, Brunella, Ceroni, Codana, Croceta, Fiasc, Lipulot, Mariondino, Monprivato, Parussi, Pernanno, Piantà, Pira, Pugnane, Rocche, Scarrone, Serra, Solanotto, Valentino, Valletti, Vignolo, Villero.

GRINZANE CAVOUR: Bablino, Borzone, Canova, Castello, Garretti, Gustava, La Corle, Raviole.

LA MORRA: Arborina, Bricco Chiesa, Bricco Luciani, Bricco Manescotto, Bricco Manzoni, Bricco Rocca, Bricco San Biagio, Brunate, Capalot, Case Nere, Cerequio, Ciocchini, Conca, Fossati, Galina, Gattera, Giachini, La Serra, Monfalletto, Rive, Rocche, Rocche dell'Annunziata, Rocchette, Rocchettevino, Roere, Roggeri, Roncaglie, Sarmassa, Serra dei Turchi, Silio

MONFORTE: Arnulfo, Bussia, Castelletto, Cerretta, Conterni, Dardi, Gavarini, Ginestra, Gramolere, Le Coste, Manzoni Soprani, Mosconi, Pianpolvere, Pressenda, Ravera, Santo Stefano, Visette.

NOVELLO: Bergera, Cerviano, Ravera, Sottocastello.

SERRALUNGA: Arione, Badarina, Baudana, Boscareto, Bricco Cerretta, Briccolina, Boscareto, Broglio, Carpegna, Cerrati, Cerretta Cappalotto, Cerretta Piani, Collaretto, Colombaro, Costabella, Damiano, Falletto, Fontanafredda, Francia, Gabutti, Gianetto, La Serra, Lazzarito, Le Turne, Lirano, Manocino, Marenca, Margheria, Meriame, Ornato, Parafada, Prabun, Pradone, Prapò or Pra di Pò, Rivette, San Bernardo, San Rocco, Sorano, Teodoro, Vei, Vignarionda, Vughera.

VERDUNO: Boscatto, Breri, Campasso, Massara, Monvigliero, Pisapla, Pria, Riva, Rocca, San Lorenzo, Sottocastello.

It is important to be clear that the above are names of officially recognized sub-zones, which may in geographical terms be owned by a single producer or divided among several. Below the official sub-zones may be parts of sub-zones, such as (to take an example from Monforte's Bussia) Bussia Soprana or Bussia Sottana; and below these may be single vineyards, such as Vigna Colonello or Vigna Cicala, whose names may be more familiar to Barolo lovers than most of the areas scheduled for official designation. Readers are therefore warned, with apologies for the prevailing confusion, that attempts to match the names of the *crus* of producers discussed below with the sub-zone names above will in many cases prove fruitless. For the future, however, the idea is that single vineyard names will not be allowed on labels except in the context of an officially recognized sub-zone.

The producers

Considering Barolo to represent the highest level of wine generically in northern Italy, I have devoted more space to this section than I have been able to do in respect of subsequent sections. This having been said, one must admit that a detailed discussion of Barolo and its producers would require a book to itself, and in many cases I have had to be all too brief.

There are those who would exlude from the hall of fame all the 'traditionalists' and include only the *avant-garde*, and only a few of them at that. And there are those who consider the new wave's ways anathema, and would strike all of *them* from the list, saying that over-dependence on oak and the fanatical avoidance of 'defects' has destroyed the soul of the wine. I have toyed with the idea of separating producers according to type, according to length of establishment regardless of type, or according to quality, and have decided eventually that the only reasonable division is according to commune, by alphabetical order. Producers of Barolo whose *cantine* are situated in the Barbaresco zone will be considered under Barbaresco (see page 82).

It is to be hoped that the descriptions themselves will give sufficient indication as to the style and the quality of the producer. Of course, there is no substitute for tasting, provided you can afford it and acquire the bottles. If you get a chance to taste the production of the following please do not take me to task if certain examples don't knock you out. By no means all of the wineries here featured are capable of such a feat, and some of the wines, especially the cheaper blends, or *crus* from lesser years, are ordinary to poor. The only claim I make for these producers is that they are *capable*, at their best, of making wine which is at least very good, sometimes excellent, very occasionally superb.

BAROLO (COMMUNE)

Fratelli **Barale**. Sergio Barale has breathed new life into this *azienda*, since 1870 one of the most respected guardians of quality. Barolo Castellero and Barbaresco Rabajà, fermented in wood and aged in Slavonian-oak *botti*, and also Dolcetto d'Alba Bussia, are the stars.

Giacomo **Borgogno** & Figli. Established 1761 (no less), long controlled by the Boschis family, this traditionalist *azienda* specializes in non-*cru* Barolo capable, from good years, of lasting and improving over several decades, though young wines can be difficult for the modern palate to approach.

Giacomo **Brezza** & Figli. Another arch-traditionalist, founded 1885, Brezza produce sturdy Barolos for laying down from such top vineyards as Cannubi, Cannubi Muscatel, Sarmassa and Castellero.

Tenuta **La Volta**. The Cabutto family control this *azienda* which has been going since 1920. Their Barolo Riserva del Fondatore is one of the pillars of traditional Barolo: long maceration without temperature control, punching down of the cap, five years' maturing in *botte*.

Marchesi di Barolo. The story of modern Barolo effectively began in the mid-nineteenth century when the Marchesa di Barolo, Giulia Falletti, whose family had been owners of the land south of Alba for centuries, began producing with the help of the French oenologist Oudart a rich red, *dry* Nebbiolo wine that subsequently took on the name of the producer's commune. (The firm's wine library, which boasts numerous bottles of principal vintages going back almost a century and a half, contains an 1859 labelled 'Cannubio' and an 1861 labelled 'Barolo' – probably representing the first example of that name generically. An interesting aspect is that, in those days, the stopping of the bottle was achieved, not by cork, but by corncob, hardened and shaped.)

Since 1929 controlled by the Abbona family, Marchesi di Barolo have in recent years emerged from the mediocrity in which they had temporarily mired themselves with some outstanding *crus* from their own vineyards at Cannubi, Brunate and Sarmassa. Methods are a mix of the traditional and the modern, there being glass-lined concrete vats and huge, century-old 180-hectolitre chestnut barrels for fermentation and ageing respectively, as well as some brand new rotating fermentors and numerous French oak *tonneaux* and French and American oak *barriques* for maturation, the latter being used for Barbera (*cru* Ruvei *et al.*), the former in particular for a recently developed international-style Barolo called Estate Vineyard.

Their ordinary Barolo, made from grapes bought in (they remain one of the principal *commercianti* of the zone, although in recent years they have halved total production from the previous 3 million bottle mark), remains, however, very ordinary indeed.

Bartolo **Mascarello**. Bartolo, grand old man and self-proclaimed *tradizionalista* of Barolo (wine and commune), is no longer able to tend his beloved vineyards in Canubbi (as he spells it), San Lorenzo, Ruè and Rocche dell'Annunziata (the last named in La Morra), but the philosophy of the *azienda* remains safe in the hands of his only daughter, Maria Teresa, and as steadfastly old-fashioned as it has for most of the twentieth century. Long maceration on skins without any attempt to regulate temperature, lengthy ageing in large old chestnut and Slavonian oak *botti*, minimal handling – these are Mascarello's methods, together with a refusal to budge from the now archaic practice (for top Barolo) of selling the wine as a blend rather than as a *cru*. 'I may be the last of the Mohicans,' he declares with a jovial wave of the hand, 'but my customers appreciate the fact that I still make my wine as the land dictates. A single site does not necessarily come good every year – especially in dry years – and Barolo to be consistently good needs the mutually compensating characteristics of different vineyards.'

Enrico **Pira** & Figli. Though dating back to the early twentieth century, this *azienda* was taken in charge recently by the charming Chiara Boschis from Borgogno (above) who, in keeping with her family traditions, makes blended Barolo and Barolo Riserva to a high standard, even if Chiara, modestly, is still seeking her way.

Giuseppe **Rinaldi**. Barolos Le Coste and Brunate are made at this 100-year-old plus estate in the time-honoured fashion: strong, tannic and rich of extract thanks to a maceration of traditional length and a good four years' maturation in large-format Slavonian oak barrels.

Luciano **Sandrone**. Sandrone learned the art of making great Barolo as oenologist at Marchesi di Barolo. He began producing wine from his own grapes in the late 1970s, and increasing fame induced him in the early 1990s to leave Marchesi and concentrate on his own thing. Today his *cru* Cannubi Boschis and blend Le

Vigne, wines at their best miraculously combining power and concentration with elegance, are among the most sought-after Barolos internationally, almost impossible to obtain even at high price. Generally associated with the modernists, Sandrone uses French oak *tonneaux* for ageing Barolo, *barriques* in the case of his Barbera d'Alba. The non-oaked Dolcetto is another impressive mouthful of sheer fruit, but with guts.

Giorgio **Scarzello** & Figli. Another of Barolo town's old-time players, Giorgio Scarzello is scion of a family of growers going back three generations. Despite the traditonalist bent, however, his Barolo Vigna Merenda, from the Sarmassa hill, can be surprisingly fruity and soft.

Sylla Sebaste. A great name in the 1980s, Sebaste fell victim to squabbles among owners and went downhill dramatically. Today, under the direction of the owners of the excellent Colle Manora estate in Monferrato, and benefiting likewise from the consultancy of Donato Lanati, the *azienda* is making a comeback, lead wines being Barolo Bussia and the Nebbiolo/Barbera blend Bricco Viole.

Aldo **Vajra**. A nicer man, with a nicer family, than this you will not find in the wine game – quiet, modest, but with a steely purpose to make the best possible wine from his carefully tended grapes, some 20 hectares of them, though with barely two of these planted to Nebbiolo, his vineyards being mostly at altitudes to which that fussy grape does not take kindly. In terms of wood-ageing he remains steadfastly traditional, sticking to the time-honoured *botte*, but when it comes to vinification he is right at the technological forefront, with a computer-controlled battery of stainless steel fermentors fitted with paddles capable of various complicated manoeuvres for the extraction of aromas and colours, both of which can indeed at times be amazing. Best known for his Barolo Bricco delle Viole, he also makes a *cru* Fossati and a Barolo *normale*, all wines of uncompromising character, not sexy, but magnificently pure, concentrated and aristocratic, as are Aldo's other wines – Dolcetto d'Alba Coste & Fossati, Langhe Freisa Kyè (read *Chi è?*; who are you?) and especially Barbera d'Alba Bricco delle Viole.

CASTIGLIONE FALLETTO

Azelia. Luigi Scavino has the good fortune to own a sizeable slice of the Fiasco hill from which he makes his lead Barolo, Bricco del Fiasco, a wine of modern tendency in that tannins are soft and French oak, though used for only a small proportion of the blend, is evident. Not a wine of fearsome structure, rather one of richness and balance, inviting almost immediate consumption (and therefore a candidate for the Elio Altare Award for Fine Barolo – see below). Scavino's Barolo Bricco Punta, too, is a leader of its type, as is his Dolcetto Bricco Oriolo.

Brovia. Giacinto Brovia was making wine in Castiglione Falletto in 1863, and Giacinto Brovia is making it today – admittedly not the same one (man or wine). The house-style remains on classic lines, however, and the quality is consistently high – not surprisingly, considering the situation of their vineyards, in such *crus* as Rocche, Villero, and Garblèt Sué.

Cavallotto. The Cavallottos have been growing Nebbiolo grapes here since 1929, making wine since 1948. Owning 23 hectares on the *cru* Bricco Boschis, they name their rich and structured wines, still aged for years in large Slavonian oak, after the sections of the hill, notably Colle Sud-Ovest and Vigna San Giuseppe.

Fratelli **Monchiero**. The Monchieros are reconstructed peasants who only within the past few years have noted the advantages of making and marketing their own wines rather than selling their grapes to the co-op or to the merchants. They happen to have a couple of very fine sites, at Rocche and Montanello, from whose fruit they are making increasingly interesting Barolos with a tendency towards the classic style. Their Barolo *normale* is, for an estate-bottled wine, particularly good value for money.

Gigi **Rosso**. Updated tradition probably best describes the philosophy of this family winery. They own some 30 hectares of relatively recently replanted Nebbiolo vineyard in a variety of prime sites of the Albese, pride of place going to the *cru* Barolo Sorì dell'Ulivo at the peak of Serralunga's Arione, all 4 hectares of which are owned by the Rossos. Medium-length maceration and maturation in traditional Slavonian oak *botte* is practised for all Nebbiolo wines, which include Barolo Castelletto in Monforte and Barbaresco

Vigneto Viglino in Treiso. At their best, Rosso's Nebbiolos are carefully crafted, subtle if fairly austere versions of their type, wines which may not floor you to begin with but which tend to open out slowly, revealing hidden depths, so that a bottle one may have begun without great enthusiasm may leave one at the end with a feeling of regret that there is not just one more glass to pour.

Paolo **Scavino**. Established in the early part of the twentieth century and run since the 1980s by Paolo's son Enrico, this *azienda* is today seen as among the most representative of the modernists, complete with rotating fermentors, high initial fermentation temperatures, termination of fermentation in *barrique*, with resulting full colours and soft tannins. Nevertheless, all Scavino's Barolos – *normale*, Cannubi, Rocche dell'Annunziata Riserva and the most famous, Bric del Fiasc – receive time in *botte* as well as in *barrique*. They, like his delicious *barrique*d Barbera d'Alba, are all marked by an almost sexy lushness of fruit which seems a million miles from the tough and leathery dried-out style of yesteryear (or yesterday).

Terre del Barolo. This is the *cantina sociale* responsible for transforming all that Nebbiolo, Barbera, Dolcetto and others not vinified by the enotechnically unequipped small growers of the Albese into Barolo etc. Given the volumes it turns out the *cantina*'s peaks are not high, but the wine is genuine and the *cru* Castiglione Falletto is valid for its combination of correctness of perfume, sheer drinkability and affordability in these days of runaway Barolo prices.

Vietti. One of the great names in post-war Barolo, run by Luciana Vietti's husband Alfredo Currado and their son Luca, Vietti turn out, from vineyards acquired in recent years in various communes, (they used to buy in grapes but switched to land purchase when more and more growers began making their own wines), a range of *cru* Barolos of classic concentration and structure, even if certain concessions to the contemporary requirement for greater softness and roundness have recently been noted. Top wines include Lazzarito, Brunate, Rocche and Villero.

LA MORRA

Lorenzo **Accomasso**. The essence of the gruff, prickly Albese,

Accomasso has been turning out long-macerated, long-aged Barolo from grapes grown on his diminutive patches at Rocche and Rocchette for forty-odd years, though not always as *crus*. Of the two, Rocchette is the more austere, which is saying something since Accomasso is not your man for easy-drinking reds.

Elio **Altare**. The most cogent and radical voice of the modernist school, a fanatical experimenter in pursuit of quality, Elio, influenced by his trips to Burgundy, began the process of *diradamento* – cutting away some bunches of grapes in order to increase concentration in those remaining – in 1978 to his father's horror and disbelief. It resulted in his expulsion from the Eden of the 1948-founded Cascina Nuova family estate. He later returned, introduced French oak *barriques* (in 1983, one of the first *in zona*) and took to horrifying just about everybody with maceration periods for Nebbiolo so abbreviated that the pulp had scarcely the time to introduce itself to the skins before it was racked away, often into small barrels to finish the fermentation and do the malo-lactic. But for all his experiments *in cantina* it is in the vineyard, he maintains, that great wine is made, the key to fruit quality being very low production per plant to achieve high concentration in each berry. He also works organically and is particularly sensitive to the rhythms of nature. His drastically limited maceration times aim to produce burgundy-like wines, svelte in youth yet capable of ageing; wines that can be drunk with pleasure at any time. Nebbiolo wines include a Barolo *normale* as well as a much sought-after Barolo *cru* Vigneto Arborina and an even more sought-after Super-Piemontese called, simply, Arborina, which is aged exclusively in *barrique* (Barolos are allowed a whiff of *botte*). It is essential also to mention here Altare's famous *barrique*-aged Barbera, Larigi, a classic of the modern style, a veritable emblem, indeed, of the revolution that Italian wines in general and Piemontese wines in particular have undergone in the past twenty-five years or so. To complete the picture, La Villa is one of the best of the Nebbiolo/Barbera blends; and in the pipeline lurks a Cabernet which should prove one of the most exciting introductions of recent years.

Batasiolo. With well over 100 hectares of vineyard planted mainly to Nebbiolo, plus a significant amount of Chardonnay and Moscato, Batasiolo are the largest producers of wines from vineyards of property in the Albese. The *azienda*, previously known rather ingloriously as Kiola, was bought by the Dogliani brothers in 1978, after which it went through a bad patch (even worse patch) from which it emerged with a run of three outstanding Barolos Corda della Briccolina between 1988 and 1990. Other Barolo *crus* are Bofani and Boscareto, made these days by oenologist Giorgio Lavagna, with the brilliant but wayward Giorgio Grai of Alto Adige helping out on the white side.

Enzo **Boglietti**. One of the most exciting of the new wave *barolisti*. Boglietti makes two *cru* Barolos: Case Nere, aged in *barrique*, and Brunate, aged in *botte*; the comparison of styles is interesting, and I have to say that the Case Nere tends to come off better. Read more about Boglietti under Barbera (page 102).

Gianfranco **Bovio**. Gian Bovio is most famous for his spacious Belvedere restaurant in the high square at La Morra, previously mentioned as *the* position for a panoramic view of the Barolo zone. His 5 hectares in prime positions on the slopes of *crus* Arborina, Gattera and Ciotto, however, would be sufficient grounds for fame on their own, the wines being capable of greatness, especially in the case of Arborina. Production tends towards the traditional, though there is one aspect of tradition which, with the swinging pendulum, is trendy again: no fining or filtering.

Ciabot Berton. Luigi Oberto worked this 9-hectare estate for decades, selling his grapes to *commercianti*, before his daughter Paola and son Marco took on the vineyards and *cantina* respectively in 1990. Early results are promising, the Barolo *normale* and *cru* Roggeri benefiting from a policy of *poco ma buono* – little but good – in the vineyard and care plus cleanliness in the *cantina*. In their quiet way they could be heading for something seriously good.

Giovanni **Corino**. Renato and Giuliano Corino are growers' sons who themselves 'grew up' in the white heat of the Albese revolution, when men like Elio Altare and Luciano Sandrone, the Corinos' gurus, were already assiduously storming the palaces of the old guard. Their wines are excellent examples of what Dante might have called the *dolce stil nuovo*, the new style characterized by soft tannins and sweet ripe fruit coming from very low production in the vineyard, abbreviated maceration times, and a goodly dose of small French oak. Barolos Rocche and Vigna Giachini are the very antithesis of the traditional style, but they're what the world wants today, and they're damned good, so who's worried?

Silvio **Grasso**. Barolo producers since the 1920s, this *azienda* didn't start bottling and marketing its own product until the 1980s. Federico Grasso, representing the generation in charge today, has taken a judicious view of the precepts of new wave viniculture, reducing maceration times to under two weeks – a lot shorter than that of traditionalists, a lot longer than that of certain radicals – and preferring *tonneaux* to *barriques* for maturation, avoiding excessive wood aromas. Barolos Bricco Luciani and Ciabot Manzoni have earned him a place among the most respected of the young up-and-comers of the Albese.

Gromis. This is the new name for what was Marengo-Marenda, whose Barolo Cerequio regularly figured among the best wines of La Morra even before the vineyards and *cantina* were rented out to Angelo Gaja (see page 84) in 1994.

Marcarini. Growers and winemakers since the middle of the nineteenth century, Marcarini have been noted since the early 1960s as producers of a Barolo Brunate of consistently high quality and, since the 1970s, for Barolo La Serra, perhaps generally a touch lighter but reliably well made. See also under Dolcetto (page 109).

Mario **Marengo**. A small producer making modern-style Barolo Brunate, sufficiently good that it stood out among the best in a recent comprehensive blind tasting of Barolos.

Mauro **Molino**. Coincidentally, another grower I'd never heard of whose wine (Barolo Vigna Conca) made its presence positively felt in the tasting just referred to. It turns out that Molino has been making his own wine (as distinct from selling grapes, as his father had always done) since the mid-1980s, but it was only in 1992 that he turned his hand to wine production full-time, replanting his vineyards in Monforte, Barolo and La Morra to give him the 8 hectares (6 owned, 2 rented) he presently works. His Barolo Conca is unashamedly of the modern style, with five to six days' maceration and two years in *barriques*, of which half are new, though he manages to avoid excessive wood perfumes. His non-*cru* Barolo is fermented slightly longer and aged in *botti*, and represents evidence that in some cases the modern methods are indeed superior.

Molino also makes a steadily improving *barrique*-aged Barbera/Nebbiolo blend called Acanzio – into which, as into his production on the whole, has been blown the inspiring breath of the philosophy of his neighbour just up the hill, Elio Altare.

Monfalletto. This estate, nearly 30 hectares, once belonged to the Falletti, Marchesi di Barolo, from whom it passed to the Cordero di Montezemolo family in 1920. The two flagship wines have always been Barolo Monfalletto, from the Gattera hill, and the *cru* Enrico VI from Villero. But the family are updating and modernizing in various ways, with new styles and new wines emerging after something of a lean spell in the 1980s.

Andrea **Oberto.** Perhaps better known as a Barbera specialist, with his *crus* Giada and Boiolo (see page 105), Andrea and his son Fabio turn out an attractive Barolo Rocche following, once again, the Altare precepts of short maceration time and ageing in small *fusti*, small barrels of new French oak. The non-*cru* Barolo goes into the used barrels.

Fratelli **Oddero.** The estate has been in the hands of the Oddero family since the latter half of the nineteenth century, since when they have been picking up vineyards in some of the finest sites of the Langhe, such as Villero, Fiasco, Bussia Soprana, Rocche di Castiglione and Rionda. With 45 hectares, one of the largest privately owned properties, their potential is enormous, and if the reality has been somewhat less so, that was before the highly regarded oenologist Donato Lanati stepped in. Meanwhile, Oddero's straight blended Barolo continues to represent the genuine article at unusually good value for money in these inflationary times.

Renato **Ratti,** Abbazia dell'Annunziata. Renato Ratti was, until his premature death in 1988, one of the prime movers of modern Barolo, not in the sense of radically abbreviated maceration and *barrique* ageing but in that of elimination of oxidation and other defects which, when Ratti began in 1965, were all too prevalent in the Albese. Since his passing the 7-hectare estate (at La Morra; they also have vineyards at Costigliole d'Asti and at Mango) has been carried forward with enthusiasm and vision by nephew and erstwhile acolyte Massimo Martinelli, joined more recently by Ratti's sons Pietro and Giovanni. The house Barolo, Marcenasco, is generally correct rather than inspired, but the *crus* Rocche and Conca (the latter recently replanted) can reach considerable heights of complexity and refinement. One of Ratti's most creative vinous works is the SuperPiemontese Villa Pattono (a blend of 85% Barbera plus 10% Freisa for aroma and Uvalino to soften Barbera's acidity). Planting Cabernet Sauvignon for the *cru* I Cedri, although carried out after his death, was Ratti's own inspiration, but Martinelli claims the credit for being one of the first to plant Merlot. Both are grown at Costigliole and receive about fourteen months ageing in French *barrique*.

Fratelli **Revello**. From nowhere, in the mid-1990s, Enzo and Carlo Revello came up with a stunning new-wave Barolo blended from the grapes of three vineyards: Rocche, Gattera and Giachini. It is to be hoped that the wine will not lose its complexity when the best grapes are fed into single *crus*. Barbera Ciabot du Re and Dolcetto are also highly appreciated.

Rocche Costamagna. With a history going back to the first half of the nineteenth century, this is one of the longest-standing Barolo producers in the zone. Present owners Claudia Ferraresi, heiress to the Costamagna estate, and her husband have handed over responsibility to their oenologist son Alessandro Locatelli, who turns out consistently good Barolo from the vineyards Rocche dell'Annunziata and Vigna Francesco (on the high slopes of Rocche), even if his passion for the French *barrique* can occasionally produce some pretty woody aromas. The *barrique*d Barbera d'Alba Annunziata is also impressive.

Aurelio **Settimo**. Settimo's father Domenico began here as a grower back in the 1950s, and Settimo himself has been bottling since the 1970s – so a borderline case in terms of style, except that his Barolo and Barolo Rocche wines are made on classic lines, long aged in *botte* even if the stay on the skins has been reduced since earlier days.

Eraldo **Viberti**. Those who only offer a Barolo non-*cru* are generally producers of the old school, yet Eraldo Viberti's Barolo is made with short maceration, fermentation at high initial temperature, ageing in French *barrique*. His success has been to blend the oaky vanilla and toast of the barrel with the fruit and flower of Nebbiolo, with neither really dominating the other – in short, an archetypal new-wave wine, as are his delicious Barbera d'Alba Vigna Clara and his Dolcetto d'Alba.

Gianni **Voerzio**. Colourful not to say absurd tales surround the split of brothers Gianni and Roberto Voerzio in the mid-1980s, but tittle-tattle is never accurate (even if interesting) so we'll leave it out. Gianni seems to have gone the way of diversity and technology, creating a wide range of wines of which the Nebbiolo/Barbera blend Serrapiù and the Barbera d'Alba Ciabot della Luna are perhaps the most interesting. Gianni's Barolo La Serra, however, is a consistently serious contribution to the genre, nothing flashy, requiring attention on the part of the taster.

Roberto **Voerzio**. A perfectionist in the vineyard, tending to modernist in the *cantina*, Roberto Voerzio has, since the late 1980s, been seen as one of the major forces in Barolo. The estate, under father Giacomo, has actually been bottling since the 1950s, which accounts perhaps for Roberto's undisguised contempt for those growers who aim for volume to sell to the co-op or the merchants. Best known for his outstanding Cerequio, he also makes excellent *cru* Barolo from Brunate and La Serra.

MONFORTE D'ALBA

Gianfranco **Alessandria**. Not many people had heard of this one until mighty recently, then whoosh! – he rises like a rocket out of the Arizona desert. Alessandria's 1993 Barolo has attracted immense praise, though production so far is very limited. If I say that in future the wine will all be 'educated' in *barrique* you will grasp which side of the fence he prefers.

Bussia Soprana. Having acquired sites considered among the finest of Monforte, in Bussia and Mosconi, Silvano Casiraghi has begun turning out Barolos of impressive dimension, including a Vigna Colonnello about which neighbour Aldo Conterno might not be so happy, given that until now he has had virtually exclusive use of the name.

Domenico **Clerico**. A founder member of the modernist school of Barolo, even if (as he maintains) quite by chance, Domenico is a firm believer in ageing Nebbiolo in *barrique* rather than in *botte* for purposes of obtaining a rounder, fruitier, earlier-drinking wine than ever the traditionalists might envisage. His best-known Barolo is Ciabot Mentin Ginestra, but the relatively new Pajana is opening a few eyes. Clerico's Arte, which now rejoices in the denomination Langhe Rosso, was prototypical of the first *barrique*-aged Nebbiolos (it also contains 10% Barbera).

Aldo **Conterno**. No one is more popular with fellow Langhe producers than this affable, ever-helpful gentleman; the younger set refer to him reverentially as 'my inspiration' or 'like a second father'. The same holds true for buyers, journalists and wine lovers generally, and consequently the front room of his magnificent winery on the road to Monforte seems eternally occupied by the great and the humble, tasting, sipping, discussing, lapping up the pearls of wisdom from his mouth (he speaks excellent English, having spent several years in California) together with the pearls of wine: *barrique*-aged Barbera (Conca Tre Pile), a prototype of its now increasingly popular genre; Chardonnay *barricato* (Bussiador) and non-*barricato* (Printanié), outstanding wines both in any company; Dolcetto, Freisa, even Grignolino. All these will be served in elegant glasses as often as not by himself or his wife, although in truth he no longer needs to sell anything as there's a line a kilometre long of punters just begging to buy.

And if he's not in his winery you'll most likely find him in the *caffè* in the square in Monforte, amid a card-playing, dialect-babbling crowd of locals. Aldo seems to value his origins, which go back in this zone, viticulturally speaking, at least to the eighteenth century; and somehow you sense that it is in the deep appreciation of where he comes from and what his *terroir* stands for, more than in this virtue of a vineyard or that innovation in *cantina*, that the secret of great quality lies: roots.

When it comes to Nebbiolo, though he broke with his strictly traditionalist brother in 1969 to found his own winery, Aldo could not be accused of being a modernist. His Barolos could perhaps best be described as of classic style without the defects, packing as he does into his finest bottles just about every nuance of which great Barolo is capable. And one feature above all others, perhaps: balance. Aldo's top *cru*, only produced in the best vintages, is Granbussia, a blend of vineyards on the Bussia slope which in good years are also made separately, to wit Vigna Cicala and Vigna Colonello. Bussia Soprana is his mainstay Barolo, produced in every year except bad ones, and can be particularly fine in lesser years when it contains all the best grapes.

Aldo is on record as being against the use of French *barrique* for the ageing of Barolo. He does use it for his Langhe Nebbiolo from young vines, called Il Favot, although he refers to this as his sons' wine – his three boys, Franco, Stefano and Giacomo, all having followed him into the business, Stefano taking on the crucial role of winemaker. Tradition, yes, maintaining however the ability to bend with the times without losing sight of the past – such seems to be the secret of what can only be described as the stunning success of the house of Aldo Conterno.

Giacomo **Conterno**. Aldo's elder brother referred to above (his name is actually Giovanni, Giacomo having been their father) could not be more different from his extrovert sibling in character. An intense, serious man, one has the impression that he is so absorbed by his wines that he doesn't quite notice what's going on

in the world around. I had been to his winery – both the old and the new, an impressive structure which dominates the view as you drive up to Monforte from Castiglione Falletto – on various occasions over a fifteen-year period and he never until very recently gave any indication of having seen me somewhere before, not even when I assured him that he had. One was more than happy, however, to lay aside the pangs of wounded ego in the interests of tasting some of the finest wines of Italy. Indeed if I was given the choice of one bottle of Barolo before I die (I have more than once maintained that Barolo will be my deathbed tipple) I would choose Monfortino. And if the grim reaper will consent to turn a blind eye to me for another twenty years or so, please make that a 1990.

Signor Conterno (one would not call him Giovanni, nor use the familiar '*tu*', although his youngest son Roberto, now taking over, is a lot less formidable) is marginally less of a traditionalist than he was when the fraternal disputes were taking place in the 1960s, especially in respect of length of wood-ageing, but he still turns out Barolos of heroic structure capable of lasting a human lifetime. His top *cru*, the above-mentioned Monfortino, the 1974 vintage of which was still in barrel when I first visited in 1983 (it still gets six or seven years in *botte*) is sought by wine collectors the world over, and even his Barolo Cascina Francia is sold out virtually before it hits the market.

The difference between these two wines resides entirely in the vinification, since only top quality grapes from the 16-hectare property of Cascina Francia in Serralunga are used for both. Whereas the Barolo is macerated for three to four weeks maximum at controlled temperature (under 30°C.), Monfortino will get a good five weeks on the skins with no attempt to keep down the temperature, which can climb in the early stages to the high 30s with consequent risk of a blocked fermentation (it happened once; they had to throw the whole lot away). On the other hand, the wine displays a complexity of aroma and a breadth and depth of flavour only possible in a wine which has teetered on the very brink of existence and, triumphantly, survived.

Paolo **Conterno**. This Conterno somehow tends to get forgotten when more illustrious holders of the name are spoken of, but he regularly turns out good Barolo of a fairly traditional style from his vineyard in the *cru* Ginestra.

Conterno Fantino. A partnership between winemaker Guido Fantino, who started out working with the great Beppe Colla at Prunotto, and brothers Diego and Claudio Conterno, this relatively recently established winery, with its breathtaking hilltop position above Monforte, has established itself as a leading modernist, and a meeting point for 'Barolo Boys' and others who fancy themselves as being in the *avanguardia* of Albese production. Principal Barolos are Sorì Ginestra and Vigna del Gris, while *barrique*-aged non-DOC Monprà brings Nebbiolo together with Barbera in one of the most successful blends of its type in Piemonte.

Alessandro and Gian Natale **Fantino.** You could get lost in the forest of Conternos, Fantinos, Grassos, Seghesios, Mascarellos, Voerzios, etc. that have accumulated in these parts over the centuries. These brothers Fantino are recent arrivals on the viticultural scene and have decided to carve their niche by producing, as well as Barolo *cru* Vigna dei Dardi, a Nebbiolo *passito* from the same vineyard. A wine of great concentration, whose sweet over-ripe fruit is cut by some pretty hefty tannins, it is more or less unique in Piemonte although Giuseppe Quintarelli in Valpolicella and Mario Pasolini in Brescia have done something similar, in both cases with impressive results.

Giacomo **Fenocchio.** The Fenocchios were among the first to bottle Barolo under their own name, although it wasn't until the 1980s that they took the decision to bottle the whole of their production. The style has remained distinctly traditional, however, with long fermentation at high maximum temperatures and protracted ageing in large Slavonian oak. Their *crus* are Bussia Sottana and Cannubi.

Riccardo **Fenocchio.** This *azienda*, founded by current proprietor Ferruccio Fenocchio's great grandfather in 1920, has maintained its traditionalist approach to winemaking until the present, renewing and updating equipment only when necessity decrees. Barolo Pianpolvere Soprano is thus a wine in the classic mould – austere, concentrated, yielding nothing to the superficial gods of charm, but deep of character.

Attilio **Ghisolfi.** This is a young grower-producer, recently arrived on the scene, whose property is on the lesser-known *cru* of Visette, between Arnulfo and Pianpolvere. Those in the know reckon that

Ghisolfi has done enough in recent vintages to be a force to be reckoned with in years to come.

Elio **Grasso**. Scion of a long line of growers, Elio started his professional life as a banker and only turned to wine when his family estate, an impressive 14 hectares in Ginestra and Gavarini, found itself with no one else to look after it. Always willing to learn, Elio proceeded step by step until he reached the position he holds today as one of the leading *barolisti*, with *crus* Ginestra Vigna Casa Maté and Gavarini Vigna Chiniera vying with each other to take the honours. A self-confessed disciple of Aldo Conterno, Elio's style stands, like the master's, mid-way between the traditional and the modern. Barbera Vigna Martina and Dolcetto Gavarini Vigna dei Grassi are also among the best of their respective genres, as is the *barrique*d Chardonnay Educato. Now that he has moved out of his restricted *cantina* in Monforte to the spacious architect-designed (the architect being his brother) establishment amid the vines things can only get better.

Giovanni **Manzone** – **Ciabot del Preve**. Another *azienda* which until fairly recently sold its grapes to major *commercianti* of the area, since the mid-1980s Manzone have been making their own wine. Their Barolo Gramolere, middle of the road in terms of style, consistently scores well in tastings, having a structure such as to render it suitable for fairly long ageing.

Armando **Parusso**. Marco and Tiziana Parusso are carrying forward their family tradition as growers straddling the border between Monforte and Castiglione Falletto, although oenologist Marco has greatly modernized the style set by his late father Armando, drastically reducing maceration time and introducing French oak *tonneaux* to combine with the traditional *botti*. Barolos include Bussia Vigna Munie and Bussia Vigna Rocche as well as the more established Mariondino.

Ferdinando **Principiano**. When Principiano's *cru* Boscareto (the vineyard is in Serralunga) first burst upon the Barolo scene everyone wondered where it was coming from. The answer was: out of a well-established viticultural *azienda* of Monforte, some of whose production, normally sold as grapes, the young, recently qualified Ferdinando had decided in 1993 to use to make Barolo as well as a highly prized Barbera Pian Romualdo. The fact that the Barolo was so successful, being considered by some as the best of its vintage, may have been due in part to the tiny production (around 100 cases), in part to its unreservedly international style (two years' ageing in new French oak barrels of 3.5 hectolitres). Most credit, however, must go to Ferdinando, whose problem in future will consist in living up to the promise.

Rocche dei Manzoni. Valentino Migliorini is one of the most conspicuous figures on the Barolo scene, and certainly one of the great experimenters, being unquestionably the leading *spumantista* with his Valentino Brut Zero and his Riserva Elena Spumante, not to mention being one of the first to introduce Pinot Nero and perhaps the first to blend Nebbiolo and Barbera in his now renowned Bricco Manzoni. An ex-restaurateur of Emilia Romagna, Migliorini purchased the property where his magnificent winery now stands, just outside Monforte on the way up from Barolo, in 1974, and has transformed it into a temple for wines of the international style with occasionally, for my taste, rather an excess of oak aromas. Much-lauded Barolos include Vigna Big and Vigna d'la Roul.

Aldo & Riccardo **Seghesio**. Yet another long established producer of grapes and wine, the younger generation of which decided in the late 1980s to market their own bottled product, following the modernist line of friends and gurus like Elio Altare. Barolo Vigneto La Villa is matched by an equally impressive Barbera d'Alba Vigneto della Chiesa.

SERRALUNGA D'ALBA

Tenimenti di Barolo e **Fontanafredda**. A romantic story of illicit royal passion is usually the preamble to descriptions of this estate; we'll skip that part, except to say that the property was founded in 1878 by King Vittorio Emmanuele II's bastard son Emanuele Guerrieri di Mirafiori. Less romantically, the enormous operation – 70 hectares of prime-site vineyard, grapes bought in from over 600 growers of Piemonte and beyond, plus a production of over 6 million bottles of which some three-quarters of a million are Barolo (!) and nearly 4 million are Asti Spumante (!!) – has been owned, since 1931, by a bank, the Monte dei Paschi di Siena. That's right, Mirafiori's son blew the inheritance as your silver-spoon nobles will do and the bank foreclosed. Biggest Barolo production by far is of the ubiquitous *normale*, rarely very inspired since they started making *crus* commercially in the early 1970s. But the traditionally crafted single vineyard wines – La Rosa, La Delizia, La Villa, Gattinera, Lazzarito to name a few – can be impressive. I have to confess, for all my dislike of banks, that it was thanks to a 1970 Fontanafredda, I forget which one, that the mysteries of Barolo were first revealed to me, and if that sounds kooky ask other Barolo-heads and they'll talk about revelation too. I remember just going off in a cloud of recognition that all these disparate parts – the acidity, the tannins, the alcohol, the sweet fruit, above all the aromas! – were not all over the place as I had always thought but actually *came together in a beautiful harmonious whole*, and that compared with this sublime experience the chunterings of my very attractive dinner companion were of *no interest whatsoever*. There you are, I've ended on a romantic note even if I shunned one at the beginning.

Gabutti. Franco Boasso's 4 hectares of vineyard are nicely situated on a south-facing slope between the hamlets of Gabutti and Parafada. Both the Barolo and the *cru* Gabutti attest to the quality of the site and of the people who make them.

Ettore **Germano**. With a history of tending vineyards behind them – not just their own but those of Batasiolo (such was Sergio Germano's job till the mid-1990s), plus a site of the quality of the south-east facing Cerretta, from which the grapes for their lead *cru* come, it is not surprising that the reputation of this estate, which started bottling only in 1982, is growing. They incline slightly left of centre in the great debate, employing an average length maceration and smallish barrels (*barriques* and *tonneaux*) – new for the *cru* and used for the Barolo *normale*.

Sergio **Giudice**. This is a small property (3.5 hectares) with a long history, the Giudice family having been here as growers and bottlers, as well as vendors, since the 1920s. Alberto Giudice makes Barolo Riserva in the classical mode, *ma non troppo*, using medium-length maceration, ageing in smallish 20-hectolitre *botti*.

Vigna Rionda. The grandfather of present proprietor Giovanni Massolino, also Giovanni Massolino, was selling Barolo in bottle a century ago, and the present Giovanni's son, Franco, seems set to carry the family glory on at least a few decades yet. Sixteen hectares in prime sites provide the experienced Massolinos with the raw material they need to make seriously good Barolo. *Crus* are Vigna Parafada, Vigna Rionda and Vigneto Margheria.

In addition to these principal communes there are others that should be considered briefly:

ALBA

Aziende Vitivinicole **Ceretto**. Taken over in the 1960s from their father Riccardo Ceretto by brothers Bruno (responsible for marketing) and Marcello (oenologist), this is a largish and very high-profile producer of a wide range of Piemontese and international-style wines from vineyards in various parts of the Langhe. *Crus* Barolo and Barbaresco are a speciality, of which the best known are probably Barolos Bricco Rocche and Prapò, and Barbaresco Bricco Asili. Ceretto are leaders in Piemonte in experimentation with, and production of, French varietal wines (Cabernet Sauvignon, Chardonnay, Pinot Nero, Syrah and Viognier all from the La Bernardina estate near Alba, under the Monsordo label), apart from which they make the high-profile Arneis Blangé as well as the usual range of Alba varietals: Barbera (Piana), Dolcetto (Rossana) and Nebbiolo (Lantasco). It was thought by some that they were going off the boil in the 1980s after a period at the top, but there are signs that the 1990s are seeing a revival, especially since they took on the eminent oenologist Donato Lanati as technical consultant.

Poderi **Colla** (see after Prunotto).

Pio Cesare. Founded in 1881 by Cesare Pio (Italians have this habit of turning their names back to front), this once arch-traditional winery today combines the best of the old and the new in Albese wines. Great-grandson Pio Boffa continues as a *commerciante*, buying in grapes from growers with whom the firm of Pio Cesare has worked for decades to make blended Barolo and Barbaresco in the time-honoured style. But the *azienda* is also now substantially *agricola*, owning prize vineyards in Barolo (Ornato in Serralunga) and Barbaresco (Bricco di Treiso) from which they produce *cru* wines of very modern concept. Both *botti* and *barriques* are used in all four styles, but the percentages vary. The less convincing Langhe Nebbiolo Il Nebbio, on the other hand, is made without ever coming into contact with oak at all, demonstrating perhaps the need of Nebbiolo for wood-ageing of some sort.

Prunotto. Beppe Colla, who from Alfredo Prunotto's retirement in 1956 until 1989 controlled this high-class *commerciante* establishment (buying grapes on long-term contracts from top growers), was for years one of the quality leaders and trend-setters of the Albese. It was he who introduced the concept of the single-vineyard *cru*, way back in the early 1960s. For all that he remained of the view that great Nebbiolo and *barriques* have no business together. Predictably, new owners Antinori are modernizing practices (in 1995, after the end of Colla's post-sale consultancy, they began using 5-hectolitre *fusti* of French oak for the ageing of some Barolo and Barbaresco, as well as shortening maceration time; also, perhaps most importantly, they began purchasing vineyards). Even so, Prunotto remain one of the pillars of classic Albese wine. Barolos Bussia and Cannubi, Barbaresco Montestefano, have all impressed recently, as have Barbera d'Alba Pian Romualdo, ever one of the outstanding examples of its genre, and the Nebbiolo d'Alba Occhetti di Monteu.

A recent vertical tasting of Prunotto Barbaresco *normale* back to the still excellent 1971 showed that a place does indeed remain for the seemingly outmoded high-quality non-*cru* blend, and it would not surprise me to see it making a comeback in the hands of winemaker Danilo Drocco who, having understudied Colla for four years, has now most ably taken the oenological reins, while the administrative ones are in the hands of Piero Antinori's eldest daughter and heiress apparent, Albiera.

Poderi Colla. Beppe Colla's daughter Federica and his much younger brother Tino have created, with the master's help, and his sense of purity and quality, a new 'Prunotto' turning out a range of Albese wines including Barolo Bussia Dardi Le Rose, Barbaresco Tenuta Roncaglia and the famous Dolcetto/Nebbiolo blend, Bricco del Drago.

Mauro Sebaste. The real heir of the well-known Sebaste family of Barolo has re-established himself in the local capital and declared himself ready, with an excellent Barolo Monvigliero and an equally fine Barbera/Nebbiolo blend called Centobricchi, to reclaim the glory of the family name.

BRA

Giacomo **Ascheri**. Matteo Ascheri, like his late father Giacomo, has the body of two men and the energy of three. Apart from being involved in various producers' groups and committees he is a passionate experimenter in vineyard (of which the family own some 25 hectares in the Barolo and Roero zones) and *cantina* (new wines, from new grapes and old, are continually popping out of the system). Bric Mileui, a *barrique*d Barbera/Nebbiolo blend, Rocca d'Aucabech (Freisa) and Costa d'Fey (Verduno Pelaverga) are recently developed wines based on Piemontese grapes, while Syrah and Viognier, planted in their Roero vineyards, are examples of experimental grapes. But given a family tradition going back centuries as growers, and over a century as producers and merchants, the Ascheri still put most of their emphasis on Barolo. Their *normale* may not be a classic, but it is certainly the best, and most correct, of the few relatively inexpensive versions going; Vigna Farina, their *cru* from Serralunga, is however the star – a wine of classic structure, needing years in bottle before achieving its full potential.

CALAMANDRANA

Michele **Chiarlo**. Founded in 1956 as a typical volume winery of that time, Chiarlo over the years have collected enough real estate, owned and rented, to stand today among the major growers of Piemonte, with important sites in Barolo (Cerequio, Cannubi, Vigna Rionda), Barbaresco (Rabajà), Asti (Valle del Sole) and Gavi (Fornaci di Tassarolo). They are leaders, too, in the field of new-wave Piemontese wines, main examples being Barilot (Nebbiolo plus Barbera) and Countacc! (the same plus Cabernet Sauvignon). It is for their Barolos, however, that they have attracted the greatest attention and esteem, these including some of the most prestigious *cru* names: Brunate, Cannubi, Rocche di Castiglione, Vigna Rionda and, at the summit, Cerequio, this being the only one for which French oak *barriques* are employed.

CANELLI

Giuseppe **Contratto**. Long known as a producer of good industrial Piemontese wines, notably Asti, this house was purchased from the Contratto family in the mid-1990s by Antonella and Carlo Bocchino, who have promptly set about upgrading the wines. A particular beneficiary has been the *cru* Tenuta Secolo from the Cerequio sub-zone in La Morra, now challenging for a leading spot among Barolos of the modern style.

Fratelli **Gancia**. Founded in 1850 by Carlo Gancia, following an extended visit to France's Champagne region, this house has always been best known for sparkling wines, and expecially for Asti (although they also turn out a fine bottle-fermented champagne-style wine called Riserva Carlo Gancia). A few years ago they purchased at what was then considered a staggering price a very choice 2.5-hectare site in Barolo's *cru* Cannubi, and although they have now sold the land to Poderi Einaudi of Dogliani they will, it seems, continue to produce, with grapes purchased under contract, their highly acclaimed Barolo Cannubi Cà dei Gancia.

MONCHIERO

Giuseppe **Mascarello**. Mauro Mascarello's riverside winery was viciously attacked by the floodwaters of 1994, but he still shows no sign of moving it up to his prime site, the superb 7-hectare Monprivato in Castiglione Falletto. Mauro toyed with, and rejected, the modernist approach to vinification way back in the early 1970s, when some of the present young turks were still running around in short pants. His wines have great intensity of perfume and wonderful balance despite a tendency to light colour – proof, he maintains, that they are not blended with you-know-what, although the wonderful primary aromas he gets in his Barolos, such a relief in a blind tasting after copious waftings of toasty oak, is proof enough. Monprivato, obviously, is the principal Barolo, but he produces a good Villero too, as well as an excellent Nebbiolo d'Alba San Rocco. His Dolcettos can be phenomenal – a twelve-year-old *cru* Gagliassi, tasted recently, was magnificently youthful and still bursting with fruit, when it should (by most people's standards) have been dead years earlier. Punctilious to a fault, Mauro has been criticized as a fanatic, but now that his oenologist son, Giuseppe, has come in to help him he positively shines.

NOVELLO

Poggio Petorchino. This 7-hectare estate, between Castiglione and Monforte in the commune of Novello, was purchased in 1990 by Elvio Cogno – for years the guiding genius of Marcarini in La

Morra – and his son-in-law Walter Fissore. Since then they have been making predictably reliable Barolo *cru* Ravera, more or less along traditional lines, sturdy yet attractive, of classic perfume. The *barrique*d Barbera Bricco del Merlo is good too, as is the Dolcetto Vigna del Mandorlo. A curiosity of their production is the slightly aromatic, spicy Nas-Cetta, a varietal white from the eponymous grape, exclusive, it seems, to Novello.

VERDUNO

Castello di Verduno. This imposing eighteenth-century castle, after passing through royal hands, was acquired by Commendatore Giovan Battista Burlotto in the early twentieth century. His grandson, same name, initiated the *cantina* in the late 1960s, and today it is in the hands of his daughter, Gabriella, married to Franco Bianco of Barbaresco. Their Barolos Monvigliero and Massara are made in the traditional manner, as are Barbaresco's Faset and Rabajà. A peculiarity – of theirs, of this commune – is the Verduno Pelaverga, a light-bodied spicy-fruity red aged in *botte*.

BARBARESCO

The Barbaresco zone is similar in virtually every way – soil, altitude, type of exposure, style of producer – to that of Barolo, and some of the best producers make wines in or from both. They might almost have been brought together under one name, as indeed they have for their non-Nebbiolo production (Barbera d'Alba, Dolcetto d'Alba, etc.). In marketing terms, such a marriage would probably have done Barbaresco a power of good, since everyone is reasonably clear as to what Barolo is whereas over Barbaresco there is some confusion, even among so-called pundits. It almost sounds like a made-up name, something to do with Barbera, perhaps, having pretensions to becoming Barolo. No wonder the most famous producer, Gaja, has reduced the official denomination on his label to a minimum while maximizing the space given to his family (effectively his brand) name.

Of course, *we* know that Barbaresco has nothing to do with Barbera (except that Barbera is coincidentally also grown in Barbaresco), being not a grape variety but a village, like Barolo, which gives its name to a zone specializing in 100 per cent varietal Nebbiolo. It is in fact a very small zone, the production of which is about one third that of its more famous neighbour on the other side of Alba. The only other communes of note are Neive and Treiso.

The same debates about vinification and maturation rage in Barbaresco as in Barolo, although with less intensity, since in the case of Barbaresco they are less hemmed in by the law. Indeed, the less rigorous requirements of Barbaresco might reduce the amount of cheating (clandestine chaptalization, large barrels for display purposes only) going on in Barolo, especially in lesser years. There are producers in either denomination who would argue that it is essential to cheat in order to make (their idea of) a successful wine.

Barbaresco's *disciplinare* may call for a slightly lower minimum alcoholic degree (12.5 as opposed to 13 per cent) and less ageing time (now 21 months from the previous 24 for *normale* with 9 months – from 12 – in oak; 45 months for Riserva); but these are slight variations on a familiar theme, and in practice it is very difficult to distinguish Barolo from Barbaresco in a blind tasting with communes and perhaps vintages all mixed together. Perhaps Barbaresco is – in general, certainly not invariably – less structured, less robust, more 'feminine' than Barolo. But then so is La Morra compared with Serralunga. It is merely a matter of degree, not of fundamental difference. On the other hand, you could say the same of neighbouring sub-zones in the Côte d'Or.

The best sites
While Barolo's *sottozone* remain the subject of debate, those of the Barbaresco area have been finalized; otherwise, remarks made in the context of Barolo are true for Barbaresco. Below is a list by commune.

BARBARESCO: Asili, Cà Grosso, Cars, Cavanna, Cole, Cortini, Faset, Martinenga, Montaribaldi, Montefico, Montestefano, Muncagota, Niccolini, Ovello Montefico, Pajè, Pora Asili, Rabajà Bas, Rabajà, Rio Sordo, Roccalini, Roncaglie (incorporating Sorì Tildin and Cossta Russi), Roncagliette, Ronchi, Secondine, Tre Stelle, Trifolera, Vicenziana.
NEIVE: Albesani, Balluri, Basarin, Bordini, Bricmicca, Bricco, Canova, Casasse, Cottà, Currà, Gaia-Principe, Gallina, Marcorino, Rivetti, San Cristoforo, San Giuliano, Serraboella, Serracapelli, Serragrilli, Starderi.

TREISO: Ausario, Bernardot, Bricco, Bungiovan, Canta, Casot, Castellizzano, Ferrere, Garassino, Giacone, Giacosa, Manzola, Marcarino, Meruzzano, Montersino, Nervo, Paiorè, Rizzi, Rombone, San Stunet, Sant'Alessandro, Valeriano, Vallegrande.

The producers

There follow profiles of the most prominent producers whose *cantine* are situated in one of the three communes of Barbaresco. A few of the best Barbaresco producers also make Barolo, and they will have been mentioned above. The phenomenon is, however, more common in reverse.

BARBARESCO (COMMUNE)

Angelo **Gaja**. A legend in his own lifetime, Angelo Gaja deserves, and receives, much of the credit for dragging the wines not just of Barbaresco but of Alba – of Italy! – to the top of the world wine tree. He began in the family business – already the major vineyard-owner of Barbaresco – in the early 1960s, and after trips to France to study the techniques of the great, and various stormy disputes with his father, introduced severe *diradamento*, thermo-controllable fermentation equipment, malo-lactic fermentation, French *barriques*, French grape varieties, single vineyard production and *grand cru* prices into the bargain (except that there's no bargain where Angelo Gaja is concerned).

Having shocked the old guard he then proceeded to rock the establishment further by planting Cabernet Sauvignon in a prime Nebbiolo site in Barbaresco in the late 1970s. Then, having for twenty-five years worked solely with the grapes of his own estate, in the 1980s he started buying or leasing property in other blue-chip zones of Italy, starting with Barolo, then Montalcino, then Bolgheri.

His principal Barbarescos are the *crus* Sorì Tildin, Sorì San Lorenzo and Costa Russi, plus one which could be described as *normale* except that there's nothing normal, either, where Angelo Gaja is concerned. In Barolo, since 1989, he has produced the *cru* Sperss (dialect for 'nostalgia', indicating the longing that Gaja had felt to return to the making of Barolo after so long) from a 12-hectare site purchased at Marenca e Rivette in Serralunga. More recently he has taken on production at the property now called

84

Gromis in La Morra (see above), with its *cru* Conteisa Cerequio. He also makes a *barrique*-aged Nebbiolo-based (plus Merlot plus Barbera) SuperPiemontese of distinction called Sito Moresco. His Cabernet Sauvignon, Darmagi, is probably the best of its type in Italy, as is his Chardonnay Gaia & Rey (see International Varieties, page 276).

Producing and marketing wine (in the former category credit is due to his faithful and talented oenologist Guido Rivella; the second he handles magnficently by himself) does not exhaust the range of Angelo Gaja's activities. He runs a company called Gaja Distribution which, as the name implies, distributes wines and wine-related articles throughout civilized Italy (his agencies include Domaine de la Romanée Conti and Riedel glasses); and he is on the road to becoming one of Italy's poshest hoteliers – his Castello di Barbaresco is across the street from his amazing winery, which descends four levels below ground level.

One cannot leave the subject of Gaja, without touching on his pricing policy, which has always seemed to some outrageous. If his square-jawed intransigence in this respect has caused him trouble in the past he has disguised it well. Today his policy seems to be paying off handsomely, with international buyers willing to spend any sum for a top name, and if criticism has saddened him he is no doubt crying all the way to the bank. One thing one can say about Gaja's wines, however: at least when you hock the house to buy a bottle, you know you're in for a bloody good drink.

I Paglieri. Alfredo and Giovanni Roagna were considered among the earliest innovators of the 1970s, in particular for their *barrique*- and *botte*-aged Nebbiolo *vino da tavola*, Crichet Pajè. The innovations have kept coming: an entirely *barrique*d Nebbiolo called Opera Prima; a Cabernet Sauvignon plus Nebbiolo blend called Soleo, and a Chardonnay plus Nebbiolo *in bianco* called Solea (now Langhe Rosso and Bianco DOC respectively). But the basis of production remains Barbaresco, still aged in *botte*, not a *cru* but often a *Riserva* from top years. This has been joined by Barolo La Rocca e La Pira aged, again, in *botte*.

Marchesi di Gresy/Cisa Asinari. Considering the antiquity of this sizeable estate – it has been in the hands of the Marchesi di Gresy for over 200 years – and the excellence of their vineyard sites, wines of greater impressiveness have been expected by some than have been delivered. Perhaps the disappointed tasters have been overlooking subtlety and grace in their wish for power and intensity, a common enough tendency in our time. Midway between the traditional and the modern, the estate produces three Barbaresco *crus* – Camp Gros, Martinenga and Gaiun – of which the first two are aged exclusively in *botte*, the third also partly in *barrique*. The Langhe Nebbiolo and the Nebbiolo/Barbera blend Villa Martis are also worth tasting.

Moccagatta. Franco and Sergio Minuto are third-generation growers who started bottling only in the mid-1980s, almost instantaneously finding themselves fêted for their wines, of which they have a wide range (three *cru* Barbarescos, two Barberas, a Dolcetto, a Freisa and a Chardonnay *cru* Buschet considered among the best in Piemonte). The most interesting aspect of their production consists in the contrast between their lead Barbarescos, Vigneto Cole being matured in traditional *botte* while Bric Balin goes into French *barriques*. Both are capable of achieving significant levels of quality.

Produttori del Barbaresco. No cooperative in Italy, perhaps none in the world, enjoys such a reputation for quality and consistency as does this one. Founded – or re-founded – in 1958 (the origins actually go back over 100 years), they work by committee ably led by Celestino Vacca, aided by his son Aldo, once of Gaja. They process only the Nebbiolo grapes of their sixty-odd members, controlling around 100 hectares, mostly in the commune of Barbaresco: around one quarter of total Barbaresco production. Vinification and maturation are along traditional lines. Their *crus* include Asili, Moccagatta, Montefico, Montestefano, Ovello, Pajè, Pora, Rabajà and Rio Sordo, and they also produce a good value Barbaresco and Langhe Nebbiolo.

Albino **Rocca**. The *azienda* makes a pair of Barbarescos of quite different types: Vigneto Brich Ronchi, a wine of structure, aged in new *barriques*, and Vigneto Loreto, lighter and more fragrant, matured in Slavonian oak *botti*. Both are consistently good, even in off years, and good value to boot. Barbera Gepin and Dolcetto Vignalunga can also be good news. A peculiarity of Rocca's production is the *barrique*-aged Langhe Bianco La Rocca, made from the Cortese grape which it is most unusual to find around here.

Bruno **Rocca**. Bruno Rocca, who took over this small *azienda* in 1978, is one of the most respected of the modernists in Barbaresco. His enthusiasm for the French oak *barrique* may have led to excesses early on, when the delicate aromas of Nebbiolo stood in danger of being overwhelmed by woodsmoke and lead-pencil. But the producer himself has seen the peril and has taken a few steps backward, relying today more on *botte* for the ageing. His sole *cru* is the famous Rabajà. He also produces a respectable non-oaked Langhe Nebbiolo called Fralù.

NEIVE

Fratelli **Cigliuti**. This diminutive *azienda* on the edge of the Barbaresco zone was producing grapes for resale for generations before they started bottling in the mid-1960s. Today, under the aegis of Renato Cigliuti, their Barbaresco Serraboella is considered consistently one of the finest of the modernist style, even though wood-ageing is still in *botte*. The SuperPiemontese Briccoserra, a blend of Nebbiolo and Barbera, is, on the other hand, matured in *barrique*.

Gastaldi. Bernardino Gastaldi, whose 14 hectares of vineyard are distributed between Neive and the commune of Rodello d'Alba (outside the Barbaresco zone), with 1 hectare in Monforte, has in the decade of his winery's existence carved himself an enviable reputation for Dolcetto (Moriolo, from Rodello, unoaked) and, in particular, for his Rosso Gastaldi, a non-oaked Nebbiolo of unusually deep colour and richness of fruit. Now he is also making Barbaresco, more elegant than full, but attractive of aroma. Given his clear vocation to make wines of personality and class, Bernardino's Barbaresco is likely to go from strength to strength, as no doubt will the Merlot from vines grafted on to Dolcetto in Monforte, when it gets going. His Bianco Gastaldi – DOC Langhe now, like the Rosso – is an impressive blend of Sauvignon and Chardonnay, also unoaked.

Bruno **Giacosa**. The common factor between the top producers of Barolo and Barbaresco, given that we speak of individuals of highly developed and utterly distinctive personality, is consistency. Their bottles are never mediocre, sometimes sensational. In my experience, no one's Nebbiolos have been more consistently wonderful over a such a long period than those of this morose, introspective genius of Neive. Certainly no one could be more different from the flamboyant, forceful marketeer, Angelo Gaja, nor could their *cantine* be more diverse, the one displaying all the grandeur of a top French establishment, the other looking more like a rented garage where the proprietor can as often as not be found helping out on the bottling line.

The Giacosa tradition is that of the *commerciante* on the highest level. Bruno and his father before him have always bought grapes from growers with whom they have enjoyed life-long relationships, growers having some of the finest vineyards in Christendom. Today, with the rise and rise of the grower-bottler ('They're sprouting like mushrooms', snorts Giacosa) the *azienda* is beginning to acquire vineyards, starting with Falletto in Serralunga and Asili in Barbaresco. The oenological philosophy could be best described as updated traditional: they continue to macerate up to thirty days on the skins, but no longer at fifty-plus as in days of yore; they still use 50-hectolitre *botti* for ageing, but the oak now is French, not Slavonian. Giacosa is contemptuous of people who reduce maceration time to a few days ('They're insane') and who dose their wines with Cabernet or Merlot or wood aromas ('. . . like cooks who drown the primary flavours with sauce'). He is very strict about what he deems suitable to be bottled under his label: his *cru* Barolos and Barbarescos were all sold *sfuso* – in bulk – in 1991, 1992 and 1994.

Apart from Falletto, Giacosa also produces Barolo *cru* Collina Rionda (Serralunga) and Villero and Rocche (Castiglione Falletto). In Barbaresco his most famous wine is Santo Stefano di Neive. He makes a traditional *botte*-aged version of Nebbiolo d'Alba from Valmaggiore di Vezza d'Alba. He is also Barbaresco's star *spumantista*, using Pinot Nero vinified *in bianco* to make what some consider one of Italy's finest *metodo classico* wines (see page 313).

Pasquero Elia-Paitin. With a history as *viticoltori* going back to the nineteenth century, you would think the Pasquero Elia family would be among the most traditionalist producers in the area. Instead they, that's to say the young brothers Giovanni and Silvano, are willing to experiment not only with French *barrique* (as who isn't?) for Barbera Serra Boella and Langhe Rosso Paitin (80% Nebbiolo/20% Barbera) but also with foreign grape varieties like Chardonnay, Sauvignon, Pinot Nero and Syrah. Obviously, however, Barbaresco is the heart of the matter, and their *cru* Sorì Paitin, aged partly in *botte*, partly in *barrique*, is a particularly successful example of the genre. Having been their UK agent for a period (during which I learned how difficult it is to sell Barbaresco to Brits even when it represents brilliant value for money) the beautiful balance and aromatic intensity of this wine stand out in my memory.

TREISO

Orlando **Abrigo**. Giovanni Abrigo, who took over from father Orlando in the late 1980s, is a man of strong ideas. It was he who started selling the product of the *azienda* in bottle, and he who began experimenting not only with unusual varieties like Chardonnay and Merlot (one of the few in Piemonte), but also with late-harvested Barbera and, of course, *barrique* ageing. Barbera Mervisano, produced only occasionally from old vines with very low production, combines both of the latter features. His Barbarescos can be relied on to be pure, Giovanni being an avowed opponent of the new wave's practice of blending foreign grapes or wines in with Nebbiolo to compensate for deficiencies in colour and fruitiness. Of his two *crus*, Vigna Pajorè generally has the beating of Vigna Rongallo.

Fiorenzo **Nada**. The father of the family, Fiorenzo, has looked after the vineyards of this estate on the outskirts of Alba so well over the years that it is possible for son Bruno to make his wines secure in the knowledge that he can rely on fruit of exceptional quality. Wines are limited in number and classic of style: first the Barbaresco, a non-*cru* aged in traditional *botti*, reliably among the best of the zone because, if it isn't, Bruno declassifies it; then the Dolcetto d'Alba, a wine of unusual intensity thanks to Bruno's insistence on severe *diradamento*; and last but far from least the now famous Seifile, two-thirds Barbera old vines, one-third Nebbiolo, aged at least a year in *barrique*.

Giorgio e Luigi **Pelissero**. That the enthusiastic Giorgio Pelissero is numbered among the in-group of young turks of the Albese owes as much to his labours and sacrifices in *vigneto* as to his experimental approach in *cantina*, the latter being a recently constructed mini-shrine of wine in a commanding site over the Barbaresco hills. Though the building is full of barrels of all sizes Giorgio does not go excessively far down the road of *barrique* maturation, preferring to play with the factors of size, age and provenance. He produces from his 15 hectares of vineyard two Barbarescos of which the *cru* Vanotu is the more highly regarded, dependably full and aromatic even in off years. But he is almost as well, if not better known for his Dolcetto Augenta, which like the Vanotu he ages in oak of various dimensions.

Vignaioli Elvio Pertinace. Talk about tradition – if Elvio Pertinace were alive today he would be 1,870-odd years old. Seriously though, this private cooperative curiously named after Roman Emperor Publius Helvius Pertinax actually dates back to the 1970s, when a dozen or so producers with some 80 hectares of vineyard in Treiso and surrounds got together round Mario Barbero to confront the difficulties of those times (funny how things change). Today they produce *cru* Barbarescos of traditionalist tendency (though they are now increasingly using *barrique*) including Vignetos Casotto, Castellizzano, Marcarini and Nervo. The worthy Pertinax lasted less than a hundred days as Emperor before he was assassinated, but the *cantina* which honours the local boy made good, is heading for its thirtieth year and going from strength to strength.

Other producers of Barolo/Barbaresco

Despite devoting a lot of space to Barolo and somewhat less to Barbaresco, I have not been able to profile all producers capable of making good quality classic wine. There follows a list of others by commune. The name of the producer or *cantina* is followed (in brackets) by the producer's principal wine or wines, where relevant; i.e. no mention may be made where the wine is merely generic.

ALBA. Armando **Piazzo** (Barbaresco Sorì Fratin); Francesco **Rinaldi** (Barolo Cannubbio).

BARBARESCO. Mauro **Bianco – Cascina Morassino** (Barbaresco Vigneto Ovello); **Cà Romè** (Barbaresco Maria di Brun; Barolo Vigna Carpegna); Giuseppe **Cortese** (Barbaresco Vigna in Rabajà); Carlo **Giacosa** (Barbaresco Narin, Barbaresco Montefico); Luigi **Minuto – Cascina Luisin** (Barbaresco Rabajà); Walter **Musso** (Barbaresco Bricco Rio Sordo).

BAROLO. Serio e Battista **Borgogno** (Barolo Cannubi); **Borgognot** (Barolo Vigna Sarmassa); Giovanni **Canonica** (Barolo).

CASTIGLIONE FALLETTO. Cascina **Buongiovanni** (Barolo); Gigi **Rosso** (Barolo Cascina Arione Sorì dell'Ulivo; Barbaresco Vigneto Viglino).

DOGLIANI. Poderi Luigi **Einaudi** (Barolo Costa Grimaldi). Einaudi have recently purchased the vineyard previously belonging to Gancia in Cannubi.

GRINZANE CAVOUR. Cantina **Le Ginestre** (Barolo).

LA MORRA. **Dosio** (Barolo Vigna Fossati); Gianni **Gagliardo** (Barolo Preve; see also under Favorita); **Erbaluna** (Barolo Rocche); Oreste **Stroppiana** (Barolo San Giacomo).

MONFORTE D'ALBA. Flavio **Roddolo** (Barolo).

NEIVE. Piero **Busso** (Barbaresco Vigna Borgese); **Cantina del Glicine** (Barbaresco Vigneto Curà; Barbaresco Marcorino); **Castello di Neive** (Barbaresco Santo Stefano); Fratelli **Giacosa** (Barbaresco Rio Sordo; Barolo Bussia); **Parrocco di Neive** (Barbaresco Gallina); **Prinsi** (Barbaresco); **Punset** (Barbaresco Campo Quadro); **Sottimano** (Barbaresco Brichet).

NIZZA MONFERRATO. **Scarpa** (Barolo Tettimora; Barbaresco Tettineive); see under Rouchet (page 115).

SERRALUNGA D'ALBA. Giacomo **Anselma** (Barolo); **Cappellano** (Barolo Otin Fiorin Gabutti); Virginia **Ferrero** (Barolo San Rocco).

TREISO. **Cà del Baio** (Barbaresco Asili); Fratelli **Grasso** (Barbaresco Sorì Valgrande); Eredi **Lodali** (Barbaresco Vigneto Rocche dei 7 Fratelli; Barolo Vigneto Bric Sant'Ambrogio).

Other Nebbiolos of the Albese
ROERO

From the opposite or left bank of the Tanaro comes Roero DOC, effectively a pure Nebbiolo despite the tradition of adding a splash of the local white Arneis, a measure increasingly ignored by those who consider it absurd to use white grapes in a serious red. Roero (the name on its own always refers to Nebbiolo, whereas the related white has to be called Roero Arneis) has in the past been conceived as a lighter and less complex wine than its counterparts from the right bank, but a couple of producers, namely Malvirà (Roero Superiore; Roero Renesio) and Correggia, have recently taken upon themselves the task of proving that their Nebbiolos can be every bit as deep and complex as the greatest Barolos. This they claim already to have achieved in blind tastings, and from what I have tasted the claim has real substance.

NEBBIOLO D'ALBA DOC, from the same area as Roero or from that part of the commune of Alba, on the Tanaro's right bank, which is sandwiched between Barolo and Barbaresco, is of a similar if normally lesser ilk compared with the big three. As a matter of fact, Correggia's top Nebbiolo (La Val dei Preti) has in the past been classified as Nebbiolo d'Alba DOC, though he's thinking of switching to the more prestigious Roero denomination for future vintages.

Apart from Correggia and Malvirà, among those making decent Roero are the following producers of the commune of Canale: Carlo **Deltetto** (Madonna dei Boschi); Filippo **Gallino**; **Monchiero Carbone**; Marco e Ettore **Porello** (Bric Torretta); Funtanin **Sperone**. Elsewhere in Roero good producers include: Giovanni **Almondo** (Bric Valdiana) at Montà d'Alba; Emilio **Marsaglia** at Castellinaldo; Angelo **Negro** (Prachiosso) at Monteu Roero.

As for Nebbiolo d'Alba DOC, apart from Correggia good producers include: Ascheri (San Giacomo); Poderi Colla; Bruno Giacosa (Valmaggiore); Prunotto (Occhetti); Ratti (Occhetti); Flavio Roddolo; Luciano Sandrone (Valmaggiore).

LANGHE NEBBIOLO has been created as a fifth category of DOC Nebbiolo into which any of the above four – Barolo, Barbaresco, Roero or Nebbiolo d'Alba – may 'cascade' should a producer wish to downgrade his classification in an off year. The denomination is also used, however, for Nebbiolos which began life as renegades outside the system – *barriquey* jobs like Altare's Arborina or Aldo Conterno's Il Favot – and which, under the new regime, are obliged to take on a controlled denomination of some sort or lose the right to use a grape name, place name or vintage year on the label. Indeed, Langhe Nebbiolo, or even Langhe Rosso, will tend to be used for anything that might not meet a producer's criteria for a classic denomination for whatever reason, including marketing hype (via that curious psychological contortion by which Italians have managed to persuade themselves, and others, that outside the system is best for image).

In relation to Nebbiolo's colour problem, one major producer of classic Barolo has gone on record as saying that any Barolo or Barbaresco of a deep, purply hue *must* be blended with another variety. Others pooh-pooh that as self-justification and say it's just a matter of vinification. While the latter undoubtedly have a point, the former are not entirely whistling in the wind. We have already heard of illicit blending with Cabernet and Merlot, but this is a relatively recent development. Traditionally some of the best Barolos/Barbarescos have been blended with Barbera or other local varieties in order to lower tannins and heighten colour.

At least if it's Barbera (or indeed Cabernet) the grapes could have come from the producer's own vineyard. Less defensible would be the use of wines trucked in from the south, a practice all too well ensconced in the nether levels of the area's tradition.

One solution to the colour problem, proposed by a growing number of producers, is to follow the Tuscan logic and openly declare one's intention to, indeed practice of, blending. Until 1994 this would have meant declassifying down to *vino da tavola* but today a Nebbiolo–Barbera blend would qualify as a Langhe Rosso DOC. As in Tuscany, such a SuperPiemontese would probably be aged in French *barrique* rather than in the traditional *botte*.

Good examples of Nebbiolo–Barbera (most of which have been mentioned above) are Elio Altare's La Villa, Enzo Boglietti's Buio, Michele Chiarlo's Barilot, Cigliuti's Briccoserra, Cisa Asinari's Villa Martis, Clerico's Arte, Conterno-Fantino's Monprà, Gaja's Sito Moresco (also with 10% Merlot), Mauro Molino's Acanzio, Parusso's Bricco Rovella, Pasquero's Paitin, Rocche Costamagna's Rocche delle Rocche, Rocche dei Manzoni's Bricco Manzoni, Sylla Sebaste's Bricco Viole, Gianni Voerzio's Serrapiù, Roberto Voerzio's Vignaserra.

There is also the phenomenon, touched upon above, of the pure Nebbiolo SuperPiemontese which certain Barolo/Barbaresco producers have developed as a response to constraints on minimal wood-ageing or expectations of typicity. In other words, such wines, which may very well come from Barolo grapes (but from young vines, perhaps), will have been aged in non-traditional containers such as French *barriques* or even stainless steel. The highest profile of the style would be Altare's Arborina and Aldo Conterno's Il Favot. Roagna at I Paglieri in Barbaresco make a version which is aged partly in *botte* and partly in *barrique* called Crichet Pajè, and another aged solely in *barrique* called Opera Prima. Pio Cesare's version, called Il Nebbio, is aged entirely in stainless steel, as is Martinenga from Cisa Asinari.

Other Nebbiolos of Piemonte
GATTINARA, GHEMME AND THE WINES OF NOVARA/VERCELLI

In the zone of Novara/Vercelli blending is part of the official profile, the secondary grapes being Vespolina, Croatina and the local version of Bonarda, sometimes called Uva Rara; but 'official' is the word, because at least one major Gattinara producer uses Nebbiolo (historically known as Spanna) at 100%. To speak of major producers, however, is misleading, since there are only a handful of wineries of any size at all in the entire area, most significantly in Gattinara. The fact that Gattinara and Ghemme were elevated in the 1990s to DOCG status owes more to their historic standing than to their present-day importance. Or perhaps there's an element of good old Italian politicking in there too. Qualitatively there is not much here that will stand comparison with any number of Barolos or Barbarescos. As for Boca, Bramaterra, Fara, Lessona and Sizzano, historic DOCs all, there is precious little viniculture in those areas.

Gattinara DOCG, like Barolo, must be aged for three years of which two must be in wood. It may be called Riserva if aged for four years. Good versions are produced by: **Antoniolo**, whose Vigneto Osso San Grato and Vigneto San Francesco are aged in *botte* and whose Vigneto Castelle is matured in *barrique*; **Nervi**, whose Vigneto Molsino is matured in a combination of *botte* and *barrique*; and **Travaglini**, the biggest producer, whose lopsided bottles are described simply as Gattinara or Gattinara Riserva, the latter having a greater proportion of *barrique*-aged wine in the blend.

Ghemme, recently elevated to DOCG status boasts one solitary producer of note, Antichi Vigneti di **Cantalupo**, which turns out wines of some polish and personality under the names Collis Breclemae and Collis Carellae (both *botte*-matured), as well as the more recently introduced *barrique*-aged Signore di Bayard.

Boca is represented by Podere ai **Valloni**, whose *botte*-aged Vigna Cristiana is the best wine; also by the house of **Vallana**, once famed for their magnificent, and inexpensive, old Spannas.

In Bramaterra one producer has been flying the flag since the 1980s: Luigi **Perazzi**, who makes not only the blended wine required of the DOC (Nebbiolo plus Croatina, Bonarda and Vespolina), aged a minimum of two years, but also a *barrique*-aged 100% Nebbiolo SuperPiemontese called La Sassaia. A good Bramaterra is also made by the long-established and much respected growers **Sella**, who are better known for Lessona, where they also have a vineyard.

In Sizzano Giuseppe **Bianchi** is the main presence, backed by Piemonte's most prestigious roving consultant, Donato Lanati. The house also produces Gattinara and Ghemme at good quality level.

The house of Luigi **Dessilani**, at Fara, makes a good-value DOC under the subtitle Caramino. Dessilani also turn out Gattinara and Ghemme.

At Suno, in the province of Novara, the grower Luciano **Brigatti** makes a SuperPiemontese, 70% Nebbiolo plus Uva Rara plus Vespolina, aged *botte* and *barrique*, called Mot Ziflon, which has a certain reputation for quality.

Nebbiolo or Spanna may also be grown under the DOC heading Colline Novaresi, in the province of Novara, or under that of Costa della Sesia in the province of Vercelli.

CAREMA

The tiny area of Carema, just inside Piemonte at the beginning of the Aosta Valley, produces 100% varietal wines from Nebbiolo, locally called Picoutener. Carema is capable of considerable perfume and elegance, although weather conditions, not to mention topographical ones, are so often adverse, and therefore the return is so small, that it is hard to understand why the growers continue to break their backs working these ridiculous but wonderful mountain terraces. Many don't, in fact, and the wine is disappearing from view; less than 300 hectolitres were declared in 1995. It doesn't help that the law insists on a minimum ageing period of four years which, for Carema *normale* certainly and for the selection usually, is far too long.

Of what is left, about half is produced by the **Cantina Sociale di Carema** who turn out a good Carema *normale* as well as a special selection called Carema di Carema Etichetta Bianca. Both are aged in *botte*. The only other producer of note is Luigi **Ferrando** of Ivrea who, like the cooperative, makes a *normale*, confusingly known as Etichetta Bianca, plus a selection, in this case called Etichetta Nera.

LOMBARDY

Lombardy's Valtellina is the only major production area outside Piemonte of wines based on Nebbiolo (here called Chiavennasca, after the town of Chiavenna). Some 30,000 hectolitres of DOC wine are produced annually on very steep terraces, this fact being responsible, no doubt, for the epithet 'heroic' being applied to the viticulture of the zone.

Production is divided between Valtellina *normale*, which may be liberally blended with a number of other red grapes (Rossola, Pignola, Brugnola, Pinot Nero and Merlot, to be precise), and from which an Amarone-like strong dry red called Sforzato (or Sfursat, in dialect) may be made; and Valtellina Superiore. The wines of Valtellina Superiore, with the sub-denominations Sassello, Inferno, Grumello and Valgella, have the distinction of being the best Nebbiolos in the world outside Alba, which is another way of emphasizing just how limited is the area of great Nebbiolo. Blending in these cases with other red grapes is limited to 5%. The best wines from Valtellina, with the exception of Sfursat, are generally labelled Superiore of which the minimum ageing period is two years; a Riserva would have to be aged four years.

The biggest market for these wines is nearby Switzerland, followed by Bergamo and Milan, and they are not much seen in the rest of Italy, let alone in the rest of the world. In middle age (four to eight years) they can be complex and seductive but there is all too much of a tendency towards thinness and hardness. They're not great, perhaps, but I owe them a debt, since it was the wines of Valtellina, of which I had occasion to drink numerous bottles in Bergamo in the early 1970s, which first alerted me to the fact that Italian wine didn't *have* to be cheap and nasty and could in fact display some considerable individuality and fascination.

The major producers of Valtellina wines tend to combine operations as merchant and grower. Perhaps the best known is:

Nino **Negri**, Chiuro. This firm, which today is owned by Gruppo Italiano Vini (otherwise known as GIV – a large conglomerate with estates in various parts of northern and central Italy), was founded in 1897 by Nino and his son Carlo, the latter qualifying ultimately as one of Italy's first oenotechnicians. Today, under long-serving director/oenologist Casimiro Maule they have earned a reputation as serious producers, making over a dozen wines from all areas of the Valtelline – Inferno, Sassella, Grumello and Valgella. In Valgella they own a particularly prized *cru* called Fracia. Another speciality has been their Sfursat 5 Stelle, a pure Nebbiolo vinified traditionally with twenty-five days maceration on the skins, yet aged in accordance with more modern precepts, around twelve months in small French *barriques*. Sassella Botti d'Oro and Negri Riserva Oro are another pair of distinguished wines, more intense than full as is characteristic of the zone, and able to play various notes on the olfactory scale.

Other worthy producers of Valtellina include:

Enologica Valtellinese, at Chiuro, whose three *barrique*-aged Riservas – Antica Rhaetia, Castel Grumello and Vigna Paradiso – are all highly rated. Also in Chiuro is the merchant **Nera** whose Sassella and Signorie, both Riserva della Casa, are of a more traditional style. Here too are Aldo **Rainoldi**, who cover the gamut of Valtellina Superiore wines with their Inferno, Sassella, Grumello and Valgella, not to mention Sfursat; all are aged in *botte* except their top *cru*, Inferno Riserva *Barrique*.

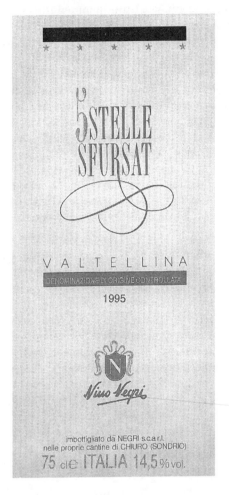

Other producers to look for are **Polatti, Marsetti, Triacca** and **Conti Sertoli Salis**. A grower, unusual in this area, is Sandro **Fay** of Teglio with his *cru* Valgella Cà Morei.

BARBERA

As a variety, Barbera is often attributed with the feminine gender, perhaps because of her seductive fruitiness, perhaps because of her sometimes catty acidity. For these qualities, as for her relatively low tannin coupled with high anthocyanin (colour) levels, her ability to produce acceptable quality even at volume, her versatility in wine form, she has found her way to almost all parts of Italy. Nostalgic ex-pat Italians have whisked her off to the far corners of the globe – Argentina, Australia, California. Of the few Italian international varieties she is probably still number one in hectarage, though increasingly outshone in market terms by Sangiovese, to which, among red grapes, she comes second only in terms of hectares planted in the motherland. In Italy, outside the North West (as defined here) Barbera is used as an anonymous minority blending component only. As someone has said, you would not believe the number of wines Barbera has crept inside.

Barbera's spiritual home, however, is Piemonte and, more specifically, the zone of Monferrato in central-south-east Piemonte, an ancient marquisate/duchy which largely overlaps, and historically engaged in endless disputes with, the free province of Asti. It is in these bosom-shaped hills that what has been called *Vitis vinifera montisferratensis* is presumed to have originated, no one knows how long ago, developing spontaneously, it has been supposed, from the seed of some more ancient variety. In any case, the first documented reference goes back only as far as 1799.

Today it remains in the Monferrato, and in the Astigiano, that Barbera enjoys the finest sites, having to settle, in the Langhe villages of Barolo, Barbaresco *et al.*, for second best. Even so, some would claim that she is capable of greater heights in the Langhe, where these days she is sometimes harvested even after the late-ripening Nebbiolo in order to achieve full ripeness and lower acidity. It has even been suggested, by no less an ampelographer than Molon, that the smaller-berried Langhe Barbera is a different sub-variety. But Dalmasso and his colleagues, in the Ministry of Agriculture's study on the wine-grape varieties of Italy undertaken in the 1960s, seem convinced that such differences are entirely accountable for by factors of soil, exposition and the health of the plant.

After phylloxera, Barbera became so widespread that, following the Second World War, she represented about 80 per cent of all Piemontese plantings. Today she still claims almost 50 per cent, maintaining popularity in an increasingly quality-conscious era because she is one of the few varieties to combine consistency, reliability and real character.

Wine-wise there exist some curiosities in the form of *blanc de noir*, *frizzante* and *passito*, and Barbera is frequently a major or minor ingredient of blends. But Barbera (as a wine, in Italian, 'she' would become 'he', though I prefer 'it') peaks qualitatively in the *barrique*-aged form, giving a mellow, sappy, moreish red with a nice balance of seriousness and drinkability. While the war continues to rage as to whether Nebbiolo ought or ought not to be refined in small French oak (partly because there is a legitimate doubt as to whether it is wise to add wood tannins to the already hefty grape tannins, partly because Nebbiolo's subtle aromas stand in danger of being covered by the grosser ones of the barrel), a growing majority seems to agree that Barbera is ideal for *barrique* treatment, because the tannins fortify the structure, and because the grape's naturally high acidity seems to be mitigated in the process, while its perfumes marry nicely with those of vanilla and wood-smoke.

But if Barbera *barricato* (i.e. matured in *barrique*) has become chic today, and in some cases very expensive, there remains a school of thought which stoutly maintains that wood-ageing in the more traditional *botte* remains the best method. Of course, there is a third school which considers that a mix of the two methods is the way to go, and a fourth which holds that stainless steel followed by maturation in bottle is the only course. Italy wouldn't be Italy without these contradictions.

THE WINES IN PIEMONTE

Evaluating Piemontese Barbera producers according to denomination, one would have some difficulty in choosing between Barbera d'Alba and Barbera d'Asti as the most important (although at around 140,000 hectolitres the latter produces three times the quantity of the former). There are big names among top producers on either side, perhaps a little bigger in the Astigiano, perhaps a few more of them in the Albese, if you take into account that just about every producer of good Barolo/Barbaresco also makes good Barbera; indeed some of the French *barrique* festishists seem better qualified to vinify Barbera than Nebbiolo. Another difference seems to be that researching the mysteries of Barbera-making seems to have taken on the character almost of a group activity in the Albese, as I discovered at a recent gathering of producers of the modernist persuasion for purposes of tasting and comparing notes. The young wines I tasted there, from producers like Altare, Clerico, Conterno-Fantino and Scavino were just sensational – masses of mouth-filling, lipsmacking, cherry and berry fruit which didn't seem on the whole to be overwhelmed by the none the less plentiful wood. They may lack the subtlety of Nebbiolo, but these are undoubtedly wines for our fruit-driven times.

Barbera del Monferrato, the production of which is only slightly less than that of Barbera d'Asti, is not without its quality exponents either. Langhe Barbera is coming into its own as a replacement for Barbera *vino da tavola* in the province of Cuneo. Colli Tortonesi seems to be a local phenomenon, or perhaps it all goes to Milan, in any case it is rarely seen in the outside world. Piemonte Barbera has so far been used mainly for wines at the cheap end, but it is one option for producers who will no longer be able to label their wines *vino da tavola*.

The producers

Braida, Rocchetta Tanaro/Asti. If anyone put Barbera on the map as a potentially great wine-grape (I choose my words carefully, since although it is possible to make an outstanding wine using just Barbera, Barbera is not in itself a great grape variety, only a very good one) it was the late Giacomo Bologna. His estate, Braida, now run by his children Raffaella and Beppe, must come first even at the expense of alphabetical sequence.

A rotund, jovial man who always attracted swarms of the serious and the curious to his stand at Vinitaly, Bologna was one of a band of enthusiastic oenologists who, in the 1970s, began visiting the classic zones of France to study the ways of the great French winemakers. The most important lesson he learned was the need, especially with the hyper-acidic Barbera, to complete the malo-lactic fermentation expeditiously and in the organic medium of wood. He learned, too, that the *barrique* was not merely something for adding flavour and nuance to one-dimensional wine, but was primarily a marvellous tool in the hands of the intelligent *cantiniere* for rounding out the sharp and rough edges of an otherwise all-too-rustic wine.

Bologna's most renowned creation is Bricco dell'Uccellone, today recognized as one of the classic *crus* of Italy. Another *barrique*-aged Barbera is the *cru* Bricco della Bigottà. Ai Suma is a

1995

Bricco dell'Uccellone

Barbera d'Asti
denominazione di origine controllata

Imbottigliato da "*Braida*"
di Giacomo Bologna s.r.l.
Rocchetta Tanaro (Italia)

13,5% Vol.
750 ml. ℮

Product of Italy
NON DISPERDERE IL VETRO NELL'AMBIENTE

substantial quasi-meditation wine made from late-harvested grapes, while La Monella is a light-hearted quaffer brightened by a touch of that fizz which the Piemontese have always appreciated in their swigging Barbera, though the first thought of ignorant foreigners is that the wine is 'off'. Far from it: 'off' wine has never issued from the *cantina* of Giacomo Bologna, and it is less likely to than ever now that the family have built an impressive technological temple to Bacchus.

Enzo Boglietti, La Morra/Alba. A young man in his early thirties, on the scene really only since the beginning of the 1990s, the cool and casual, apparently easy-going Enzo does not at first give the impression of being an artist – more that of a hippy. The *cantina*, in which one tastes from barrel, is tiny and the kitchen, where the bottles are brought out, was a bit of a mess until Enzo got married not long ago (losing his mother at an early age, there had been no women in the house for years). But the vineyards, cared for lovingly by Enzo's father and brother, are tended impeccably; herein the secret of his – their – success.

Being a denizen of La Morra, producer of two outstanding *crus* in Case Nere and Brunate, one's first inclination is to profile him as a *barolista*. Yet there are few *barolisti* who put so strong an emphasis on the quality of their Barbera as does Enzo, and it is generally agreed that the *azienda*'s most exciting *cru* is in fact their Barbera d'Alba Vigna dei Romani, from old vines on the Fossati slope. This is a wine which demonstrates to perfection the harmonies and mutual enhancements arising from the marriage between Barbera grapes in perfect condition and high quality small French oak – berry-fruit aromas mingling happily, and without loss of character, with the vanilla and toast of the barrels. Let us hope Enzo's marriage proves as successful.

Enzo also makes a good Barbera d'Alba *normale* from second-selection fruit which gets less barrel-time, and the SuperPiemontese called Buio – a beautifully judged *barrique*-aged blend of Nebbiolo and Barbera – a word which means darkness and is Enzo's nickname, even though his smile and his wines are full of light.

Matteo **Correggia**, Canale/Roero. Matteo's father and grandfather were growers here in Canale, selling their grapes to *commercianti* and *privati*, but when in 1987 he took control of the 10-hectare estate (soon to increase) he began doing things his way, which largely means the Altare way. It wasn't long before he started making a name for himself, not just with the outstanding Nebbiolo d'Alba referred to above, but also – mainly – with his Barbera d'Alba Bricco Marun. These wines come from separate selected vineyards on sandy-calcareous slopes near the winery. Despite the differences, however, he makes them both in exactly the same manner, macerating for six to eight days depending on the condition of the grapes at vintage time, then decanting the wines straight into new French *barriques*, heating the environment to bring on the malo-lactic fermentation. The barrels are then put outside in the cold for two days for the wine to settle down. The ageing period in *barrique* is approximately eighteen months with limited rackings, and the wine is bottled in the spring of the second year without fining or filtration.

Matteo takes a poet's approach to wine, rather than a scientist's. 'I trust more to my palate than I do to analyses,' he says. 'That way I get better wine and it costs me less.' That his wines are seriously good has been widely recognized – Bricco Marun's feat of taking Tre Bicchieri in the Gambero Rosso/Slow Food Guide to Italian Wines in back to back vintages has only, to my knowledge, been equalled by the Vigna Larigi of Altare himself. 'Barbera is

wonderful', says Matteo, 'but it doesn't have the character of Nebbiolo.' Agreed.

Araldica Vini Piemontesi, Castelboglione/Monferrato. The significance of this producer is that it represents the vast majority of Barbera production in Piemonte – that of the *cantine sociali*. In fact,
Araldica is an umbrella-name for three large *cantine*, Mombaruzzo
and Ricaldone as well as Castelboglione. Average annual production of Barbera, of which about 70 per cent is DOC Asti, the rest
being classified as Piemonte Barbera, is about 50,000 hectolitres. In
other words, the Barbera production of this one group is roughly
equal to the entire production of Barolo and Barbaresco combined.
Think about it.

But Araldica is not just about quantity, it is a quality producer
too. Run by Claudio Manera, an oenologist, whose oenologist wife
Lella reigns in the laboratory, and who is assisted technically by
oenologists Daniela Pesce at Mombaruzzo and Paolo Pronzato at
Ricaldone, with help on the commercial side from oenologist Luigi
Bertini, and enjoying the input of flying oenologist Matt Thomp-
son from New Zealand, having enjoyed that of Australian Martin
Shaw for several years, the place is crawling with oenologists.

But that doesn't mean that the wines are 'technological'. The key
to quality in an operation of this size is selection. As the grapes
arrive at vintage time they are graded according to sugar content
and health (freedom from rot). Growers who produce to Araldica's
exacting specification are given a significant bonus payment for
their grapes. They have even, under antipodean guidance, taken
this one step further back and begun identifying best vineyards
among the 700 hectares of Barbera planted by their members or
soci. 'Best vineyards' generally means those with old vines, low in
production, high in quality.

After vinification the wines from the best grapes are further
selected to determine whether they should be included in the *cru*
Vigneti Croja, a wine of classic style, concentrated and firm, aged
in large *botti* for an average of fifteen months; or in the 20% *barrique*-aged Ceppi Storici (old vines), softer and more rounded,
which has had its share of successes in competitions round the
world; or in the Alasia Barbera d'Asti, from a line of varietals (Barbera, Dolcetto, Chardonnay, Cortese), developed by Australian
Martin Shaw, which combines the fruit and/or the wine styles of

the old world with the almost obsessively anti-reductive methods
of the new). If none of these, it will go into the normal Barbera
d'Asti, a wine which represents excellent value for money since we
are talking about a very modest price for a wine of selected grapes
made to a high standard by professionals. Value for money is
indeed what the cooperatives can offer in spades, and if Araldica
can do it, why not others of their ilk?

Just ship in a few more oenologists?

As regards other producers of good to excellent Piemontese Barbera I have thought it clearest to divide them by zone or category.
(Only producers that have not been previously mentioned have
their names printed in **bold** and their communes recorded.)

BARBERA D'ALBA. Brovia (Sorì del Drago); Aldo Conterno (Conca
Tre Pile – perhaps the first to be aged in *barrique* and among the
greats); Giacomo Conterno (Cascina Francia); Conterno-Fantino
(Vignotà); Corino (Vigna Pozzo); Ghisolfi (Vigna Lisi); Elio Grasso
(Vigna Martina); Silvio Grasso (Vigna Fontanile); Giuseppe Mas-
carello (Pian Romualdo); Moccagatta (Vigneto Basarin); Angelo
Negro (Bric Bertu); Andrea Oberto (Giada; Vigneto Boiolo); Paitin
(Serra Boella); Parusso (Ornati); Pelissero (Piani); Prunotto (Pian
Romualdo – a classic of the genre); Revello (Ciabot du Re); Albino
Rocca (Gepin); Bruno Rocca; Rocche Costamagna (Annunziata);
Paolo Scavino (Carati); Aldo & Riccardo Seghesio (Vigneto della
Chiesa); Aldo Vajra (Bricco delle Viole); Viberti (Vigna Clara);
Vietti (Scarrone Vigna Vecchia – sixty-year-old vines); Vigna
Rionda (Vigneto Margheria); Gianni Voerzio (Ciabot della Luna);
Roberto Voerzio (Vignasse).

BARBERA D'ASTI. **Bava** (Stradivario), Cocconato d'Asti; **Bertelli** (Giarone; San Antonio Vieilles Vignes; Montetusa), Costigliole d'Asti; **Boffa** (Collina della Vedova), San Marzano Oliveto; **Brema** (Le Cascine), Incisa Scapaccino; **Bricco Mondalino** (Il Bergantino), Vignale Monferrato; **Cascina Castlet** (Policalpo; Passum – a rare example of Barbera *passito*), Costigliole d'Asti; Michele Chiarlo (Valle del Sole); Giuseppe Contratto (Solus Ad); Luigi **Coppo** (Pomorosso; Camp du Rouss), Canelli; **Forteto della Luja** (Le Grive), Loazzolo; **La Barbatella** (Vigna dell'Angelo), Nizza Monferrato; **Marchesi Alfieri** (Alfiera), San Martino Alfieri; **Martinetti** (Montruc), Calliano; **Rivetti** (Cà di Pian), Castagnole Lanze; Scarpa (La Bogliona); Cantina Sociale di **Vinchio e Vaglia** (Vigne Vecchie), Vinchio; **Viticoltori dell'Acquese** (Bricco), Acqui Terme.

BARBERA DEL MONFERRATO. **Cave di Moleto** (Mulej), Ottiglio Monferrato; **Colle Manora** (Pais), Quargnento; **La Guardia** (La Vigna di Dante), Morsasco; **Nuova Cappelletta** (Vigneto Minola), Vignale Monferrato.

BARBERA-BASED SUPERPIEMONTESE. This is a catch-all for anything which has Barbera at at least 50%. Needless to say the rest could contain all manner of things, including Barbera itself. These are generally classified as DOC under denominations like Piemonte Barbera, Langhe Barbera, Langhe Rosso, Monferrato Rosso. Those mentioned below are all made to a high standard and virtually all matured in *barrique*.

Abbazia di Vallechiara (Torre Albarola, plus Dolcetto and Lancellotta), Lerma; Altare (Larigi, 100% Barbera – see under Barolo, La Morra, page 65); Ascheri (Bric Mileui, plus Nebbiolo); **Cà Viola** (Bric du Luv), Montelupo Albese; Colle Manora (Manora Collezione); Gaja (Sito Rey, 100% Barbera); **La Tenaglia** (Emozioni, 100% Barbera), Serralunga di Crea; Malvirà (San Guglielmo, plus Nebbiolo and Bonarda); Mauro Molino (Acanzio, plus Nebbiolo); Nada (Seifile, plus Nebbiolo); Azienda Agricola **Pira** (Bricco Botti, 100% Barbera), Monforte; Ratti (Villa Pattono, plus Freisa and Uvalino); **Sant'Evasio** (Rosignolo, 100% Barbera), Nizza Monferrato; Mauro Sebaste (Centobricchi); Renzo Seghesio (Ars Vivendi, 100% Barbera); **Viarengo** (Il Fale'), Castello di Annone; **Villa Fiorita** (Il Giorgione, 100% Barbera), Castello di Annone.

THE WINES IN LOMBARDY

From Lombardy the denomination under which Barbera is most likely to appear on shelves is Oltrepò Pavese, either varietally (i.e. minimum 85%) or as the basis of a blend (Oltrepò Pavese Rosso). Producers capable of turning out a good product include **Cabanon** (Infernot Riserva), Godiasco; **Doria** (Roncorosso Vigna Siura), Montalto Pavese; **Frecciarossa** (Villa Odero), Casteggio; **Le Fracce** (Cirgà), Casteggio; **Mazzolino** (Terrazze), Corvino San Quirico; **Monsupello** (Podere la Borla), Torricella Verzate; **Montelio**, Codevilla; **Piccolo Bacco dei Quaroni** (Fornacione), Montù Beccaria; **Vercesi del Castellazzo** (Orto di San Giacomo), Montù Beccaria.

THE WINES IN EMILIA

From Emilia there is Colli Piacentini Barbera and Gutturnio, which may be excellent. The best producer I've come across is **La Tosa** of Vigolzone, whose Gutturnio *cru* Vignamorello can be amazingly rich and deep. **La Stoppa** of Rivergaro make a varietal and a *barrique*d blend of Barbera and Bonarda called Macchiona. Sisters Giovanella and Maria Giulia Fugazza, of **Castello di Luzzano** in Rovescala, just inside the Oltrepò, make a *barrique*d Gutturnio (Romeo), as well as an Oltrepò Pavese Barbera aged in *botte*, just to emphasize their borderline position both geographically and oenologically.

As for Colli Bolognesi Barbera, a small amount is produced but it is rarely seen outside the zone. **Cantina dell'Abbazia**, in Monteveglio, turn out a respectable version.

DOLCETTO

Generally placed third in the Piemontese red grape hierarchy, this characterful variety seems to have originated in the area of Acqui/Ovada, from which it has spread to various other parts of Piemonte. Outside Piemonte it is rarely found except in Ligure di Ponente, where it is known as Ormeasco. Like Barbera it is first mentioned in print in 1799, by Count Nuvolone who refers to it by one of its synonyms: Dosset (others include Uva d'Acqui, Uva di Ovada and Uva del Monferrato). And like Barbera it is thought to have developed from seed.

Dolcetto is an accommodating variety, being easy to grow even in lesser sites and ripening ten to fourteen days before Barbera, helping growers thus to make multiple use of their vinification equipment. The same feature, however, makes it vulnerable to early September rains. The name is said to relate to the sweetness (*dolcezza*) of the grape at harvest time, despite the fact that Dolcetto is not particularly impressive for its sugar accumulation, but rather for its balance between sugars, acids and polyphenols.

THE WINES IN PIEMONTE

There are seven separate, relatively historic DOCs for Dolcetto in Piemonte: D. d'Acqui, D. d'Alba, D. d'Asti, D. Langhe Monregalesi, D. di Diano d'Alba, D. di Dogliani and D. di Ovada; to which we must now add four sub DOCs: Colli Tortonesi, Langhe, Monferrato and Pinerolese. *Un bel casino*, as they say – a fine mess. Despite its third-fiddle status in Alba, it is from there that the best wines generally come, and certainly the greatest volume of DOC (around 50,000 hectolitres). Alba is followed in volume by Ovada (around 25,000 hectolitres), which also is capable of some impressive quality. Dogliani (around 15,000 hectolitres), which specializes in the variety, probably has the highest proportion of good wines to total production. Diano d'Alba (around 5,000 hectolitres) is another specialist zone having a few good producers. Of Dolcetto d'Acqui there is a total production of around 15,000 hectolitres, most of it the work of the local cooperative. As for Dolcetto delle Langhe Monregalesi, it hardly exists, nor in reality do Colli Tortonesi and Pinerolese. Langhe Dolcetto and Monferrato Dolcetto are beginning to catch on as useful DOCs to cascade into.

Of moderate acidity, rich in anthocyanins, Dolcetto can with a quite brief maceration give an impressively purply wine of moderate tannicity thanks to the limited requirement for its presence on the skins.

Most Piemontese Dolcetto is, therefore, straightforward, fruity, easy drinking wine, making it the favoured everyday mealtime wine of the Piemontese. From low-producing vineyards, however, and given a longer maceration, it can yield a deep-coloured, rich and tannic wine capable of medium to long-term ageing. Such versions are rare, not least because there is little market credibility for top-level Dolcetto and therefore the price they fetch is unlikely to justify the effort and expense involved.

The producers (by DOC area)
DOLCETTO D'ALBA

Among Dolcetto producers in the Alba zone a number stand out. One is Cà Viola of Montelupo Albese, already cited for their outstanding *barrique*-matured Barbera, Bric du Luv. In fact Cà Viola are, if anything, even better known for their Dolcetto d'Alba Barturot, a wine of deep colour, powerful and compact in the mouth with quantities of damson fruit and a sturdy structure of ripe tannins. Another is Mauro Mascarello of Giuseppe Mascarello at Monchiero, whose stunning 1985 Gagliassi, referred to on page 81, seemed but a babe when tasted in 1998. Alas, Mauro is no longer able to acquire grapes from Gagliassi, but his Bricco is heading in the right direction.

Perhaps the most remarkable of Dolcettos from Alba, however, is the Boschi di Berri of Marcarini at La Morra. The secret here is the age of the vines, believe it or not over a hundred years old and still planted on their own rootstocks, propagation taking place by the ancient method of layering. The wine is soft and elegant having great intensity and a range of fruit aromas (no oak is used).

Other good to very good producers of Dolcetto d'Alba include (no *cru* mentioned where the wine is simply Dolcetto d'Alba DOC): Gianfranco Alessandria; Altare; Azelia (Bricco Oriolo); Barale (Bussia); Boglietti (Vigna dei Fossati; Tigli Neri); Clerico; Aldo Conterno (Bussia); Giacomo Conterno; Gastaldi (Moriolo); Germano (Pra di Po); Elio Grasso (Vigna dei Grassi); Manzone (La Serra); Nada; Oberto (Vantrino Albarella); Pasquero Elia (Sorì Paitin); Pelissero (Augenta; Munfrina); Prunotto (Mosesco); Revello; Albino Rocca (Vignalunga); Rocche dei Manzoni (Vigna Matinera); Roddolo (Monforte); Sandrone; Scarzello; Vajra (Coste e Fossati); Viberti; Vietti (Tre Vigne); Vigna Rionda (Vigneto Barilot); Gianni Voerzio (Rocchettevino); Roberto Voerzio.

DOLCETTO DI DOGLIANI

Three producers stand out in Dogliani. Quinto **Chionetti** produces *crus* San Luigi and Briccolero, from old vines, low production, that are almost legendary, especially the Briccolero, more structured and of greater extract. Luigi Einaudi have already been mentioned for their Barolo (see page 91) but are better known for their constantly improving *crus* Dolcettos, the non-oaked, ripe and fruity Vigna Tecc and the fuller, more complex *barrique*d I Filari. Fratelli **Pecchenino** produce *crus* Pizabò (the fresh fruity one with minimal maceration, aged in stainless steel), Bricco Botti (heavily *barricato*) and, most prestigious of all, Sirì d'Jermu, which despite a mere two days on the skins is deep of colour, full of ripe tannin and extract, the whole overlayed by a marvellous wealth of fruit – a wine whose complexity-cum-balance won it the coveted Tre Bicchieri in 1998.

A producer that has recently begun making a name for itself is **Manfredi**, of Farigliano in the Dogliani zone. These merchants, representing a range of good-value Piemontese wines from Moscato to Barolo (they also go under the name of Patrizi), have been busily upgrading their production in recent years, acquiring vineyards in La Morra (for Barolo) as well as in Farigliano, where they produce a tasty Barbera d'Alba as well as a high-quality Dolcetto from the vineyard Torralta del Bricco Rosso.

Other worthy producers of Dogliani include: Francesco **Boschis** (Sorì San Martino; Vigna dei Prey); Antonio **Del Tufo** (Vigna Spina); **Devalle** (Bric Sur Pian); Carlo **Romana** (Vigna Bric dij Nor); Adalberto **Schellino**.

DOLCETTO DI DIANO D'ALBA

Good wines are produced by Matteo e Claudio **Alario** (Costa Fiore; Montagrillo) and **Bricco Maiolica** (Sorì Bricco Maiolica).

DOLCETTO D'ACQUI

Production in Dolcetto's homeland is dominated by the Cantina Sociale **Viticoltori dell'Acquese**, who have been through some hard times but are coming out of them now with ex-Antinori winemaker Dora Marchi as resident oenologist, backed by consultant Donato Lanati. One of the biggest and best producers of Moscato in the zone, with plenty of Barbera and a limited amount of good quality Chardonnay, Viticoltori because of their position are particularly focused on Dolcetto. Their standard product is light and fruity, an easy drinker of no great substance. The recently introduced *cru* Statiellae, however, carries the wine on to another level, the wine having an entrancingly plummy aroma and a very attractive sweet fruit-juicy style on the palate, cut by firm but not excessive acidity and just a twist of bitterness at the back of the palate, rescuing it from possible accusations of frivolity. Tasting a wine like this, one can understand why Dolcetto is sometimes called the Beaujolais of Italy; this would be on the level of a single *Village*.

Other valid makers of Dolcetto d'Acqui include: **Banfi** (Argusto), Strevi; **Cascina Bertolotto** (La Muiette), Spigno Monferrato; **Marenco** (Marchesa), Strevi; **Villa Sparina** (Bric Maioli; d'Giusep), Gavi.

DOLCETTO D'OVADA

Good producers include: **Abbazia di Vallechiara** at Lerma; **Castello di Tagliolo**, Tagliolo Monferrato; **La Guardia** (Villa Delfini; Gamondino; Vigneto Bricco Riccardo), Morsasco; **La Slina** (Pianterasso), Castelletto d'Orba; **Ratto** (Gli Scarsi), Roccagrimalda; **Verrina** (Vigna Oriali; Podere Semonina), Prasco.

DOLCETTO D'ASTI

Brema (Vigna Impagnato), Incisa Scapaccino.

LANGHE DOLCETTO

Gaja (Cremes).

DOLCETTO-BASED SUPERPIEMONTESE

This is a rare breed. The best-known wine of the genre is Bricco del Drago from Poderi Colla, a *botte*-matured Dolcetto (85%) Nebbiolo blend. **Trinchero**, at Agliano d'Asti, makes an interesting Dolcetto/Merlot blend called Le Taragne.

THE WINES IN LIGURIA

Easily the best-known producer of Riviera Ligure di Ponente Ormeasco is **Lupi** of Pieve di Teco, who make an Ormeasco Superiore under the name Le Braje and a rosé called Ormeasco Sciactrà.

FREISA

Like Barbera and Dolcetto, Freisa's first recorded mention was made by Count Nuvolone in 1799, though in a different context. It had certainly, however, existed in strength in Piemontese vineyards prior to that time, for it was much written of by ampelographers of the nineteenth century. Said to have originated in the hills of Chieri between Asti and Turin, Freisa almost died out after phylloxera and began only a few years ago to make a serious comeback. Today it is appreciated for its versatility either as a blender or as a varietal in two styles, generally reflecting the two distinct types of Freisa to be found in Piemontese vineyards, which may in fact be distinct sub-varieties, although they may just be the same variety behaving differently in different conditions (cf. Barbera).

In any case, there do indisputably exist a large-bunched, large-berried Freisa known suitably as Freisa Grossa and a small-bunched and -berried version called Freisa Piccola. The former is given to high acidity and makes a pleasant if rather insubstantial *frizzante* style, often sweet, not dissimilar to Lambrusco (in fact one of the synonyms it has acquired is Freisa Brusca, meaning acidic). In the sweet version the sharpness is offset by residual sugar while the carbon dioxide accentuates the strawberry-raspberry aromas (the name may derive from the French *fraise*). The dry style is somewhat more difficult to bring off but can be amazingly aromatic and refreshing.

Since the 1980s there has been a resurgence of the serious small-berried Freisa di Chieri, a grape of distinctly superior polyphenolic endowment, capable of making a wine not dissimilar in structure to Nebbiolo, while having quite distinctive aromatic characteristics; similar, in fact, to those of Freisa Grossa, but more complex and more subtle. Needless to say the various DOCs, which include Asti, Chieri, Langhe, Monferrato and Pinerolese, do not distinguish between the two types. It is wise to know the producer's style before purchasing.

The greatest concentration of producers of the serious still red style is to be found under the DOC Langhe. Good producers include: Ascheri (Rocca d'Auçabech); Aldo Conterno (La Bussianella); Giacomo Conterno; Giuseppe Mascarello (Vigna Toetto); Giuseppe Rinaldi; Aldo Vajra (Kyè). Bartolo Mascarello makes an unusual Freisa Nebbiolata, one which has been passed over the skins of Nebbiolo after racking following fermentation, in the manner of Valpolicella *ripasso*.

A good example of the dry *frizzante* style from the Langhe is La

Bastiana from Caudrina at Castiglione Tinella (see under Moscato, page 125).

In the Monferrato two serious producers of dry still Freisa are Luigi Coppo (Valdivilla Mondaccione) and Scarpa (La Selva di Moirano).

There doesn't seem to be much activity left Freisa-wise around Chieri, but two wines under that DOC are made by Azienda Vitivinicola **Balbiano** at Andezeno, one still and dry, aged in *botte*, called Punta d'Vigna Veja, the other, distinguishable by the description Vivace, dry and *frizzante*.

Freisa d'Asti is likewise produced in two versions – aged in *botte* (Vigna del Forno) and Vivace – by Cascina **Gilli** at Castelnuovo Don Bosco. **Biletta**, of Casorzo, makes a *cru* called Moncucchetto.

BRACHETTO

An aromatic red variety grown mainly in eastern Piemonte, Brachetto reaches its vinous apotheosis in the commune of Strevi, a *frazione* of Acqui Terme, where it has scaled the dizzy heights of DOCGdom. Brachetto may have hailed from Provence, where it is apparently known as Braquet and figures in the wines of Bellet, near Nice; but this hypothesis has come under heavy fire from certain ampelographers and is by no means proven. Wherever it came from, its perfumes, which are wonderfully flowery-raspberry, suggest to some that it may be related to Moscato, although others deny the possibility saying that Brachetto lacks the characteristic 'muskiness'. It generally but not invariably comes sweet and *frizzante* or *spumante* but it can also be dry and still, and there is a super-sweet *passito* version capable of remarkable longevity.

A grower once told me the story of his ancient grandfather who, about to pass on to the next world around the middle of the twentieth century, called for a bottle of the excellent 1864 Brachetto Passito to be brought from the *infernot*, or family cellar. 'But grandfather, don't you think you should have a nice cup of camomile tea instead – alcohol wouldn't be good for you.' An argument ensued, a compromise was found: first the Brachetto, then the tea. The bottle was duly fetched and lovingly opened, the old man drank a wholesome draft and promptly expired, a happy smile on his face. No time for camomile tea.

Considering the DOCG status it is surprising how few producers are attempting BRACHETTO D'ACQUI. Those located in Strevi include: Banfi (Vigneto la Rosa); **Contero**; and **Marenco** (Pineto). Viticoltori dell'Acquese also make an excellent version of the sweet sparkling style. As for the *passito* version – a wine of infinitely greater intrinsic character – outstanding producers include Domenico **Ivaldi** and Giovanni **Ivaldi,** both of Valle Bagnario in Strevi. It was the latter who told me the above story.

From Canale, in the Roero, mysteriously omitted from DOC status, Brachetto often goes under the locally invented name of Birbèt, indicating a wine that may be sweet or dry, perhaps with a touch of CO_2. Producers include **Cascina Chicco** (Dolce), Malvirà (Dolce) and **Porello** (Secco), all of Canale. Matteo Correggia calls his excellent dry version Anthos.

Piemonte Brachetto may take any of the possible forms. Bertolotto produces a sweet, semi-sparkling version called Il Virginio. Scarpa's La Selva di Moirano, on the other hand, is dry and serious.

MALVASIA DI SCHIERANO

Another aromatic red variety, which we shall meet again in Tuscany and in particular in Puglia, Malvasia Nera is produced in two very restricted DOC areas north of Asti: Casorzo and Castelnuovo Don Bosco. Between them they manage about 5,000 hectolitres per year of sweet, sparkling wine of a subtly flowery fragrance, not dissimilar to Brachetto. Producers of Malvasia di Castelnuovo Don Bosco include Balbiano and Gilli; of Malvasia di Casorzo, Biletta (all mentioned under Freisa).

GRIGNOLINO, PELAVERGA, ROUCHET

These native Piemontese are among Italy's more distinctive varieties, not necessarily in the best sense. Grignolino wine tends to have a pale, onion-skin hue with a somewhat vegetal aroma and, frankly, not a great deal of taste. Or put it this way: it's an acquired taste which I personally have failed to acquire.

Three DOCs exist: G. d'Asti, G. del Monferrato Casalese and G. Piemonte. To my surprise I discover that some 33,000 hectolitres are produced from the three – double the production of Barbaresco. The surprise comes from the fact that you almost never see Grignolino outside Piemonte, and it's too pale and delicate to be of any use in blending. I suppose the natives, at least, enjoy the stuff.

Well-known producers are Braida, Coppo, Rivetti and Scarpa, while other names we have come across before include Biletta, Villa Fiorita, La Tenaglia, Boffa and Nuova Cappelletta. **Bricco Mondalini** of Vignale Monferrato make a *cru* called, funnily enough, Bricco Mondalino, and Livio **Pavese** of Treville makes one called Podere Sant'Antonio. **Brichet**, at Isola d'Asti, makes an intriguingly named Grignolino d'Asti called Non Ti Scordar di Me (Don't forget me); Luigi **Spertino**, at Mombercelli, produces Grignolino Vendemmia Tardiva (late harvest).

Pelaverga is said to have been brought to Verduno in the eighteenth century by a Piemontese priest called Beato Valfrè. It comes a somewhat deeper ruby, but it too tends towards the vegetal and rather acidic, though with a spicy-fruit component. It is a peculiarity of the Saluzzesi hills in the province of Cuneo, and in particular of Verduno, one of Barolo's minor communes, where it rejoices in its very own DOC. It is frankly difficult to get enthusiastic about; even one of its major producers admits that he personally doesn't like it.

In Verduno, good producers include Fratelli Alessandria, Burlotto and Castello di Verduno (Massara). Ascheri's is called Costa dei Faggi.

Rouchet (sometimes spelled Ruchè), with a bright ruby colour and something of a floral aroma, is probably the most interesting, or rather most approachable of the three. But the market for these wines is minute, they are little produced and therefore generally too expensive for their quality. Representative producers are Biletta with their *cru* Moncucchetto, while DOC Ruchè di Castagnole Monferrato is made by Bava (Casa Brina).

Just a few words here about a producer whose name has cropped up a few times and which represents not just an exceptional example of the old style but which stands in a way for the guardianship of Piemonte's ampelographical patrimony: the Antica Casa Vinicola **Scarpa** of Nizza Monferrato. Mario Pesce, who heads up the firm in this medium-sized town in the heart of the Monferrato hills, is a *signore* of the old school, correct in speech, dress and manner, gently anathematizing the innovations of the past few decades while stoutly maintaining that Scarpa, for their part, will never change. Their wines are living proof that the traditional style does not necessarily entail faulty wine, every bottle in their range being technically impeccable if perhaps a little unyielding, offering few concessions to modern requirements for sweet fruit, low acidity and soft tannins, and then only by chance. All wines are from Piemontese varieties and are recommended to those who are looking for classic benchmarks: Nebbiolo (Barolo Tettimora and Barbaresco Tettineive); Barbera d'Asti La Bogliona; Dolcetto La Selva di Moirano; Freisa La Selva di Moirano; Grignolino d'Asti Sandefendente; and, most successful of all, Rouchet Bricco Rosa – light of colour, somewhat aromatic of bouquet, having a penetrating fruity acidity on the palate and generally most admirable for its purity of conception and execution.

BONARDA ('UVA RARA'), CROATINA ('BONARDA'), VESPOLINA ('UGHETTA')

We have already come across instances of the demonic plot on the part of Italians to confuse us (and themselves); they don't come a lot more fiendish than this one.

What is called Bonarda in the Novara/Vercelli area of Piemonte, and is used as one of the back-up grapes to Nebbiolo (Spanna) in wines like Gattinara and Ghemme, *is* Bonarda. Another of the back-up grapes here is Croatina. However, in Oltrepò Pavese and Colli Piacentini what is called Bonarda is *not* Bonarda, it is Croatina. Another name for *real* Bonarda (from Novara/Vercelli) is Uva Rara, and it is as Uva Rara that this Bonarda makes its appearance in Lombardy and Emilia, alongside what is *called* Bonarda but is *actually* Croatina.

Clear? No, it's not to me either, and I am not at all sure I've got it right, but if I'm wrong so is the latest *Guide to the DOC and DOCG Wines* put out by the Enoteca Italiana of Siena; whose interpretation, I am bound to say, does not seem to mesh very well with the punditries of Messrs Dalmasso *et al.* of the Ministry of Agriculture's commission for the study of the principal wine-grape varieties of Italy, this latter study being, however, considerably older.

Just to mix it a bit more, the folk of Novara/Vercelli make a distinction between Bonarda di Gattinara, from the west bank of the Sesia river (province of Vercelli), and Bonarda Novarese, from the east bank (province of Novara). This may mean that the latter is what Dalmasso calls Bonarda Piemontese, but who can say for sure? – not I. It's all too exhausting, and not really important, since none of these grapes, by whatever name you please to call them, is of any great importance in our time, with the exception of Croatina.

As for Vespolina, the third of Novara/Vercelli's back-up grapes, it is planted also in Oltrepò and Colli Piacentini; but there it is called Ughetta.

In terms of wines, Bonarda exists as a sub-DOC under Piemonte and also under Colline Novaresi together with Croatina and Vespolina. Actual production, however, is very limited. The only varietals out of Piemonte I have come across are from Brigatti (Bonarda and Vespolina).

So-called Bonarda (Croatina) from Oltrepò Pavese (around 75,000 hectolitres) and Colli Piacentini (around 17,000 hectolitres) is relatively plentiful, on the other hand, and can make wines of very deep-coloured, soft and plummy fruit, almost to the point, sometimes, of seeming jammy; they may be attractive and easy-drinking but tend to be somewhat one-dimensional. Good examples come from Mazzolino, Vercesi del Castellazzo (Fatila), Castello di Luzzano (Carlino), Monsupello and **Orlandi**, at Rovescala.

OTHER RED GRAPE VARIETIES

Other red grapes of the North West (not counting international varieties) include the Valle d'Aosta group of native obscurities such as **PETIT ROUGE, FUMIN** and **VIEN DE NUS**. The **Institut Agricole Régional** at Aosta makes a representative Petit Rouge and **La Crotta di Vegneron** at Chambave produces a Fumin.

Lombardy too has its share of oddities, including **ROSSOLA, BRUGNOLA** and **PIGNOLA**, which still support Nebbiolo in the blend of Valtellina, as they have done for centuries, but are not to be found varietally. Then there is **GROPPELLO**, a grape of considerable character, grown exclusively on the western shores of Lake Garda, and giving a wine of firm acidity, middling tannins and a fruity-spicy palate. The principal DOC is Riviera del Garda Bresciano, with a varietal and a Groppello-based Rosso and Chiaretto (rosé). The best producer is perhaps **Cascina la Pertica** at Polpenazze del Garda, with the following all capable of turning out good quality: **Comincioli** and **Monteacuto** at Puegnago del Garda;

Costaripa and **Monte Cicogna** at Moniga del Garda; **Redaelli da Zinis** at Calvagese della Riviera.

Although **MARZEMINO** is today more associated with Trentino, it has a certain tradition and continuing presence in Lombardy. The best wine from this grape is Mario **Pasolini**'s Ronco di Mompiano, a blend with Merlot (see Blends, page 298).

Then there is the **ROSSESE** of Liguria's Ponente, which makes the easy-drinking Rossese di Dolceacqua DOC over near the French border. A good example comes from **Tenuta Giuncheo** (Vigneto Pian del Vescovo), and the *barrique*-aged *crus* Vigneto Luvaira and Vigneto Morghe, by **Foresti** at Camporosso, are worth tasting should you by some miracle ever find them. **POLLERA** is an indigenous variety at the other end of Liguria, in the Colli di Luni of the Levanto. I am told that on its own it doesn't stand up to ageing, and I'd better believe it because the man who told me was Pieralberto Ferro of **La Colombiera** at Castelnuovo Magra, maker of the best red wine I have tasted from Liguria, a Tuscan/Bordeaux style blend (no Pollera), based on **SANGIOVESE**, called Terrizzo.

For its part, Emilia has one minor and one major red variety to offer. Minor in reputation, if certainly not in vineyard presence, is **ANCELLOTTA** (or Lancellotta), a grape of deep colour, high sugar and polyphenolic content, and neutral aroma mainly used for blending with Lambrusco, Chianti, Sangiovese di Romagna and other wines in which it is perhaps not supposed to find itself but somehow does. Somewhat surprisingly, the variety, whose name may derive from that of a fifteenth-century grower of the Modena area called Tommasino Lancillotto, turns out to have over 5500 hectares planted to it in Emilia alone, putting it among the top thirty most planted grapes in Italy. Nor is it unknown in Tuscany, where at least one major grower has grafted it on to his Trebbiano and Malvasia as an insurance against the poorly endowed Sangiovese of lesser years. Anyone itching to know what it tastes like can refer to the versions of Stefano **Spezia** of Mariana Mantovana in Lombardy, who produces an oak-aged version as well as one made by secondary fermentation in bottle.

The Emilian variety of major importance is one of those that Ancellotta is often blended with, to wit:

LAMBRUSCO

The main point about Lambrusco is that there is a world of difference between the industrial screw-cap stuff which sells in such amazing quantities (though distinctly less today than at its peak in the 1980s) and the cork-closed DOC wines, usually dry and produced in much lower numbers because the industrial product has convinced international markets that Lambrusco has got to be cheap. I suppose I didn't make that point clearly enough when I wrote *Life Beyond Lambrusco*, because now when I go to Emilia the Lambrusco producers – even the good ones – snub me. Let me then emphasize: THERE IS SUCH A THING AS GOOD LAMBRUSCO AND I PERSONALLY ENJOY DRINKING IT VERY MUCH. La!

Lambrusco is actually not a single grape variety so much as a family of kindred varieties. The parent grape (deceased) was a wild thing, of the family of *Vitis vinifera silvestris*, which crept out of the forests of the Apennines, who knows how many thousands of years ago, and settled in Emilia, mainly in the vicinity of the city of Modena. Over the centuries it developed different characteristics according to local conditions, so that today there are noticeable differences between the three quality sub-varieties, which are: Grasparossa, of the red stems, from around the village of Castelvetro, south of Modena on the lower slopes of the Apennines; Sorbara, the most delicate, most prized and most pricey, from the plain-lands surrounding the village of that name north of Modena; and Salamino (little salami, so named for its sausage-shaped bunches) from around the village of Santa Croce, east of Sorbara. Salamino will often be planted in with Sorbara as the latter has pollination problem, though the wines are generally vinified apart.

Other sub-varieties, more associated with volume production of the type needed to churn out rivers of cheap sweet frothing stuff for consumption by the MacDonald's patrons of this world, are Marani and Montericco, also Mastri, sometimes prefixed by the name Grappello, as is the sub-variety Viadanese, which latter is mainly grown in the Lombard section of the Po Valley plain round the city of Mantua. Yet another sub-variety, if not a different variety altogether, is Trentino's Lambrusco a Foglia Frastagliata.

Not so long ago Lambrusco vines were trained up tree trunks and along their branches. Today this Etruscan viticultural practice is continued in a more rational fashion by training up stakes in a *pergola* formation with, often, two long cordons for volume production per plant. Producers more concerned with quality are increasingly turning to training on Geneva Double Curtain.

As indicated, Lambrusco doesn't necessarily equal super high production for medium alcohol at low cost. Most 'Lambrusco' consumed outside Italy is, it is true, cheap, sweet *vino da tavola* in the true sense (except who would want to drink that sickly stuff with food?). But self-respecting Emilians rarely if ever touch it in this form, preferring the dry, strawberry-fruity, low-tannin high-acid versions which cut so nicely through the grease and fat of their pork- and dairy-dominated diet; or at most the *amabile* or slightly sweet style, more suitable for after dinner or mid-afternoon sipping. '*Lo amo brusco*' – I like it sharp – is one Emilian myth-version of the origin of the name, and even the *amabile* style has plenty of fruity acid to keep it lively.

Lambrusco has been made frothing since the discovery of the cork closure – according to one producer such a style is favoured by the climate. Fifty years ago the best Lambruscos were still being made by the traditional bottle-fermented method. Even in the 1960s one firm was still making a million bottles a year by this method, leaving the deposit in the bottle. But tastes changed, as did laws, and today the firm produces a mere 1 per cent of that figure by the traditional method, having along the way, under government pressure, introduced *dégorgement* – removing the sediment from the wine. Almost all DOC Lambrusco today is made from grape-must stored under pressure at 0°C, fermented slowly in pressure-and-temperature-controlled tanks called *autoclavi*. Dry versions may be left for two months or more on the lees before decanting. Sweeter wines are taken off the lees immediately. Some of the real cheap-and-nasties may be given their sparkle by the 'bicycle pump' method – addition of CO_2 gas.

DOC Lambruscos – which must, by law, have a cork closure – are named after the area of production plus, in two cases, the sub-variety. Thus Lambrusco di Sorbara – generally a light, pale-coloured wine of delicate perfume, vinified off the skins after a few days' cold maceration; Lambrusco Grasparossa di Castelvetro, deep-hued and robust, with a certain earthy gutsiness to it; Lambrusco Salamino di Santa Croce, somewhere between the two. Lambrusco Mantovano, from Lombardy, is not much seen outside Mantua. As for Lambrusco Bianco, it is not a DOC, and there exists no white Lambrusco grape. The wine is from black grapes vinified *in bianco*, a post-war phenomenon devised to satisfy a market for sweet, white, frothing wine, nothing more.

As far as producers are concerned, by far the most important in terms of quality Lambrusco is **Cavicchioli** of San Prospero di Modena, the largest private firm in a land of giant cooperatives. Cavicchioli, the firm alluded to above in respect of bottle-fermented Lambrusco (incidentally, the wine is called Vigna Due Madonne), own around 150 hectares of vineyard, making them the biggest growers in Modena. Nevertheless, having an annual production of some 130,000 hectolitres, most of which, admittedly, is everyday plonk and 95 per cent of which is sold on the home market, they still have to buy in the vast majority of their grape requirement, equalling about a third of the total; the rest they buy as wine. Their *crus* include a L. di Sorbara Vigna del Cristo, dry, light and aromatic, and a L. Grasparossa di Castelvetro Col Sassoso with more colour, body and depth to it.

Other producers turning out good wine include: Casimiro **Barbieri** (L. Grasparossa di Castelvetro Magazzeno), Savignano sul Panaro; **Barbolini** (L. di Modena il Maglia; L. di Sorbara), Formigine; Francesco **Bellei** (L. di Sorbara Capsula d'Oro), Bomporto; **Casali** (Roggio del Pradello; Bosco del Fracasso), Scandiano; Vittorio **Graziano** and Enzo **Manicardi** (L. Grasparossa di Castelvetro), Castelvetro di Modena; **Moro Rinaldo Rinaldini** (Metodo Classico Pjcol Ross and Vecchio Moro), Sant'Ilario d'Enza.

Grapes, wines and producers – white

MOSCATO BIANCO

In the beginning the god made the grape. And the god said: Let it have company. And the grape became twain: aromatic, and non-aromatic. And the god said: Let them multiply. And the grapes procreated and became many, of each type. And the god of grapes created insects, that he might through them savour the sweetness and swoon to the scent of his fruit. And he noted the particular partiality of his winged creatures for the progeny of the aromatic grape, and he named it (for his language was Greek, as for so many of the best gods): *kanathelicon moschaton*.

Moscato (Muscat) is a direct descendent of the first aromatic grape. Since its early appearance on the Italian peninsula, nature, servant of the gods, has kindly provided a diversity of sub-varieties spread across multiple regions: Moscato Bianco (what the French call Muscat à Petits Grains), Moscato Giallo (in the German-speaking South Tyrol called Goldmuskateller), Moscato Rosa (German: Rosenmuskateller). These may be of different hues and may have slight variations of aroma but are essentially Moscatos of the small-berried, rose and peach-perfumed type. The larger-berried Moscato di Alessandria, essentially a table grape, is a cousin.

It is in Piemonte that Moscato Bianco, or Moscato di Canelli as it is also called after one of the important growing communes, has found its principal home. Here it thrives in the light, chalk and limestone soils of the hills of the provinces of Asti and Alessandria, with a bit of Cuneo attached.

Despite its charms, the grape was never, until the latter half of the twentieth century, a favourite with growers, owing to a long ripening season which renders it vulnerable to the weather's vagaries. Its early popularity with wine-bibbers in positions of power, however, ensured continuity in Piemontese vineyards; in 1511 a statute issued in the Langhe village of La Morra decreed that *muscatellum* had to constitute one-fifth of any new-planted vineyard. Over the past half-century, however, and particularly since improvements in wine-making technology made it relatively straightforward to deal with, it has increased its share of plantings in eastern Piemonte by leaps and bounds.

Today, Moscato Bianco is second only to Barbera in Piemontese hectarage, and by far the most planted of Italy's various Moscati. Being grown at altitudes ranging from 160 metres, around Strevi in the eastern part of the zone, to 550 metres, around Mango in the west, it varies both in ripening time and style – the high, steep (in some cases practically perpendicular) slopes of the Santo Stefano/Castiglione Tinella *conca* giving a later-ripening, lighter, more acidic, more floral wine, while the lower, less dramatic slopes of Strevi yield wines of greater body and substance, more fruity-peachy than floral. The sub-regions centred on Canelli (east of Santo Stefano) and on Alice Bel Colle (west of Strevi) tend to a combination of characteristics.

THE WINES IN PIEMONTE

Nothing in the wine world is more delightful in its context than a fragrant, flowery-fruity, sweet but fresh, lightly frothing Moscato d'Asti (DOCG, along with its more famous but less refined cousin, Asti – the word 'Spumante' has been eliminated from the title since 1994). The style was first developed by Giovan Battista Croce, a gentleman viticulturist of the early seventeenth century, who wrote a booklet on the method of making sweet, aromatic, low-alcohol wine. At that time the processes of wine-production were not fully understood, but Croce observed that continued fermentation was associated with loss of sweetness, and devised a method, based on multiple racking from barrel to barrel, cooling by immersion of barrels in water, and filtration using hempen sacks, of reducing (if not altogether eliminating) the risks of refermentation. His wine was not conceived of as sparkling, but no doubt slight refermenta-tion did occasionally occur, the result having all the characteristics of the wine we know today.

In the mid-nineteenth century Carlo Gancia of Canelli began to apply the knowledge he had gained in Champagne to Moscato production, his principal concern being how to inhibit excessive refermentation in bottle. With the help of a team of oenologists he came up with a method of removing the nitrogenous substances necessary for yeasts to work, and Asti (then dubbed 'moscato champagne') was born.

Today, bottle fermentation is a thing of the past and production methods have been streamlined – Asti Moscato being surely one of the world's wines to have benefited most from the development of technology. The basic tool of the modern technique is the *auto-clave*, a pressurized, thermo-controllable stainless steel tank which enables the producer to hold the freshly pressed must at around 0°C in temperature and 0–2 or 3 degrees of alcohol until ready to complete the process. In the case of Moscato d'Asti, parting from a must with a potential alcohol of 11 degrees, about half of the sugars will be transformed into actual alcohol, the rest remaining in the wine as natural sweetness. The ripest grapes go into Moscato d'Asti, because it may not be enriched by saccharose (in poor years enrichment by addition of concentrated Moscato grape must is permitted). The sparkle is, of course, natural, carbon dioxide gas being a by-product of the fermentation process, here trapped in the wine held under pressure at a maximum of 1.7 atmospheres.

The producer of fully sparkling Asti is allowed to add sugar to increase the actual alcohol content, which must be not less than 7 degrees. Here the pressure must not be less than 3.5 atmospheres and is usually more like 4.5 to 5; and again it must be natural, no added gas permitted. Unfortunately, Asti has an unenviable recent history of having been handled by 'industrialists', not to say crooks, who have not scrupled against employment of various cheapening devices. Today, however, the Consorzio per la Tutela dell'Asti has taken over control of the regulations for all producers, and fraudulent, and therefore cheap, Asti is becoming (they say; or they hope) a thing of the past.

Another significant difference between Asti and Moscato d'Asti is that the latter is increasingly becoming a *cru* wine, reflecting the differences of *terroir* as described above, while Asti remains with few exceptions a blended mass-market product of standardized quality according to the brand.

At the time of researching *Life Beyond Lambrusco* it would not have seemed appropriate to feature a producer specializing in a wine so obscure as Moscato d'Asti. In the past few years, however, the style has taken off to such an extent that it seems right to cast the spotlight on the estate which, more than any other, deserves credit for having developed *cru* Moscato:

Caudrina, Castiglione Tinella. When, in the years following the Second World War, Redento Dogliotti first started making Moscato from the grapes of his vineyards – splendidly exposed on super-steep slopes in the commune of Castiglione Tinella – he was reviving a tradition that had all but died out. It turned out to be extremely hard work for little return, and he was obliged to give up, but not before firing his son Romano with a passion to take up the challenge, which he duly did in the late 1960s.

At first Romano's wine was made in bottle, with all the attendant problems of unwanted refermentation and sediment. But the coming of refrigeration and the *autoclave* enabled him, in the early 1980s, to perfect his technique. His Moscato La Caudrina, from grapes grown anywhere on the 19-hectare estate, is today considered not just the archetype but also one of the finest of the genre, so that the more recently developed single-vineyard La Galeisa, with a more floral bouquet and a touch more concentration, may be considered different but scarcely superior.

Following Romano's lead several others have come to challenge him for quality in the Moscato d'Asti stakes, but I have not found a *spumante* to rival his intensely delicious La Selvatica, one of the

REDENTO DOGLIOTTI

La Caudrina®

MOSCATO D'ASTI

DENOMINAZIONE DI ORIGINE CONTROLLATA E GARANTITA

Imbottigliato all'origine da Redento Dogliotti & Figli - Castiglione Tinella - Italia

75 cl ℮   5,5% vol.

few examples of estate-bottled Asti, the first production of which was in 1993. Romano also makes traditional *frizzante* reds from his few Barbera and Freisa vines.

Other top grower-producers of Moscato d'Asti include:

Bera (Su Reimond), Neviglie; **Ca d'Gal** (Vigne Vecchie), Santo Stefano Belbo; **Cascina Fonda/Secondino Barbero**, Mango; **Cascina Pian d'Or** (Bricco Riella), Mango; **Degiorgis** (Sorì del Re), Mango; Icardi (La Rosa Selvatica), Castiglione Tinella; **Il Falchetto** (Tenuta dei Ciombi), Santo Stefano Belbo; **La Morandina**, Castiglione Tinella; La Spinetta (Bricco Quaglia); Marenco (Scrapona); **Perrone** (Sourgal), Castiglione Tinella; **Saracco** (Moscato d'Autunno), Castiglione Tinella; **Scagliola** (Volo di Farfalle), Calosso; **Vignaioli di Santo Stefano**, Santo Stefano Belbo. Of these, Bera, Cascina Fonda and Cascina Pian d'Or also make Asti of particular worth.

These, of course, are all small fry. Production of Moscato d'Asti, and especially of Asti, is dominated by large-scale private and cooperative producers, some of which are capable of wines of real quality. Among the privates are such well-known names as Banfi, Cinzano, Contratto, Fontanafredda, Gancia, Martini Rossi. Of the *cantine sociali* good producers include Araldica Vini Piemontesi and Viticoltori dell'Acquese. The latter's *cru* Casarito, from vineyards in the Valle Bagnario sub-zone of Strevi, is among the best in absolute terms.

Quite a lot of Moscato is grown in the Oltrepò Pavese, from whence, horrid rumour-mongers have mooted, Piemonte derives goodly amounts of grapes and grape-must. And not only from the Oltrepò, these dreadful voices whisper, but from all parts of Italy including even from Pantelleria where the sub-variety grown is not even Bianco but Moscato di Alessandria.

Before our friend Croce got going most Moscato from Piemonte was made by the *passito* method – another reason why the growers didn't like it, since in the old days grape-drying was carried out under the sun, and in October there is more likely to be rot-forming mist in northerly Piemonte than hot sunshine. This process, when successful, produced a wine of amazingly concentrated sweetness and perfume, and such wines exist to this day, though in tiny quantities, the grapes being dried in more protected locations such as under the winery eaves. Particularly prized areas for such production are Loazzolo, which boasts a DOC for the style and whose prime producer, Forteto della Luja, makes a wine called Piasa Rischei, considered by some among the greatest of Italy's many dessert or *meditazione* wines; and the Valle Bagnario in the commune of Strevi, near Acqui Terme. Here Ivaldi Domenico (Casarito) and Ivaldi Giovanni (Eliodoro) are top exponents. Icardi of Castiglione Tinella makes a particularly rich *passito* called Muscatel.

THE WINES IN VALLE D'AOSTA

Muscat de Chambave, from Valle d'Aosta, is a little-produced but occasionally available – and potentially delicious – wine of the *passito* type; best producers are La Crotta di Vegneron and Ezio **Voyat**. There is also provision for Moscato Passito in the *disciplinari* of Valcalepio and Valcalepio Scanzo, in Lombardy's Bergamo area, but precious little actual wine emerges.

CORTESE

Although it is grown as far east as Lake Garda, where under the name Bianco Fernanda it forms part of the blend of grapes, the *uvaggio*, for Bianco di Custoza, Cortese's true home is the Alto Monferrato, where it remains widely planted, despite a decrease in hectarage during the 1980s. The first reference to it in wine literature is attributed, as in the case of several Piemontese red varieties, to Count Nuvolone in 1799, although it has almost certainly been in the vineyards of the province of Alessandria a lot longer than that.

Cortese's chief characteristic is its ability to maintain high levels of acidity even in very hot years, making it a good candidate for wines destined to be served with fish, as, for example, in the tourist resorts of the Ligurian coast. Conversely, in cool years, or cool climates, full ripening can be a problem, the acidity can be bitingly high, and the sugar level quite low, so that enrichment with MCR (*mosto concentrato rettificato*, or concentrated rectified grape must) is almost always resorted to and malo-lactic fermentation, preferably partial so as not to lose aroma, is becoming increasingly common. The ideal is to achieve balance in the grape itself, which requires not just favourable climatic conditions but also restricted yields, not an easy matter given its tendency to high productivity.

Easily Cortese's best-known vinous manifestation is Gavi, after the eponymous town in the south-east corner of Piemonte. Gavi is a (supposedly) 100% varietal wine which rejoices in the reputation, not totally justified according to some, of being one of Italy's finest whites. That it has been one of the most hyped is beyond dispute, and when it's good – full enough of body to match the acidity, with a twist of lime cordial on the nose and finish – it can, in the right context, be just the thing. Almost inevitably, some producers are resorting to barrel fermentation in an attempt to increase complexity.

There are those who claim that Gavi does not reveal its quality until it has had a good two years in bottle, perhaps longer. As most Gavi is consumed young the theory is not often put to the test. Certainly the wine has the acid structure to withstand the trials of time, but may lack the body to make such maturation worthwhile.

The phrase 'Gavi di Gavi' indicates a Gavi from the commune of Gavi, which includes most of them. It is taken by the market to indicate a wine of a quality superior to that of simple Gavi, and while this is often the case, it is by no means an inevitability.

Good producers include (*barrique*d examples marked by *): Banfi (Vigna Regale); Nicola **Bergaglio** (Minaia), Gavi; **Broglia** (*Bruno Broglia), Gavi; **Castellare Bergaglio** (*Barric), Gavi; **Castello di Tassarolo** (*Vigneto Alborina), Tassarolo; Michele Chiarlo (*Fior di Rovere); **La Giustiniana** (*Vignaclara), Gavi; **La Scolca** (Gavi dei Gavi Etichetta Nera), Gavi; **Tenuta San Pietro** (Vigneto la Gorrina), Tassarolo; Villa Sparina (La Villa).

The La Scolca estate, which under Vittorio Soldati established itself after the Second World War as the flag-bearer of Cortese di Gavi production (until the early twentieth century Gavi had been mainly a red-wine zone), has today under son Giorgio Soldati made itself the front-runner in the production of Cortese *spumante* with their Brut and Extra Brut.

Other Corteses of DOC status include Alto Monferrato and Piemonte, which are allowed to blend in other grapes to a maximum of 15%, as is Oltrepò Pavese Cortese in Lombardy. Piemonte's Cortese Colli Tortonesi, which is only separated from Oltrepò Pavese by the regional border, does not enjoy this freedom, but it is in any case a very obscure wine.

Good producers of Cortese Alto Monferrato include the previously mentioned cooperatives Araldica Vini Piemontesi (Alasia) and Viticoltori dell'Acquese (Terme I). Among privates, worthy of a mention are: Bertolotto (Il Barigi); Marenco (Valtignosa); **Scrimaglio**, Nizza Monferrato.

ARNEIS

The name, according to documents of 1478 and 1528 referring to the transactions of the Counts Roero, appears to derive from the site known then as Renesium, or Renexii. Through marriage, the site subsequently passed to the counts Malabaila of Asti, the present proprietors, although the historic *cru* Renesio or Bricco Renesio is today leased and worked by the Damonte brothers of the Malvirà estate.

Despite its antiquity Arneis was never planted in any great quantity in the Roero, probably because it is a naturally low yielder and, while generally achieving good sugar levels by mid-September, it tends to lose acidity rapidly near ripening time. Traditionally it has been used as a blending variety for the softening of Nebbiolo, and would have occupied perhaps two or three rows of a vineyard. Thus this small-bunched, small-berried variety was sliding gently towards extinction when, in the 1970s, Vietti and Rabezzano took it in hand, buying tiny quantities from this grower and that in order to make up sufficient for purposes of vinification.

Recent research and revised viticultural practices have resolved to some extent the problem of low acidity, as well as its tendency to oxidation. Arneis is prized today for its unique range of aromas and flavours, and increasingly considered one of Italy's most characterful native white varieties. Its preferred *terroir* is the relatively light, chalky-sandy *terra bianca* of the Roero hills; from heavier, more clay-based soils on either side of the Tanaro it will be less short-lived. Plantings to Arneis are still very limited, but increasing every year as growers recognize its potential as a good earner. Between 1992 and 1996 the area planted in the Roero increased from 287 to 395 hectares, and production rose from 11,500 hectolitres to nearly 20,000.

The town of Canale in the Roero can be considered the centre of production for the DOC Roero Arneis (the name Roero on its own refers to Nebbiolo). The aforementioned **Malvirà**, of Roberto (the oenologist) and Massimo (responsible for the vineyards) Damonte, is probably the *azienda* most widely respected. Their *cru* Renesio is vinified without wood, *cru* Trinità partially fermented in 4.5-hectolitre French oak *fusti*, and *cru* Saglietto is wholly oak fermented and aged.

Another producer of excellent *cru* Arneis is my old friend Luigi **Bertini** of Monticello d'Alba in the Roero. The Arneis grapes for the wine he calls Sorilaria (*sorì* = exposed towards the sun in Piemontese dialect; Ilaria is the name of Luigi's delightful elder daughter) are grown in a small (1.2 hectares) vineyard which was planted as far back as 1979 – one of the first specialist Arneis vineyards – two-thirds of it being on white calcareous soil (good for acidity and structure), one-third on sandy-clay soil necessary to give the wine perfume. In good years (for white, not necessarily for reds) the wine can have an unusual longevity, but the mature vines regularly bring forth a melony, slightly tropical-fruity wine having a luscious drinkability well beyond its modest price.

Other good to excellent producers of Arneis based in Canale include: Cascina Chicco; **Cornarea**, who also make a *barrique*-aged *passito* called Tarasco; Correggia; Carlo Deltetto (San Michele Daivej), also makers of a *normale* and the *passito* Bric Tupin; **Serafino** (Chiosso); **Malabaila di Canale** (Pradvaj); Marco e Ettore Porello (Camestrì); Funtanin Sperone (Pierin di Soc).

Elsewhere in the Roero notable producers include: **Almondo** (Burigot), Montà d'Alba; Negro (Pedaudin), Monteu Roero; **Rabino**, Santa Vittoria d'Alba; **Tenuta Carretta**, Piobesi d'Alba; **Teo Costa** (Serramiana), Castellinaldo.

The most important Arneis producers situated outside the Roero, whether the DOC of their wine is Roero Arneis or Langhe Arneis, are Vietti, the originators, Bruno Giacosa, and Ceretto, whose Blangé is probably the best-known Arneis worldwide.

ERBALUCE

The history of the white wine of the area of Piemonte south of Ivrea (of Olivetti fame) and north of Turin (Fiat *et al.*) goes back, some say, beyond Roman times – Roman settlers having, apparently, found it sufficiently irresistible to inspire them to organize the thitherto random vines into proper vineyards with a training system known as *topia*. However that may be, the first mention of Erbaluce, under the name Erbalus, is recorded by G.B. Croce in his 'curious little work' of 1606, and the same spelling was used by good old Count Nuvolone in his *Instructions on the cultivation of the vine* . . . at the end of the eighteenth century, although he mistakenly refers to it as a synonym of Arneis.

The nineteenth-century ampelographer di Rovasenda talks of a Greco Bianco from Ghemme which seems to him to be identical with 'Erbalus', but any connection with other grapes called Greco, all found much further south, is unlikely. Erbaluce, or Albaluce, so named because it displays a fiery copper colour in the light of the sun, in autumn, seems to have originated in the sub-alpine zones of Piemonte, where it has steadfastly remained, never travelling in any direction, though experiencing in the course of its history divers ups and downs. At present the downs have it as potential field-workers prefer to make their living in the nearby industries. But one or two brave souls continue struggling against the tide.

Like other native Piemontese varieties Erbaluce can have a particularly mordant acidity, which may be useful in the sweet, raisined-grape style (Caluso Passito) but can be off-putting in the dry (Erbaluce di Caluso). The *passito* is the more interesting wine, but it is in very short supply, and the dry can be interesting when made from fully ripe grapes in a good year. There is also a small production of *metodo classico tradizionale*.

Probably the best, certainly the longest-serving producers – since 1894, in fact – are **Orsolani** of San Giorgio Canavese, whose *cru* La Rustìa covers the dry and the sweet, and who also make an Erbaluce Brut Nature Cuvée. Luigi Ferrando of Ivrea makes a good dry *cru* Vigneto Cariola and a delicious late-harvest wine called Solativo. The fact that Antoniolo of Gattinara have recently introduced an Erbaluce is perhaps a sign of modest revival.

FAVORITA

This late-ripening variety is said to have arrived in Piemonte some 300 years ago, brought from its Mediterranean base by Ligurian oil merchants. Although grown today in various parts of the Astigiano and Langhe, where it is sometimes called Furmentin, it is in the Roero that it made its main home, in particular in the light, sandy soils of Corneliano, becoming known as Favorita di Corneliano.

If the name, as has been surmised, refers to the preference of the good growers of that commune for the variety, the reason for the preference would probably not relate to its performance as a wine grape but rather as a table grape. The berries are large and fleshy, the high acidity (almost but not quite on a level with Cortese in this respect) preserves it through the winter, and the loose bunches help it resist mould.

As a wine today Favorita is dry, firm of acidity unless the malolactic is completed, and non-aromatic – any scented character it may have coming by illicit blending (for example, with Moscato). In the past it was often made sweet, or, as often today, used as a blender, particularly with Nebbiolo. As a wine grape it seems to have peaked around the turn of the nineteenth/twentieth centuries, since when, and particularly since the Second World War, it has declined dramatically in plantings. The Alba producer Franco Fiorina (now defunct) revived Favorita in the 1970s, and today, with the help of an active producers' association, it is making something of a comeback. In the past five years or so production has doubled and now stands at over 1 million bottles. But its popularity is much more modest than that of Arneis (which produces three times as much) or Chardonnay, and it seems destined to continue to play a minor role in Piemontese viticulture in years to come.

The only DOC is Langhe Favorita. Cascina Chicco, Deltetto, Malabaila and Malvirà produce good examples, the wine from the last-named being much broader and more unctuous than most – almost like a good Vermentino from the Tuscan coast. Indeed, Favorita is said by some to be closely related to Vermentino, while others say it *is* Vermentino, which stacks up with the story that it arrived from Liguria where Vermentino grows in abundance. On the other hand, Piero Romisondo of the Ministry of Agriculture's ampelographical study commission (1964) reports that differences in the bud, bunch and leaf lead him and his colleagues to conclude that 'Favorita and Vermentino must be considered as two distinct cultivars'.

One producer has made himself something of a champion of Favorita. Gianni Gagliardo (mentioned under Barolo), the head of the aforementioned producers' association, makes from his vineyards in Monticello d'Alba two *crus*: Casa and Neirole, the latter being half *barrique*-fermented.

BLANC DE MORGEX

This is Valle d'Aosta's main contribution to the world's collection of white grape varieties, making, at best, a clean, mountain-fresh but not very complex dry wine. Practically all production is in the hands of the **Cave du Vin Blanc de Morgex et de La Salle**, a cooperative with 95 members from the two communes (of Morgex and La Salle) whose vineyards scale the mountains up to a height of 1,300 metres. Apart from the DOC and a table wine called Blanc des Glaciers there is also a *metodo classico* sparkler made, needless to say, with the local grape.

TREBBIANO DE LUGANA

This will be considered together with Trebbiano di Soave in the North East.

VERMENTINO

In pan-Italian terms Vermentino is a much more important variety than its presumed first cousin, Favorita, but its glory comes from Tuscan and Sardinian manifestations rather than any from the North West. Nevertheless it is dominant in Liguria, whose Colline di Levanto becomes by extension Tuscan, and whose ports, particularly Genoa, are traditionally the main continental points of connection with Sardinia.

It is probable that Vermentino arrived in Liguria from Sardinia, having arrived on that island from Spain (where, however, it is not known by that name) being in all likelihood an Iberian sub-variety of Malvasia. At any rate it is recorded as having been present here since around 1300, time enough to have developed some forty of its own sub-varieties distributed in vineyards the length of the region and beyond.

Lupi are reliable producers of Vermentino, their best *cru* being called Le Serre. In the Levanto's Colli di Luni **Il Torchio** and La Colombiera at Castelnuovo Magra are good. But no one (in northern Italy) can rival Ottaviano **Lambruschi**, a small but dedicated specialist Vermentino grower whose *normale* and *crus* Costa Marina and Sarticola are sold practically before release.

PIGATO, BOSCO, ALBAROLA, LUMASSINA AND BIANCHETTA

Pigato is said by some to be a relative of Vermentino, by others to be a native of the Castelli Romani, planted in Liguria by Caesar's legions, by others still to be an import from Greece, and by yet others to relate to Arneis. They cannot all be true, the relationship with Vermentino being perhaps the most probable (Vermentino *pigato* or spotted Vermentino being referred to in the *Bollettino Ampelografico* of 1883), although Pigato's wine is distinctly robust and fruity in comparison with the more austere, herbaceous Vermentino. Pigato is so named, they say, because of the spots of pigmentation on the grape's skin when ripe. It is grown almost exclusively in the Liguria's Riviera di Ponente, where it is generally considered superior to non-spotted Vermentino.

La Vecchia Cantina, of Albenga in the province of Savona, make a wine of good weight and concentration. Also from Albenga, con-

sidered incidentally the variety's place of origin, is the *cru* Cascina Fèipu from **Parodi**. Other good producers of Savona include **Terre Rosse**, Finale Ligure; Lupi (Le Petraie) and **Bruna** (Villa Torracchetta), Ranzo.

Other Ligurian white varieties include, mainly, Bosco, the main grape of the Cinque Terre blend: strange, but not so wonderful. Walter **De Battè** is as reliable a producer as you will find; he also makes the rare Sciacchetrà (see page 48). The Cooperativa Agricola di **Riomaggiore** also make various *crus* as well as Sciacchetrà.

The second grape of Cinque Terre is Albarola, said to be a type of Trebbiano, as is Lumassina, used in certain whites of the Riviera di Ponente; that of Stefano **Centa** is an example. On the other hand the Bianchetta of Genoa province seems to be a one-off. An enterprising producer is the Enoteca **Bisson** of Genoa itself.

PIGNOLETTO, MALVASIA

Despite its almost total obscurity in international terms, Pignoletto makes a significant volume of wine in Emilia's Colli Bolognesi (around 12,000 hectolitres of DOC), some of which is sufficiently good to make you wonder why the grape is not better known. Wines tend to be *frizzante* in the favoured Emilian mode; representative producers include Tenuta **Bonzara** of Monte San Pietro and Cantina dell'**Abbazia** of Monteveglio. More impressive, however, are the still versions, capable of being impressively full-bodied and melony as in the version by **Gaggioli** of Zola Predosa.

White Malvasia, specifically Malvasia di Candia, is, like Pignoletto, a favourite of locals in Emilia, having its own sub-DOCs in Colli di Parma and Colli Piacentini, provision being made in both cases for the wine to be dry or sweet, still, fizzy or sparkling. There is little market for such wines beyond a fairly restricted radius, but, provided the aromatic character of the grape is captured, in whatever style, they can hit the spot when one is on the spot. A good producer of the dry version is **Forte Rigoni** of Pilastro in Colli di Parma. The Fugazza sisters at Castello di Luzzano in Colli Piacentini produce a very scented and feminine version, delicately frothing. **Monte delle Vigne**, of Ozzano Taro, again in Colli di Parma, make a luscious sweet wine.

II
THE NORTH EAST
Veneto, Friuli-Venezia Giulia, Alto Adige, Trentino

N
0
50
kilometres
Switzerland
ALT
Stava
Merano
Bolzano
Nalles
Caldaro
Alto Adige
see Classic Map IV
Termeno
Mezzocorona
Mezzolombardo
Lavis
San Michele all' Adige
Faedo
Santa Massenza
Padergnone
Pergolese Sarche
Lasino
TRENTIN
Arco
Nogaredo
Isera
Volano
Rovereto
Ala
Avio
Borghetto
Lago di Garda
MONTI LESSINI
Bardolino
S. Pietro in Cariano
Negrar
Verona
Adige
Custoza
Soave
Veronese
see Classic Map II
See North West area map
Bologna
Key to Wine Zones
(DOC)
Veneto
1 Garda
2 Colli Berici
3 Colli Euganei
4 Montello & Colli Asolani
5 Piave
6 Lugana
Friuli-Venezia-Giulia
7 Grave
8 Carso
9 Collio
10 Ramandolo
11 Colli Orientali del Friuli
Alto Adige
12 Alto Adige
13 Valle Isarco
14 Santa Maddalena
15 Val Venosta
Trentino
16 Trentino
17 Campo Rotaliano
18 Valdadige
19 Val di Cembra
underlined Towns giving their name to Wine Zones
Main wine towns
Other wine towns
Regional capital
Provincial capital
Regional boundary
International boundary

The North East.

Austria

ADIGE

• Bressanone

hiusa

Generally, but not invariably, where wine zones or
sub-zones derive their names from wine towns, the
latter are underlined (e.g. Breganze, Aquileia), and
further zonal indication is not given. Zones which are
numbered generally lack such town-based
identification (e.g. Alto Adige, Colli Berici).
No hierarchy of importance is intended.

FRIULI-

Belluno □

Pinzano al
Tagliamento •   Nimis ○   ⑩

Spilimbergo •   ⑪
Taurino •   Udine   Cividale
                                   del Friuli

VENEZIA-   ○ Buttrio

San Pietro   ⑦   Codroipo •   Cormons •
di Felletto ●   Pavia di Udine
Miane ●   ○Pieve di Soligo   ● Sacile   Gorizia ○
Valdobbiadene ○   ○Conegliano   Gonars ●   ⑨
        ○Vidor   Susegnano ●   Gradisca
Nervesa della Battaglia ○ ●Tezze di Piave   Talmassons ●   d'Isonzo
assano   ④   ●Volpago del Montello   GIULIA Bagnaria   ⑧
Crappa • Asolo   ● Montebelluna Pramaggiore● Portogruaro●   Arsa
ganze   ● Trevignano   ● Aquileia
        Treviso □   Salgaredo ● Lison ○ Latisana ●
        VENETO   Trieste
cenza   ⑤

                    Venezia ○

□ Padova

③
aneo
  Arqua
• Petrarca
• Monselice ● Bagnoli di Sopra
i   Adige
ganeo

□ Rovigo

                Po

                        Adriatic Sea

ROMAGNA

Pordenone □

Friuli-Venezia Giulia
see Classic Map III

Slovenia

139

As in the North West, mountains and pre-alpine hills are a dominant feature of the North East's topography, in the form of Dolomites to the west, becoming Carnic Alps further east, and running down Italy's eastern frontier in the form of the Slovenian hills.

In Italy's northernmost province, Bolzano (Alto Adige or South Tyrol), viticulture has been practised since time immemorial on the lower slopes of valleys squeezed between towering mountains. Today, vineyards are moving higher up the slopes, a tendency which has been gathering pace in recent times thanks to the market's willingness to pay higher prices for the superior product of lower-yielding, more difficult to work, significantly sloping vineyards. This is something of a compensation for the not-inconsiderable viticultural exploitation of the valley floor, a reclaimed marshland whose rich soil is fine for growing Golden Delicious apples and other fruits in abundance but not, in most cases, quality wine-grapes.

But if valley-floor viticulture is a minority feature in the South Tyrol, it is most of the show south of the narrow Salorno pass which separates South Tyrol from Trentino. Here the mountains on either side of the Adige river loom skywards no less awesomely than in South Tyrol, but the plain is broader and far more vine-covered than north of Salorno. This does not necessarily mean lower quality: one of the (potentially) finest reds in Italy, Teroldego Rotaliano, is produced in the Campo Rotaliano, the plain in the vicinity of Mezzolombardo, above Trento. And from the hills above San Michele all'Adige, in the village of Faedo and up the Val di Cembra, come some of the region's finest whites and delicate reds. But the majority of Trentino wine is none the less of fairly ordinary quality from high-producing *pergola trentina*-trained vineyards in high-yielding flatland sites.

The Adige valley once again closes to a narrow pass below Avio, on the southern side of which it emerges into western Veneto, just east of Italy's largest lake, Garda. An arc drawn from the south of Garda north and east above the towns of Verona, Vicenza, Treviso, Conegliano, Pordenone, Udine and Gorizia would, roughly speaking, separate the mountains from the alluvial/maritime plain, *la pianura*. Much of the best viticulture of the regions of Veneto and Friuli-Venezia Giulia is practised in the foothills where these two zones meet: Bardolino, Valpolicella, Soave/Gambellara, Breganze, Montello e Colli Asolani, Valdobbiadene and Conegliano, Colli Orientali del Friuli and Collio Goriziano, to mention the main areas. Other hilly zones of significance are Colli Berici and Colli Euganei, both outcrops in the plain which stretches south from the foothills.

There is, too, plenty of flatland viticulture, most of it of a good standard, some industrial, some on the other hand excellent. The 'good' would include Veneto's Piave and Lison/Pramaggiore, and Friuli's Grave, capable of producing good if not outstanding wines on gravelly, well-drained soil. The 'excellent' would certainly include Isonzo, where some of finest white wines in Italy today are produced. The 'industrial' comes mainly from the more fertile sites such as those tacked on to the Valpolicella Classico and Soave Classico in the first half of the twentieth century, to cash in on the historic names; as well as from Friuli's lowland *bassa pianura*.

The climate here is not radically dissimilar from that of Piemonte and Lombardy, although in this context it is worth observing that the classic viticultural areas are well to the north of those of the North West, putting them roughly in line with southern Burgundy as distinct from Bordeaux. This partially explains why white wines achieve a higher level of excellence here than do reds, especially in respect of the international varieties.

The Alps constitute a protection from cold north winds, but also form a wall against which fog may accumulate. As the mountain air becomes increasingly less pure this is a growing problem, especially in Valpolicella and Soave following the vintage, when humid smog can cause moulds to form on the *recioto* grapes in the first stages of *appassimento*. Hail, too, can be devastating, as in June 1996 when it destroyed the vineyards of Oslavia in eastern Collio so comprehensively that not only the fruit but the very leaves were stripped from the vine, endangering future harvests and even the life of the plant. Seasons in this mostly continental climate are strongly differentiated, and there is marked variation of conditions from year to year so that vintage variation is no less significant than it is in the North West. Clean air can be positively influential, especially in the mountains, where industrial haze is not a problem, and in areas near to bodies of water. The western end of Valpolicella, for example, enjoys proximity both to the Adige and to Lake Garda. These two bodies of water are said to have a marked effect on fruit quality, not only for their contribution to photosynthesis but also for their regulating influence on the mean temperature.

The people are mixed, ethnically, linguistically and historico-traditionally. The South Tyroleans of Brennero down to Salorno are scarcely Italians at all, having been citizens of the Austrian Empire until 1919. Even now they have Germanic names, Germanic architecture, Germanic habits and, most importantly, the German language, which remains most people's preference. South Tyroleans look down on Italians, tending to despise their anarchic ways and resent their political presence. Wine producers have, however, made a good thing out of being members of the European Union, since the white styles in which they excel are far more prized in the red-wine regions of the south than in the rival white-wine areas of Austria, Switzerland and Germany.

On the eastern frontier of Italy, in the Colli Orientali and the Collio Goriziano of Friuli, there is a certain Slavic influence, as reflected in names like Princic or Radikon. These people, however, are far more Italian-orientated than the South Tyroleans, and certainly have no desire to join Slovenia. There is here, too, a certain German influence, the area having for a long time been part of the Austrian Empire. This may be noted in names like Jermann and Vazzoler.

Between these extremes are the region of Veneto and sub-region of Venezia Giulia, the heart of what used to be the Venetian Republic. Remnants of Venetian glory are scattered through the hills of the Veneto in the form of grand patrician villas, inspired by such sixteenth- and seventeenth-century architects as Palladio. It is a land of individualists, as well as of internationalists, the Venetians having been in their heyday great seafarers and merchants, deriving their enormous wealth from exchange and interchange with foreigners from Greece to China.

In terms of wine styles, it is true to say that the production of red wine here outstrips that of white in volume terms. Nevertheless, the zone as a whole is primarily known for its white wines, and while, in the 1970s and 1980s, Italian reds were working their way towards international recognition in places like Tuscany and Piemonte, the same was true of Friuli and to a lesser extent South Tyrol and Trentino in the white department.

In both departments – red and white – there is a much greater preponderance of 'foreign' grape varieties here than in any other macro-zone of Italy, mainly from France, but also from Austria and Germany. But whereas the foreigners are, elsewhere, almost entirely of post-war introduction, here they have a tradition dating back at least a century and a half – not very long, perhaps, in Italian terms, but not much less than certain 'New World' countries whose justification for planting French and German grapes is never challenged.

Another traditional wine style of significance in these parts is the sparkling or semi-sparkling, especially in the form of Prosecco from the Conegliano-Valdobbiadene area north of Venice; indeed, it is La Serenissima's favourite tipple, to be found in various forms (the most interesting being the most artisanal, or least refined) in every bar in the city. There is, too, the odd very fine French-style champagne-method (or should I say *metodo classico*?) wine from various sources scattered around the North East.

The wine style perhaps most peculiar to the zone – specifically to the Veronese hills – is the *passito*, or semi-dried-grape style. This is a classic process for making highly concentrated wines, red and white, of which probably the most important repository in the world today is Verona. The ancients needed wines which had the structure and style to withstand time and oxidation, and the power to be able to be mixed with weird and wonderful aromas and liquids, including mainly water.

Production areas

VENETO

In terms of volume, the region of Veneto easily outstrips any other in northern Italy, having more than double the production of Trentino-Alto Adige and Friuli-Venezia Giulia combined. It usually vies with Emilia-Romagna for third place in Italy, after Puglia and Sicily, but in terms of volume of DOC wines produced Veneto is number one in Italy.

Veneto's association with wine goes back at least three millennia, and even 2,000 years ago Roman writers, followed by Longobards, were singing the praises of Reticum and Acinaticum, considered to be the direct ancestors of the quality Veronese wines of today. For most of the last millennium the influence of Venice has been crucial, however, creating an internationalist atmosphere in respect both of the export of Veneto wines and of the import of foreign grapes and wine styles. Tradition here has thus never enjoyed the quasi-holy status that it has in other parts of the peninsula, which has made it relatively easy for international varieties, in the past one and a half centuries or so, to infiltrate to all parts. Only in the areas of Conegliano and especially Verona have native grapes retained the upper hand. Indeed a consideration of the significant viticultural areas of the North East ought properly to begin with VERONA, the Bordeaux of Italy. This historic city, with its Roman arena and its medieval streets and architecture, to say nothing of its super-stylish shops, is not only the centre of production of one of Italy's three classic red wines, it is also the site of the annual April wine fair called Vinitaly. From a smallish affair in the mid-1960s, Vinitaly has, like Bordeaux's Vinexpo, become an unmissable appointment for just about every wine producer in the land, not to mention a growing number from abroad, plus buyers, journalists and assorted wine buffs and winos from every corner of the

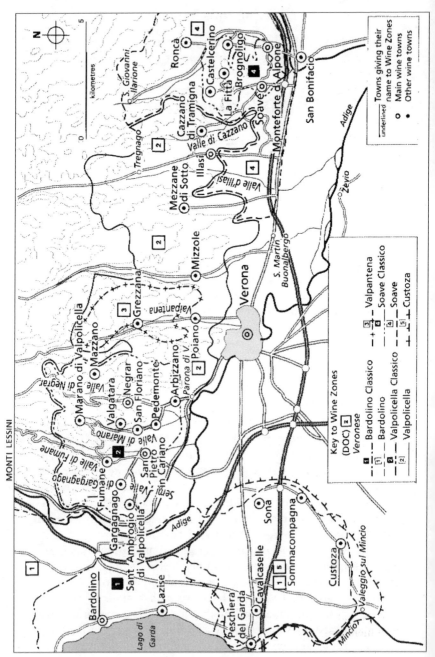

CLASSIC MAP II: Principal zones/towns of Verona.

146

universe. Today, despite a five-day duration, it is impossible to cover even a fraction of the event in any depth – it can take half a day just to get from the entrance to the farthest reaches of Pavilion 38, what with all the stops for visits, tastings and chats that such a journey might entail.

Also like Bordeaux, Verona (city or province) is home to some of Italy's largest and most internationally famous *négociant* houses such as Bolla, Pasqua, Montresor, Sartori, Fabiano, GIV (Lamberti and Santi) – large-scale producers whose main criterion in the past may have been volume at low price but who have been making great efforts to upgrade their production in recent years, fighting to rid themselves of the 'industrial' reputation that they created not just for themselves but for the Veneto region, indeed the Italian nation, as a whole. To some extent they have dug a hole for themselves, for much as they may wish to move upmarket, their more powerful customers, mainly supermarkets, want them to continue churning out the cheap and cheerful. But with production costs continuing to rise in Italy, not least thanks to government taxes, and other low-cost production zones coming on-stream round the world, the days of cheap table wines from Verona are over. The question that remains is whether the world will accept that better quality Veronese wines are worth paying significantly more for.

The category 'wines of Verona' is considered to consist principally, west to east from Lake Garda along the lower slopes of the Lessini massif, of BARDOLINO, VALPOLICELLA (both blended reds based on the Corvina grape) and SOAVE (a white based on Garganega). Each has a historic Classico sub-zone surrounded on most if not all sides by a non-classic or (as Italians would unofficially refer to it) *normale* zone, tacked on in the twentieth century by the industrialists (see page 24).

BIANCO DI CUSTOZA, an *uvaggio di vigneto* (Trebbiano, Garganega, Tocai or Trebbianello, Cortese or Bianca Fernanda, Malvasia, Pinot Bianco, Chardonnay and Riesling Italico, if you please) from the south east corner of Garda, is largely overlapped by the southern sector of Bardolino *normale*, and is today generally included among the wines of Verona. The white Trebbiano-based LUGANA, at the southern end of the lake, is generally considered to be a member of the Veronese family even though most of the DOC area is technically in Lombardy.

A recent addition to the already swollen ranks of DOCdom is

GARDA, whose multi-DOC allows for all manner of local and international varietals – the classic grapes of the area, Corvina and Garganega, being joined by the Bordeaux and Burgundy families plus Rieslings Italico and Renano, and others. The purpose of this newcomer to the official ranks is to act as a catch-all for wines of good to high quality of the provinces of Verona in Veneto, as well as of Brescia and Mantua in Lombardy, which would not otherwise be sanctified by the law.

The zone of Valpolicella, the 'valley of the many cellars', is in fact a series of ridges, like fingers stretching north–south from the arm of the mountainous massif, separated by valleys named after the main town in all but one case (Valpantena). Thus, a hiker starting from Superstrada 12 slightly east of the Adige River would cross the La Grola hill and arrive at the semi-valley of GARGAGNAGO; he would then go up and over into the valley of FUMANE; up again and down into the valley of MARANO; up again and into the valley of NEGRAR, these four constituting the Classico zone, but only half of the extended zone, for climbing again towards the east he would descend into the VALPANTENA, then up and over into the valley of ILLASI, completing his trek in the valley of CAZZANO, well to the north-east of Verona, having started out well to the north-west.

If our hiker was not yet exhausted and carried on due east, he would, over the next ridge, enter the hills of Soave Classico, an amazingly beautiful sweep of vineyards running upwards into the hinterland behind the picturesque village of Soave itself and of MONTEFORTE D'ALPONE. A characteristic of the Soave Classico hills is that they are full of marine fossils, dating back millions of years, indicating that the land was once under the sea.

Due east again, crossing the invisible dividing line between the provinces of Verona and Vicenza, he would enter the small DOC area of GAMBELLARA, a virtual extension of Soave. Like its more illustrious neighbour Gambellara produces from the Garganega and Trebbiano grapes a range of wines including dry white, a *passito* white and a sweet sparkling *passito*. Higher up in the Monti Lessini, behind Soave and Gambellara, is the area of LESSINI Durello, normally producing a *frizzante* wine made from grapes of that name, little seen outside the area.

Almost contiguous with Gambellara, south of the small but elegant city of Vicenza, is the zone called COLLI BERICI, a hilly area including in its *disciplinare* various sub-DOCs based on Garganega, Merlot, Cabernet, Pinot Bianco, Chardonnay, Tocai Italico and Tocai Rosso. The cooperative here has the surprising if dubious distinction of being, so they claim, the largest producing *cantina* in Italy.

COLLI EUGANEI is an outcrop of pimple-like hills sandwiched between Colli Berici to the north-west and the city of Padua to the north-east. Some of the hills in this striking, slightly other-worldly land are of volcanic origin, and the area is still known for its hot springs. Other hills are of strongly chalky composition, favouring white grape production, the volcanic soils being better for reds.

Colli Euganei has a wide-ranging DOC which embraces the Gallic group of Chardonnay, Pinot Bianco, Merlot and Cabernet (generically, as well as Cabernet Franc and Cabernet Sauvignon specifically, wines which must include at least 90% of the stated sub-variety), not to mention the autochthonous white selection of Tocai Italico, Pinello and Serprino (Prosecco). The Colli Euganei boast of being the only part of Italy to grow both Moscato Bianco and Giallo, although the latter, here called Fior d'Arancio, is much more in evidence. Colli Euganei Rosso and Bianco are blends from the various permitted non-aromatic grapes, therefore excluding Muscat.

The recently created DOC zone BAGNOLI DI SOPRA is also in the province of Padua, its sub-DOCs having largely a French flavour except for Friularo, a red wine based on Raboso Piave.

The zone of BREGANZE, centred on the town of that name, lies a few kilometres north of Vicenza. The Breganze DOC, a name made famous in wine circles by Maculan, covers a range of French-type varietals including Cabernet, Pinot Nero, Pinot Grigio and Pinot Bianco; plus one surviving Italian, Vespaiolo, from which Maculan's famous sweet wines are made; as well as Breganze Rosso and Breganze Bianco, blends based on the above plus some.

From Breganze to enter the zone of MONTELLO E COLLI ASOLANI our intrepid one need only cross the town of Bassano del Grappa. Montello etc. is another of those multi-DOCs of the Veneto whose varietals include most of the usual French brigade plus Prosecco. There is a red blend based on the Bordeaux mix. The only well-known producer is Loredan Gasparini, who produce a slightly anomalous non-DOC red called Venegazzù.

Crossing the Piave River he now arrives at VALDOBBIADENE,

which together with CONEGLIANO gives its name to an area famous for well over a century as a producer of sparkling and *frizzante* wines based on the indigenous Prosecco grape. More recently the area has become doubly DOCified under the COLLI DI CONEGLIANO rubric, a more-than-usually enterprising denomination whose white is based on Incrocio Manzoni 6.0.13, whose red includes Marzemino and Incrocio Manzoni 2.15, together with the inevitable French varieties, and which includes a sweet red Refrontolo Passito based on Marzemino and a sweet white 'naturally dried' (presumably including either late-harvest or the *appassimento* process) Torchiato di FREGONA based on the local trio of Prosecco, Verdiso and Boschera.

Our man now plunges into the PIAVE (the wine zone, not the river), which extends from Conegliano practically all the way to the coast east of Venice. This large alluvial-plain DOC area is named after the river which flows through its centre. Its multi-DOC embraces the French brigade (including Pinot Nero) plus the characterful Raboso (red) and the white varieties Verduzzo and Tocai Italico.

From Piave he heads east into LISON-PRAMAGGIORE, sandwiched between the Livenza river and the Tagliamento which separates Veneto from Friuli. This is another alluvial-plain zone. The multi-DOC is very similar to that of Piave, the major exception being that instead of Veneto's Raboso there is Friuli's Refosco. The wines, like those of Piave, are generally of a good but unexceptional standard. From here our indefatigable explorer would enter Friuli-Venezia Giulia.

FRIULI-VENEZIA GIULIA

Friuli is a region whose viticulture has been taken over to a very large extent by the international varieties, especially the French: Merlot, Cabernets Sauvignon and Franc, Pinot Nero on the red side; Chardonnay, Pinot Grigio, Pinot Bianco, Sauvignon on the white side. Of the native varieties the only one to have survived in substantial numbers is Tocai Friulano, although Verduzzo, Ribolla and Malvasia Istriana have maintained a respectable presence among whites. As for reds, apart from traces of Schioppettino, Tazzelenghe and Pignolo, only Refosco today has held its own.

Mind you, Friuli is today a land of white wines – at least, that is

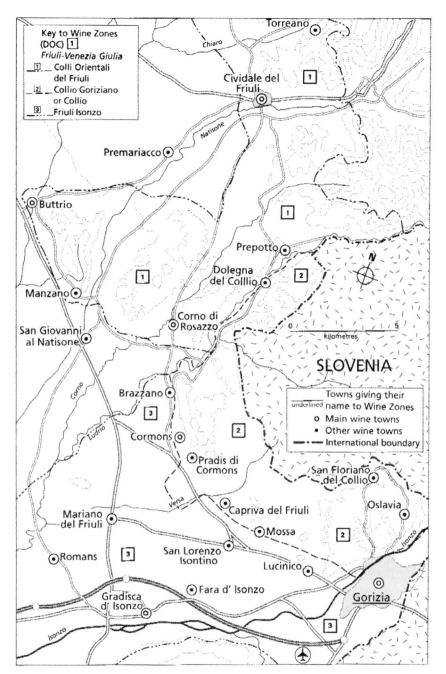

CLASSIC MAP III: Principal zones/towns of Eastern Friuli.

what the world looks to her for. From that latter statement perhaps one should subtract the Anglo-Saxon world, since countries like the UK, USA and Australia seem somewhat underwhelmed by Friuli's charms. The Italian, and to a lesser extent the Teutonic worlds, on the other hand, appear to be quite smitten, and there certainly is no problem selling the top wines – on the contrary, the problem is getting them. Perhaps it is this expectation on the part of a home market thirsty for white wines of excellence that has brought about the realization of the desire. Certainly the best whites from these parts are about as fine as anything from anywhere, while the reds, good though they may be, never quite make it to the top.

It is important, in considering the region as a whole, to make a clear distinction between the areas capable of good quality, which is all of them; and the areas from which outstanding wines may come, which obviously doesn't mean that they invariably do. The latter are all in the extreme east of the zone, over near the Slavonian border, and include Collio, Friuli Isonzo and parts of Colli Orientali del Friuli.

This distinction is one reason why Collio Goriziano, the zone of greatest prestige, has fought to maintain its independence against the bureaucratic plot to lump all sub-zones together under the general heading of Friuli. Had the desk-dwellers had their way we would today have Friuli Collio, just as we now have Friuli Isonzo and Friuli Aquileia (or Aquileia del Friuli). For the lesser sub-zones, like Aquileia, the general title may be an advantage in terms of consumer recognition, but producers in the better ones tend to see it as planification in a downward direction.

Our hiker, now heading north from the coast, finds that Veneto's Lison-Pramaggiore DOC area extends slightly into Friuli, although it soon becomes FRIULI GRAVE (ex Grave del Friuli). As the name suggests, the soil here on the *altopiano*, the high plain, is gravelly from alluvial deposits; similar, in other words, to the soil of Bordeaux. The multi-DOC varietals are even more numerous here and include Pinot Nero, Traminer and Riesling Renano as well as the inevitable Bordeaux grapes – minus Sémillon, strangely; it would probably do quite well. Blends may also be fashioned under the names Bianco (Chardonnay and Pinot Bianco plus others), Rosso, Rosato and Novello (based on Cabernet together with others).

Crossing the Tagliamento river and heading once again in a southerly direction, our tireless trekker crosses into FRIULI LATISANA, a denomination of the low coastal plain where the usual ampelographical fare is on offer but where wines rarely reach levels which might be interesting abroad. Nevertheless, the Latisana multi-DOC provides for no less than sixteen varietal wines (including Franconia and Malvasia Istriana) plus Spumante and Rosato.

Moving eastward along the coast he comes next to the recently created (as if we needed it) FRIULI ANNIA, whose *disciplinare* is nothing if not familiar, and whose wines display an equally familiar lack of distinction.

Similar thoughts will perhaps arise in his mind as he crosses, next, into FRIULI AQUILEIA, where at least the house of Zonin has organized its extensive vineyards in such a way as to produce a range of wines that are good value for money if hardly very exciting.

Just as our traveller starts thinking that one can have too much of a good thing, he comes (in his eastward odyssey) across a sub-zone which he finds truly exciting: FRIULI ISONZO. Alas, the bureaucrats have had their way with this denomination, but the quality of the wines continues to defy gravity, or expectations of quality, given that wines of such sublime character ought not, he might think, to come from vineyards which are so impressively pancake flat. The *disciplinare* is not especially innovative. On paper it may place more emphasis than the previous on Italian or at least non-French varieties, like Moscato Giallo and Rosa, Malvasia, Franconia, Refosco and Schioppettino, but in reality its great wines are from French white varieties.

Quality-wise, or certainly reputation-wise, the most important sub-zone of the region is the one he comes to next, as he heads eastward and northward into COLLIO, otherwise known as COLLIO GORIZIANO after the provincial capital, Gorizia. Passing through GRADISCA D'ISONZO, an outcrop of Collio surrounded by the Isonzo plain, then heading north-east, skirting Gorizia to the west and climbing into the hills at OSLAVIA, round to SAN FLORIANO, turning westward now towards RUSSIZ and then on to CORMONS and points north along the international border, he passes the vineyards and wineries of some of Italy's greatest white wine-makers.

Again, the Collio *disciplinare* is not radically different from others of the region, but its nineteen possibilities, including varietals associated with France, Germany and even Italy, give winemakers ample scope to express themselves with what they've got. This is especially significant for Collio Bianco, an *uvaggio* which until recently has been based on native varieties but has now been opened to include practically anything white in practically any proportion – an important point because some of Collio's most famous wines are white fantasy blends typified by Jermann's Vintage Tunina.

The traveller will complete his Friulian journey by heading back in a slightly westward and northward direction into the hills south of CIVIDALE DEL FRIULI in which are concentrated most of the best producers of the DOC zone COLLI ORIENTALI DEL FRIULI. The *disciplinare* is not radically different, but a more diverse selection is liable to come from these parts, including some impressive reds of indigenous varieties and the best of Friuli's sweet wines from Picolit and in particular Verduzzo. In this context, the famous RAMANDOLO comes from a tiny sub-zone well to the north of Cividale.

Sharp-eyed readers will have noticed that our traveller has missed out on the sub-zone of CARSO, a less ambitious multi-DOC covering most of the land-strip between Gorizia and Trieste. Particularly prized from this area is Terrano, a type of Refosco as we shall see. The principal white wine is a varietal Malvasia. But production in any case is tiny.

ALTO ADIGE/SOUTH TYROL

Technically Alto Adige is the northern half of the region Trentino-Alto Adige. In reality it is quite separate, operating independently for all practical purposes, and certainly in a wine context it should be considered apart.

South Tyrol, as we shall occasionally refer to it in English (German Südtirol; Italian Alto Adige; administratively equivalent to the autonomous province of Bolzano or Bozen) became part of Italy only in 1919, although the majority of its German-speaking inhabitants might consider that it never has been and never could be truly Italian. Previously it was the southernmost outpost of the Austrian Empire, the place to which the emperors repaired in summer, long-time supplier of light red and cheap white wines to Teu-

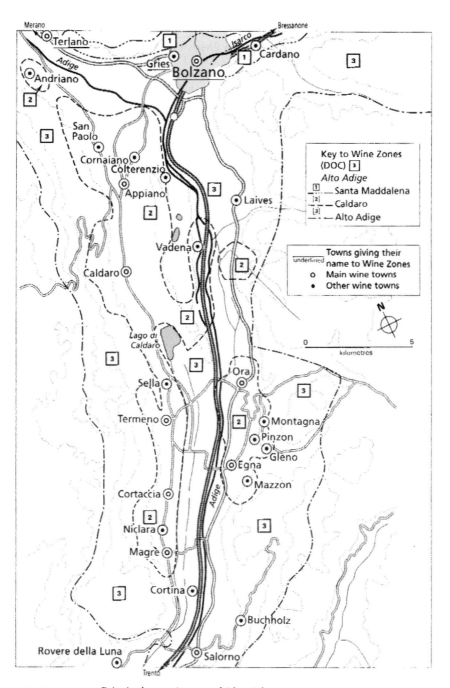

Merano
Terlano
Adige
Andriano
[2]
San Paolo
[3]
Cornaiano
Colterenzio
Appiano
[2]
Caldaro
[3]
Lago di Caldaro
Sella
[3]
Termeno
Cortaccia
Niclara
[2]
Magrè
Cortina
[3]
Rovere della Luna
Trento

Bressanone
Isarco
[1]
Gries
Bolzano
[1]
Cardano
[3]

[3]
[3]
Laives
[2]
Vadena
[2]

Ora
[3]
Montagna
[2]
Pinzon
Gleno
Egna
Mazzon
[3]
Buchholz
Salorno

Key to Wine Zones (DOC) [3]
Alto Adige
[1] — Santa Maddalena
[2] — Caldaro
[3] — Alto Adige

underlined   Towns giving their name to Wine Zones
o   Main wine towns
•   Other wine towns

N

0   5
kilometres

CLASSIC MAP IV: Principal zones/towns of Alto Adige.

155

tonic markets, always looking north, never south.

South Tyrol's viticultural history is long and honourable, pre-dating the arrival of the Romans. Until very recently the vast majority of production was red, mainly from the Schiava variety, and all vines were trained on the picturesque but questionable (from a quality viewpoint) *pergola trentina*.

Today the zone's vocation for fine white wine, and indeed for fine red wine from varieties other than Schiava, is being recognized, as is the importance of limiting yields and experimenting with training systems of lesser productivity and greater ability fully to ripen grapes. Thanks to some considerable talent in the human department excellent wines are already emerging, although one senses that the quality potential here is enormous and that the journey towards higher levels is only beginning, feeling its way towards a market which is more oriented in a southward and outward rather than in an exclusively northward direction.

Apart from Schiava there is only one significant native variety here – the red Lagrein; and that might be claimed by Trentino – so that most of South Tyrol's grapes and producers will be considered in the section on international varieties (see page 225). One might, it's true, wish to include Traminer among the natives, as it is named after the South Tyrol village of Termeno (Tramin), but it is probably best included with the Germanics, of which there are, not surprisingly, quite a number in these parts.

If we were to airlift our intrepid traveller to South Tyrol from where we last left him – in the Colli Orientali del Friuli – we would station him in the capital, Bolzano, a city which stands at the central junction of a Y-shaped viticultural area. In all three directions, but mainly to the south, are the vineyards of the multi-DOC ALTO ADIGE (Etschtaler), which not only embraces over twenty sub-DOCs including various Schiavas and Lagreins, the Bordeaux gang, the Burgundy mob, various German whites, not to mention two types of Moscato (Giallo and Rosa) and Malvasia, but also does umbrella duty for other sub-multi-DOCs such as Terlano, Valle Isarco and the recently established Valle Venosta, involving in the process not a little apparently pointless repetition; the final count, of wines coming under the overall Alto Adige rubric, being no less than fifty-eight.

Two of these, SANTA MADDALENA (St. Magdalener) and Santa Maddalena Classico, are at the very heart of things, the city of

Bolzano itself. Breathtakingly exposed on steep slopes above the city (which incidentally is quite capable of recording the highest daytime temperatures in all of Italy thanks to its position at the bottom of a mountainous basin), this is a prime example of the wrong grape (Schiava) being trained in the wrong way in the right place. The potential for making great red wine in this sun-soaked south-facing situation is fabulous, and one can only regret that so much of the vineyard area is still devoted to Schiava. Mussolini, for political reasons, may have included Santa Maddalena among the three most important wines of Italy, but no one in their right mind would do so today.

From the hills round the city – the COLLI DI BOLZANO (Bozner Leiten) – comes another, lesser Schiava. Let's just say that it will never set the markets of the world on fire. From a western suburb of the city, on the other hand, comes Lagrein di GRIES, this being a prime site for what is doubtless the region's most interesting native red variety.

At this point, our traveller might elect to carry on up the north-west arm of the Y, passing the vineyards of the multi-DOC TERLANO (Terlaner) on slopes either side of the Adige river. Terlano is particularly noted for the quality of its Sauvignon, although it produces a considerably greater quantity of Pinot Bianco.

Further upriver he will come to the vineyards of the *elegantissimo* town of MERANO (Meran), where European royalty was wont to summer in the golden days before the First World War, when Kaisers were Kaisers and Tsars were Tsars, and above which can be seen, halfway up the mountain, the Castle of Tirolo from which the region takes its name. Meranese di Collina (Meraner Hügel) is another Schiava-based light red the loss of which would not cause excessive grief in the vinous world.

Returning to Bolzano and following now the north-east arm of the Y our traveller finds himself ascending the Isarco (Eisack) Valley in the direction of the Brenner pass. In so doing he would encounter vineyards of the multi-DOC VALLE ISARCO (Eisacktaler), the varietals of which would all fit in a southern German or Austrian context even if they are not all pure German: Pinot Grigio (Ruländer), Sylvaner, Veltliner, Müller-Thurgau, Kerner, Gewürztraminer and Schiava (Vernatsch). Around BRESSANONE (Brixen) the name of the town may be added, and since even Valle d'Isarco comes under the all-embracing Alto Adige denomination the full official name would be Alto Adige Valle Isarco Müller-Thurgau (for example) di Bressanone.

Returning again to the city and heading south, now, he notes that the Terlano sub-zone continues on the right bank, to some extent overlapping the only pure Tyrolean denomination – CAL-DARO (Kalterer) or Caldaro Classico – which is not preceded by the words 'Alto Adige'. This Schiava-based wine, famous throughout the German-speaking world, is mainly a right-bank phenomenon – after all, the eponymous lake is on the right – and extends from north-west of Bolzano to the southern limit of Alto Adige. Indeed, the zone continues on into Trentino on the other side of the Salorno pass, adding 30,000-odd hectolitres to the 70,000-odd produced in Alto Adige to make it the region's number one wine – in volume, at any rate.

Much more interesting from a quality point of view are the Alto Adige-plus-varietal vineyards clinging to the low and middle slopes of the valley on either side. Place names likely to catch our enchanted traveller's eye here include (on the right bank) NALLES (Nals), ANDRIANO (Andrian), SAN PAOLO (St. Pauls), APPIANO (Eppan), CORNAIANO (Girlan), COLTERENZIO (Schreckbichl), SAN MICHELE (St. Michael), CALDARO (Kaltern), TERMENO (Tramin) and CORTACCIA (Kurtatsch), all of which are home to quality cooperatives. A small detour at Cortaccia will bring him to the charming village of NICLARA (Entiklar), where he will be able to refresh himself at the *weinstube* of Schloss Turmhof (Tiefenbrunner), one of the region's best private producers. Finally he will arrive at MAGRÈ (Magreid), where another of the top privates, Lageder, have their winery. And if he should climb to a high vantage point at, say, Termeno, he will be able to gaze across the valley and see the town of ORA (Auer), with EGNA (Neumarkt) to the south and, perched on a ledge above the valley, the town of SALORNO (Salurn), at the gateway to what is truly Italy. Higher up the mountain, between Ora and Egna, he will spot the villages of MONTAGNA (Montan), PINZON and MAZZON (Mazon). At that moment he will be gazing upon the finest Pinot Nero vineyards in the land.

TRENTINO

Although similarities inevitably exist between Alto Adige and

Trentino, there are some important differences which taken together add up to a quite distinct personality.

Similar, as we have seen, is the lie of the land, except that in the Trentino one has less often the impression of being dwarfed by enormous rock formations looming almost vertically overhead. Similar is the style of viticulture, especially in respect of the near-ubiquity of *pergola trentina*; in Trentino, however, there is much more valley-floor planting, and rather less exploitation of the higher slopes.

Grape varieties are similar, with Schiava playing a major role in the sector north of Trento, decreasing as you move south. In Trentino there is generally less emphasis on the Germanic varieties, more on the French. Most importantly, Trentino has varieties which don't exist in Alto Adige, notably Teroldego and Marzemino among reds and Nosiola among whites; these are responsible for some of Trentino's best and most distinctive wines.

Similar, also, is the fact that production is controlled to a very large extent by *cantine sociali*, although in Trentino they tend to be larger and fewer. Small individualist producers are developing in both zones, with examples in both cases of very high quality production. But there are more of them going further in Alto Adige.

Mean temperatures in Trentino are that bit higher than in Alto Adige, giving the former an edge in the production of full-bodied, serious reds. On the other hand, although white grapes grow in great profusion – Chardonnay is the most planted variety – the quality does not at its best match that of Alto Adige in respect of aroma, elegance and complexity. But these are generalizations; you've only got to find one exception in order to indicate that the fault lies with the people and not the *terroir*. And that one exception does exist.

There are two wine styles in which Trentino specializes which are less important further north: one is champagne-style sparkling; the other is dessert wines, using both the *vendemmia tardiva* (late harvest) method, usually with Moscato Giallo or Moscato Rosa, or the *appassimento* (semi-dried) method, as in the case of the regional speciality based on Nosiola and called, as in Tuscany, Vino Santo.

Trentino is less homogeneous than Alto Adige, less easy to categorize. There are more bits and pieces off the beaten track, more one-offs. In a nutshell, Trentino is more Italianate, Alto Adige more Germanic.

Our intrepid one, having squeezed through the pass at Salorno, immediately finds himself in the TRENTINO multi-DOC zone which follows the Adige all the way down to the border with Veneto, with bits sticking out as in the case of the VAL DI CEMBRA in the north, or on their own as in the area of Lakes Toblino and Cavedine in the centre-west, and above Riva del Garda in the southwest. Trentino, like Alto Adige higher up, is a catch-all denomination for red, white and rosé table wines of various indigenous, Gallic and Germanic types, as well as for the sweet wines – Vendemmia Tardiva, Vino Santo – mentioned above.

Still in the north, around MEZZOLOMBARDO and MEZZO-CORONA, both towns with large and important cooperatives, is the CAMPO ROTALIANO, the gravelly plain on which are grown the grapes for the province's most distinguished wine, Teroldego Rotaliano. Lagrein also does well here. Across the Adige, on the left bank, is the village of SAN MICHELE ALL'ADIGE, site of one of Italy's most prestigious oenological academies. If our man felt like a brisk hike into the heights above he would shortly come to the village of FAEDO, made famous from the 1970s by the activities of small quality-dedicated grower-producers of which Pojer & Sandri are the prototype. Müller-Thurgau is a speciality of this area.

Back down the mountain, proceeding southward along the valley, he comes to LAVIS, site of another major cooperative, and a few kilometres later to the provincial capital Trento, site of some of the most important wineries of the province including the massive *cantina sociale di secondo grado*, Cavit, as well as the famous sparkling wine (not motor car) producers, Ferrari. In fact, TRENTO is the name given to the province's sparkling wine denomination, modelled in all particulars on champagne (even Pinot Meunier is included in the *disciplinare*, as well as Pinot Nero and Chardonnay), and second in importance in Italy after Franciacorta.

The next town downriver is ROVERETO, surrounded by vineyards mainly on the flat or on gentle slopes, and home to many of the best-known producers of Trentino. The traditional speciality here is Marzemino, though the international grapes are gaining an increasing hold.

South of Rovereto the valley narrows again, preparatory to squeezing through into Veneto, but just before it does so our trekker, an avid claret fan as it happens, is able to satisfy his craving with a taste of the consistently excellent bordeaux-style San Leonardo at AVIO.

Before leaving Trentino, it is necessary for form's sake to mention three other DOCs of the province. SORNÌ refers to wines, rarely seen, made in the red version from Schiava and Teroldego or, in the white, from Nosiola and others around San Michele and Lavis. CASTELLER is a red wine produced in some volume from Schiava, Merlot and Lambrusco grapes grown virtually anywhere in the province of Trentino and south into the province of Verona. VALDADIGE (Etschtaler) is a catch-all DOC for red, white and rosé blends, plus the varietals Chardonnay, Pinot Grigio, Pinot Bianco and Schiava, produced anywhere along the Adige river in the provinces of Bolzano, Trento and northern Verona.

ATESINO, an adjective meaning 'of the Adige', is a name seen often in the past on wines downgraded to *vino da tavola*. This has changed and Alto Adige has already settled on its alternative, for IGT wines, namely MITTERBERG. In Trentino, from the vintage of 1997, the equivalent IGT is VIGNETI DELLE DOLOMITI, a name also available to, but unlikely to be used by, Alto Adige producers.

Grapes, wines and producers – red

CORVINA, RONDINELLA, CORVINONE, MOLINARA AND NEGRARA

Corvina, the mainstay of Valpolicella, is presumed to have been present in Veronese vineyards for hundreds if not thousands of years. The first written reference to the grape or wines called 'Corvini' dates back to 1627, but the first description of Corvina Veronese goes back only as far as 1818, when Pollini speaks of a 'Corvina . . . cultivated throughout the Valle Pulicella'.

Corvina is characterized by an aromatic fruitiness, high total acidity and a low phenolic content, being poor in both tannins and pigments. When overproduced in *pianura* vineyards, which it all too often is due to its great vigour, it can also be poor in extract, giving rise to some pretty short-lived and mediocre wines (don't we know it). When grown on hillside sites it can produce a grape of more concentration, capable of yielding a wine of moderate ageing potential. Grown in what is known here as *toar* – a volcanic soil, rich in minerals like basalt, potassium and magnesium, which disintegrates easily – grapes can be very perfumed, if a little thin in substance. But, though one hears a lot about them, *toar* soils are in fact rare – more common are those derived from the sedimentary deposits of calcareous rock of the Eocene era, rich in fossils, while alluvial deposit soils predominate on lower slopes.

Corvina is generally, even today, trained in the *pergola veronese* manner – high, with a horizontal arm as distinct from one upwardly angled arm, as in the case of *pergola trentina*. The reason for this is that, in the words of one grower: 'Corvina is a great grape variety with a great defect', namely that it doesn't fruit on the first few buds on the cane. So it needs the long arm, and plenty of space, even where, as is increasingly the case, it is trained to the *spalliera* formation. Corvina is a relatively late ripener, its thickish skin making it reasonably resistant to rot during the drying-off-the-plant process known as *appassimento*, which is really its salvation as a quality grape.

Corvina is accompanied in vineyard and wine by the earlier-ripening Rondinella, a more robust and reliable, but less perfumed or elegant variety, planted precisely to give the grower a more consistent crop and a more balanced wine. Some consider Rondinella a mere workhorse, others see in it considerable character. Its small berries make it a good candidate for *appassimento*, evaporation occurring more rapidly where there is a higher skin-to-pulp ratio, so although it starts off with a lower sugar content it may catch up in the drying.

The grape called Corvinone, which literally means 'big Corvina', has traditionally been considered to be a sub-variety or mutation of Corvina, although more and more experts today seem to be of the opinion that it is at most a distant relative, perhaps having a common ancestor. Corvinone *does* fruit on the first few buds; it has deeper colour, higher sugar and firmer tannins than Corvina; its berry is distinctly larger, making it the last of the trio to dry in the *appassimento* process, which is where Corvina catches up. Like Corvina, it does well in hillside sites, but is rather unproductive and disease-prone in the valley compared with Corvina. I recently participated in a controlled experiment, carried out by the Valpolicella Consortium, in which clones of Corvina, Corvinone and Rondinella from different parts of the Valpolicella zone were vinified separately under identical conditions, and my notes confirm that Corvinone gave wines of noticeably fuller colour, higher tannicity and greater concentration than did Corvina.

In any case, the extent of the difference has not yet been recognized by most growers, who consider them as different clones of the same thing, and Corvina and Corvinone continue to be found in a confusion of plantings on the terraces of Valpolicella, both referred to as Corvina. Even the grape's official existence is a phenomenon of the very recent past, before which it enjoyed no separate mention either in the *disciplinare* or in the list of recommended or authorized varieties for the zone.

Another component of the Valpolicella *uvaggio* has traditionally been Molinara, favoured by growers wishing to bulk out the wine rather than those who seek greater concentration and depth. Molinara may be juicy and easy-drinking, as in the light but intense version produced by the legendary Giuseppe Quintarelli, but it is distinctly weak in extract and colour, and so is quietly being excluded from the blend, rather as Canaiolo is in Tuscany.

Negrara, part of a large family with numerous sub-varieties and name variations, has never been much more than a minor blender, used for body and colour rather than flavour in which it is somewhat deficient. Other Italian grapes which may be found in the Valpolicella blend, licitly or illicitly, include Sangiovese, Croatina (sometimes known here, confusingly, as 'Barolo'), Dindarella (or Pelara), Oseleta and Rossignola.

More favoured these days, however, are the Bordeaux grapes, for purposes of increasing colour, weight and extract. When the rules for Valpolicella were changed in the early 1990s, when wines or musts from other parts of Italy – read the south – were finally expelled from the blend, there was a big struggle on the part of certain large-scale producers to have Cabernet and Merlot allowed at up to 15%. They lost, on paper, being allowed only 5%. But a taste of a range of Valpolicella wines today indicates that producers are doing as they think best, never mind the law, as is customary in Italy.

The struggle to minimize the Bordeaux influence (which is not entirely new, by the way; Quintarelli has had Cabernet Franc in his vineyard for years) was led by the Valpolicella producers' consortium, mainly in the person of its director, Emilio Fasoletti, who maintains that Corvina's delicate perfumes are all too easily overwhelmed by the aggressive aromas of Cabernet and Co. This, incidentally, is one of the more active and on-the-ball consortia of Italy, counting among its membership most of the small, medium, and even large growers of the area, the main outsiders being Masi and Sartori, who exclude themselves in order to be able to follow their own path in respect of publicity and marketing, rather as Antinori, a couple of decades ago, excluded themselves from the Consortium of Chianti Classico producers in order to go smoothly on their own way without having to deal with the riff-raff.

THE WINES

VALPOLICELLA: RECIOTO, AMARONE, AMANDORLATO, RIPASSO

Valpolicella has two main divisions: Classico, the area historically associated with the quality red wines of Verona, and non-Classico: the area added on in 1968 to exploit the commercial properties of the name. It is sometimes said that all the quality stuff comes from Classico and all the rubbish from non-Classico, but this is not the case; there are excellent wines from the hills east of Verona, as well as plenty of rubbish from Classico. The quality division is, rather, between hill-grown and plain-grown, more particularly between high yield and restricted yield.

There are three styles of Valpolicella: (1) *normale*, made in the way of all red table wine, with generally a relatively short maceration period; (2) Recioto (including Amarone), made from grapes dried for up to four months, occasionally even longer, in the lofts of Veronese wineries; (3) *ripasso*, a method unique to Valpolicella, whereby the *normale* wine is 'passed back over' the lees of the Recioto in the spring after vinification of the latter is complete, causing a minor refermentation. (I put the words *normale* and *ripasso* in italics because, unlike Recioto and Amarone, they are not, at the time of writing, officially recognized terms, although *ripasso* is set to become one.)

Valpolicella *normale* is at best light and fruity, without great body or much pretension to longevity. This is certainly true of the wines of the *pianura*, though there are, increasingly, serious reds coming from recognized quality sites, no doubt in some cases thanks to assistance from the Gallic contingent. There is, in fact, a movement afoot to re-evaluate Valpolicella *normale*, the proponents of which wonder rhetorically how anyone can expect to make a great wine from second-choice grapes, given that in most cases the first choice tends to go into Amarone.

When critics wonder how Valpolicella ever got to be considered a great wine they forget that it was never for the *normale* but for the Recioto that it was so highly prized. This bittersweet red, together with its dry companion Amarone, is unique among wines and deserves recognition as one of the world's great classics. Admittedly it is only since the 1980s, with the help of refrigeration and greater understanding of wine chemistry, that it began to overcome problems of oxidation and volatility to emerge, or re-emerge, as a contender for such a position, so tasters have not yet had a chance to orient their taste buds to its charms; it takes time to come to terms with such a complex taste-touch-smell experience. And of course it has had the bad name of Valpolicella hanging over it.

Recioto today is made essentially as it has been for 2,000 years or so, with the major difference that today's best versions bring primary fruit flavours and not tertiary aromas to the fore. The method consists basically in a natural concentration of the sugars and extract of the picked grapes by way of the drying process called, as we have seen, *appassimento,* during which the grapes will lose approximately 25 to 30 per cent of their original weight. The process also involves certain chemical and biological reactions within the semi-raisined grapes giving rise to substances unique to the genre.

It is no wonder that Recioto/Amarone is expensive – it is very expensive to make, not to say a labour of love. Consider the work involved in selecting only perfect bunches; in transporting them single-layer to the winery; in laying them out on bamboo canes or, as happens increasingly, in shallow wooden fruit crates; in nursing the bunches through the crucial first ten days of drying, when practically any excess humidity can get grey rot running rampant through the room (but see 'tunnel' in the Glossary); in continuing over a period of months to weed out berries with negative rather than noble rot (the latter being to some extent desirable in sweet Recioto, less so in Amarone); in trying to get a fermentation going in deepest winter with ambient temperatures rock-bottom and a must thick with sugar and substances; in controlling the fermentation in such a way as to end up with a particular level of residual sugar (some producers don't bother – they let nature take its course); in ageing the result, as happens in some cases, in barrels of different sizes and different woods, including cherry and acacia as well as various oaks. The process is labour-intensive in a most unmodern, cost-ineffective way, not to mention the fact that the partially raisined grapes will only yield around half the quantity of wine that they could otherwise give.

People often 'ooh' and 'aah' when they taste Recioto, but then dismiss it, saying: 'But when would you drink it: a sweet red?' I am tempted to answer: whenever you would drink port; and you'll feel a lot better for it in the morning, since there's no added alcohol in Recioto. In fact, I would say that Recioto is a more modern wine than vintage port, especially in the youthful-fruit-packed style that many producers are aiming for today. You don't have to wait years for it to come round, it's a great warmer in winter and delicious chilled from the fridge on a hot summer's day, especially when it comes with a slight fizz as do certain traditional producers' wines.

Have I overstated the case? Probably, as far as Recioto is concerned. Sweet wines of any type are not of our time. On the other hand, Amarone is, very much so.

Amarone, the full, dry version of Recioto, is not the recent development that some would have us believe (at least two of the major names in the game claim to have 'discovered' it since the war). As previously stated, the wine's fermentation has traditionally been 'left to nature', that is to say the battle between yeasts and sugars was allowed to proceed in every vat. When the sugars won, you got sweet Recioto. When the yeasts won, you got what is today known as Amarone. In between, you got what some call Amandorlato. Some have suggested that Amarone was in the past considered a Recioto gone wrong, a sort of vinous aberration fit only for field-workers and such-like. But while this may have been true in some cases, there is evidence that Amarone has had its devotees in the past – only they have not been so vociferous as those of sweet Recioto.

Some say the phenomenon is old, only the name is new, although there is evidence that the name was applied to the style as early as the eighteenth century. However that may be, Amarone is certainly the 'serious' Valpolicella of our time, the one into which producers pour the greatest efforts, the one which gets the most complex and expensive barrel-ageing and which is capable, in the top examples, of long bottle maturation. By law, Amarone must have not less than 14 degrees of alcohol, and some producers, aiming at a product which can be considered as a normal table wine, limit themselves to this and even complain that the minimum should be reduced. These would also be inclined to limit if not eliminate noble rot in the drying grapes in the interests of minimal oxidation, reduction of volatile acidity and consequent reduction of the need for high levels of sulphur. Others just let the wine hang right out, achieving 15 and 16 degrees plus of alcohol together with tremendous concentration of flavour. The 'light' brigade regard such creations as dinosaurs; the 'heavies' see them as the ultimate expression of the genre.

Personally, I see a place for both types, though I incline to the latter view: as one of the few wines of the world capable of inducing awe in the beholder, why not let it go all the way? You wouldn't want to drink it every day, admittedly. But every now and then you look for something to knock your socks off. Italians call this style *vino da meditazione*. In my view, the world needs true meditation wines – it's not as if there's much volume of the top stuff anyhow, and a bit of meditation never did harm to any third party or anything but good to the meditator.

Ripasso is another wine style unique to Verona – it would not, after all, be possible without the Recioto/Amarone element. Potentially this is the most interesting of all Valpolicella styles for general consumption at a high level of quality and authenticity, because the boost in glycerol and alcohol that comes from the passing-back-over method confers upon the resulting wine a roundness and richness that the *normale* never achieves and which the Amarone achieves in excess. Blends involving non-traditional grape varieties may and do achieve a similar object, but at the cost of typicity.

There is some confusion as to nomenclature, since Masi, who claim to have discovered or re-discovered the process in the 1960s with their Campo Fiorin, have registered the name 'Ripasso' for their exclusive use, others having to allude to the process by different spellings or other subterfuges. For the most part, users of this method call their wine Valpolicella (Classico) Superiore, but this is not by any means an infallible indication that the wine is a *ripasso*; it may be a single vineyard wine, or a special selection, or a wine special for the maturation process employed. It may also be a partial Amarone in the sense of being blended with 10–20 per cent of the fuller wine, as in the case of Dal Forno's outstanding Valpolicella Superiore Vigneto di Monte Lodoletta.

A recently developed version of *ripasso* consists in passing the wine directly over partially or lightly raisined grapes in the manner of *governo all'uso toscano* (see Glossary). However, whereas in Chianti this method will be used at a very low percentage of the total wine, around 5 per cent, in Valpolicella the dried grapes on to which the freshly fermented wine will be poured directly for refermentation may contribute up to half of the total resultant wine, so that it is to all intents and purposes a semi-Amarone. An example of this is Allegrini's Palazzo della Torre.

The best sites

As in other classic zones of Italy, the concept of *cru* is becoming rapidly more important in Valpolicella. Herewith a list of some of the more highly prized sites – the list is not exhaustive.

VALPOLICELLA CLASSICO: Armaron, Brigaldara, Cà del Monte, Calcarole, Cerè, Conca d'Oro, Crosara, Fieramonte, Figari, Gnirega, Jago, La Grola, La Poja, Le Ragose, Maregnago, Mazzano, Mezzanella, Monteleone, Monte Sant'Urbano, Moron (sic), Palazzo della Torre, Pojega, Roccolo, Sassine, Siresol, Torbe, Tramanal, Villa.
VALPOLICELLA: Boiaigo, Castalde, Lodoletta, Monte del Drago, Ronchi.
VALPANTENA: Carrare, Lumiago, Mezzomonte, Romagnano.

The producers
The following producer profiles should give a good overall picture of both status quo and developments in Valpolicella at the present time. The communes are listed in geographical sequence, moving, like our intrepid traveller, west to east. As before, the communes are those where the wineries, not necessarily the vineyards, are situated. (Producers having very short descriptions, in quasi-note form, are not necessarily of minor significance; it's just as likely to mean that I know less about their production.) Classico in brackets after a commune's name indicates that it is situated within the Valpolicella Classico zone.

SANT'AMBROGIO DI VALPOLICELLA, FRAZIONE GARGAGNAGO (CLASSICO)

Aleardo **Ferrari**. Traditionalist grower-producer particularly well known for his Recioto, also making good classic Amarone and Valpolicella Classico Superiore without resort to *cru* names.

Masi. Probably the highest-profile *azienda* on the contemporary scene, this dynamic group run by the Boscaini family (growers here since the late eighteenth century) under the genial Sandro Boscaini, have been leading innovators since the 1960s. They were among the first to introduce *cru* Amarone with Mazzano and Campolongo di Torbè, plus *cru* Recioto with Mezzanella. They were certainly the first, during the 1970s, when the wizard of Valpolicella, Nino Franceschetti, was still with them, to re-establish the *ripasso* method with their Campo Fiorin.

In the 1980s they took the neighbouring estate of Serego Alighieri, property of the heirs of Dante, under their oenological wing, widening their range with Amarone Vajo Armaron and

Recioto Casal dei Ronchi. Today they control production in some 160 hectares, owned or rented, in the Verona area.

For decades Masi have been at the forefront of experiments with training systems, clones and forgotten varieties, and the upmarket table wine Toar, a blend of Corvina and Rondinella together with the obsolescent Oseleta, Rossignola and Dindarella, is one fruit of this activity. This should be enough to earn them widespread respect, without referring to their unceasing work to promote the wines of Valpolicella by organizing seminars, award foundations and a variety of other activities. Indeed they are highly respected abroad, if rather less well-liked by certain locals who resent aspects of their independent stance.

FUMANE (CLASSICO)

Allegrini. One of the earliest pioneers of quality Valpolicella for our time was Giovanni Allegrini who, a few years prior to his premature death in 1983, purchased the La Grola hill in Sant'Ambrogio for the purpose of producing fine *cru* wines with new methods of planting and vinification. His work has been carried forward famously by sons Walter (vineyards) and Franco (winery), and daughter Marilisa (sales/PR). All their wines are from grapes grown in their own vineyards (nearly 50 hectares) situated in the communes of Fumane and Sant'Ambrogio. They include La Poja, from *spalliera*-trained Corvina vines planted at the top of the Grola hill, probably the single greatest table wine (i.e. unaided by semi-dried grapes, though what grapes it may be aided by nobody is quite sure) ever to come out of Valpolicella; La Grola, a single-vineyard Classico Superiore aged in French oak *fusti*; Palazzo della Torre, mentioned above; an outstanding Amarone of the modern, relatively light type; and an intensely fruity Recioto named, appropriately, Giovanni Allegrini. Allegrini are, and will remain for the foreseeable future, leaders of the modernist school in Valpolicella.

Corteforte. Relatively recently appeared on the scene, this grower's wines have maintained an impressive and improving standard. Valpolicella Classico Superiore Podere Bertarole and Amarone are firm of structure while displaying modern-style rich non-oxidized fruit. Even the unusual Amandorlato, with its somewhat traditional aromas and bittersweet palate, manages to display a modernesque intensity of fruit.

Le Salette. Franco Scamperle's modernized *cantina* in the quiet heart of Fumane turns out reliably good, and good-value, Amarone (Marega) and Valpolicella Classico Superiore (Cà Carnocchio), plus a modern-style, fruit-driven Recioto (Le Traversagne) from well-sited vineyards *in zona*.

SAN PIETRO IN CARIANO (CLASSICO)

Stefano **Accordini**, *frazione* Pedemonte. This small family winery, run by Tiziano Accordini and his father Stefano, enjoys the benefit of an expert and experienced oenologist in the form of the technical director of the local *cantina sociale*, who happens to be Tiziano's brother Daniele. They may not have much in the way of hectares of vineyard, but they make the most of what they've got, turning out modern-style, fruit-packed Amarone and Recioto under the ancient name of Acinatico (see also Bertani), plus a *cru* Amarone called Vigneto il Fornetto which, with few others, must be a beacon towards the future of this wine which is capable, we realize increasingly, of combining power and elegance – and, crucially, freshness, that is absence of oxidation – like few other wines in the world. The only problem about making outstanding *passito* wine from a limited vineyard area is that, when the best grapes go for drying, what's left for the making of *normale* and *ripasso* may not be capable of keeping up the standard.

Lorenzo **Begali.** A small and dedicated grower who bottles only the cream of his production, selling the rest to the merchants. A *passito* specialist, both his powerful Amarone and his fresh intensely fruity-spicy Recioto, sold without *cru* identification, regularly give an impression of having been made with great care.

Brigaldara, *frazione* San Floriano. Stefano Cesari is a mover and shaker who knows how to get things done without getting too caught up in the red tape that invariably, in Italy, attempts to smother organized activity like a blood-sucking creeper. This energy and intelligence he applies equally to the various committees on which he serves and to his own production. He began working his 15 hectares of vineyard as a hobby in 1978 and he has been steadily improving and updating ever since, developing a passion for wine-making, which he now does full-time, in the process.
    Stefano is of the modernist school in the sense that he aims to

minimize oxidation and maximize fruit. The style is best exemplified by his Valpolicella Classico Superiore Il Vegro, a *ripasso* which spends a mere six hours, rather than several days, on the lees of the Recioto.

The Recioto itself accentuates cherry fruit while the Amarone (he only makes one and intends not to make a *cru*) is perhaps his most classic wine, a drinking style, characterful and structured but appropriate – unlike so many Amarones – as an accompaniment to the Sunday roast.

Giuseppe **Brunelli**. Luigi Brunelli is a young man who, apart from using relatively small and relatively new barrels for ageing purposes, sticks for the most part to traditional principles of Amarone production. It is, in fact, for his Amarones that he is particularly well regarded, wines which from a successful year can display all the opulence and concentration of which the genre is capable combined with a certain smoothness and brightness of cherry acid-drop fruit which makes them distinctly moreish despite a hefty alcoholic degree.

Giuseppe **Fornaser**. Amarone Monte Faustino and Valpolicella Classico Vigneto La Traversagna are the stars of this property's production.

Nicolis. Medium-sized producer with properties in Bardolino as well as in Valpolicella. Good Recioto of the youthful style and a decent Amarone, *cru* Ambrosan.

Santa Sofia, *frazione* Pedemonte. Once a big name in the Veronese, Santa Sofia's attempts at a comeback have been more successful in respect of Soave and Bardolino than of Valpolicella, although the recently undertaken restructuring of the *cantina* at Pedemonte points to a firm determination to return to the days of glory.

Fratelli **Speri**, *frazione* Pedemonte. The extent to which the Speris have stuck together since their ancestor initiated the business of producing, bottling and commercializing their own wines in 1874 is testified to by the complex of family residences surrounding the winery in Pedemonte. Carlo Speri, current *capo*, youngest of four brothers, presides over the activities of various sons and nephews whose impressive teamwork convincingly continues the making of one of Valpolicella's longest-standing *crus*, Monte Sant'Urbano.

This hilltop vineyard, whose 20 plus-year-old vines are perfectly positioned at around 230 metres of altitude, regularly produces strapping Amarone and a Valpolicella Classico Superiore, lightly *appassito*, which typifies the best of the traditional table wine style. A more recent star, sign that the younger generation are being allowed, indeed encouraged, to have their say, is the amazing Recioto La Roggia, whose grapes are dried till February and macerated a couple of weeks in naturally cold conditions. The wine is then transferred to *barriques* to complete the fermentation, after which it spends an appreciable time in *botte* and bottle before being released. The densely concentrated, aromatically complex, sweet but balanced result is emblematic of the new Recioto – not a revolutionary wine but one, like a latter-day saint sitting on the shoulders of his elder, whose elevation could not be achieved were it not for the foundation of tradition.

Fratelli **Tedeschi**, *frazione* Pedemonte. Renzo Tedeschi, alongside his business as a medium-sized *commerciante*, was one of the late twentieth-century pioneers of fine *cru* production from own grapes in Valpolicella, though his style now situates itself towards the right wing of the traditionalist-modernist dividing line. Regular winners have been Amarone Capitel Monte Olmi, Recioto Capitel Monte Fontana and the *ripasso* Capitel San Rocco. His white Recioto, Vin de la Fabriseria, has occasionally been stupendous.

Fratelli **Tommasi**, *frazione* Pedemonte. One of the most dynamic and forward-looking of the established *commercianti*, with a large technologically advanced winery on the one hand, and no fewer than 78 hectares of vineyard in various sectors of the Veronese on the other, Tommasi's strength on the ground in Valpolicella is beginning to show through. No fewer than three *cru* Amarones are on offer – Villa Girardi, Il Sestante and Cà Florian Tommasi – as well as the *normale*, and if great heights are generally not to be expected, nor are great disappointments. Apart from which there is a complete range of the wines of Verona at the various commercial levels.

Massimino **Venturini**, *frazione* San Floriano. Traditional Amarone, Recioto (Le Brugnine) and Valpolicella Classico Superiore (Semonte Alto) from own vineyards in excellent sites.

Villa Bellini. Small property, upgraded and organicized by recent purchasers Marco Zamarchi and Cecilia Trucchi. One of the few which produces, apart from Amarone and Recioto, the in-between style known as Amandorlato.

MARANO, FRAZIONE VALGATARA (CLASSICO)

Paolo **Boscaini.** Sister-*azienda* to Masi of Sant'Ambrogio (it's all in the Boscaini family, consisting of numerous brothers and cousins), this establishment has specialized in large-volume middle-of-the-road Veronese wines on the one hand and on own-vineyard production on the other. Indeed they own or control 110 hectares throughout the region, and under the direction of Dario Boscaini, ex-director of the regional viticultural school at San Floriano, have achieved a measure of success with *cru* Amarone Cà de Loi and the *ripasso* Le Cane, traditional-style wines of good if rarely inspired quality.

Giuseppe **Campagnola.** There are several wineries run by people named Campagnola in the area – this is the big one, with an annual production of some 3 million bottles. Campagnola's range is pan-Veronese and their production is vast, but the wines are correct and of ever increasing quality as the policies of the young Giuseppe, who recently took over from father Luigi, take effect. The basis of the business, however, remains the bread and butter lines of consistency and good value for money – and why not? There's a place for everything.

Fratelli **Degani.** Brothers Aldo and Angelo Degani look after the vineyards while Luca takes care of the *cantina* at this small *azienda* turning out artisanal versions of the Valpolicella range which can be quite exciting and delicious. Amarone, Recioto and Valpolicella Classico Superiore are non-*cru* as far as the rather old-fashioned label is concerned, but the contents are personalized to such an extent that you can almost taste the *terroir* – in the nicest possible way.

La Bionda. The production of brothers Piero and Sergio Castellani does not seem to have suffered since they divided the property between them. Wines under the La Bionda label, intended for a relatively large market in the distribution of which neighbours Boscaini are involved, have proved correct and of good depth of flavour. It is under the I Castei label, however, that the higher selection wines are bottled.

San Rustico. This is one of those Campagnolas which is not *the* Campagnola, indeed no relation; hence the name, which may be complemented on the label by that of their principal vineyard, Il Gaso. From their 40 hectares of vineyard they produce reasonably priced Amarone, Recioto and Valpolicella Classico of good, if rarely excellent, quality, including in the range a sparkling Recioto of a type once popular but rarely today made in the zone.

NEGRAR (CLASSICO)

Bertani, *frazione* Arbizzano, *località* Novare. Founded in 1857, Bertani have all the trappings of an *azienda-leader* for Valpolicella, including a splendid villa at Novare, capacious cellars at Grezzana in Valpantena and some 135 hectares of vineyard in Valpolicella and Soave. Unfortunately the family factions could never in recent years get on, so in 1993 production and marketing were turned over to a consortium headed by Emilio Pedron of Gruppo Italiano Vini (GIV). Bertani remain by far the biggest producers and stockholders of Amarone, with 15,000 hectolitres' wood capacity mainly in the form of 80-hectolitre old Slavonian-oak *botti*. They have been making Amarone deliberately dry since 1959, before which (under the name Recioto) it was sweet, and they still have vintages back to 1962 commercially available – some stored in *botte*, some in bottle (the 1967 was bottled in 1985; even the 1983 didn't see bottle until 1993). Other specialities include a *ripasso* called Secco-Bertani, from Valpantena; a Recioto Spumante, one of the few examples of this wine in fully sparkling form (bizarre but delicious!); and several thousand bottles of a 1928 Recioto which they call Acinatico, a name which harks back to the days of the Longobards in the early Dark Ages, as recorded in a letter written by one Cassiodorus, minister of King Theodoricus, who describes 'acinaticum' as having a 'sweetness of incredible suavity' and the density of 'meaty liquid, of a drink meant for eating'. This cache of old Acinatico was found by builders in 1984 behind a brick wall, having been hidden there in the 1940s as protection from German predators. There's something to meditate on – if you can wangle a bottle.

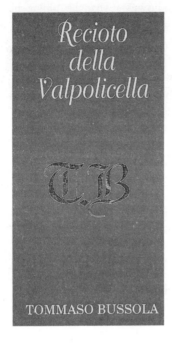

Tommaso **Bussola**, *frazione* San Peretto. When asked who he particularly recommended among the younger generation in Valpolicella, Giuseppe Quintarelli (see below) gave only one name: Tommaso Bussola. This producer does not come from a wine family, but his uncle, Giuseppe, was a grower who took Tommaso under his wing when the young man decided that an indoor career was not for him. The function became a passion, Tommaso being a single-minded man, and the passion for the vine developed into a passion for making wine, so that in the early 1990s he mortgaged himself and his family to the hilt to build a house-cum-winery adequate for his needs. And indeed, Tommaso moves among his many barrels of cherry, chestnut, French and Slavonian oak with the same reverence as I noted in Quintarelli when I first visited his premises in the early 1980s, almost as if this were not a winery but a temple. He takes a sample from this *barrique*, that *fusto*, that *damigiana*, that stainless steel *serbatoio*, and peers at you as you taste, as if your opinion were a matter of real importance to him.

With such a number and diversity of containers one feels he must fall into a hopeless confusion, but he seems to know what's what. When it comes to bottles he presents two ranges each consisting of a Valpolicella Classico Superiore, a Recioto and an Amarone, the 'bg' (for Bussola Giuseppe) selection representing wines of less age and relatively contained price, having less expensive wood-treatment; and the 'TB' range for the wines whose cost of production is entirely dictated by the necessities of creative expression. All the wines have a marvellous aromatic character, based on maraschino cherry, the TBs displaying a depth and intensity of sheer fruit difficult to find anywhere in the world of wine, with nary a trace of oxidation. The *capolavoro*, the masterpiece, if one had to pick one, would have to be Amarone Vigneto Alto, although the amazingly rich yet balanced Recioto runs it close.

Le Ragose, *frazione* Arbizzano. Marta and Arnaldo Galli, in the early 1970s, were virtually the first to bring quality viticulture back to the heights above the *pianura*, growing at 500 or so metres of altitude where stony soil and terraces make for hard labour and low yields, an area that had been abandoned when Valpolicella became an industrial wine sold on price alone. Since the beginning their wines have commanded great respect, if somewhat less enthusiasm, having something of that austerity of the *terroir* from which they spring. Stars are the Amarone and the Valpolicella Classico Superiore Le Sassine, to which more recently they have added a Cabernet which ranks among the best of the zone.

Roberto **Mazzi** & Figli, *frazione* San Peretto. Roberto Mazzi, a third generation grower-bottler, may incline to the making of wines of the old school – big, powerful, concentrated, with plenty of extract – but his sons Stefano and Antonio are gradually bringing the winery into the modernist mould. The *pièce de résistance* has always been their Amarone Punta di Villa, a dry, rather austere wine aged in traditional *botti* after a long maceration. The dreaded *barrique*, however, is beginning to make its appearance, for Recioto le Calcarole (in part) and for the relatively newly developed Valpolicella Classico *cru* Colle Crosetta. My personal favourite, however, has been the Valpolicella Classico Superiore Vigneto Poiega, a model combination of subtle power and finesse which keeps you sipping, trying to unlock the secret you know is in there somewhere.

Giuseppe **Quintarelli**. The Quintarellis have been working their vineyard at Monte Cà Paletta since 1924, and third-generation Giuseppe Quintarelli, who took over from his father in the mid-1950s, introducing exportation shortly thereafter, still stands as a living monument to the splendour of traditional Valpolicella. He is the ultimate believer in nature-doing-her-thing, allowing each individual wine to make itself according to its own biochemical lights, tending to each drying berry, each gently bubbling barrel, each humble demijohn with the loving care a father would bestow upon his children. One realizes in his presence, as he draws samples from this barrel and that, intently studying your expression and your words as you taste and comment, that it is this attention to every detail which constitutes the difference between the great and the good in artisanal wine-making.

Undoubtedly Quintarelli's wines can be great in terms of wealth of extract and complexity of aroma (dried fruits, herbs, spices, tar, leather), and if to get to that point they must spend seven to ten years in barrel, so be it. But being a traditionalist does not mean that Signor Quintarelli does not experiment. He was the first, he maintains, to bring Cabernet into the Valpolicella equation, and he still makes *passiti* from Cabernet Franc (the much sought-after Alzero) as well as from Nebbiolo. His *passito* whites, from Garganega, Tocai and the local Saorin, sometimes having a high percentage of grapes which have developed noble rot in the drying process, are equally amazing.

Casa Vinicola **Sartori**. One of the most successful post-war 'industrials' having made a huge success in the United Kingdom and the United States, Sartori supply at various levels – from supermarket own-label cheap-and-cheeerful to mid-quality *cru* – the entire range of Veronese wines, plus some from beyond. Like others of their type, noting the increasing inability of Verona to provide grapes or bulk wines at prices sufficiently low to make them competitive at the cut-throat end of the international market, they have been making strenuous efforts of late to upgrade.

C.S. **Valpolicella**. Founded in 1933 to serve the growers of Negrar, the *cantina* expanded in the 1950s to become a production centre for grapes from Valpolicella generally. Unlike most of the cooperatives in Verona and indeed in Veneto (and indeed in Italy) they have pursued a policy of high quality bottled product. This manifests today under the Domini Veneti label which applies to the cream of Amarone, Recioto and Valpolicella Classico Superiore production. They also, increasingly, make wines of limited areas, examples being Amarone Vigneti di Jago and Recioto Vigneti di Moron.

Villa Spinosa. Enrico Cascella Spinosa, whose 15-hectare vineyard is situated at Jago (made famous by Bolla), is a fairly recent entrant into the world of wine-production. The quality of his site, his policy of low production helped by vines trained to *cordone speronato* (see Glossary), has allowed him to make Amarone, Recioto and Valpolicella Classico Superiore of real character, even if continuity has been a bit lacking. He has also planted, and vinified, Cabernet as a varietal wine. One to watch.

Viviani. Claudio Viviani's ace in the hole is his vineyard in the hills above Negrar, in the sub-zone Mazzano, made famous by Masi (to whose wine it is not impossible that Claudio's grapes have made their contribution). To this must be added the enthusiasm and perfectionism of a young man determined to climb to the top qualitatively as well as geographically. Given his position he has to play on aroma and elegance rather than on power and depth, and he has proved that in the better vintages he is well equipped and able to do this. His wines, which embrace the Valpolicella gamut of Amarone, Recioto, Classico Superiore and straight Classico, stood out for these qualities in a blind tasting not long ago. The problem has been that, in the lesser vintages, being more exposed than the growers of the valley, he suffers more from the vagaries of the weather, especially in respect of high acidity in the straight Valpolicella Classico.

VERONA

Bolla. For a good many of the years, since 1883, that the Bolla family has controlled this vast enterprise, and especially since the Second World War, their name has been synonymous with Soave, especially in their biggest market, the USA. In recent times, however, while maintaining a huge production of their lead wine, they have been intent on shifting the publicity spotlight away from the mundane towards the particular. Hence *cru* wines like Valpolicella Classico Superiore from the Jago vineyard – given two years' ageing in large *botti*, and like Soave Classico Castellaro, made sturdier and more concentrated by twelve hours' crio-maceration on the skins. Hence, too, experimental 'world-market' style wines like Creso Rosso, two-thirds Cabernet Sauvignon and one-third Corvina given a light *appassimento*; like Merlot Colforte; and like Sauvignon Lunaia – wines which might not shine sufficiently to sell on their own but fit conveniently into a package. Hence, finally, the renewed emphasis on a wine for which the firm claims credit for developing (or redeveloping) way back in the 1950s: Amarone. Their version went through a dip in the 1980s when, against many newer, fresher versions, it began to look tough, tired and desperately old style; but recent bottles have shown that they have understood the new exigencies of the market, and while it retains its old power and concentration, today's wine is much less oxidized and tannic.

Montresor. See under Bianco di Custoza, page 147.

Pasqua/Cecilia Beretta. Having been founded in 1925 and grown into another of the post-war industrial giants, Pasqua's answer to the shifting requirements of the market has been to buy vineyards. So far they have acquired over 100 hectares, including the Cecilia Beretta estate at Mizzole, where they are busily replanting, using French-style cordon training methods. They have also teamed up with the Sagramoso family, giving them control over a further 60 hectares in Valpolicella and Soave. And they have enjoyed for a few years now the services of certain high-flying Italian oenological consultants. So far, Cecilia Beretta, under the labels Terre di Cariano, Terre di Brognoligo and Roccolo di Mizzole, have perhaps promised a bit more than they have delivered, but the potential and the will for greater things is certainly there. Were one to criticize the operation in one aspect it would be for a too-much-too-soon alienation of the wine style from the traditional in the direction of the 'international' (oak, French varieties in the blends). There is elegance, yes; but is it Veronese?

Verona lives, however, in the parallel upgrading of the production under the Pasqua label. The bread-and-butter lines continue to roll out in their millions (how do you think they are financing all this?) but the special selection wines are gathering force. Amarone and Valpolicella Vigneti di Casterna and Villa Borghetti are capable of figuring among the leaders in Verona tastings these days without excessive sacrifice of *tipicità*. The straight Cabernet Sauvignon Morago would not convince many Frenchmen, but maybe it's not supposed to. As for the effect of their recently established joint venture in Puglia's Salento, that remains to be seen.

MIZZOLE

Baltieri. This emerging estate, in a commune slightly north-east of Verona, is one of the few to make a clear distinction between vineyards destined for the production of *passito* wines (the 30-hectare Il Bosco estate) and those whose grapes go to make Valpolicella Superiore (10 hectares at I Ronchi, where they also grow various experimental varieties). At the moment the *passiti* are the most successful wines, especially the Recioto called Praedium, so thick with cherry fruit that it almost seems a syrup. For those of the sweet-tooth disposition it can be addictive; those of a drier inclination will not be disappointed by the carefully crafted Amarone.

MEZZANE DI SOTTO

Corte Sant'Alda. We are now well to the east of the Classico zone of Valpolicella but not, it would seem, east of Eden. This small estate, which began life as a hobby for Marinella Camerani and became her prime focus, has elicited much praise in recent years for its ability to turn out wines which bring elegance and concentration of fruit to the fore rather than power. Not that her wines, made from vines trained to *spalliera* and therefore tending to considerably lower yields than is the norm in these parts, lack the necessary backbone for ageing, indeed improving, over a goodly period in bottle. Wood-ageing, too, is modernist in style, the barrels being French oak *barriques* and *tonneaux*. Production embraces the Valpolicella range, the mention 'Mithas' being made on the label of Amarone or Valpolicella Superiore of selected quality.

Villa Erbice. This is a small estate producing Amarone and Recioto of grace rather than muscle, as befits the zone. Silvio and Alberto Erbice have the enthusiasm and the ability to raise their wines to the level of the higher echelons of Classico.

ILLASI

Romano **Dal Forno**, *frazione* Cellore. This estate, founded only in the 1980s, *has* climbed to the maximum heights which Valpolicella, Classico or otherwise, is capable of attaining. Dal Forno's wines were already being hailed among the best before he started introducing new French oak in 1990. Today there are those who consider Dal Forno the quality king of Valpolicella, combining as he does, in his Amarone Monte Lodoletta, a mighty structure with a concentration of flavours and perfumes scarcely paralleled anywhere in Italy. The Valpolicella Vigneto di Monte Lodoletta too can be quite stunning. I have never tasted a Valpolicella (though it's blended with a bit of Amarone) with so much personality, so finely tuned in respect of wood treatment and fruit quality, and in particular with such a chromatic scale of intensely individual aromas, as the 1990. Nor is the Recioto Monte Lodoletta any less of a liquid bombshell.

To Romano Dal Forno must go credit for two things: for proving conclusively that great Valpolicella can be made outside the Classico area; and for demonstrating how principles of modern

oenology can be employed to enhance the properties of an ancient wine without in any way compromising typicity. Dal Forno's wines are profoundly revolutionary and yet profoundly Valpolicella. This is an approach that all Italian wines might do well to emulate: Yes to modernity; No to loss of soul.

Santi. One of two *cantine* owned by Gruppo Italiano Vini in the area, Santi produce large volumes of the Veronese standards plus a few reasonably successful *crus* such as Valpolicella Superiore Castello d'Illasi and Soave Sanfederici. Their Amarone is middle-of-the-road, nothing wrong with it, nothing special about it.

Trabucchi. Giuseppe Trabucchi is a lawyer who has revived his family estate, complete with new *cantina*, along organic, semi-modernistic lines. Given the conditions in Illasi – stonier, harsher, drier than in Classico – he turns out wines which make up in aromatics (flowers, soft fruits) for what they lack in structure. That's when they succeed, which they don't always. But then it is always harder to get an organic operation off the ground; once it's established, it should gain in strength.

PRODUCERS BASED IN OTHER AREAS

Guerrieri Rizzardi, Bardolino. With an astonishing 150 hectares of prime vineyard property in the classic areas of the Veronese, the

Counts Guerrieri Rizzardi enjoy a potential second to none. Their Valpolicella range comes from vineyards surrounding the Villa Rizzardi at Poiega in Negrar, and include a Valpolicella Classico, the Classico Superiore Villa Rizzardi Poiega and Amarone Calcarole, all made in classic style. The main estate is at Bardolino, a superb establishment on the shore of Lake Garda, and indeed Bardolino *crus* Tacchetto and Fontis Mina Munus are among the best-expressed wines of their production.

Zenato, Peschiera del Garda. See under Lugana, page 210.

Zeni, Bardolino. A medium-sized grower-*commerciante* producing the wines of the three classic Veronese zones, this *azienda* under the direction of Gaetano Zeni has earned itself a reputation simultaneously for serious quality on the 'commercial' level and for top quality on the *vino di pregio* level. Amarone has succeeded for them in various guises – *barricato* and aged in *botte*, selected (Vigne Alte) and *normale*; if indeed Amarone can ever be described as 'normal'. The 'Vigne Alte' rubric is used for selected wines in various denominations – Valpolicella, Bardolino, even Bianco di Custoza.

Zonin, see under Gambellara, page 208.

BARDOLINO

Apart from Valpolicella, Bardolino is the only other wine of significance made from Corvina and company. The *uvaggio* is the same, but soil types are different – lighter, more calcareous and pebbley, less clay. The conditions here do not lend themselves to that *appassimento* process which is the secret of quality in Valpolicella. Here there is no history of drying grapes. Instead the direction is towards even greater lightness than that which one finds in Valpolicella *normale*. Historically, one of the important wine styles has been a type of rosé called Chiaretto. Today, the fashion is for Novello, Italy's answer to Beaujolais Nouveau. The prospect of neither is likely to bring the serious wine-bibber out in a sweat of anticipation, although great efforts are made to whip up enthusiasm for Novello every year in early November.

Bardolino's position on the south-eastern shore of Lake Garda, western Europe's largest lake, is probably the secret of its continuing success – these light fruity wines of little structure, which lend themselves to a light chilling, being perfect accompaniments to the salady and picnicky fare on offer to the Italic and Teutonic hordes that swarm round the lakeside in holiday season. Light reds are in any case much to the Germanic taste, and there is healthy demand for Bardolino in the lands to the north. Whatever the reasons, production figures remain buoyant, with around 200,000 hectolitres of Bardolino and Bardolino Classico being churned out yearly.

But perhaps I am being too harsh. There are *some* Bardolinos of concentration and structure – although far fewer than there are Valpolicellas. In the town of Bardolino the long-established noble house of Guerrieri-Rizzardi (see above) makes good *crus*, and **Cavalchina** at Custoza produce a Bardolino Superiore Santa Lucia which has a bit more to it than most. I have been impressed with the wines of **Corte Gardoni**, of Valeggio sul Mincio; also of **Le Fraghe** at Cavaion Veronese. The *cru* San Pietro, from Le Vigne di San Pietro, of Sommacampagna, is among the best, although the reputation of this producer rests perhaps more with other wines (see under Moscato Giallo, page 214).

RABOSO

According to experts, Raboso Piave (a.k.a. Raboso Friularo or just Friularo) and Raboso Veronese, despite their sharing of the principal name, are two distinct grapes. And, despite clues provided by secondary names, they probably originate neither from Friuli nor from Verona, but are natives of the eastern Veneto wine area called Piave after the river of that name with its tributary (you guessed it) Raboso. Certainly the Piave plain is the only place where they are, or ever have been (since the first mention of Raboso in the seventeenth century), grown in any volume, with the exception of Bagnoli. Both are deeply coloured and rather light in grape sugar while being heavy on acidity and tannin – hence another, less plausible derivation of the main name, from the word *rabbioso*, angry. Of the two, the Veronese is less temperamental and so tends to be taking over from its rival, though both are on the decline, these days being used more as blenders than as varietals.

The DOC Piave Raboso allows both types. Because of a tendency to uppish acidity Piave Raboso is best with a bit of age, and indeed the *disciplinare* calls for a three-year minimum ageing period. A good producer, managing to capture the intense fruit of the variety along with its wild-fruit acidity, is Giorgio **Cecchetto** of Tezze di Piave; another is **Cescon** of Salgaredo.

There is also a wine called Friularo included under the recently established multi-DOC Bagnoli, which requires 90 per cent of the grapes included to be Raboso Piave, and which also provides for a dried-grape version, by late harvest or *appassimento*. The sole producer of any size is Lorenzo **Borletti** of the Il Dominio estate at Bagnoli di Sopra, whose *passito* combines some complexity with relatively easy drinkability for a sweet red, though it lacks the concentration of a top Recioto di Valpolicella.

REFOSCO

Said to be of ancient origin, this native Friulian (as far as we know) has developed over the centuries a number of sub-varieties, the best quality one being Refosco dal Peduncolo Rosso (of the red stem, or foot). The first reference to Refosco dates back to 1390 when Francesco di Manzano mentions it as having been offered by 'Roman ambassadors' to the general of the Dominicans. Refosco is a late ripener, the grapes being vermilion of hue, *selvatico* of style – i.e. having a sort of wild-berry perfume and pointed acidity, with a tendency to greenish tannins. Indeed, Refosco wines are generally best drunk young while that fresh, vibrant, wild-fruit character prevails.

Refosco is thought to be related to the Mondeuse Noire of France's Savoie, and is grown as Refosco in California. Other grapes which go by the name of Refosco in the North East include Refosco Nostrano, or R. d'Istria, or R. del Terrano. This latter is grown mainly in the Carso zone of Friuli, and is linked with the Teran of Slovenia across the border to the east, as well as with the Cagnina of Romagna. It is often described as a close kin of Refosco, indeed Pittaro and Plozner (*L'Uva e il Vino*, 1982) go so far as to state categorically that it is 'undoubtedly a Refosco'. On the other hand, according to Cosmo *et al.* of the Ministry of Agriculture's commission for the study of the principal wine-grapes of Italy, 'Refosco del Carso has nothing to do with the many "Refoschi" which once grew in Friuli and which today, if we except "Refosco nostrano" or "Refosco dal pecol rosso", have almost disappeared.' The DOC Carso does in fact legislate for two separate sub-DOCs: Terrano, and Refosco dal Peduncolo Rosso. So you can take your pick.

Most of Friuli's multi-DOCs embrace Refosco as a varietal, the exception being Collio from where, none the less, come some good wines, including that of Marco **Felluga** of Gradisca d'Isonzo, Bottaz from **Venica & Venica** of Dolegna del Collio and the Carpino Rosso from **Il Carpino** of Oslavia (a blend with Merlot).

Most of the best, however, come from the Colli Orientali, above-average versions being produced by the following: **Dorigo**, Buttrio; **Le Due Terre** (Sacrisassi Rosso, blend with Schioppettino), Prepotto; **Livon** (Riul), San Giovanni al Natisone; **Meroi**, Buttrio; **Ronchi di Cialla**, Prepotto; **Ronchi di Manzano**, Manzano; **Volpe Pasini** (Zuc di Volpe), Torreano; **Zamò e Zamò**, Buttrio.

A good example from Aquileia is the *cru* Villa Chiozzo, made by the **Cantina Produttori Cormons**. A reliable if unexciting Refosco of Friuli Grave is produced by **Collavini** of Corno di Rosazzo in the Colli Orientali del Friuli.

As for Terrano, no one makes a better version than Edi **Kante** of Duino Aurisina; **Castelvecchio**, of Sagrado, is another good producer.

Russolo in Pramaggiore make I Legni, one of the few examples of Refosco to come out of the Veneto.

Refosco also makes not-infrequent appearances in red blends of Friuli. Example: Giovanni **Dri**, of Nimis, makes Il Roncat Rosso from 50% Refosco and 30% Schioppettino, the rest being Cabernet. Enzo Pontoni, of Azienda Agricola **Miani**, Buttrio, makes his highly rated Miani Rosso with Refosco, Cabernet and Tazzelenghe.

SCHIOPPETTINO, PIGNOLO, TAZZELENGHE

Until around the end of the nineteenth century, when following phylloxera they were replanted largely with French varieties, the vineyards of the Colli Orientali del Friuli were chock-a-block with native grapes, most of them either very acidic or very tannic or both. Apart from Refosco, they all were heading quietly towards the great vineyard in the sky until the latter half of the twentieth century, when they (these three, anyway) began something of a revival.

The most diffuse is certainly Schioppettino (a.k.a. Ribolla Nera), which derives its name, it is said, from its way of 'crackling' (from *schioppettare*, to crackle) on the tongue, when made young and fizzy as it may be locally, though outside the area one is not likely to find this style. It tends to be of interesting fruit character – wild raspberry or blackberry – but low in alcohol and almost citric of acidity.

Good producers, all in the Colli Orientali, include: **Casa di Legno**, Prepotto; **Petrussa**, Prepotto; Ronchi di Cialla; **Ronco del Gnemiz**, San Giovanni al Natisone; **Rubini** (Villa Rubini), Cividale del Friuli; **Vigne dal Leon**, Premariacco.

More promising, perhaps, if much less widespread, is Pignolo, whose firm acidity is more than compensated for by good grape sugar, wild-fruit flavours and soft tannins. It is beginning to catch on today around the area of Buttrio-Manzano-Rosazzo in the Colli Orientali south of Cividale del Friuli; indeed Rosazzo has its own sub-multi-DOC, which includes Pignolo, under the umbrella multi-DOC Colli Orientali del Friuli. The outstanding producer is Giro-lamo Dorigo of Buttrio – see under Cabernet in International Varieties (page 243). The version of **Abbazia di Rosazzo**, of Manzano, can also be very good.

Tazzelenghe, or Tacelenghe, so called because the acidity and tannins of the wine made traditionally (it was once very diffuse) are so strong that it seems to cut (*tagliare*) the tongue (*lingua*), is the least likely to become a universal best-seller, but it is re-appearing slowly in the south-west corner of the Colli Orientali.

Marina **Danieli**, of Buttrio, with her famous consultant Giorgio Grai, has tried to smooth the wine out by wood ageing. The only other producers that I know of are Vigne dal Leon and **La Viarte**, Prepotto.

LAGREIN

The theory that the name of this native of Trentino-Alto Adige stems from Val-Lagarina has been disputed by Cosmo and Polsinelli on the grounds that no evidence exists for Lagrein's presence in Trentino until the twentieth century, whereas it has been cultivated by monks in Bolzano since the seventeenth century. This grape has the advantage of considerable depth of colour and extract without tremendous tannin; but the disadvantage of a bitter twist at the back which seems difficult to tame except by ageing in *barrique*, to which a growing number of producers are therefore resorting. At its best, this interesting variety can harmonize rich gameyness with smooth fruitiness in a way which makes its rusticity seem almost sophisticated. As the wines get better, so do Lagrein's plantings increase in South Tyrol, mainly at the expense of Schiava (see page 191), to which it used to be regarded as inferior.

The DOC in South Tyrol is Alto Adige, and there is even provision for a Cabernet-Lagrein blend. As a varietal it may be a full-bodied red ('Scuro' or 'Dunkel') or a rosé ('Rosato' or 'Kretzer'). The sub-denomination 'di Gries' or 'Grieser' may be added if it comes from the Bolzano suburb of that name. Indeed, the best wines come from vineyards planted on the outskirts of the city, in or near the classic sub-zone of Gries, where the terrain is an alluvial mix of gravel and sand, ideal for big-but-balanced red wines.

C.S. **Gries**. Founded in 1908, in the heart of a busy metropolitan suburb, this cooperative, which processes grapes from some 190 hectares of vineyard has, like so many in South Tyrol, chosen the way of quality, not flinching at the necessity of spending on modern technology in order to reap excellent results. Production is divided in three categories corresponding to three levels of quality – basic, middle (the Serie Collection) and top (Prestige). Even at the 'Collection' level they make a fine Lagrein Scuro in the form of *cru* Barone Carl Eyrl. The top wine, understandably, is however the *barrique*d Prestige Riserva, in which the bitter tannins which can make Lagrein seem quite rough on the back-palate are transformed into aromas of coffee and dark chocolate, underlying the abundance of plummy fruit. C.S. Gries also make a nifty Merlot Siebeneich in the Prestige line and an interesting *barrique*-aged Lagrein/Merlot blend.

Cantina Convento **Muri-Gries**. Virtually across the street from the secular winery is the holy one, whose cellars lie underneath the church of the convent. The building goes back to the eleventh century, it has been used as a monastery for nearly six centuries (previously by Augustinians) and has been occupied by its present tenants, the Benedictine monks originally of Muri, in Switzerland, since 1845. They have been making wine mainly for sale in bulk to Switzerland since their inception, but in the last twenty years or so the emphasis has been on fine bottled product, with Lagrein, which occupies about a third of their 30 hectares of vineyard, in the principal role.

Muri-Gries make three styles of Lagrein: a fresh, full-flavoured Kretzer (rosé), a Dunkel (dark) Gries, and a Riserva called Abtei Muri. The Kretzer is one of the best of its type in South Tyrol and indeed one of Italy's best rosé wines, Lagrein being well suited to this style because of its abundance of anthocyanins which eliminates the need for prolonged maceration, which might bring harsh tannins into play. The Dunkel, aged in traditional *botti*, is a dark, brooding wine, with firm tannins overlain in good years by an abundance of fruit. The Abtei Muri, which *kellermeister* Christian Werth refines in *barrique*, is a wine of greater roundness and elegance than its partner, full of soft blackberry fruit with a backdrop of ripe tannins.

C.S. **Santa Maddalena**. See under Schiava, below.

Other good to excellent producers of Alto Adige Lagrein Scuro include: C.S. **Andriano** (Tor di Lupo), Andriano; **Gojer** (Glögglhof Riserva), Bolzano; **Kossler**, Appiano; **Martini & Sohn** (Maturum; Ruslhof), Cornaiano; Josephus **Mayr** (Riserva), Cardano; Thomas **Mayr** (Selezione), Bolzano; **Niedermayr** (Riserva Gries), Cornaiano; **Niedrist** (Berger Gei, Gries), Cornaiano; Heinrich **Plattner**, Bolzano; Hans **Rottensteiner** (Riserva Select, Gries), Bolzano; **Thurnhof**, Bolzano; **Tiefenbrunner** (Castel Turmhof), Niclara; **Viticoltori A. Adige** (Pischlhof), Appiano; Clemens **Waldthaler** (Raut), Ora.
  Of the above, reliable Lagrein Kretzer can be obtained from C.S. Gries (Baron Carl Eyrl); Thomas Mayr; Hans Rottensteiner; C.S. Santa Maddalena.

South of Salorno the DOC for Lagrein is Trentino. But while the grape's name may hint at origins south of Trento, what there is of Trentino Lagrein – much less than in Alto Adige – is almost entirely to be found north of Trento, playing second fiddle to Teroldego. Representative producers include:

TRENTINO LAGREIN SCURO: **Barone de Cles**, Mezzolombardo; **Cooperativa Rotaliana**, Mezzolombardo.
TRENTINO LAGREIN ROSATO: **Dorigati**, Mezzocorona.

SCHIAVA

Meaning 'female slave' in Italian, the grape variety most planted in the Alto Adige may have Slavic (precisely, Slavonian) origins, although the name for the grape in Germany, Trollinger, suggests a Tyrolean provenance. This would be supported by the name used in German-speaking South Tyrol, where it is known as Vernatsch, comparable with Italian Vernaccia, indicating a local grape variety. In other words South Tyroleans look upon Schiava as 'our own home-grown grape'. Another interpretation of the origin of the name relates to an early system of training involving binding or 'enslaving' the canes, as distinct from allowing them their natural freedom.

Records of vines of the Schiava family go back at least to the thirteenth century. It is in fact quite a numerous family, the members of which are not necessarily even related by blood, as it were, as distinct from adoption. It consists of several sub-varieties (if indeed they're not different varieties) including Schiava Grigia (Grauvernatsch), followed in quality terms by Schiava Gentile (Kleinvernatsch; possibly also Mittervernatsch) and Schiava Grossa (Grossvernatsch). Despite its weakness of structure or perfume, the big-producing Schiava Grossa was the one most planted in the mid-twentieth century to satisfy a seemingly inexhaustible Germanic thirst which in the 1980s did, however, begin to exhaust itself, leaving many growers in a quandary. Today Schiava production, in South Tyrol as in Trentino, remains vast although on the decline, and the decline will doubtless continue unless more serious quality wine is made from the superior sub-varieties (or varieties). That having been said, even a better Schiava, like Grauvernatsch for example, is dull compared with a grape of real character and presence like Lagrein. If I say that the height of Schiava's ambitions is decent mediocrity, I do so truly in the hope if not the expectation that someone some day will prove me wrong.

The most famous Schiava DOC in quality terms is Santa Maddalena (St Magdalener), which comes from vineyards on the outskirts of Bolzano, more notable for their exquisitely sloping beauty than for the quality of their wine. With a judicious dollop of Lagrein or Pinot Nero in it, Santa Maddalena can be quite pleasant, though rarely (never, in my experience) exciting. The oldest part of the vineyard is called Classico (Klassisch). Equally well known in the Germanic world is Lago di Caldaro (Kalterersee), of which there is reputedly a great deal more in labelled bottle form than there are vineyards to support such production. Great expectations should not be raised by the sighting of descriptives like Scelto (Auslese) or Classico (Klassisch) on the label.

Various other Schiava-based DOCs exist in Trentino-Alto Adige, including Casteller, Sorni Rosso and Valdadige Rosso. In Lombardy it pops up as part of the blend of Botticino, Cellatica and Garda Bresciano Rosso (whoopee!).

An excellent producer who also happens to be, by the very nature of its establishment, a Schiava specialist, is:

C.S. **Santa Maddalena**, Bolzano. This cooperative was founded in 1930 and still occupies its somewhat cramped position near the middle of the city of Bolzano, not that far, however, from where the mountain rises with its splendid steep canopy of vines. This has been a viticultural paradise for centuries, the only shame being that in recent years the vines have been mainly Schiava Grossa rather than something more valid. Insofar as excellent Schiava is not a contradiction in terms, however, the winery produces it, in the form of *crus* Huck am Bach and Stieler. Both are blended with a bit of Lagrein for added colour and body, and while neither has much substance the Huck am Bach has at least the benefit of lashings of ripe fruit and a pleasant creamy texture (practically no tannins). For some reason Oz Clarke's description 'banana yoghurt' comes to mind.

With grapes of real character, however, winemaker Stefan Filippi can do *much* better. His Lagrein Taberhof displays amazing density of extract, with fruit successfully covering structure (the 1997, indeed, is positively mind-blowingly concentrated). Cabernet Mumelterhof, a back-to-back Tre Bicchieri winner in 1994 and 1995, has the same density and depth and, lacking any greenness of aroma, almost comes nearer to ripe coffee-chocolatey Lagrein in style than it does to herbaceous or brambly Cabernet. His whites are impressive too, led by a distinctly varietal Sauvignon Mockhof, followed by a *barriqued* Chardonnay Kleinstein of beautifully ripe fruit and nicely judged alcohol/acid structure, capped by a rich, perfumed Gewürztraminer from a vineyard planted to *spalliera* with Alsatian clones – a wine, indeed, that would not fear inclusion in an Alsatian line-up.

Other representative producers of Schiava (I had almost forgotten) include:

SANTA MADDALENA/CLASSICO: Gojer (Rondell); C.S. Gries (Maso Trögler); Josef Mayr (Unterganznerhof); Hans Rottensteiner (Premstallerhof); **Waldgries**, Bolzano.

LAGO DI CALDARO/CLASSICO SUPERIORE/SCELTO: C.S. **Caldaro** (Pfarrhof), Caldaro; Niedermayr (Ascherhof); **Erste & Neue** (Leuchtenberg), Caldaro; **Schloss Sallegg** (Bischofsleiten), Caldaro.

ALTO ADIGE SCHIAVA GRIGIA: C.S. **Andriano**, Andriano; C.S. **Cortaccia** (Sonnentaler), Cortaccia; **Kossler**, Appiano.

ALTO ADIGE SCHIAVA: C.S. **San Michele Appiano** (Pagis), Appiano.

ALTO ADIGE MERANESE: C.S. **Burggräfler** (Schickenburg), Marlengo.

MOSCATO ROSA

One of the great moments of my vinous career was my first encounter with Rosenmuskateller, in Bolzano, years ago. The experience is recorded in *Life Beyond Lambrusco*, pages 185–7, and at the request of my editor I précis it here.

> It was getting near the end of the tasting and the white table-cloth was littered with scores of tasting-glasses, mostly containing light red fluid, this being the predominant colour of wines of that area. Most recently we had been trudging through a selection of (to me) indifferent Schiavas of one denomination or another, and I was getting rather bored. More pink-red wines were set before me. Desultorily, expecting nothing, I brought one of them to my nose.
>
> Instantly, bells began clanging in the olfactories. My God! What was this? It smelt like roses. Yes, pure, real, fresh, sweet, Nature's own roses. I brought it to my lips. Nectar! Surely I had been transported out of this humdrum hotel with its hundreds of wine-swillers into some other-worldly Elysium! This Rosenmuskateller was sweet, it was rich, it was perfumed, it was concentrated, it was forceful, it was discreet, it was complex, it was divine! I had never tasted anything like it and almost had difficulty in accepting that it was natural wine.

Certainly the variety is aptly named, its scent being unmistakably that of roses. If someone sticks a glass under your nose and says: 'You're an expert – what's that?' (a nightmare experience which occurs all too frequently), the best grape it can happen with is Moscato Rosa.

There seems to be a great lack of knowledge as to where it comes from – some say from Sicily, some from Dalmatia; more probably the latter, via Venice. The first mention of it in ampelographical literature appears as late as 1913, referring to a wine in Istria. These days the usually – but not invariably – sweet wine, from late-harvested grapes, is more often found in Alto Adige and Trentino, each of which make provision for the varietal under their multi-DOC. In Friuli it is DOC under the Isonzo heading, though it is found in other parts. Occasionally it crops up elsewhere in Italy (Tuscany, Latium). Wherever you find it it is in short supply – an addendum to the list rather than its central focus (like how often do you want to drink sweet alcoholic rose-essence?)

One winery which is as well known for its Moscato Rosa as for any other wine it produces is Franz **Haas,** of Montagna in South Tyrol. The *azienda* was already over 100 years old when, in the 1980s, the current Franz Haas decided to upgrade viticulturally and technologically with the aim of becoming one of the major forces among private producers in the burgeoning Alto Adige. Since that time, right up to the present and doubtless on into an undefined future, Franz and his oenologist Martin Abraham have engaged in a flurry of improvements, experiments, new plantings (featuring *guyot*-trained vines with up to 12,500 plants per hectare), new varieties (including Pinot Nero from Burgundian clones), Syrah, Merlot, Cabernet and Petit Verdot from French clones, Sauvignon, Petit Manseng, Sémillon, Tempranillo, even – perhaps most unexpected of all, because so close yet hitherto so ignored in Alto Adige – Teroldego, as well as the more predictable Pinots Bianco and Grigio, Chardonnay and Gewürztraminer. So far his greatest success has probably been with Merlot, his soft, attractively fruity version being one of the best to emerge from the Alto Adige in the modern era. His greatest efforts, doubtless, and longest sleepless nights, have been poured into Pinot Nero, long a stalwart on this side of the mountain but never before subjected to so many trials; his efforts have been rewarded by a 1995 *cru* Schweizer, complex of aroma yet approachable of palate, which might almost have sprung from the Côtes de Beaune. Another speciality is his developing white IGT Mitterberg Manna, a blend of Riesling, Traminer, Chardonnay, Pinot Bianco and Sauvignon (Sauvignon, incidentally, does not work as a pure varietal on the east side of the mountain, and he will be abandoning it).

As for the Moscato Rosa, it comes rather as an afterthought, almost as if he is saying: this one is too easy. He sticks it under my nose, blind of course, but there's no mistaking it: great waftings of rosewater, a sweet, flowery, almost syrupy palate, saved by a firm line of acidity. I am inclined to agree with the pundits who declare Haas's the best Moscato Rosa in South Tyrol today.

Other good examples of Alto Adige Moscato Rosa include:

Erste & Neue; Schloss Sallegg (authors of the wine in the experience mentioned above, now coming back to glory after a lean period); Heinrich Plattner; Tiefenbrunner; Elena **Walch** (Kastelatz), Termeno.

TRENTINO MOSCATO ROSA: **Endrizzi**, San Michele all'Adige; **Gaierhof**, Rovere della Luna; **Istituto Agrario**, San Michele all'Adige; **Letrari**, Nogaredo.

FRIULI: Marco Felluga; **Jermann** (Vigna Bellina), Farra d'Isonzo.

TEROLDEGO

The grape Teroldego is said by some to have come up the Adige Valley from the Veronese in the nineteenth century, and evidence is put forward in the form of the similarly named Teroldico which grows still in a tiny volume in the province of Verona, especially on the banks of Lake Garda. But Pittaro and Plozner reject any affinity between Teroldego and the similar-sounding Terodola, also existent in Verona, while Cosmo and Polsinelli (Ministry of Agriculture) assure us that there is in fact no relation between the two. One might have thought that the presence of 'terol' in Teroldego indicates a Tyrolean provenance rather than a Venetan one. Whatever the case may be, today Teroldego is almost absent in South Tyrol, as it is in the Veneto, being grown virtually exclusively on the gravelly soil of the Campo Rotaliano plain in Trentino, north of Trento, from Mezzocorona down to Lavis.

Teroldego is called the 'prince' of Trentino red wines, prized for its elegance, complexity and harmony. Overcropped, as it too often is, it can be very ordinary, at best a pleasant wine for early drinking. But in the hands of a quality producer it can reach impressive

VIGNETO SGARZON

TEROLDEGO ROTALIANO
DENOMINAZIONE DI ORIGINE CONTROLLATA

IMBOTTIGLIATO ALL'ORIGINE DALLA
AZIENDA AGRICOLA FORADORI   12,5 vol.
MEZZOLOMBARDO (TN) ITALIA   750 ml ℮

heights of breeding and concentration. The only DOC is the varietal Teroldego Rotaliano, which may be Rosso, Rosato or Superiore, the latter qualifying as Riserva after two years' ageing.

These days the undisputed top producer of Teroldego is Elisabetta **Foradori** of Mezzolombardo. Scion of a family with deep roots in this part of the world (her uncle is Paolo Foradori of Hofstätter in Alto Adige), Elisabetta studied agronomy at the Institute of San Michele all'Adige. Her father having died prematurely, she assumed with her mother the running of the family estate at an early age. Having to learn as she went, she began experimenting with *barrique* to tame the toughness of the Teroldego tannins, in which she was getting increasing concentration thanks to low yields, both per hectare and especially per plant, having made the important viticultural decision to train her vines by the *spalliera* system, with high density per hectare, coupled with rigorous *diradamento*.

Apart from a highly rated Teroldego Rotaliano *normale*, Elisabetta produces two DOC *crus* – Vigneto Sgarzon and Vigneto Morei. Her *capolavoro,* however, is the *barrique*d Granato, a wine which in many people's view has raised Teroldego to the highest level internationally. In fact, although she persists in her deep commitment to the Teroldego grape, Elisabetta is increasingly experimenting with international varieties like Syrah (*cru* Ailanpa), Cabernet Sauvignon, Merlot and Petit Verdot (for the blend of *cru* Karanar).

Other good producers of Teroldego, all based north of Trento, include: Barone de Cles (Maso Scari); **Conti Martini** (Le Razli), Mezzocorona; Dorigati (Diedri), Mezzocorona; C.S. **Lavis** (Ritratto – blended with Lagrein); Cooperativa Rotaliana (Riserva); **Sebastiani**, Lavis.

MARZEMINO

Blessed with numerous synonyms, including Berzamino (by which name it is referred to in early texts), Marzemino is the only member of a fairly extensive family of grapes to have survived in any volume, others having disappeared for lack of character or inability to resist cryptogamic attacks. The variety has been grown in north-eastern Italy since at least the sixteenth century; it is mentioned by Agostino Gallo in 1569 in his *Le Vinti Giornate dell'Agricoltura*. Today it is most intensively cultivated in Trentino's Vallagarina, though it may be found playing supporting roles in several red wines of the North East, not least in Veneto where it appears in DOC form in Colli di Conegliano Rosso (as part of a blend), Refrontolo Passito and Garda Orientale. It also has a certain presence in the province of Brescia in Lombardy.

As a wine, Marzemino is most famous for having been described by Mozart's Don Giovanni, on the brink of falling into everlasting damnation, as '*eccellente*'. Certainly it did enjoy a devoted following in Austria – still does to some extent. The wine may be anything from light and herbaceous to fairly full-bodied and structured.

In Trentino its principal manifestation is as a varietal under the regional multi-DOC. There is no producer today, as far as I am aware, whose wine may be described as '*eccellente*', but then even a hamburger might be delicious if your next stop is hell. The following are capable of providing worthy examples: **Cavit** (Terrazze della Luna), Trento; **Concilio Vini** (Monografie), Volano; **De Tarczal**, Isera; **La Cadalora** (M. della Vallagarina), Ala; **Letrari**, Nogaredo; **Simoncelli**, Rovereto; Enrico **Spagnolli**, Isera.

OTHER GRAPES OF THE NORTH EAST

Other, rather obscure, red grapes of the region include Veneto's **TOCAI ROSSO** (according to some derived, like the Rhône's Grenache and Sardinia's Cannonau, from the Spanish Garnacha). This variety makes rather wishy-washy light reds in Veneto's Colli Berici (doesn't sound like Spanish Garnacha, does it). Then there's **INCROCIO MANZONI 2.15** (Prosecco × Cabernet Sauvignon), an optional part of the blend of Colli di Conegliano Rosso. The **REBO,** of Trentino, is a Merlot × Marzemino whose exponents include **Maso Solengo** at Volano and Dorigati at Mezzocorona. Lambrusco a Foglia Frastagliata (already mentioned under Lambrusco, probably unrelated to the Emilian sub-varieties), is grown mostly in the southern section of Trentino and used in the blend for the Schiava-based Casteller.

Grapes, wines and producers – white

GARGANEGA

The prolific Garganega, Italy's fifth most planted white variety, can be found in various vineyards of the North East, but its historic home is the western Veneto in the provinces of Verona and Vicenza. It is a grape of great vigour which, like its red mate Corvina, requires training on a long arm. Maturity occurs between the last third of September through to the middle of October, depending on altitude and the degree of ripeness in the grapes desired by the producer.

The first mention of this grape in literature comes in the early fourteenth century, when in Pier de' Crescenzi's *Ruralium Commodorum* we find reference to 'Garganica'. For centuries prior to this it would have fallen under the more general rubric 'Retica', which would have included other grapes of the Veronese, including black ones. That Garganega has a long tradition of high quality may come as a surprise to those who associate it with industrial plonk, but grown on the slopes where yields are self-regulating Garganega can bring forth a wine of great delicacy and finesse, not to mention versatility and durability.

Recent research suggests that Garganega is probably related to that Grecanico of presumed Greek origin so diffuse today in Sicily, from where it might have travelled to other parts of Italy and found a home from home in the hills of Verona. The theory is based on a great resemblance between the respective bunch, berry and leaf shapes, together with a similarity of aromas and wine styles. It would also explain the curious pronounciation of Garganega (Gar-**ga**-ne-ga, as Gre-**ca**-ni-co, rather than the expected Gar-ga-**ne**-ga).

THE WINES

SOAVE

Easily Garganega's most important wine is Soave, over half a million hectolitres of which are produced annually, representing almost half the DOC production of the Veneto. The wine is named after a medieval walled town of great charm which stands, dominated by its imposing castle, at the lower slopes of an intensively cultivated vineyard area rising ever upward into the hills east of Verona. It is said that the town's name derives from 'Svevi' or 'Suavi', after the Swabians who invaded Italy in the sixth century AD. Already in the fifth century, as we have seen, the minister of the king of the Longobards had in a famous letter sung the praises of both the red and the white *acinaticum* of the area, and it is thought that this was a reference to the *passito* wines today called 'Recioto di Valpolicella' and 'Recioto di Soave'.

An attempt has been made to attribute to Dante an etymological link between the name of the town of Soave and its 'nettare soave' (suave nectar), but even if Dante did pen the poem attributed to him by Pietro Zannari the name-connection is of doubtful accuracy. Dante did use the name 'Soave' in *Paradiso III*, but it was to indicate the country Swabia.

It is crucial, as already indicated, to distinguish between Soave Classico and just plain Soave, 'plain' being the *mot juste* for the wine of overproduced grapes as well as something of a pun. On the flat expanse of the *pianura* it is easy to produce the 140 quintals of grapes per hectare allowed by the *disciplinare* (with a possible 20 per cent bonus depending on the vintage); indeed it is perfectly possible to churn out 200 quintals plus, and many do. But only on the Classico slopes behind the towns of Soave and Monteforte d'Alpone is production sufficiently limited to ensure good concentration of sugars and extract in the grapes.

Within Soave Classico there are three main styles: dry table wine, Spumante and Recioto, the last a *passito* made from semi-dried grapes, being the wine historically considered to represent the peak of Soave quality. Today the dry version is being taken increasingly seriously, especially with the gradual establishing of the *cru* sites. In 1993 the DOC regulations were altered to allow blending of up to 30% of Chardonnay and/or Pinot Bianco, as well as of the more traditional Trebbiano (supposedly Trebbiano di Soave, a relatively high-quality variety, but too often Trebbiano Toscano, despite the law), in order to give the sometimes rather thin wine some added substance. Another recent trend is the burgundy-style vinification of the wine in French *barriques*. The jury is still out as to whether Garganega on its own has the guts to stand up to oak treatment, the prevailing view being that it doesn't without the addition of Chardonnay. The word 'Superiore' indicates a higher alcohol level and a bit more ageing but not necessarily better wine.

The dry Spumante has never made any waves, and is not likely to, although there is such a thing as sparkling Recioto which can be tasty. Normally still, Recioto di Soave suffered something of a fall from grace in the period following the Second World War, but sweet wines have begun recently to make a comeback and the market seems to think there is a place for one which is not too thick or overpowering and whose clean acidity is able to overcome any cloying character the residual sugar might impart. Under the new Recioto di Soave DOCG regime the permitted yield in grapes is 9 tonnes per hectare with a yield of wine from 100 kilos of grapes of 40 per cent.

The *cru* sites are in process of being established, but among the principal ones are the following: Calvarino, Capitel Croce, Capitel Foscarino or Col Foscarin, Capitel Pressoni, Carbonare, Castellaro, Colbaraca, Col Federici, Fittà, Froscà, La Rocca, Mons Fortis, Monte Grande, Monte Tenda and Posara.

The producers

There has been something of a mini-boom in quality Soave production recently, with several individual grower-producers rising up to challenge the hegemony of the *cantine sociali*. Meanwhile the few traditionalists have been refining their methods with the help of modern technology. The producers profiled here represent the various positions occupied between *avant-garde* and old guard.

SOAVE (COMMUNE)

Cantina del Castello. Arturo Stocchetti has for the past few years been trying to coax ever better wines from his vineyards on Monte Pressoni and Monte Carniga and, vintages permitting, he has by and large been succeeding. Something of a Recioto specialist, he makes three types: unoaked, oak-matured and, most unusual and delicious of all, a version which undergoes secondary fermentation in bottle and, not being disgorged, remains on the lees until consumed.

Coffele. Owners of some of the finest vineyards in the Classico zone, on terraces high above the town of Soave, Coffele have recently expanded the production of their own wine in bottle now that young Alberto Coffele has taken over. Apart from a normal Soave Classico Superiore of good character they produce a *cru* Cà Visco of distinctly greater breeding as well as a couple of particularly well-made *spumante* wines. A *barrique*d Soave Classico and Recioto (Le Sponde) are now being added to the list.

Leonildo **Pieropan**. No producer in Italy has been more faithful and courageous than the house of Pieropan, which for three generations has suffered the gross industrialization of their precious product, quietly continuing to turn out, year after year, wines of which it was often said: 'Too good to be Soave'. With outstanding vineyards at La Rocca, behind the famous castle, and at Calvarino,

further up in the hinterland, Nino Pieropan and his wife Teresita, now being joined by their sons, not only continue, with intelligent modifications, to fly the traditionalist flag but match, quality for quality, the young turks who have risen like chest-beating Tarzans during the past ten to twenty years, claiming the 'new Soave' as their territory. Nay, Pieropan has more than matched them, for although he does not resort to Chardonnay, or Sauvignon (for his dry wines), or use *barrique* in the making of anything but sweet wines (he has, however, recently taken to fermenting his *cru* La Rocca in *tonneaux*, after which it spends a year in *botte grande*), his wines not only perform well in professional tastings but also have several times proved their ability to age amazingly, well into their second decade. Garganega!

But if his dry wines are good, his sweet wines can on occasion be exceptional. The classic one, Recioto le Colombare, a Garganega dried conventionally on *graticci*, the traditional cane or bamboo mats, until February, is a model of restraint and balance, perhaps not the type of wine that wins blind tastings, rather the type of which you actually want to drink more than one glass of. Pieropan also makes a Passito della Rocca, a blend of Sauvignon, Riesling Italico and Trebbiano di Soave dried slightly less time on *graticci*, fermented and aged in *barrique*; plus, two or three times a decade, when conditions are right, a mind-blowing *vendemmia tardiva* wine from Garganega grapes left to dry on the plant until mid-December, developing about 40 per cent noble rot.

C.S. **Soave**. From the sublime to the – enormous. With nearly 800 members working 2,500 hectares of vineyard producing a quarter of a million hectolitres of wine per year, this is one of Italy's largest and most politically active cooperatives. Founded in 1930, having shares in the huge private producer, Gruppo Italiano Vini, a supplier in bulk and bottle of many of the major *commercianti* of Verona, as well as of major importers and supermarket chains internationally, not to mention its links with other non-bottling cooperatives in the Soave zone, the establishment is on course to reach its target of controlling 80 per cent of all Soave production. Sort of reminiscent of the multi-nationals and the governments of the western world, isn't it?

Anyway, C.S. Soave, like other operations of such size, have a policy of creaming off the best of their members' production for bottling an assortment of Soave Classicos under labels which include CADÌS (**Cantina di S**oave – geddit?), PAS (Produttori Associati di Soave), Viticoltori di Soave and Rocca Sveva, this last being the restaurant line. They also produce what are not exactly single-vineyard, rather single-zone bottlings that include Fittà and Castelcerino, one good step up in quality. Considering the massive volumes they handle, and the very high average production per hectare of their members (however hard they try to get it down) the overall quality is very acceptable, and good value for money.

Viticola Suavia. The winery of Giovanni Tessari and daughters enjoys a beautiful position high in the hills behind Soave town, near the *paese* of La Fittà. They tend their vines, some of them very old, all of them on rocky, infertile soil capable of bringing forth only a fraction of the yields possible in the *pianura*, with loving care, bringing forth real Soave Classico in the form of a good *normale*, an even better *cru* Monte Carbonara, and a sound if simple Recioto La Boccara.

MONTEFORTE D'ALPONE

Roberto **Anselmi**. The name today is world famous, and the man behind the name – cigar-smoking, fast-driving, expansive Roberto Anselmi – is rightly credited with being the other major force (apart from Pieropan) behind the revival of this ancient but industrially degraded wine. While the Pieropans were against all the odds holding the fort for quality, Anselmi's father at his sizeable winery at Monteforte was churning out the volume stuff that was undermining the building's fabric. Roberto, from the moment he entered the business in 1974, began turning things round. In the vineyard, he was the first to introduce French-style viticulture – high density planting on *guyot*, low yield per plant – and worse than that, a French grape, Chardonnay. He also brought in staggered picking (ensuring ripe, healthy fruit) and *diradamento*, for which he was cursed by the old boys who hissed: 'God will punish you'. For the winery he purchased the newest technology and, most significantly, introduced (probably the first in Italy for white wine) *barriques* in which to ferment and mature certain of his *crus*.

In the beginning, and for quite a while, his father didn't like what his son was doing, but was obliged to change his tune as Roberto's policies began paying off, and they became known world-wide for the quality of their wines, sold at significantly higher (though still reasonable) prices than they ever had before. Like other revolutionaries of the new wave – Angelo Gaja, Elio Altare, Maurizio Zanella, Fausto Maculan, Marco de Bartoli – Roberto is first and foremost an inspired publicist, but like them he had to make sure before he hit the publicity trail that the product he was pushing was genuinely valid on an international level.

Today, Anselmi the pioneer is almost establishment, but the dynamism continues and the enthusiasm lives. Perhaps his most successul wine has been the *barrique*-aged Recioto I Capitelli, others having succeeded famously being the Soave Classico Capitel Foscarino and the revolutionary *barrique*-fermented Soave Classico Capitel Croce. Almost as revolutionary was his introduction, into the temple of whites, of the Cabernet Sauvignon grape, from which he makes a sleek bordeaux-style wine called Realdà.

And we'll be hearing of more new things from Anselmi before long, you may be sure of it.

Cà Rugate. Amedeo and Giovanni Rugate were for years the apple of other bottlers' eyes, providing from their ten hectares in prime positions in the communes of Monteforte and Soave some of the best grapes in the area, until – alas for the big names – they decided to vinify and bottle for themselves. Today they are seen as among the top producers with wines like Soave Classico and *cru* Monte Fiorentine, both unoaked, as well as the *barrique*-fermented Monte Alto, the latter being one of the happy few in Soave to obtain Tre Bicchieri from the *Vini d'Italia* guide.

Gini. Claudio and Sandro Gini have built on to the strong foundations of their lineage – the family have been present here since the eighteenth century – a new and far-seeing reality in the form of new vineyards (10 hectares of densely planted *guyot*-trained vines), new varieties, new small French oak and a new *cantina*.

Their wines reflect both the traditional and the modern. Soave Classico and the *cru* La Froscà are made without recourse to oak, and reflect the crisp, nutty, penetrating character typical of the genre. The Classico Superiore Contrada Salvarenza, on the other hand, while coming from old vines, is fermented in *barrique* and displays all the weight and complexity, if not the aromas, of a fine Chablis. Not many would take experiment so far in this traditionalist stronghold as to vinify three French varietals, Chardonnay

(Sorai), Sauvignon (Maciete Fumé) and, most unusual of all, Pinot Nero (Sorai Campo alle More), but Gini's success with each has been notable. Nor must we forget the excellent Reciotos Col Foscarin and Renobilis, the latter being a particularly luscious representative, still rare in northern Italy, of the botrytized style.

La Cappuccina. Pierantonio and Sisto Tessari come of a family well-established in the Soave zone, while forming a fully paid-up part of the new wave. Keen students, travellers and tasters, they have applied their accumulated knowledge to the business of wine-producing in a positive way. Their *crus* include a non-oaked version, Fontego – fresh, lightly *profumato* (scented), penetrating; and the *barrique*d San Brizio, which demonstrates that a gentle toast can harmonize with the subtle apricot and almond aromas of Garganega. A surprise is the convincingly well-defined Sauvignon. A bigger surprise is Madégo, a blend of Cabernet Sauvignon and Cabernet Franc of considerable depth, concentration and balance.

Umberto **Portinari.** The *titolare* of this small property has come up with a novel way of making white wine: cutting the fruiting cane at harvest time so that one half continues to ripen and the other, while remaining on the wire, undergoes a light external *appassimento*. The resulting Soave Vigna Albare Doppia Maturazione Ragionata is unique, full of colour, rich of extract, but with a fine vein of acidity running through the middle; at once, a thinking man's Soave, and a delicious drink. *Crus* Vigna Albare (without double maturation) and Ronchetto are more typical of the genre, clean, elegant and subtle.

Fratelli **Pra.** Brothers Graziano and Sergio Pra form the ideal double act, Sergio being a dedicated vineyard man while Graziano displays a canny technique in the *cantina*. They do not go in for fireworks, but rather aim to produce the finest expression of Garganega from the 20 or so hectares of vineyard they possess or lease. Their Soave Classico is, indeed, one of the classic expressions of the genre year after year, while *cru* Monte Grande (the non-oaked one) brings an extra complexity and structure to the equation. They also make a *barrique*d *cru* Sant'Antonio. Currently they are demonstrating their faith in Garganega as distinct from trendier French varieties, by planting five new hectares to the variety on the Ponsara slope of Monte Foscarino. A small section will also be reserved for the real

Trebbiano di Soave, as distinct from the much inferior Trebbiano di Toscana previously planted by growers in the interests of volume.

SAŇ BONIFACIO

Inama. Stefano Inama is a young man with big ideas. Fortunately for him he has behind him one of the biggest prime-site vineyards in private hands in the Soave Classico area, his father having intelligently purchased, in the 1960s when land was cheap, 25 hectares on Monte Foscarino (Soave Classico's most famous *cru*, thanks to Anselmi) plus a further 5 in other parts. Stefano's work-experience in California has prepared him mentally for taking on the traditions of his homeland, and he is already part-way into a programme that will see all of his vineyards replanted to *cordone speronato* in the next few years. Stefano has made a speciality of Sauvignon, producing no less than three versions (unoaked, oaked, *vendemmia tardiva*), of which the oaked version, Vulcaia Fumé, has in particular won him some rave reviews (on the other hand, early trials on the oaked dry white were catastrophic). Raves have also come his way for Soave Classico Superiore Vigneto Du Lot and Vigneti di Foscarino. Nor has his *barrique*d Chardonnay, Campo dei Tovi, failed to move the pundits to high praise.

Others making Soave which is decent to good, if rarely at the level of most of the those mentioned above from small growers, include large-scale *aziende* or *commercianti*, generally situated outside the area, like Bertani (Le Lave), Bolla (Castellaro), Paolo Boscaini (Monteleone), Guerrieri Rizzardi (Costeggiola), Masi (Col Baraca), Montresor (Classico), Pasqua/Cecilia Beretta (Case Vecie), Tedeschi (Vigneto Monte Tenda), Zeni (Vigne Alte).

OTHER GARGANEGAS OF THE VENETO

VALPOLICELLA

There is little tradition of white wine production in most of Valpolicella, but that doesn't mean there isn't any white wine produced. Such as there is is likely to be based on Garganega, or contain it somewhere in the blend, although Chardonnay and Sauvignon are making inroads here too. These days dry whites would come under the multi-DOC Garda, the range of whose sub-sub-DOCs we have considered earlier. Good dry whites do exist, but sweet *passiti* tend to outstrip them in terms of absolute quality. Outstanding examples include Allegrini's Fiorgardane, Bussola's Peagnà and Tedeschi's Vin de la Fabriseria.

GAMBELLARA

This, like Soave, is the name both of a village and of a DOC; indeed, it is a virtual extension into the province of Vicenza of the Soave district. The *disciplinare* more or less mirrors that of its more famous neigbour, with a *normale* and a Recioto as well as Recioto Spumante. Of interest is the fact that Gambellara still recognizes, as DOC, a 'Vin Santo', which in effect is what sweet wine from raisined white grapes used to be called in these parts up to a century ago. The difference would be in the degree of drying, the grapes for Recioto being lightly dried, those for Vin Santo receiving a more radical *appassimento*.

The genre is dominated by the giant **Zonin**, owners of numerous sizeable estates in five regions of northern and central Italy, whose headquarters are in Gambellara where, at their Il Giangio estate, they make Gambellara Classico, Recioto di Gambellara still and sparkling, plus a *barrique*d Cabernet Sauvignon/Merlot blend called Berengario. They also have a *podere*, a small farm, at Negrar in Valpolicella Classico called Il Maso, where they make Valpolicella Classico and Amarone.

Luigino **Dal Maso** (Cà Cischele), of Montebello, and **La Biancara** (Gambellara Superiore La Sassaia; Recioto di Gambellara and Pico dei Laorenti, a *barrique*d Garganega) are the only other significant producers in Gambellara that I know of.

In COLLI BERICI the wine of the grape is called Garganego, one producer whose wine is at least correct, if little more, being C.S. **Colli Vicentini** at Montecchio Maggiore.

COLLI EUGANEI Bianco is a complex wine based on Garganega. Notable producers include: **Borin** (Vigna dei Mandorli), Monselice; **Cà Lustra**, Faedo di Cinto Euganeo; and especially **Vignalta** (Marlunghe Bianco), of Arquà Petrarca.

TREBBIANO DI SOAVE/DI LUGANA

For general remarks on the Trebbiano family of grapes see Central Italy, Volume II.

The sub-variety Trebbiano di Soave, a.k.a. Trebbiano di Lugana or Trebbiano Veronese, is sufficiently distinctive, in the context of Trebbiano generally, to be considered independently. Despite its name, it is a minor component of the Soave *uvaggio*, vastly superior in quality and lower in productivity to the Trebbiano Toscano which, via the Trojan horse of a name, is today far more widely planted in the Soave zone than growers will admit. Trebbiano di Soave ripens slightly earlier than Garganega, making it a particularly important component in a difficult year.

LUGANA

The only area where this Trebbiano shines on its own is at the southern tip of Lake Garda, where it is the only grape used in the making of Lugana (from Latin *lucus*: a wood, wooded area). There is evidence to suggest that this Trebbiano, planted here since about the end of the nineteenth century, is a version of the Marche's Verdicchio, with the quality of which it would indeed appear to be more closely related than to that of the very ordinary Trebbiano Toscano. Two outstanding Lugana producers are:

Cà dei Frati, Sirmione. This winery technically finds itself in the region of Lombardy, but since they are Lugana specialists and since Lugana is to all intents and purposes one of the Verona family of wines, we will consider them here.

Igino, Franco and Anna Maria dal Cero, with the enthusiastic support of their parents, have turned this at-first-view unprepossessing property, whose vineyards are all on the flat near the southern tip of Lake Garda, into one of the most perfect *boutique* estates in the land. The vineyards are tended with meticulous attention and the *cantina*, which winemaker Igino built up section by section over several years as and when they could afford it, is a model of intelligent design, advanced technology and impeccable hygiene. On their 20 or so hectares of vineyard they produce an unoaked Lugana I Frati of so much character you wonder whether it could really be a pure Trebbiano, plus a superior *cru* Brolettino which spends a few months in new and second-passage *barrique*, and a fresh, light rosé called Garda Bresciano Chiaretto. The range is completed by the white blend Pratto (Trebbiano di Lugana, Chardonnay and Sauvignon), the red blend Ronchedone (Cabernet Franc, Cabernet Sauvignon and Merlot) and the sweet Tre Filer (as

Pratto, but *vendemmia tardiva*), all three receiving *barrique* treatment, all wines to be proud of, as the dal Ceros plainly are, puffing
up visibly if modestly as you praise their babies. The only blight on
the property – not from their point of view, but from that of
would-be exporters with a large requirement of wine – is the huge
number of Italian, Austrian and German tourists who swarm here-
abouts in summer, buying up all the Cà dei Frati wines they can
carry home. I would too, in their place.

Zenato, Peschiera del Garda, *frazione* San Benedetto di Lugana.
This medium-large family operation has built up quite a reputation
for itself over the years as a quality *commerciante*. The reputation
is founded mainly on the astute purchasing acumen and unerring
palate for selection and blending of *paterfamilias* Sergio, whose
function it is to seek out gems in the various sectors of the Veronese
vineyard. His success has even been crowned by the accolade of the
Tre Bicchieri for the Amarone aptly named Sergio Zenato. Another
Valpolicella with which he consistently scores is the *ripasso* which
they call Ripassa, a neat way of getting round the problem discussed above (see page 165).

But their pride and joy is their own estate in the Lugana area,
Santa Cristina. Here they grow the Trebbiano grapes which go into
their *cru* Lugana, as well as Cabernet Sauvignon and Chardonnay
which get the full bordeaux and burgundy treatment respectively.
Sergio's children Alberto and Nadia have now entered enthusiast-
ically into the business, ensuring both continuity and even
improvement over the coming decades.

Others capable of turning out good Lugana are: Montresor (Lis-
sara Vecchia); **Ottella** (Le Creete), Peschiera del Garda; **Tenuta
Roveglia** (Vigne di Catullo), Pozzolengo; **Visconti** (Sant'Onorata),
Desenzano del Garda.

PROSECCO

Some maintain that this is originally a native of Friuli, specifically
from around the village called Prosecco on the Slovenian border
(where today the wine is called Glera). Others say it came from the
Colli Euganei near Padua, where it is known as Serprino. Still others consider there is too little hard evidence either way to make
pronouncements. Whatever is the truth, Prosecco has been planted

in Treviso province, north of Venice, at least since the early nine-teenth century, and has been the major presence in the area since the end of the nineteenth century. From that time, indeed, it has been used mainly for the production of fully or lightly sparkling wines, for which there was and is a ready market in the bars of nearby Venice.

Prosecco lends itself well to the sparkling mode, being light of body, not particularly rich in sugar, having highish acidity and clean fresh primary aromas which, like the family of Pinot grapes, marry well with the yeasty perfumes arising from secondary fermentation. It is a late ripener – generally not coming to full maturity until mid- to late October. In times past, this meant a slow winter fermentation, and wines that naturally maintained a certain sparkle and often a certain residual sugar.

But it was a certain Cavaliere Carpenè, oenologist of the oenological society of the province of Treviso, who adapted champagne techniques to the making of Prosecco in the late nineteenth century, bringing method to what was previously a haphazard operation.

Today the vast majority of Prosecco di Conegliano/Valdobbiadene is dry or off-dry (although the sweeter styles are recognized) and is made by the *charmat* method – the best undergoing that prolonged contact with the lees (*charmat lungo*) which can turn it from a rather ordinary sparkler into one which can have the kind of yeastiness and creaminess one associates with champagne. Most of it is fully sparkling, and as such has been a firm favourite with Venetians and other Italians for decades. However, for tax avoidance and other marketing reasons there is today an increasing quantity of *frizzante* wine, which arguably lends itself better to the style of the grape as well as being more traditional. Only a tiny proportion of total production is still, although it can be the most interesting.

Though among the top thirty grape varieties of Italy in terms of hectares planted, those hectares are almost all to be found in the the zones of Valdobbiadene and Conegliano in the province of Treviso, and in that of Colli Euganei in the province of Padua (mainly in the blend of Colli Euganei Bianco). Most of the establishments authorized to carry out the process of *spumantizzazione* are in or around Valdobbiadene. It is also from the commune of Valdobbiadene, in the sub-zone called Cartizze, that what are considered the best grapes are grown. The sub-denomination Superiore di Cartizze indicates a wine from this area having a slightly higher alcoholic degree.

Over the past twenty-five years or so Prosecco's popularity has really taken off. Between the early 1970s and the late 1990s plantings in the DOC zone almost tripled to around 3,500 hectares, and production almost quintupled to around 30 million bottles, of which something over a million are Cartizze. The home market is still by far the most important, but the Germanic lands are guzzling increasing quantities. In Anglo-Saxon countries, on the other hand, sales have never risen very far off the ground.

The best Proseccos I have tasted have been from small artisanal producers who as often as not leave the wine on the lees in bottle. Unfortunately these wines are rarely commercially available. Of the establishment producers among the best are the following:

VALDOBBIADENE

You could get quite confused by the Ruggeris and the Bisols of Valdobbiadene. There's the firm of **Angelo Ruggeri**, who turn out a good Spumante Brut as well as Prosecco di Valdobbiadene (Dry Funer, Funer being the name of a particularly prized site) and Cartizze; then there's **Le Colture**, run by Cesare and Renato Ruggeri, who also do a Prosecco di Valdobbiadene Dry Funer as well as a very good Extra Dry and an unusual still wine, Tranquillo Masarè. The firm of Desiderio **Bisol**, one of the best known, make Cartizze and a range of sparklers under the Prosecco di Valdobbiadene DOC (Dry Garnei, Dry Salis, Extra Dry Colmei, Brut Crede, Extra Dry Vigneti del Fol); and **Ruggeri & C.**, today run by Paolo Bisol, having been founded in 1950 by Giustino Bisol after whom one of their top *crus*, Giustino B., is named; it used to be called Giustino Bisol, written right out, but presumably the other Bisols objected, the two firms being rivals for the top spot here, one (Bisol) having taken Tre Bicchieri in 1997 for their Dry Garnei, the other (Ruggeri & C.) winning the same accolade the same year with their Dry Santo Stefano, as well as awards for their Cartizze and their Tranquillo.

Other good producers based in Valdobbiadene include: **Bortolin; Canevel; Col Vetoraz; San Eurozia di Geronazzo; Tanorè;** and C.S.

Valdobbiadene. In the commune of Conegliano recommended producers include: **Bernardi**; the historic **Carpenè Malvolti**; and **Zardetto**. And in the commune of Vidor: **Adami**; **Bronca**; **De Faveri**.

VESPAIOLO

This variety is also known as Vespaiola and Vesparola, under which latter name it first appears in print, in the *Bullettino Ampelografico* of 1881. It is so called because the wasps (*vespe*) are particularly drawn to the sweet ripe grapes at vintage time and during the subsequent drying period. In the past it is said to have thrived, or at least to have been present, in the provinces of Alessandria in Piemonte, Siena in Tuscany and Chieti in Abruzzo, although it seems to have practically disappeared in all three. Today it is virtually confined to the Breganze area of central Veneto, where it makes a light, acidic, non-aromatic white of some character under the umbrella of the Breganze multi-DOC. Far more important than the dry version, however, are the sweet ones, either from *passito* grapes, called Torcolato, or from late-harvested ones which have contracted noble rot.

The most famous producer of Torcolato, by far, is **Maculan** (see under Cabernet, page 241). Maculan goes one step further than mere *passito* with his Yquem-like Acini Nobili; berry-selected, late-harvested once the noble rot has struck, it is one of Italy's outstanding dessert wines. The only other producer of note, making both dry table wine and Torcolato, is the cooperative **Beato Bartolomeo da Breganze.**

MOSCATO GIALLO

(For general notes on the Moscato family of grapes see under Piemonte, page 122).

The only place where Moscato Bianco is grown in the North East is in Veneto's Colli Euganei, whose multi-DOC provides for a product made along the lines of Moscato d'Asti, although the provision is not much reflected in fact. More interesting here and throughout the North East is Moscato Giallo (Goldmuskateller), the wines from which are sometimes called, particularly in the Colli Euganei, Fior d'Arancio or Fior d'Arancio Passito. These tend to be sweet and perhaps sparkling, and can give out a really pungent flower-cum-citrus aroma.

Both the Trentino and the Alto Adige multi-DOCs provide for a Moscato Giallo varietal, which may be dry or sweet but which is, in either case, redolent of orange blossom (*fior d'arancio*). The dry Goldmuskateller of Tiefenbrunner is an excellent example. Thurnhof in Bolzano produce another good example, as well as a *passito* from Moscato Giallo, Chenin Blanc and botrytis-affected Riesling, called Passaurum. In Trentino producers of good dry Moscato Giallo include **Bolognani** at Lavis, Conti Martini and **Maso Roveri** at Avio.

An excellent sweet wine, variously called Sud, Due Cuori, and perhaps other names in future, is produced by **Le Vigne di San Pietro.** As has been mentioned earlier, this producer, based at Sommacampagna near Lake Garda in Veneto, is in Bardolino country, but excels rather in wines of perhaps less 'classic' typology but of greater imagination and creativity. Since, in the early 1990s, young Paolo Nerozzi took over the reins of the *azienda*, which even then was considered one of the few grower-producers of importance in the Veneto, quality has increased noticeably. This can be appreciated especially in wines like Refolà, made from slightly raisined Cabernet Sauvignon grapes, I Balconi Bianco, a example rare in Italy of good Riesling Renano, and I Balconi Rosso, a blend of the Bardolino grapes (Corvina, Rondinella, Molinara) and Cabernet Sauvignon. The wine he has been most lauded for, however, is the above-mentioned sticky, an all-too-rare example of how marvel-lously rich and complex sweet Moscato can be.

INCROCIO MANZONI 6.0.13

This is a cross between Riesling Renano and Pinot Bianco developed by Professor Giovanni Manzoni of the Istituto Sperimentale per la Viticoltura at Conegliano. Not the most poetic of names, but a grape of sufficient quality to work its way, over the past few years, into the vineyards of the Veneto, especially in the Conegliano district, where it is used primarily as an ingredient in the white blend.

A representative producer is **Le Case Bianche** of Pieve di Soligo (Colli di Conegliano Bianco Costa dei Falchi).

TOCAI FRIULANO

It may be known as Tocai Friulano, as produced in Friuli (where it is first among white grapes in volume terms), or Tocai Italico, as produced in the province of Venice in Veneto, although there is some disagreement as to whether the latter is a more productive clone of the former, or whether there is little or no relationship. Certainly, according to Cosmo and Polsinelli, it has 'nothing to do' with the Tocai Bianco of Breganze. While on the subject of rela-tionships, there is *none* with Tokay d'Alsace (a doomed synonym of Pinot Grigio) nor, in all probability, with the Furmint that informs the famous Hungarian Tokay. There *is*, on the other hand, apparently, with Sauvignon, this being (according to pundits) the Sauvignon Vert or Sauvignonasse so widespread, for example, in Chile, where, as here, its characteristics are considerably less dis-tinctive than those of the classic Sauvignon Blanc.

Tocai is included among the native varieties simply because no one quite knows where it came from, or when it arrived in Italy. All that is known is that it was present in north-eastern vineyards at the beginning of the twentieth century. Today it is widely planted not only in Friuli (nearly 2,000 hectares) and the eastern Veneto, but also in Emilia and as far south as Rome.

Large volumes of what Americans would call 'jug' wine are pro-duced from Tocai on the plains of eastern Veneto and western Friuli, but all the serious stuff, with a few exceptions, comes from the eastern Friuli on the Slovenian border (Collio, Colli Orientali del Friuli and Isonzo being the principal quality umbrella DOCs). It may be a bit of a struggle to wrest from your glass firm evidence that there is a relationship with Sauvignon, but if you give up and accept it for what it is Tocai can be quite a classy white wine, subtle of bouquet, with a combination of nuts and fresh fruit on the palate. One producer who exemplifies Tocai Friulano at its best is:

Schiopetto, Capriva del Friuli. Mario Schiopetto is still the ruling presence in Friuli wines, years after I did the research for *Life Beyond Lambrusco* in which I said the following (abridged), still all true:

> A legend in his lifetime, Schiopetto was the first in Friuli to set the standard of unrelenting quality which has brought the region, and in particular Collio and Colli Orientali, into the position of being seen as Italy's foremost white wine producer. He started his *azienda agricola* in 1967; by the 1970s his wines were causing a stir; today (mid-1980s) he is recognized by all as the doyen of Friulian wine production.
>
> Schiopetto is an unpretentious man. 'I haven't studied philosophy', he says, 'but it's inside.' 'To give expression to what Nature provides without varying it' is his goal. It follows that Schiopetto does not agree with the use of wood in the maturation of white wines. He is not happy about adding anything to wine, even sulphur dioxide, which he keeps to a minimum. Nor is he particularly in favour of technology *per se*. 'Anyone can know the technology. The important thing is sensitivity.'

That was fifteen years ago – so what has changed? Nothing, but things have been added. First, a magnificent new winery in the midst of the vineyards, a monument to rationality, hygiene and, one is bound to say, technology, if ever there was one (presumably technology is fine provided sensitivity leads). Second, the entry into his business of his sons Giorgio (*enotecnico*) and Carlo (*agronomo*) and daughter Maria Angela (Admin/PR) – necessary given the increasingly precarious condition of Mario's health. Third, the extension of the technique of hyperoxygenating the must even to red wines, in order to eliminate the need for addition of sulphur dioxide during fermentation and to reduce its use in finished wine to an absolute minimum. This is a technique he developed with Mattia Vezzola, today of Bellavista in Franciacorta, when the latter was with Seitz, the German wine-technology firm. Also in common with Bellavista they operate a yeast bank which allows them to experiment prior to the harvest with the yeasts best suited to the grape and the conditions.

And the wines? They are as good, as pure, as reliable, as numerous as ever, the range including Sauvignon, Pinots Bianco and Grigio, Malvasia, Riesling among whites, Merlot and the Cabernets (for the blend Rivarossa) among reds. But the real speciality, one can't help feeling, is the Tocai Friulano to which Schiopetto, as a Friulian, is particularly 'sensitive'. If you are only going to try one example to see what the grape is like in its purest liquid alcoholic state, this is the one.

A word of warning, however. Best to open a bottle between its third and fifth year – the process of hyperoxygenation does entail a slower development of the natural perfumes, just as it guarantees a longer life.

There are numerous good to excellent producers of Tocai Friulano, fairly equally divided between Collio and Colli Orientali del Friuli (COF), with the odd Friuli Isonzo producer thrown in. Even the twenty or so names which follow do not suffice to exhaust the list. They do, however, represent the best.

COLLIO

Borgo Conventi, Farra d'Isonzo; **Borgo del Tiglio**, Cormons; Marco Felluga; Edi **Keber**, Cormons; **Pighin**, Pavia di Udine; **Princic**, Cormons; **Russiz Superiore**, Capriva del Friuli; Franco **Toròs**, Cormons; **Villa Russiz**, Capriva del Friuli.

COLLI ORIENTALI DEL FRIULI

Adriano **Gigante**, Corno di Rosazzo; La Viarte; Davino **Meroi**, Buttrio; **Miani**, Buttrio; Paolo **Rodaro**, Cividale del Friuli; Ronco del Gnemiz; Andrea **Visintini**, Corno di Rosazzo; **Volpe Pasini**, Torreano; **Zamo & Zamo**, Manzano.

OTHER FRIULIANS

Di Lenardo (Friuli Grave), Gonars; Sergio e Mauro **Drius** (Isonzo), Cormons; Pierpaolo **Pecorari** (Isonzo), San Lorenzo Isontino.

BREGANZE

Even if the Tocai Bianco which informs Breganze Bianco DOC is not related to Tocai Friulano, this seems the appropriate place to name producers, who are only three in any case: C.S. Beato Bartolomeo da Breganze; Maculan (Breganze di Breganze); and **Vigneto Due Santi** at Bassano del Grappa.

MALVASIA ISTRIANA

For general remarks on the family of Malvasias see Central Italy in Volume II.

This is generally considered the best quality sub-variety, if the least productive, of the Malvasia family. It has probably been planted in this zone since the fourteenth century, presumably introduced by the much-travelled Venetians. Today it may be found growing throughout the region, though in small volume (some 140 hectares), its sub-DOCs including Carso, Collio, Colli Orientali, Latisana and Isonzo.

The style of its wines varies considerably according to *terroir*. Grapes grown on a poor soil will give a wine of some body and perfume, the reverse being true of wines from richer, flatter zones. In some cases it may be made *frizzante*.

Good producers include: Dario **Raccaro**, Cormons; Schiopetto; Vigne dal Leon; Villa Russiz.

RIBOLLA GIALLA

Ribule in dialect, Rebula in Slavic, this is undoubtedly a native Friulian, mentions of its existence stretching back as far as the fourteenth century. It is cultivated almost entirely on the slopes of the Collio and Colli Orientali over against Slovenia, as well as on those of the other side of the border. In the plain it does not perform well, for which reason it attains official status only under the multi-DOCs of the two areas mentioned. Even there its presence today is scarce.

The wines it influences are generally medium-weight, light, dry, non-aromatic, quite acidulous. Ribolla is an acquired taste, lacking perhaps the wealth of flavour of a good Chardonnay or Sauvignon, but having a certain racy nuttiness which combines well with traditional Friulan dishes.

Considering how little total hectarage it enjoys (under 100), there are a surprising number of good producers, apparently reflecting a greater interest among growers than among consumers. Good examples may come from the following:

Matijaz **Tercic**, San Floriano del Collio. This young ethnic Slovenian grower didn't start bottling until 1993, encouraged by and under the tutelage of Gianfranco Gallo of Vie di Romans (see under Sauvignon Blanc, page 257); before that time he, or rather his father, Zdenko, sold the grapes grown in their 5.5 hectares of vineyard (of which 2 are rented) to Puiatti. Gallo's influence shows in the concentration of flavour and sheer finesse of the mainly white wines produced (his yields per hectare, already low, are reduced further by bunch-thinning). He has not until recently used oak in the winemaking or maturation processes, but will henceforward be vinifying his Chardonnay in wood. But it is for his impressive demonstration that the unsung, unoaked Ribolla Gialla can make grown-up wine that he is to be regarded most seriously. His version is subtle and non-aromatic, clean and inviting of nose, with a dry, nutty palate which none the less manages to charm with hints of sweet honeyed fruit and a perfectly balanced acidity. A remarkable fact is that, although this sort of wine would be expected to lose its character within hours of being opened, Tercic's manages to stay fresh for days.

Other good examples may come from the following:

COLLIO: Bruno & Mario **Bastiani**, Cormons; **La Castellada**, Oslavia; **Primosic**, Oslavia; Tenuta **Villanova**, Farra d'Isonzo; Villa Russiz.
COLLI ORIENTALI DEL FRIULI: Abbazia di Rosazzo; **Cà di Bon**, Corno di Rosazzo; La Viarte; Davino Meroi; Lina & Paolo **Petrucco**, Buttrio; **Torre Rosazza**, Manzano.

PICOLIT

Because of a tendency to unsuccessful pollination of its flowers due to sterile pollen, a condition sometimes hilariously referred to as floral abortion, Picolit is a variety which gives a very low yield per hectare, so that the fruit sells at a very high price. At the same time there has, in the past twenty-five years or so, been a rich harvest of hyperbole to set against a very tiny quantity of actual liquid, which rarely turns out to be as exciting as the hype would lead us to expect.

The story, at least, is interesting. Picolit is, it appears, a genuinely Friulian variety, probably going back several centuries. Because of its pollination defect, it has come in and out of the picture, but certainly it was very 'in' in the eighteenth century when, among other mentions, there is a report by one F.M. Malvolti which informs us that it caused a great stir at the court of France. In the nineteenth century it continued to inspire writers, but in the twentieth it rather went 'out' again until the most recent re-awakening.

Picolit likes a hillside position and volcanic soil, and being such a cantankerous beast it is hardly worth planting it elsewhere. DOC-wise it appears varietally under the Collio and Colli Orientali umbrellas, as a sweet wine in both cases. The hectarage is difficult to assess, as it will generally occupy only a small section of a vineyard, but it has been estimated that there aren't much more than 25 hectares in Friuli, taking all the little pieces into account.

Picolit may indeed be vinified sweet but light, in which case it is (to my mind) not unlike a young Vouvray, which I personally would prefer if I am paying. I have, once or twice, tasted late-harvest versions which are delicious, in that their natural acidity keeps even great sweetness from being cloying. But again, I'd take a well-hung Vouvray, value for money, any time.

Probably Picolit's greatest value today is not as a varietal but as part of a blend, in which it is able to add a touch of aromatics and a nice line of fruity acidity.

One of the best producers of varietal Picolit is **Ronchi di Cialla** of Prepotto in the Colli Orientali, and it is appropriate here, I think, to consider for a moment this unusual producer.

It was in 1970 that Paolo and Dina Rapuzzi decided to chuck in the city life and install themselves in the country in search of self-sufficiency. The property they purchased was in a state of abandonment, but it offered good viticultural potential. At this point came the crucial decision, one which few producers have been so courageous (or so daft) as to hazard, to plant exclusively autochthonous Friulian varieties. The ones they chose were Picolit, Verduzzo, Refosco, followed some years later by the almost extinct (at that time) Schioppettino. As if that was not enough they decided to opt for an organic style of viticulture referred to in Italy as *lotta guidata ed integrata*, which translates rather Leninistically into 'guided and wholehearted struggle'. Another first they claim is that of being, since 1977, the first *azienda* in Italy to use *barriques* for the ageing of *all* their wines, red and white. And another struggle (they seem to have a taste for it) – that of establishing their locality, Cialla, whose viticultural roots they trace back to 1496, as a geographical sub-zone. But since 1995 their wines may be (and are) labelled, for example, 'Picolit di Cialla' under the DOC Colli Orientali del Friuli, permitted grapes being the four mentioned above plus Ribolla Gialla.

Today sons Pierpaolo and Ivan are qualified agronomists and working at the estate, which has some 15 hectares under vine. The wines produced by the family include varietals Refosco, Schioppettino, Verduzzo and Picolit, plus a white blend (Verduzzo, Ribolla Gialla and Picolit) as well as a red one, Ciallarosso, which of course is a mix of Refosco and Schioppettino. The Picolit – since that is the one we are supposed to be focusing on here – is a wine of light gold-green tints with a fruity-flowery bouquet, a moderate sweetness offset by a firm acid vein and an elegant rather than forceful palate with something of a green apple taste.

Other valid producers of Picolit Colli Orientali del Friuli are: **Cà Ronesca** at Dolegna del Collio; Livon; **Rocca Bernardi**, Premariacco; Ronchi di Manzano; Ronco del Gnemiz. But the best I've tasted is the *passito* of Dorigo, from the Montsclapade vineyard, a wine of golden colour displaying a bouquet of pure dried apricot, while the palate is rich and redolent of dried and candied fruits, with a hint of toast from the *barrique* and a firm acid finish, cutting through the sweetness. Abbazia di Rosazzo make a captivating *barrique*-aged blend, with Verduzzo, called Ronco della Abbazia.

VERDUZZO

There are two distinct and apparently unrelated varieties going under this name: Verduzzo Friulano and Verduzzo Trevigiano. The latter is said to have originated from Sardinia around the beginning of the twentieth century, and is a variety of little character whose main virtue resides in the fact that it churns out regularly impressive volumes of plonk, mainly in the Treviso province sub-DOCs of Lison Pramaggiore and Piave).

Verduzzo Friulano, on the other hand, while also extensively grown in eastern Veneto, is as indigenously Friulian as Refosco, a mention being made of it by Acerbi in his *Delle Viti Italiane* of 1825. Even here, however, there is a distinction between the Verduzzo Verde (green) which produces rather ordinary, light dry wines in plainland sites; and the Verduzzo Giallo (yellow) which yields delicious and quite complex sweet wines, especially in the hills of Colli Orientali del Friuli. One place, Ramandolo, has its own sub-zone denomination because of the particular finesse of its wines. Here there is said to exist yet another sub-variety, Verduzzo Rascie, good for sweet wines because of its loose or *spargolo* bunches.

Caveat emptor. In the context of the various Friuli sub-DOCs (all except Collio), if the label reads Verduzzo or Verduzzo Friulano then the wine may be dry or sweet, possibly *frizzante*.

Sweet Verduzzo from late-harvested grapes has the richness of body and concentration to stand up well to small-*barrique* ageing, especially, as is increasingly the practice; the grapes are also subsequently subjected to an *appassimento*. Good to excellent producers include: Dorigo; **Lis Neris – Pecorari** (Tal Luc), San Lorenzo Isontino; Livon (Casali Godia); Celestino Petrussa (Pensiero), Prepotto; Roberto **Picech** (Passito di Pradis), Cormons; Ronco del Gnemiz; Ronchi di Manzano (Ronc di Subule); Roberto **Scubla** (Graticcio), Premariacco.

La Viarte make a rich and complex Verduzzo/Picolit blend from *passito* grapes, having eighteen months' *barrique*-ageing, called Siùm.

Two producers of genuine Ramandolo, both with their winery in the town of Nimis, are: Giovanni **Dri**, long renowned for the excellence of his traditionally crafted sweet wines; and the relatively modernist Dario **Coos**, who takes specialization to the point of making, from his 5 hectares of vineyard, only two wines, both sweet Ramandolos. The one subtitled Il Longhino is made from grapes harvested in October to give more concentration to the remaining bunches, then vinified in stainless steel. There is no use of oak in the ageing process, so that the resulting wine keeps the accent on freshness of fruit. The more prized version, called, simply, Ramandolo, is made from bunches selected over the course of two or three further passages in the vineyard, generally during the first half of November. The grapes are then subjected to several days' maceration at low temperature, giving an unusually firm tannicity to the finished product. About a third of the grapes undergo a light *appassimento* on *graticci* – some fifteen to twenty days. The wine is fermented at length in a variety of oak barrels of Slavonian and French origin (2–5 hectolitres capacity), as well as in Italian acacia, and the malo-lactic fermentation begins in the spring and generally lasts right through the summer. Production is never more than 30 hectolitres per hectare, often less. As for the wine, at 8 per cent residual sugar it is obviously sweet but both tannins and a firm acidity help to prevent any cloying effect, while the perfumes are a seductive mix of the fruity (banana, fruit salad) and the subtly oak-scented.

NOSIOLA

With the possible exception of Traminer (named after a South Tyrolean village but dealt with under International Varieties, see page 286), Nosiola, surprisingly, is the only white variety of any significance that can be described as autochthonous in Trentino-Alto Adige, that region so noted for its white wines. Even then the significance is slight, Nosiola being grown virtually not at all in Alto Adige and in a very limited way in Trentino, where at least it enjoys DOC status both as a varietal and as one of the principal components of Sorrì Bianco.

First mentioned in a text of 1825, Nosiola has, probably for centuries, been a favourite among denizens of the upper Adige for quaffing in bars, soon after the harvest, its thin body, fairly neutral aromas and modest alcohol lending it to purposes of volume quaffing. Good to very good producers include: Bolognani; Concilio Vini; **Pojer & Sandri**, Faedo; **Pisoni**, Pergolese Sarche and **Pravis** (La Frate) at Lasino, these last two being in the sub-zone known as the Valle dei Laghi (Valley of the Lakes) which is probably the epicentre of world Nosiola production.

Thus it is from the Valle dei Laghi that the most interesting Nosiolas come in the form of a *passito* called Vino Santo, that sweet but not-too-cloying amber liquid which locals are inclined to offer their guests as a mid-afternoon pick-me-up, or as an occasional treat. Trentino Vino Santo has never had the cachet of the Tuscan version, and is produced in tiny quantities, but seems to be gaining a certain reputation these days. Principal producers include: Pisoni; Francesco **Poli** and Giovanni **Poli** at Santa Massenza, **Rigotti** at Padergnone, and the Cantina Sociale di **Toblino**.

III
INTERNATIONAL VARIETIES

The definition of an 'international' grape variety in the present context is one which is (a) non-native to Italy and (b) cultivated in a number of countries internationally.

Grapes like Corvina, Teroldego, Groppello or Arneis, are clearly both indigenous and limited to local production. A few, like Nebbiolo and Barbera, would qualify technically on the second count, being found to some extent cultivated internationally, but they are obviously of Italian origin.

What then of the likes of Moscato and Malvasia, which are indisputably of non-Italian origin and are widely distributed internationally? Here I am obliged to introduce a statute of limitations, according to which a variety becomes 'Italian' if it has been firmly established in a particular zone of Italy for at least two centuries; that's to say, before oidium, peronospera and phylloxera forced widespread rethinking in the vineyards. Most grapes in this category have in any case adapted themselves fully to their particular *terroir* or environment and have become as genuinely Italian as a descendant of an Italian-American family whose great-grandparents emigrated to the United States in the early nineteenth century has today become American.

Even then I find myself stuck with one or two borderline cases in order to categorize which I am going to have to pass from finesse to finagle. An example is Tocai Friulano, whose provenance is unknown (though thought to be non-Italian) and which has been linked, as we have seen, with the internationally planted Sauvignon Vert or Sauvignonasse; and which, while firmly established today in Friuli and eastern Veneto seems to have achieved this status only within the past century. Due to the vaguenesses mentioned I have included this one among the Italians.

On the other hand, I have considered as international that Riesling Italico whose name suggests Italian-ness but whose origin is certainly non-Italian and which, under names like Welschriesling or Olasz Rizling, is cultivated in various parts of eastern Europe.

Trickier still is the Traminer, which takes its name from a South Tyrolean village. But 200 years ago South Tyrol was politically as well as ethnically and linguistically (which it remains) part of the Austro-Germanic world with which Traminer, and Gewürztraminer, is properly associated. Therefore it is included among the internationals.

In *Life Beyond Lambrusco* I described Pinot Grigio as an 'honorary Italian' because of its widespread popularity – the 'home from home' – it has established in north-eastern Italy. But this is plain wrong – Pinot Grigio clearly belongs with the Pinot family of 'international' varieties.

But why make a distinction between Italian and international varieties anyway?

The prime purpose is to highlight what is both the glory of Italian viniculture and the aspect which makes her position in the world of wines today unique: the many local varieties surviving into the third millennium AD and which are capable of contributing such colour and – well – variety to the world wine scene. For this it is necessary to consider apart the varieties which do not fall into this category, and which, it must be said, are behind some of the finest wines that Italy has to offer.

Another major motive for separation resides in the fact that, while most of the Italian varieties are highly localized, the international varieties have in many cases spread themselves to several, if not all, parts of Italy. For this reason it is not convenient to consider them zonally, as it would involve too much repetition. It is however, I believe, valid to distinguish between their manifestations north and south of the Po Valley, because in most cases they have been established much longer in the north where they have taken on, for better or for worse, a certain *terroir*-linked character.

There is much debate in Italy, and among Italy-observers elsewhere, as to the merits or otherwise of planting non-Italian varieties in a land of such great native ampelographical wealth. There are those who maintain that the indigenous patrimony ought to be rigorously preserved, and that introduction of foreign grapes is the thin end of a wedge designed to undermine tradition; if it is not a plot by the French, or by francophile fifth-columnists wishing to keep Italy in its traditional subordinate role, it is a move by super-market giants and corporate monstrosities to reduce all wines of the world to a style easily recognized and glugged by the masses.

While sympathizing personally with the position which would resist the MacDonaldization or the Golden Deliciousification of the planet's vinous resources, I would defend Italy's right to cap-italize on the popularity of Cabernet, Merlot, Chardonnay, Sauvi-gnon, etc. The view that suggests Italians should refrain from making easy-to-sell wines strikes me as unfair not to say absurd; on the contrary, they should be applauded for sticking to their guns to the extent that they have.

There are two provisos to this. First, that where a strong varietal tradition still exists they should develop the internationals as a commercial sideline and not as a principal policy. I say 'still exists' because in certain areas – in many parts of the North East, for example – the take-over by the internationals already happened decades ago and there is now no turning the clock back.

And second, that insofar as they do turn to the internationals, they do it well, which in an increasing number of places they have demonstrated that they can, indeed up to the very highest level, as we shall see.

Why, after all, should the Italians be penalized for doing what everyone else in the world is doing merely because, unlike most others, they have the possibility of doing something different as well?

Of course, there are tricky areas in the middle, when it comes to blending the natives with the internationals, or using vinification techniques to bring local Italians into line with popular ideas as to how wine ought to taste. I am not disputing that Italy should be constantly upgrading the quality and value for money, indeed the modernity, of her indigenous varieties, and this is happening. But it cannot be denied that dollops of Cabernet together with Nebbiolo or Sangiovese risk bending wine styles away from pure typicity towards something which could be described as neither fish nor fowl.

There is a place for commercial wines of international style, although it is preferable that they should not masqurade as some-thing they are not. There is also a place for highly individual wines of unique and inimitable character arising from a combination of influences usually referred to as *terroir*, in which the grape variety (or varieties) plays what is arguably the principal role.

The arrival of the internationals

In 1903 there was published in Florence a learned and thoroughly researched book by Salvatore Mondini entitled *I Vitigni Stranieri da Vino Coltivati in Italia* (Foreign wine-grapes grown in Italy). This was the period when *Phylloxera vastatrix* was at full throttle chewing through the vineyards of northern Italy and indeed the whole of western Europe.

Mondini – whose definition of a 'foreign' variety accords pretty closely with the above – tells us that at the turn of the century these grapes were becoming quite diffuse in northern Italy. Faced with a choice between, on the one hand, grapes capable of delivering high yields and/or elevated sugar levels for purposes of making cutting wines (i.e., strong wines for improving weaker ones in inexpensive blends) for easy sale abroad at a period when such wines were in high demand; and, on the other hand, varieties of a quality capable of improving a blend or even of shining on their own but which were relatively low-yielding or little understood, growers perhaps understandably went in the main for the easier option. But a few were willing at least to experiment with grapes brought from the neighbouring lands (and sometime occupying powers) of France or Austria to see if they could give them greater protection from disease, or something they could plant in less favoured sites, or even a better wine. Mondini's book gives us an insight into the state of play from an early twentieth-century perspective.

It is clear that, at the time Mondini was writing, the French varieties – which were then and to an even greater extent than today the principal foreigners – had been in northern Italy for over eighty years, and winning increasing favour with collectors, wine schools and indeed growers for thirty to fifty years. A crucial role seems to have been played by the Sambuy family of Piemonte. 'It is, in fact,' writes Mondini, 'to Cav. Alfredo Bertone di Sambuy that we owe the first trial cultivation of Cabernet Sauvignon which he began, from 1820 on, in his vineyards of Valmagra, in the Marengo plain, near Alessandria.' This nobleman had apparently been struck, during a visit to the Gironde, by the similarities between the soil there and in his home territory, and had brought cuttings of Cabernet and other Bordeaux varieties home to his Piemonte estate. 'His effort was crowned by excellent success,' Mondini assures us. A few years later General Emilio di Sambuy is reported by Mondini as having introduced at his estate in the province of Cuneo the Burgundians Gamay and Pinot. What kind of success his effort was crowned with is not reported.

There is a theory which maintains that phenomena begin spontaneously and once in the 'ether', as it were, begin to spread and become common. Whether this is the case here or not it is not possible to know, but certainly from this modest snowflake a snowball began to form, and then to roll, slowly at first, then with increasing momentum.

Already in 1825, in the province of Mantua in south-east Lombardy, a certain Signor Acerbi was writing of the 900-plus foreign varieties being cultivated in his experimental nursery (400 from the Austro-Hungarian empire, the rest from a nursery of Chambéry in France). Unfortunately all other details concerning this collection have been lost. In 1852 Marchese Leopoldo Incisa of Rocchetta Tanaro, in the province of Alessandria, was cataloguing 'Cabernet, Verdot, Malbeck, Aramon, the Pinots and the Gamays' as part of his collection. Also in the 1850s the famous ampelographer di Rovasenda was at work in Cuneo, experimenting and cataloguing. Contemporaneously the French viticulturist Oudart, an early member of the roving consultant brigade, was helping several Piemontese growers in their struggle with the French varieties.

Despite all this early activity, however, the internationals never took off in Piemonte. Mondini reckons that the Piemontese were not 'sympathetic' to the imported grapes, having too many interesting varieties of their own. But commentators from Mondini's time onwards note a gradual eastward drift of the phenomenon, perhaps because the North East was always more cosmopolitan than the North West, especially taking into account the strong Austrian influence, perhaps because the native grape varieties of the Veneto (which at that time included Friuli) were with a few exceptions less interesting than those of Piemonte in particular.

In any case, the situation in 1903 was that of all the international grapes the most important in the north was 'Pinot', followed by 'Cabernet'. Merlot, the foreigner which was to become by far the most widespread of all by the end of the century, was relatively unimportant, following in the trail of Malbec, Grenache and

Syrah, and Mondini mistakenly considers it an unlikely candidate for future success.

One might, then, identify three phases in the development of international varieties in northern Italy. The first would be from about 1820 until towards the end of the nineteenth century; a period of experimentation, of 'getting to know you'. The second began with the scourge of phylloxera forcing all growers to rethink their planting policy, and lasted until after the Second World War; this was a time of trial and error, of the popular varieties establishing themselves while the others, notably those of the Germanic and Austro-Hungarian camps, but also the Rhône grapes, tended to fall away. The third phase, which has seen the internationals rise to absolute prominence in Friuli-Venezia Giulia and to parity at least in Veneto, Trentino and South Tyrol, began after the war and continues today.

The international varieties of northern Italy may be considered in groups according to provenance. The most important, today, is the Bordeaux contingent, closely followed by the Burgundy collection. A long way behind, in terms of spread and sheer number of vineyards planted, comes the section from the Rhône. Of considerable influence in the North East is the group associated with Germany. Finally there are the surviving stragglers from Austria and Eastern Europe.

THE BORDEAUX CONTINGENT

We have seen that the Cabernets probably made their first appearance in northern Italy in Piemonte. From there, according to one version, they travelled to the Colli Euganei in Veneto where, in the estates of Count Corinaldi at Lispida, they were being cultivated in 1870. Cabernet Sauvigno (sic), however, had been recorded as existing in Veneto earlier than this – in 1855, to be precise, at the 'Mostra dei Prodotti Primitivi del Suolo' in Vicenza (source: *Storia Regionale della Vite e del Vino in Italia*; Calò *et al.*). Indeed it is recorded that Prince Ernesto d'Aremberg of Costozza in Veneto began importing French varieties from Burgundy and Bordeaux from about 1835.

In 1877 the Cabernets were catalogued among the varieties present in the vineyards of what is today known as the Istituto Sperimentale per la Viticoltura at Conegliano, in northern Veneto. And from this time Cabernet began its spread throughout the Tre Venezie, in all parts of which it is to be found planted today.

Another version, which does not exclude the preceding as a simultaneous explanation, is that Cabernet and other Bordelais varieties arrived in Friuli in 1869 directly from France, brought by the French nobleman Comte Théodore de la Tour when he married into the Austrian family which owned Villa Russiz in the Collio.

The reason, incidentally, for the mention of Cabernet collectively is that, from the beginning until really quite recently, there has been confusion in Italy between **CABERNET SAUVIGNON** and **CABERNET FRANC.**

Cabernet Franc is a better producer than the rather miserly Cabernet Sauvignon, as well as being more precocious in terms of ripening – meaning that in a tricky year it will mature more readily than Cabernet Sauvignon. Thus did Cabernet Franc gradually pull ahead of its brother as cautious growers during the lean years of the early twentieth century considered their options.

Recent research, however, has revealed a probable association of the form of Cabernet Franc found in parts of the north – Alto Adige and Trentino in particular – with Bordeaux's **CARMENÈRE**, a subvariety of considerably less distinction than the classic Cabernet Franc of the Libournais. Some say there is an appreciable difference in quality between the two, and would only replant with material deriving from France. Others claim the difference is more due to other factors such as training systems and production per plant than to intrinsic differences between sub-varieties.

Where Cabernet Sauvignon has survived from the early days it, like Cabernet Franc, has been planted on *pergola* and has often been overproduced, to the extent that overproduction is a possibility with Cabernet Sauvignon, and so has produced wines with a grassy, vegetal character more reminiscent of its cousin in the Loire than of its brother in Bordeaux. However, once the principle of low yield is accepted, be it on *guyot* or *pergola*, Cabernet Sauvignon is generally considered (even though the assumption is now beginning to be questioned) to deliver the higher quality – deeper colour, a tremendous polyphenolic content, more fruit character, and less herbaceousness of perfume. So that today, when higher prices may be obtained for wines which merit the extra, new plantings of Cabernet Sauvignon exceed those of Cabernet Franc by more than two to one.

In fact, the lure of Cabernet Sauvignon for quality producers in the past fifteen to twenty years has been such as to constitute what could be called a second wave of introduction of the variety into northern Italy. This consists in a turning of the back on the clones of Cabernet developed in the north, considered to have deteriorated owing to overproduction and indifferent selection procedures, and a return to France for propagational material. Today, practically all of the top Cabernet Sauvignons of the north are from French material, planted (at least in recent years) on *guyot* rather than on *pergola*.

A similar picture emerges for what is today the most popular Bordeaux varietal, **MERLOT**. Under the synonym Bordò it is recorded as existing in the Veneto in 1855 (Calò). In 1880 Merlot is named as being planted at the viticultural institute of Conegliano, and in the same year it was brought directly from Bordeaux to Friuli by Senator Pecile and Count Savorgnan di Brazzà, the latter winning a gold medal with his Merlot at an exhibition in Cividale del Friuli in 1896. This despite Mondini's negative judgement on the grape's potential.

Merlot is more cooperative, earlier ripening and considerably more prolific than the Cabernets in the vineyard, being able with its higher sugar levels and less aggressive aromas to make acceptable wine at quite elevated production levels. It turns out grapes markedly less acidic than those of the local competitors, which makes it an ideal subject for improving musts. These factors, far more than the grape's only recently recognized high quality potential, are responsible for making its fortunes.

Indeed, growers wishing to make top wines will be wary of using Merlot clones of Italian origin, unless they have been tried and tested by a reliable nursery such as Rauscedo. They will prefer, as with the Cabernets, to obtain their material directly from France and in particular, obviously, from Bordeaux.

In the mid-1990s, surprisingly, Merlot was Italy's fifth most planted grape, with almost 37,000 hectares (more than double the area claimed by all other French varieties put together), of which nearly 33,000 hectares were in Friuli and the Veneto alone, where it is the most planted grape variety, with over half and one-third respectively of the total areas under vine. Every one of the eight multi-DOCs of Friuli (nine if you include Lison-Pramaggiore) provides for both Cabernet Sauvignon and Franc as well as Merlot, plus a blend of some description. The two Cabernets and Merlot are catered for in most Veneto DOCs too, if only tacitly; even in Valpolicella one is allowed the addition of '5 per cent of other red-grape varieties of the zone'.

Cabernet Franc, for its part, represents a little under 5 per cent of plantings in Veneto and nearly 6 per cent in Friuli. Cabernet Sauvignon has a 1 per cent share in the former and is not among the leading sive black varieties in the latter, though its importance increasingly outweighs its position. Nationally, Cabernet Franc is planted in something over 4,000 hectares while Cabernet Sauvignon's share is around 1,500 hectares and rising. In both cases the vast majority of plantings, if not of hype, is in the north.

The Bordelais are major players, too, in the red wine production of Trentino Alto-Adige, if less so than in Veneto and Friuli. Merlot is the second most planted red variety (if you take the Schiavas together) at nearly 6 per cent. Cabernet Sauvignon, with 125 hectares, is officially claimed to be more prevalent than Cabernet Franc, although you wouldn't guess it to taste the herbaceousness of some of the wines.

In Lombardy Merlot, despite not being central in any major producing zone, represents 6 per cent of area (1,300 hectares). Both in Bergamo's rather undistinguished Valcalepio, and in the potentially more interesting Terre di Franciacorta Rosso, Merlot is an element, but second (in theory) to Cabernet. Yet neither Cabernet manages 1 per cent of vineyard area, being out of the top 10 red varieties, which does not alter the fact that an increasing amount of top quality red wine production in Lombardy is being based on Cabernet Sauvignon.

There is a bit of Cabernet Sauvignon in Emilia's Colli Bolognesi and Colli Piacentini, and a speck of Merlot in the former, but they are overwhelmed by the oceans of Lambrusco of various types, and do not register in the available statistics. In Liguria, Valle d'Aosta and Piemonte there is no Bordelais presence at all in any official capacity, although in Piemonte Cabernet Sauvignon is grown increasingly in a clandestine way, mainly for purposes of lending a bit of help to the native varieties. Angelo Gaja was the first to challenge the law openly with his Darmagi, and the number of Cabernet-based wines or blends is beginning to get serious.

It would not be at all surprising, indeed, to see this bandwagon growing rapidly in the twenty-first century. One hopes not too rapidly.

The traditional northern Italian approach to the Bordeaux grapes has been to use them varietally, and only in recent years have growers in the North East woken up to the fact that there is a good reason why the Bordelais resort to blending. In fact there are two good reasons: one is that Cabernet Sauvignon cannot be relied upon to ripen fully every year, in which case it can be very astringent, while Merlot's thinner skin is highly susceptible to rot in wet autumn weather, so it is useful for growers to have something in the vineyard that they can fall back on. The other, as Californians have found, is that they compensate for one another's shortcomings in the blend, mitigating Cabernet Franc's herbaceousness, softening Cabernet Sauvignon's aggressive tannicity or adding a bit of spice to the less specific aromas of Merlot.

Of the other red grapes of Bordeaux, there seems to be an increasing if still minuscule interest in **PETIT VERDOT** for purposes of adding body and acidity to the blend; but Petit Verdot will never be a major variety anywhere, owing to its inconsistent performance from year to year. **MALBEC** (or Malbeck or Malbech) is, on the other hand, rapidly losing what ground it had captured, which up to the mid-twentieth century was apparently quite a lot. A small amount is still produced around the Friuli-Veneto border, without benefit of a DOC, but with the advantage of having the giant Santa Margherita as its principal proponent.

As has been suggested, the vast preponderance of Bordeaux varietal wines in the recent past, indeed in the present, have been overstretched and underwhelming to put it politely. Growers have pushed production to the limit with inappropriate training systems, *commercianti* have considered only the bottom line, and buyers have looked for the cheapest available, capitalizing on easy-to-sell varietal names. In such a context it was quite possible to conclude, which many did, that bordeaux-style wines from northern Italy were (are) a load of crap.

It took a few daring souls like Gaja to push them to the opposite limit, that of quality regardless of price, for the world to begin to glimpse that the negative image was not necessarily correct. And why should northern Italians not produce world-class claret-style wines? The latitude is right – roughly on a level with Bordeaux – and in many cases the climate in terms of mean temperature and average rainfall is at least as favourable as in Bordeaux. There are plenty of good gravelly or well-drained soils for Cabernet Sauvignon to thrive on and heavier partly clay-based soils in which Merlot can shine. Training systems like *sylvoz* or *pergola trentina*, with their low-density planting and high yield-per-plant, were plainly not suitable for these vines, but these are gradually giving way to French models, and the earliest planted vineyards by the pioneers, which only go back really to the late 1970s–early 1980s, are beginning to come into maturity.

Meanwhile cellar techniques involved in making great wines are not top secret – indeed simplicity is the key. They just cost money – for the best crushing equipment, the finest barrels, etc. There are those in northern Italy today who are willing to spend that money, and they are making outstanding wine. And in any given zone, from a given grape, if just one outstanding wine can be made, it shows it can be done. If several can be made, it shows it's not an isolated phenomenon. This is what is happening in northern Italy today, and although we are just at the beginning the future looks bright.

When it comes to white grape varieties from the Bordeaux contingent, this effectively means **SAUVIGNON BLANC**, with a smidgin of Sémillon. Mondini, noting that Sauvignon tends to be more vigorous but less productive than Sémillon, tells us that both were introduced into vineyards at Castelceriolo in Piemonte by yet another member of *that* family, Cavaliere Manfredo di Sambuy.

Cosmo and Polsinelli speak of two distinct types of Sauvignon, large or green, and small or yellow – the former being known today as Sauvignonasse, the latter as Sauvignon Blanc. Undoubtedly it is the Sauvignon Blanc, also known as Blanc Fumé or just Fumé, which gives fruit of greater distinctiveness – the well-known herbaceousness, or greenness, the vegetal character (asparagus, capsicum), the closest fruit aroma being gooseberry; 'cat's pee' being another descriptive, usually giving rise to sniggers or surprise. The character can best be summed up as *selvatico*, or wild, which indeed, according to Cosmo and Polsinelli, is behind the derivation of the name.

Cosmo and Polsinelli tell us that, according to the French ampelographer Petit-Laffitte (via Molon, 1906) little is known of the origin of Sauvignon, not even the precise date of its introduction into Italy. By the turn of the nineteenth/twentieth centuries, however, Mondini tells us it was already quite diffuse throughout the north, being present in Piemonte, Veneto and Emilia.

It was never to catch on in a big way, however, perhaps because of overcropping which robs it of its character, perhaps because its character is of a type which Italians have traditionally considered exaggerated for a white wine. So it is only in recent years, thanks in part to pressure from export markets to which a Sauvignon without the distinguishing olfactory characteristics is unacceptable, that Sauvignon in Italy has begun to spread its wings, particularly in two regions, Friuli and Alto Adige, not noted by Mondini – the first because it was then part of Veneto, the second because it belonged to Austria. Friuli is the only region in which Sauvignon represents more than 1 per cent of total area planted.

SÉMILLON's arrival in Italy seems to have coincided with that of Sauvignon, but it was never so well regarded nor so popular with growers, probably because of its well-known susceptibility to *Botrytis cinerea*, which is all very well when you are making sweet wines but not so good for the fresh and dry. In Mondini's time it was planted in Piemonte, Veneto and Emilia, and there are traces left today, but they are insignificant. As far as I know no one is making a varietal Sémillon of quality in northern Italy.

In the producer reviews that follow I have tried to consider wines by variety, taking 50% as a minimum for inclusion in any given category unless otherwise specified. For reasons explained, the two Cabernets have been taken together. Even so the blends are many and varied, and I will try to indicate blend-components where possible. For the sake of consistency I will consider the regions in the order in which they appeared in the chapters on indigenous varieties. It goes without saying that this does not in any way constitute an order of merit.

CABERNET (SAUVIGNON AND FRANC) PRODUCERS

PIEMONTE AND VALLE D'AOSTA

Angelo **Gaja**, Barbaresco (see also under Barbaresco, page 84). Gaja brought his Cabernet Sauvignon from Bordeaux's Côte de Blaye and began planting from 1978, in a prime site for Nebbiolo di Barbaresco, thus succeeding in shocking the little world of Alba to its bootstraps (think of the reaction to planting Nebbiolo on a site in Clos de Vougeot). 'Pity!' he said, and Pity he called it (or, rather, in Piemontese: Darmagi). Today, with the vines gaining in maturity, the wine is becoming ever more complex, with its severity of structure overlaid by a wealth of fruit and harmony of layered taste sensations typical of, if not similar to, the great Nebbiolos of Alba. Aromatically, on the other hand, the wine resembles top claret, with blackcurrant fruit and cedarwood coming through as in the great Pauillacs.

Darmagi is far and away the greatest example of Cabernet in Piemonte and vies with two or three others for the distinction of being the best in Italy. Considering Gaja's success, and considering how long he has been making a success of it, it is surprising how few emulators he has inspired. Bertelli (I Fossareti), Ceretto (La Bernardina) and Renato Ratti (I Cedri) make varietal Cabernet at levels from good to potentially excellent. More interesting, however, are wines like La Vigna di Sonvico from La Barbatella and Sulbric of Martinetti, both excellent blends of Cabernet Sauvignon and Barbera, as is the Virtues of Cisa Asinari. But more on this subject in Blends.

The only wine I know of from Valle d'Aosta which fits this category is from the experimental vineyards of the **Institut Agricole Régional** in the city of Aosta. Called Vin du Prévôt, it's a blend of Cabernet Sauvignon and Merlot. I have yet to taste it.

LOMBARDY

As Darmagi reigns supreme among Piemontese 'clarets', so in Lombardy does Maurizio Zanella (the wine) of **Cà del Bosco** in Erbusco, though by a lesser margin. Now classified as IGT Rosso del Sebino, this wine is deliberately intended as a Bordeaux *Premier Cru Classé* type blend, the producer being well aware that Cabernet Sauvignon needs a bit of softening. Maurizio Zanella is a blend of Cabernet Sauvignon at 45%, Cabernet Franc at 25%, and Merlot at 30%, with all procedures in vineyard and cellar following the French line, from the 9,000 plus plants per hectare, through the punching-down of the cap during fermentation, through the use of new *barriques* exclusively, right down to the fining with egg whites. Maurizio Zanella (the man) began planting his vineyards in the mid-1970s, so that today they have achieved a nice level of maturity and are capable of putting out some very soft and voluptuous Margaux-style wines at prices which also remind one of Margaux (the Château, I mean).

On a par with Maurizio Zanella is the Solesine of **Bellavista**, another IGT from the zone of Franciacorta. This is a Cabernet Sauvignon (85%) plus Merlot blend of great class from a single hillside vineyard in the commune of Adro. For more on the above two producers, see Metodo Classico (pages 315, 317).

Scattered around the region are other worthy claret-types which include Gatti Rosso from Enrico **Gatti** and Rosso dei Frati Priori from **Uberti**, both in Erbusco; Ronchedone from Cà dei Frati; Cantoalto from **Cascina del Bosco** in Sorisolo; Le Zalte Rosse from Cascina la Pertica; Vigneto Il Falcone from **La Prendina** in Monzambano; and Due Querce and Rosso del Benaco Sur from **Trevisani** at Soprazocco di Gavarardo.

Then there are the two Bordeaux-grape-based DOCs of Lombardy, starting with what is today called Terre di Franciacorta Rosso in which the Cabernets (mainly Franc) and Merlot are joined by Nebbiolo and Barbera. The wine can often be a little green and unsure of its identity, but there are some good ones, though not particularly good value for money. These, in addition to those of the Erbusco-based producers mentioned above, come from **Cavalleri** (Vigna Tajardino), Erbusco; **Cornaleto** (Selezione Poligono), Adro; **Guarischi** (Le Solcaie), Cazzago San Martino; **Il Mosnel** (Fantecolo), Camignone; and **Villa** (Riserva Gradoni), Monticelli Brusati.

Reasonable Valcalepio DOC comes from the above-mentioned Cascina del Bosco as well as from the three Grumello del Monte-based producers: **Castello di Grumello** (Colle del Calvario), **La Cornaselle** and **Pecori Giraldi Majnoni** (Villa Majnoni).

LIGURIA

In Liguria there is a bit of Cabernet and Merlot about, but their vinous manifestations are hard to find. The only one I have come across, Rosso il Poggialino from La Colombiera in the Colli di Luni, was disappointing considering the fact that the vines making up the majority Cabernet Sauvignon component of the blend, which also includes Merlot and the local Pollera, are over thirty years old; also considering how delicious their Sangiovese plus Merlot blend, Terrizzo, can be, demonstrating that Pieralberto Ferro knows how to make good wine.

EMILIA

Terre Rosse, Zola Predosa (Colli Bolognesi). The late Enrico Vallania was one of the first producers in post-war Italy to experiment with French varieties. His Cabernet Sauvignon, called Il Rosso di Enrico Vallania by his children and heirs, Giovanni and Elisabetta, who have followed faithfully in his footsteps, has for many years now been regarded as a yardstick for Cabernet in the Italian style: pure varietal aromas, with no wood component. Indeed the Cabernet Sauvignon vines at Terre Rosse have been propagated from stock planted in the vineyards over 100 years ago.

Other valid producers in the Colli Bolognesi include **Cantina dell'Abbazia** at Monteveglio, **Santarosa** (Giò Rosso) at Monte San Pietro and **Vallona** at Castello di Serravalle. Recently the Tenuta Bonzara of Professor Francesco Lambertini has come up with a *cru* Bonzarone, Cabernet Sauvignon with a modicum of Merlot, which has attracted considerable attention.

The other significant Emilian production zone for quality bordeaux-style wines is Colli Piacentini. Three serious producers are **Il Poggiarello** (Perticato del Novarei) at Travo, **La Stoppa** (*cru* La Stoppa) at Rivergaro and La Tosa (La Luna Selvatica) at Vigolzone.

VENETO

Maculan, Breganze. The *azienda leader* of the Veneto in terms of French-style production has, until recently, unquestionably been this one – not that its leadership has been lost, just challenged. It was in the late 1970s/early 1980s that Fausto Maculan, scion of a family whose wine-roots in Breganze go back generations, decided (as I put in in *Life Beyond Lambrusco*) to 'withdraw from the rat-race of low-price, high-volume production to concentrate on quality'. This, for decades in central Veneto, has meant mainly French grapes, and Fausto, ever a keen observer of French methods, decided in 1984 to plant the newly acquired Ferrata hill to Cabernet Sauvignon, Chardonnay and Sauvignon (French clones) at 10,000 vines to the hectare. The resulting *crus* 'Ferrata' have been steadily improving as the vines mature, and as Fausto's near-obsession with the latest oenological equipment has refined cellar techniques (he is particularly proud of a slow-moving belt which allows

FERRATA

Cabernet
Sauvignon

unsound or unripe grapes to be eliminated prior to crushing). To my mind the Cabernet, a wine of subtlety and finesse rather than power, is the most convincing, and stands today among the leaders of Italy, outshining his own very fine *cru* Fratta, made from slightly raisined grapes.

Serafini & Vidotto, Nervesa della Battaglia. The 'challenge' referred to above is going to come more and more, as the new century progresses, from *boutique* producers like this one in the zone of Marca Trevigiana, province of Treviso, an area rich in viticultural potential which until recently was being seriously under-exploited. The old convent of Nervesa, with its vineyards, was acquired in the late 1980s by the two young grower-enthusiasts who have proceeded to overhaul the vineyards (French-style, of course), concentrating on the two Cabernets and Merlot as well as on other French varieties, not forgetting to retain a good measure of the local Prosecco. Oenologist Francesco Serafini's *barrique*-matured bordeaux-blend Rosso dell'Abazia is star of their production, while they also make good DOC Cabernet and Merlot varietals (Montello e Colli Asolani). If the wine has not yet reached the highest levels of complexity the youth of the vines and the continuing experiments in *cantina* are partly the explanation. Excellent things can be expected in the near future from them and from young Venetans like this pair.

Other producers of good to excellent Cabernet-based bordeaux-style wines of the Veneto include: Anselmi (Realdà); **Barbarossa** (Ner d'Ala), Conegliano; **Collalbrigo** (Rosso di Collalbrigo), Conegliano; Corte Gardoni (Rosso di Corte); La Cappuccina (Madego); Le Ragose (Cabernet Le Ragose); Le Vigne di San Pietro (Refolà); **Loredan Gasparini** (Venegazzù della Casa and Capo di Stato), Volpago del Montello; **Scarpa** Afra e Tobia (Corbulino Rosso), Trevignano; Ornella **Molon Traverso** (Piave Cabernet Ornella), Salgaredo; Vignalta (Colli Euganei Cabernet Riserva).

Quintarelli of Negrar makes an outstanding Cabernet Franc/ Sauvignon blend called Alzero (see page 179), but it is basically an Amarone and a million miles from the bordeaux style.

FRIULI-VENEZIA GIULIA

Dorigo, Buttrio, Colli Orientali del Friuli. Girolamo Dorigo gave up the security of a business career to become a poet of the vine decades ago, since when he has been carefully honing his reputation as the region's best red wine producer, not only from French varieties but also from Refosco and from the fast-disappearing Pignolo, Tazzelenghe and Schioppettino. His *capolavoro*, however, is a 60% Cabernet Sauvignon/40% Cabernet Franc–Merlot blend named after the Montsclapade vineyard in which the grapes are planted French-style, high-density/guyot-trained/very low yield per plant. The *barrique*-aged wine, nicely structured, multi-layered and harmonious, is generally reckoned Friuli's finest in the bordeaux style, although Dorigo wines can take you right through the meal on a consistent high, from the outstanding Pas Dosé Cuvée Pinot through the highly rated Chardonnay out of the Ronc di Juri vineyard, and the various excellent reds, to a Picolit (also out of Montsclapade) the equal of which for complexity and balance I have not, as I have said, come across elsewhere. Make sure your wallet is well-padded.

Russiz Superiore, Capriva del Friuli, Collio. Coming down slightly from the clouds, we find ourselves in the part of Friuli best known for its lead in the white revolution, although they're making rapid strides in the red department. An excellent example is the Cabernet

Sauvignon (70–80%) plus Cabernet Franc and Merlot blend, Rosso degli Orzoni. *Barrique*-aged, of course. It began life in the mid-1980s with something of that monolinear character from which Collio reds have suffered, but as the vineyards mature (5,600 plants per hectare trained on double-*guyot*), and the techniques refine, the wine is becoming fuller with better follow-through in the mouth. The Felluga family (father Marco, son Roberto, daughter Patrizia) make their top range of wines at this ancient estate dating back to the thirteenth century (they acquired it in the 1960s), including a varietal Cabernet Franc which is about as good an example as you can find of traditional red production in these parts. They also control the separate winery named Marco Felluga, at Gradisca d'Isonzo, which produces a worthy rival to Rosso degli Orzoni called Carantan; as well as an estate recently acquired at Buttrio. Committed to experimentation in the vineyards, advised by Italy's most famous viticultural consultant Attilio Scienza, the Fellugas' is among the most dynamic operations in the region.

Other good to excellent Cabernet-based reds of Friuli come from: Abbazia di Rosazzo (Ronco dei Roseti); Borgo Conventi (Braida Nuova); **Borgo Magredo** (Braida Vieri), Tauriano di Spilimbergo/Friuli Grave; Borgo del Tiglio (Collio Rosso); Jermann (Cabernet); La Castellada (Rosso della Castellada); Livon (Plazate; Arborizza – Cabernet Franc Collio); **Mangilli** (Progetto), Talmassons; **Masut da Rive** (Cabernet Sauvignon Isonzo), Mariano del Friuli; **Midolini** (Ronco dell Regina Rosso), Manzano; Ronco del Gnemiz (Rosso del Gnemiz); Schiopetto (Cabernet Franc Collio); **Vistorta** (Friuli Grave Merlot), Sacile; Zamò & Zamò (Cabernet COF).

ALTO ADIGE

The Cabernets have traditionally had a significant if minor role to play among black varieties here. Cabernet Sauvignon has received most of the attention, even if it tends to come with a certain greenness from insufficient ripening (overproduction on *pergola* the main culprit) and a drop in mid-palate where the blended varieties ought to be – where the Bordelais put them, that is. Some growers are now leaning more to Cabernet Franc – the real thing, that is, from France; not Carmenère – as a base wine: it reaches full maturity more frequently and has less of the tough stringiness of insufficiently cooked green beans. That has not prevented producers from persevering and, indeed, from attracting some very favourable press coverage with their Cabernet Sauvignons. However, I think no bordeaux expert would be as convinced as Italian oeno-journalists appear to be by the pure varietal Cabernet Sauvignons of this part of the world. There follow profiles of two producers who have led the procession away from the old style:

C.S. **Colterenzio**, Cornaiano. The cooperative winery, known here as *Kellereigenossenschaft*, is a phenomenon of major importance in the context of wine production in Alto Adige – as a group they have even been authoritatively described, Heineken-like, as 'probably the best in the world'. A worthy representative of the genre is this one, established in 1960, today boasting a beautifully equipped modern winery and controlling over 400 hectares of well-sited and painstakingly tended, largely organically treated vineyard in various parts of the province from Merano to Salorno and at various altitudes up to 600 metres depending on varieties planted. To add to their advantages is the consultancy of Donato Lanati, today doubtless the best known of the peripatetic oenologists of northern Italy.

The range of wines produced, typically for South Tyrol, is wide – perhaps too wide – but divides for commercial purposes into three lines: the Classic line of single varietals, the Pradium Selection of single estate wines and the top selection under the Cornell label, with the distinctive black castle. Among the Cornell wines are the 100% Cabernet Sauvignon Lafoa, a wine of impressive concentration and compact flavour which has a tendency, unfortunately, to suffer from the aforementioned polo-mint syndrome (hole in the middle of the palate), and a more complete Cabernet/Merlot blend called Cornelius which, though less concentrated, has ultimately greater follow-through and finesse.

Alois **Lageder**, Magrè. The current Alois Lageder, vintage 1950, is the fifth consecutive holder of that name to head this firm since 1855. It is a task which, it must be said, he has undertaken with resounding success, the winery generally being rated today as number one among the privates in South Tyrol and one of the leaders of all Italy. They were among the first to introduce high-density planting to *spalliera* (a continuing process), organic methods of viticulture (the aim is 100 per cent conversion), restricted yields and crop-seeding between rows – this not just into their own 17 hectares of vineyard in various parts of the province, but increasingly into those of the 150 growers from whom they regularly purchase grapes. The *cantina*, too, run by Alois' brother-in-law Luis von Dellemann, is, since its transfer from Bolzano to Magrè in 1996, one of the most modern in the land, everything working on the principle of gravity duction from process to process and minimal mechanical intervention.

We have seen that South Tyroleans go in for a wide range and Lageder are no exception. Like the cooperatives they divide their premium production into three lines. The 'Classic' varietals, seventeen of them no less, include the well-known Buchholz Chardonnay and Mazon Pinot Nero Riserva. The 'Single Vineyard' selections make up a further six, including the partially oak-fermented and/or -matured Haberlehof Pinot Bianco, Benefizium Porer Pinot Grigio and Lehenhof Sauvignon, all among the finest of their type, as well as Dornach, a *barrique*d IGT Mitterberg *uvaggio di vigneto* of Chardonnay, Pinot Bianco and Pinot Grigio. The third range, the 'Estate Wines', are *barrique*-matured whites (Tannhammer Terlaner and Chardonnay Löwengang) and reds (Löwengang Cabernet and the flagship Cor Römigberg).

Lageder's 'Estate Wines' represent the two faces of South Tyrol viticulturally, Löwengang (whose blend includes 15% each of

Cabernet Franc and Merlot) coming from old vines still on *pergola*, Cor Römigberg from a 1.7-hectare site planted at high density to *guyot* by Lageder in the 1980s in the *cor* or heart of the excellent Römigberg vineyard overlooking Lake Caldaro. Impressive as Löwengang can be, it is the Cor Römigberg which, despite its near-varietal purity (it's 97% Cabernet Sauvignon plus 3% Petit Verdot), displays the kind of concentration, complexity and sheer ripe-fruitiness capable of putting it, in a few years when the vines have achieved greater maturity, among the great Cabernets of Italy and the world.

See also **Casòn Hirschprunn** in Blends (page 304).

Other producers pulling away, successfully to very successfully, from the bad old days of overproduction and underripeness include: C.S. Caldaro (Campaner; Riserva); C.S. **Cornaiano** (Optimum), Cornaiano; C.S. Cortaccia (Freienfeld; Kirchhugel); Erste & Neue; **Hofstätter** (Yngram), Termeno; **Loacker** (Kastlet), Bolzano; Josef Niedermayr (Riserva); Heinrich Plattner; Hans Rottensteiner (Riserva); C.S. Santa Maddalena (Mumelterhof); C.S. **San Michele Appiano** (St Valentin), Appiano; **Schwanburg** (Castel Schwanburg), Nalles; Thurnhof (Wienegg Riserva); Tiefenbrunner (Linticlarus); Elena Walch (Castel Ringberg; Istrice); Baron **Widman** (Feld), Cortaccia.

TRENTINO

The general comments made under Alto Adige are largely true for Trentino. In terms of specific Cabernet-based wines, certainly, two producers stand out.

Pojer e Sandri, Faedo. Established in the mid-1970s, this team effort by grower Fiorentino Sandri and oenologist Mario Pojer is today firmly established as one of the foremost *boutique* wineries of Italy. With vineyards from around 300 to 700 metres altitude on the mountain, which slopes upward and eastward from San Michele all'Adige, they are able to turn out a variety of wines ranging from the light, aromatic Müller-Thurgau, for which they were perhaps originally best known, via Chardonnay, Nosiola, Traminer, Sauvignon, Riesling, Kerner, Pinot Nero and Schiava to the Cabernet Sauvignon (50%) plus Cabernet Franc, Merlot and

Lagrein that make up the blend of the medium-full, complex Rosso Fayé for which they are most hailed in this age of red wine. From a good year this wine has all the berry-fruit aroma, firm but ripe tannins, follow-through and length you could ask for from an elegant claret-style red of medium concentration. Ask them which of their wines they feel is most representative, however, and they will answer Pinot Noir, although their *spumante*, a *cuvée brut* (no dosage) of two vintages with thirty months on the yeasts, and their extraordinary late-harvest sweet wine Essenzia, are also very special. (Not forgetting, either, their range of grappas, for which the Trentino in general, and they in particular, are famous.)

San Leonardo, Borghetto. This large (nearly 300 hectares, some 20 of which are planted to vines) and ancient estate at the southern extreme of Trentino, between the Lessini mountains which loom upward on the east, and the Adige river which flows by on the west on its way into the Veneto, seems almost a world unto itself. Eight hundred years ago it was a monastery, and since the eighteenth century it has belonged to the family of the Marchesi Guerrieri Gonzaga, whose present encumbent has maximized its outstanding viticultural potential. Marchese Carlo Guerrieri Gonzaga is in fact a trained oenologist who decades ago had a hand in creating Marchese Incisa della Rocchetta's Sassicaia, and today his San Leonardo is one of the most convincing rivals to that archetypal Italian answer to the Bordeaux *grand cru classé*; indeed the two *marchesi* are great friends and share importers in a number of export markets. San Leonardo is a classic and judicious blend of Cabernet Sauvignon (about 60%, all on *guyot*), Cabernet Franc (about 30%, on *pergola*) and Merlot (mixed systems). The estate enjoys a particularly favourable micro-climate, and the wine is kept in oak large and small for up to thirty months, followed by 8 months' bottle-age, prior to release. From a great vintage, such as 1997, San Leonardo can have an elegance-cum-depth capable of taking on the best clarets of the world.

Others capable of good Cabernet-based wines (which does not mean they always *are* good) are: **Bossi Fedrigotti** (Foianeghe Rosso; Conte Federico), Rovereto; **Endrizzi** (Collezione), San Michele all'Adige; Elisabetta Foradori (Karanar); Letrari (Maso Lodron); **Madonna delle Vittorie**, Arco; **Maso Cantanghel** (Rosso

San Leonardo

1994

VINO DA TAVOLA DI VALLAGARINA

Imbottigliato all'origine da
Marchese Carlo Guerrieri Gonzaga
Tenuta di San Leonardo s.a.s.
Borghetto all'Adige (TN) Italia

750 ml e   13% vol.   ITALIA

di Pila), Civezzano; Pravis (Fratagranda); de Tarczal (Pragiara); **Vallarom**, Avio. This last is the property of the famous Professor Attilio Scienza, late of the Institute of San Michele all'Adige, today probably Italy's highest-profile viticultural consultant. However, it seems a case of the great man giving his attention everywhere but home, as the wines of Vallarom have been distinctly weak of late. That, theoretically, should not detract from their capacity to be good again when time permits . . .

Nor should one forget the emerging **Castel Noarna** of Rovereto, whose Romeo, a blend of Cabernets Sauvignon and Franc, is a serious wine to be sought after from the mid-1990s on and whose bright, carbonic-maceration Mercuria is a Cabernet with a difference: as one pundit would call it – '*vino frutta*'.

MERLOT PRODUCERS

NORTH WEST

Merlot has virtually no presence in Valle d'Aosta or Liguria, and not a lot in Emilia despite having its own sub-DOC under the Colli Bolognesi banner. Its plantings in Piemonte are few and far between at present but may be expected to increase in the current climate of Merlot-fever. For some reason, while Merlot ripens more easily than Cabernet in the North East, according to Angelo Gaja it is a failure in Piemonte. The only varietal wine I have come across is one made by the enthusiastic Giovanni Abrigo of Orlando Abrigo at Treiso in the Barbaresco zone; it has good varietal aromas, but suffers perhaps a bit from that earthy toughness which is a characteristic of Piemontese reds. More convincing, indeed at its best quite excellent, is the Palo Alto from Colle Manora in Quargnento, where Merlot forms part of a complex blend. It will be interesting to see what Bernardino Gastaldi achieves with his Merlot planted at Monforte.

Merlot is more important in Lombardy than at first meets the eye, but mainly as a back-up grape in Valcalepio and Terre di Franciacorta. Varietally it is produced at a good level by Cavalleri (Corniole) and La Prendina (Vigneto la Prendina) but by few others.

Emilia offers one surprising exception to the rule that little Merlot of value can be found there, in the form of the Rocca di Bonacciara Colli Bolognesi DOC of Tenuta Bonzara at Monte San Pietro. Professor Francesco Lambertini and consultant Stefano Chioccioli have teamed up to produce a wine good enough to merit the top award of Tre Bicchieri in the 1998 *Vini d'Italia* guide of Gambero Rosso/Slow Food; another indication that the Bolognese hills are bristling with potential when it comes to high quality red production.

VENETO

Considering its importance in terms of hectarage, it is surprising how few varietal Merlots of real quality there are in the Veneto. They are well spread about: in Breganze Maculan makes a Breganze Rosso (i.e. Merlot) called Marchesante which has the elegance-cum-concentration one expects from the producer; in Verona Montresor have recently brought out an oaked Merlot del Veneto which is excellent value for money in these inflationary times; in Pramaggiore Iginio **Russolo** makes the interesting Borgo di Peuma, a Merlot-dominated blend with Cabernet and Refosco; in Piave, Ornella Molon Traverso produces a good Merlot Ornella; in Bagnoli di Sopra Borletti makes a pleasant mid-weight version under the Il Dominio label; and in the Colli Berici, Domenico **Cavazza** makes a varietal called Cicogna. But the only one which I have found which might lay claim to excellence comes from:

Vignalta, Arquà Petrarca, Colli Euganei. Franco Zanovello and Lucio Gomiero have taken the viniculture of these bizarrely shaped hills, where the credo has always been volume production of ordinary red to wash down meals in the nearby city of Padua, and revolutionized it with careful site and clone selection, drastic reduction of yield and painstaking attention to detail. Years of tasting the great wines of Bordeaux convinced Lucio that anything Pomerol could do he could do just as well, so when he planted his vineyards in the mid-1980s and equipped his new winery in the

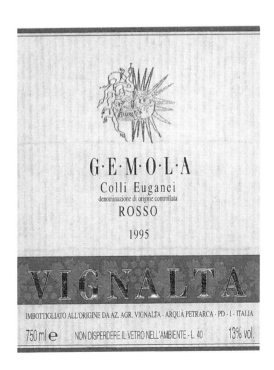

G·E·M·O·L·A

Colli Euganei
denominazione di origine controllata

ROSSO

1995

VIGNALTA

IMBOTTIGLIATO ALL'ORIGINE DA AZ. AGR. VIGNALTA · ARQUÀ PETRARCA · PD · I · ITALIA

750 ml e   NON DISPERDERE IL VETRO NELL'AMBIENTE · L. 40   13% vol.

mid-1990s he did so with the *grands crus* of the Gironde in mind. Their most celebrated wine, in fact, has been the Cabernet Sauvignon (see page 243), but the real star is Gemola, at 70% Merlot and 30% Cabernet Franc every inch a right-bank Gironde-style wine. The range they produce is extensive and includes, apart from the reds planted on the volcanic hills (the real wealth here is linked to the spa business), various whites like Chardonnay, Pinot Bianco and Moscato Giallo, planted on cooler clayey soils. Even Lucio's increasing absences in California playing *radicchio* king of the universe (the Padua area is famed for its *radicchio*, and Lucio has transferred that expertise with stunning success to the American West Coast) has not adversely affected things: there's always Franco (who also runs the second best winery in the area, Cà Lustra), and the occasional assistance of one of the most talented of the young itinerant winemakers, Roberto Cipresso.

FRIULI

Friuli is by far the most important region in northern Italy for the production of quality Merlot. Representative of the best are the following two:

Borgo del Tiglio, Cormons (*frazione* Brazzano), Collio. Nicola Manferrari comes from a long line of viticulturists. His pharmacist grandfather grew grapes on his hectare of vineyard as a hobby and his father extended the property by a couple of hectares. When his father died in 1981 Nicola, in one of the family's traditions, was practising pharmacy, but decided to turn to the other to see in the vintage. He never returned to pharmacy, but rather took the pharmacist's passion for experimentation and mixing into winemaking. On his 9 plus hectares spread over three vineyards, each with its own particular micro-climate, he produces reds and whites varietally or blended (the blends change constantly), and although most of his grapes are white, from which he produces some impressive barrel-fermented wines, he is perhaps most respected for his Rosso della Centa. This is a *barrique*-aged varietal Merlot of a concentration and complexity altogether removed from the common herd of everyday Merlots, illustrating both the versatility of the grape and the potential in Friuli, given the will, to produce top-class reds.

Villa Russiz, Capriva del Friuli, Collio. It was to this property that, it is claimed, French grapes were introduced into Friuli by the Frenchman Comte Théodore de la Tour in 1869. After his death his Austrian wife withdrew to her homeland and later donated the estate to the Italian government. It became an orphanage, supporting itself by viticultural activities, and was one of the first in Friuli to introduce estate bottling (1960s). In 1988 Dr Gianni Menotti took over the directorship from his father and relaunched the winery, since which time it has gone from strength to strength, with ambitious projects for the reconstruction of the winery and the château as well as, most importantly, for the overhauling of the vineyards. Today Villa Russiz is seen as being one of the best white wine producers of Friuli, especially for its Sauvignon and Pinot Bianco. But the pinnacle of quality in future is to be represented by the Chardonnay Gräfin (German for countess) and the Merlot Graf de la Tour. The latter already won enthusiastic plaudits for its first vintage, the 1993. Production is a miserly 35 hectolitres to the hectare, the colour is deep, the nose intense, the wine rich but not without a certain noble restraint, another convincing demonstration of Friuli's potential for high-quality red wine production.

Other Friulian producers of good to excellent Merlot-based wines, often blended with minority portions of Cabernet Franc and/or Cabernet Sauvignon, include the following: B. & D. **Buzzinelli** (Carlo Buzzinelli), Cormons; Livio **Felluga** (Riserva Sossò), Cormons; Marco Felluga (Collio Merlot); Edi Keber (Collio Merlot); **Renato Keber** (Grici), Cormons; **La Boatina** (Collio Merlot), Cormons; La Viarte (Roi); Lis Neris – Pecorari (Lis Neris); Livon (Tiare Mate); Miani (COF Merlot); Pierpaolo Pecorari (Vielj Baolar); Roberto **Picech** (Collio Merlot), Cormons; Rocca Bernarda (Centis); Ronchi di Manzano (Ronc di Subule); **Ronco del Gelso** (Isonzo Merlot), Cormons; Russiz Superiore (Collio Merlot); Schiopetto (Rivarossa; Collio Merlot); Torre Rosazza (L'Altromerlot); Vigne dal Leon (Rosso V dal L); **Vie di Romans** (Voos dai Ciamps), Mariano del Friuli; Venica & Venica (Perilla); Andrea Visintini (COF Merlot); Zamò & Zamò (COF Merlot).

ALTO ADIGE

While some very attractive Merlots and Merlot-based blends are being produced, and increasingly, in Alto Adige, they have yet to reach the levels attained in Friuli or, especially, in Tuscany. The growers here are, however, on a learning curve, Merlot having always been considered a grape of high production, therefore consigned to valley sites and equally low esteem; it is only very recently that they have been selecting quality clones and planting them in hillside sites, increasingly (as we have seen) to *guyot*, and wines full of potential are beginning to emerge. One of the earliest to do so was the Schweizer of Franz Haas (see under Moscato Rosa, page 194). Another is the Casòn of Hirschprunn (but see under Blends, page 304). Other promising producers include: Baron Widman; C.S. Colterenzio (Siebeneich); Schloss Sallegg; Clemens Waldthaler (Raut).

The Merlot that has captured the greatest attention has been the Brenntal of C.S. Cortaccia, which in its 1995 version came top of various pundits' ratings. This was also the first year of production of one of the Merlot-based wines which shows the greatest future promise, the Iugum of Peter **Dipoli** (see under Sauvignon Blanc, page 258). This is a blend with Cabernet Sauvignon at 30% from a 300 metre-high vineyard at Magrè, planted to *guyot*, three clones for each grape, imported from France. The colour is deep, the aromas of coffee and berry-fruit, the fruit on the palate soft but intense with very ripe tannins as a back-up; sexy but serious.

TRENTINO

Although, as in Alto Adige, plenty of Merlot exists in Trentino, they have not caught the same train as their northern neighbours. There are some decent wines, but nothing either exceptional or showing signs of becoming exceptional. To say that one of the best is the second wine of San Leonardo, a relatively humble Trentino Merlot, is to put the matter in perspective.

Others of reasonable value include: **Cantina d'Isera** (Trentino Merlot), Isera; de Tarczal (Merlot d'Isera); Maso Cantanghel (Tajapreda); Simoncelli (Trentino Merlot); Istituto Agrario (Trentino Merlot); **Le Meridiane** (Vigneto San Raimondo Riserva), Trento; Concilio Vini (Novaline Riserva).

SAUVIGNON BLANC PRODUCERS

PIEMONTE

Despite having been introduced to Italy via Piemonte, the region has never been noted for quality Sauvignon production. In the 1980s there were virtually no significant Sauvignon Blancs here, and such as exist today are phenomena of the 1990s, though some may have been planted in the 1980s.

Perhaps predictably, the only really good Sauvignon from Piemonte is the first, Gaja's Alteni di Brassica. Planted in 1982, first released in 1985, this is a *barrique*-matured wine of surprising complexity, having what one expert has described as a mouth-feel quite unique among Sauvignons of the world. On the other hand there is not a great deal of varietal aroma, and it is significant that Angelo Gaja has declared that he will not be planting any more Sauvignon here: Chardonnay is easier, he says. Other producers attaining a reasonable level of quality include: Bertelli (Monte-tusa); Colle Manora (Mimosa Collezione); Pasquero Elia; Parusso (Bricco Rovella).

LOMBARDY

Sauvignon Blanc is a rare phenomenon in Lombardy. The only well-known example is Cà del Bosco's Elfo, a *vino da tavola* unable to print a place name, variety name or even vintage date on the label, as Sauvignon is not an authorized variety for the region and as such is not covered by any DOC or even IGT. The vintage problem is overcome by slipping the last number of the year in question after the name, hence for example Elfo 8 (for Elfo 1998). Elfo is not technically a varietal, being 70% Sauvignon Blanc – clones from France, of course – and 30% Invernenga and Erba-matta, two obscure local grapes. The wine is clean and sharp with penetrating acidity coming apparently from the Erbamatta (or crazy grass) input, while the aromas, be they due to the supplementary grapes or the provenance, are not typically French even though recognizably Sauvignon, i.e. herbaceous. An intriguing wine, if somewhat more so intellectually than organoleptically.

Cascina La Pertica of Polpenazze on the west bank of Lake Garda make their Le Sincette Bianco with Sauvignon and Chardonnay; but it's nothing to get excited about.

EMILIA

Sauvignon has been diffuse in this region since the late nineteenth century and currently boasts a significant role among Emilian DOCs, appearing in the general Colli Bolognesi *disciplinare* and in every one of its numerous obscure offshoots, as well as in Colli Piacentini, Colli di Parma and Colli di Scandiano in the province of Reggio Emilia – either under its own name or under that adopted in the Classico zone of Spergola or Spergolina or Spargola. All this legal recognition, however, masks the fact that there is precious little – or precious little decent – Sauvignon to be found from Emilian vineyards. It may come light and *frizzante*, as from Tenuta **Pernice** in Borgonovo Val Tidone; or it may come still, as from Vallona or from Tenuta Bonzara (Colli Bolognesi Le Carrate). An example of Colli Piacentini Sauvignon comes from La Tosa, of Colli di Parma from **Forte Rigoni** of Pilastro, and of Colli di Scandiano from **Casali** of – wait for it – Scandiano.

VENETO

Until recently the highest-profile version of this variety from Veneto, a region not noted for its Sauvignons, has been Maculan's Ferrata. Indeed I have not yet tasted an outstanding example of Sauvignon from the Veneto, though there is one producer who is receiving a lot of attention for his three versions, dry unoaked (Vulcaia), dry barrel-fermented (Vulcaia Fumé) and sweet late-harvest (Vulcaia Après); this is Stefano Inama (see under Soave, page 207).

Other producers making a worthy effort with Sauvignon are: Luigino Dal Maso (Vigneto Casara Roveri) in the Colli Berici; La Prendina at Custoza (these people also have an estate in Lombardy); Gini (Maciete Fumé); La Cappuccina; Ornella Molon Traverso (Ornella Molon); and Iginio Russolo (Ronco Calaj).

FRIULI-VENEZIA GIULIA

It is in this region, and especially in the eastern section, and *particularly* on the gravelly subsoils of the Isonzo plain, that Italian Sauvignon has really come into its own in recent years, with wine styles somewhere between Bordeaux and Loire for elegance and subtlety while having a voluptuousness of texture peculiarly Friulian (none of that overstated asparagus or tropical fruit-salad that one finds in New World versions, which may be impressive but are difficult to drink in any quantity). In both *barrique*-fermented and unoaked versions there are excellent performers, but one producer stands out of the pack as being an inspiration to Sauvignon-artists Italy-wide if not one of the world's leaders in the genre.

Vie di Romans, Mariano del Friuli, Isonzo. Gianfranco Gallo (whose impertinent wish to use his own name on the label has earned him the wrath of a certain Californian of similar appellation, forcing him to change his winery's title) comes from a long line of growers of the Isonzo plain. He himself took over from his father in the late 1970s when still a teenager, and in his quiet way he has been the leading light in the transformation of Isonzo from a volume-producing flatland to a zone recognized as being one of Italy's two or three finest for white wines. Everything has changed, from the yields, the density of planting and the further impoverishment of the already unfertile soils by grassing the rows to the *cantina* itself and the methods of vinfication and maturation. His production is 95 per cent white and consists of a couple of outstanding Chardonnays (unoaked Ciampagnis Vieris and barrel-fermented Vie di Romans), a broad but structured Pinot Grigio (Dessimis) and a remarkable dry floral-aromatic blend called Flors di Uis – his only white to undergo crio-maceration.

But his greatest triumphs are his unoaked and oaked (in non-new barrels) Sauvignons, respectively Piere and Vieris. It is hard to state a preference between these two extraordinary wines. Piere's aromas are more floral than herbaceous or gooseberry, but there are hints of those varietal calling cards as well. Creaminess of texture, offset by complexity of flavour and a certain richness of body are Vieris' characteristics, but neither here nor in the case of Piere is there any obviousness, either of oak or of aroma, unlike so many supposedly fabulous New World Sauvignons and Fumés.

I asked Gianfranco Gallo how it was that such a flat land as Isonzo could produce such remarkable wines. The answer, it seems, lies mainly in the soil. The topsoil, not more than 40 centimetres deep, is alluvial marl rich in ferrous and aluminium oxide; below it there are the pebbles for good drainage. Where there are no pebbles underneath, everything changes. The other part of the explanation relates to the breeze constantly blowing on to the plain from the east through a gap in the mountains on the Slovenian side of the frontier. This helps keep the vineyards dry and maintains a mean temperature slightly lower than in surrounding areas.

Other Friulian producers capable of outstanding Sauvignon are: Borgo del Tiglio (Collio S.); Edi Kante; Lis Neris – Pecorari (Isonzo S. Dom Picol); Livon (Collio S. Valbuins); Miani (COF S.); Paolo Rodaro (COF Bosc Romain).

In the good to very good category would be included the following: Abbazia di Rosazzo (COF S.); Tenuta **Beltrame** (Friuli Aquileia S.), Bagnaria Arsa; B.& D. Buzzinelli (Collio S. Carlo Buzzinelli); **Castello di Spessa** (Collio S.), Capriva del Friuli; Livio Felluga (COF S.); Edi Keber (Collio S.); Renato Keber (Collio S.); La Castellada (Collio S.); La Viarte (COF Sauvignon); Pierpaolo Pecorari (Isonzo S.); **Pittaro** (Friuli Grave S.), Codroipo; **Polencic** (Collio S.), Cormons; Primosic (Collio S. Gmajne), Gorizia; **Puiatti** (Collio S.; Archetipi), Farra d'Isonzo; Ronco del Gnemiz (COF S.); **Roncus**, Capriva del Friuli; Ronco del Gelso (Isonzo S.); Russiz Superiore (Collio S.); Schiopetto (Collio S.); Torre Rosazza (Silterra); Venica & Venica (Collio S.); Tenuta Villanova (Montecucco); Villa Russiz (Sauvignon de la Tour); Zamò & Zamò (COF S.); **Zof** (COF S.), Corno di Rosazzo.

ALTO ADIGE

The improvement in Sauvignon in Alto Adige and Trentino over the last decade or so has been dramatic, even if there is still very little of it. Ten years ago the only wines of any varietal character at all were Lageder's Lehenhof and the DOC from the cooperative at Terlano, both of which remain very good if occasionally overtaken by new stars. Today there are several capable of impressing even on a world stage. The preferred style seems to steer away from the green, vegetal type associated with some New World Sauvignons towards riper, fuller fruit, occasionally with an oak-fermented component, though not without the requisite whiff of herbaceousness.

A wine that typifies the 'new' Sauvignon is the one out of the St Valentin range at C.S. San Michele Appiano (see under Pinot Bianco, page 272) which took Tre Bicchieri in the 1998 *Vini d'Italia* Guide, with its 'exotic, enveloping aromas', as the author put it. Another comes from:

Peter **Dipoli,** Laives. Peter is a self-described '*appassionato del* *vino*', from a family of grape and apple farmers going back generations. Although his studies at San Michele all'Adige were centred on fruiticulture, his friends were into wine, and his dream of one day owning a vineyard began there. Since that time he has travelled through various parts of the wine world and indeed, when I met him recently in Alto Adige, he had just returned from a week-long trip to the Loire. It was in 1987 that he got the chance to acquire Maso Voglar, at an altitude of 550 metres above the commune of Cortaccia. He decided that the site was ideal for the production of a great white, removed all the existing Schiava vines on *pergola* and replaced them with Sauvignon on *guyot*.

Peter limits production in the vineyard to about 85 quintals per hectare and picks his grapes as late as the beginning of October for full ripeness, the combination of altitude, exposure (east-northeast) and soil (lime-chalk with good structure) ensuring that an adequate acidity level is maintained. Winemaking is normal, no wood involved, no malo-lactic fermentation, and following a period in stainless steel and bottle the wine is released a year after the harvest. This is not a normal practice in a country which generally accepts only the most recent whites, but Peter sees his wine as one benefiting from, indeed requiring time in bottle to bring out its best. A three-year old bottle tasted recently had an evolved, honey and melon style about it, with no signs yet of suffering from advancing age; it was quite different from the recent release, still nettley and zesty with notes of ripe pineapple and grapefruit.

Other producers capable of Alto Adige Sauvignon of real interest include: C.S. Andriano (Terlano Classico); Baron Widman; **Haderburg** (Stainhauser), Salorno; Hirschprunn; Istituto Sperimentale **Laimburg**, Vadena; Ignaz **Niedrist** (A.A. Terlano S.), Cornaiano; C.S. Santa Maddalena (Mockhof); Tiefenbrunner (Kirchenleiten).

TRENTINO

There is less activity with Sauvignon in this province than there is north of Salorno, but there are none the less a few impressive wines. One which certainly deserves that description is the Trentino Sauvignon of the brothers **Cesconi** at Pressano, near Lavis; an unusually lipsmacking combination of ripe fruit and creamy texture, with a well-judged oak component at 50 per cent of the blend. The Cesconi quartet are keen to acknowledge their debt to Mario Pojer and Fiorentino Sandri of Faedo, who also make a small amount of quality Trentino Sauvignon. Other producers of good Sauvignon are Graziano **Fontana**, also of Faedo, and Nicola **Balter** as well as the brothers Zani of **Castel Noarna**, both of whose wineries enjoy vineyards on medium high slopes on opposite sides of the valley at Rovereto. The Castel Noarna, like Cesconi's being from fully mature grapes and having a certain oak component, has a ripeness-cum-typicity that few achieve.

THE BURGUNDY COLLECTION

Historically, it is a little difficult to separate red from white. For one thing, Mondini and other commentators before his time were in the habit of referring to the family collectively as, simply, 'Pinot', generally but not invariably referring to Pinot Nero, of which Pinot Grigio and perhaps Pinot Bianco are considered by ampelographers as genetic mutations (Cosmo and Polsinelli, quoting Frenchmen Viala and Vermorel). In any case, Pinot Grigio is in fact grey, or copper-coloured, nearer to red than white in appearance even though, today, its wines are almost invariably white.

To add to the confusion, Chardonnay in Italy has traditionally been lumped together with Pinot Bianco, both in vineyard and in wine, and it is only recently that the real distinction has been recognized *de facto* as well as *de jure*. At most its separate existence was recognized in the past under some hybrid name. One grower is cited by Mondini as obtaining, from a very low-yield crop of 'Pinot Bianco Chardonnay', a highly appreciated 'Chablis'.

It was inevitably a Sambuy, General Emilio di Sambuy in this case, who first introduced 'Pinot' into his vineyards in the province of Cuneo in Piemonte in 1825, together with 'Gamay'. Even before phylloxera struck Pinot was widespread throughout northern Italy (and the rest), being the subject of numerous direct importations from France rather than the result of propagation from originally imported stock. In 1903 Pinot was present in fifty-three out of sixty provinces throughout Italy, compared with second-place Cabernet's forty-five out of sixty. As for Gamay, it had achieved fairly wide distribution by Mondini's time, but presumably all experiments failed, since it is today virtually non-existent in Italy.

Pinot does not seem to have been considered a success in the trial years, being seen by growers as giving very early ripening grapes prone to grey rot and berry-loss, with very low acid content, deficient colour and, worst of all, a relatively low price on the grape market. Insofar as it was prized at all, it was mainly for purposes of blending with native varieties of high acidity (usually red) such as Raboso, or for the making of sparkling wines. The House of Gancia, following the lead of a certain Cavaliere Boschiero of Asti, whose scholarly approach to winemaking led him to use the original champagne grapes for the making of his *spumante*, seems to have been particularly active in this regard. Gancia encouraged growers in the district of Canelli in Piemonte and in Lombardy's Oltrepò Pavese to carry on trying when otherwise they might have been tempted to rip out their vineyards, as many indeed did.

As the twentieth century proceeded the Pinot family caught on more and more, even if the general quality level on the whole was somewhere between mediocre and poor by world standards. Industrialists learned how to make vaguely acceptable products out of overproduced grapes on ill-suited training systems, and as long as it remained possible to keep prices at rock bottom level there were always buyers.

But by the 1970s, when I first became aware of Italian wines, the outlook for the Pinot family was looking pretty grim. Such Pinot Neros as did exist, from the Oltrepò Pavese, for example, and from Alto Adige, were worlds removed from the *crus* of Burgundy (one or two old bottles from Hofstätter subsequently proved the exception to this rule). The confusion between Chardonnay and Pinot Bianco (to the Germanics conveniently rolled up in a single word: Weissburgunder) was still very much a reality, and the wines in either case were usually either incredibly neutral or faulty. The one exception was Pinot Grigio, which was then in the early days of its take-off; I remember even being quite excited by a bottle of Santa Margherita, at a time when production was relatively limited; in those days it was a wine of real character, a feat which is admittedly difficult if not actually undesirable when you are trying to please all of the people all of the time.

The situation today has evolved – is evolving – dramatically, with the now clearly identified and distinguished Chardonnay in the van. We shall consider that situation in relation to the individual varieties, taking, as ever, red before white.

PINOT NERO

Burgundy's Pinot Noir, Italian Pinot Nero, is, as everyone knows, one of the most difficult yet potentially sublime of all grape varieties. Pinot Nero presents problems relating to a thin skin (paucity of colour and susceptibility to rot in damp conditions at vintage time), early ripening (restricted aromatic-maturation season), and low fixed acidity in warmer climates. Further problems have been self-imposed historically by producers in the form of inferior clones, although this is being addressed by growers who are going now directly to France for their material; and in that of inappropriate training systems (for purposes of quality, without which Pinot Nero is nothing); needless to say, new plantings are all to high-density *guyot*. Today, in certain zones having the kind of day–night temperature fluctuation that characterizes the top growing areas of Burgundy, the search is on for the definitive Pinot Nero. In most cases the goal is frankly a long way off, but in Alto Adige there seem to exist real hopes of competing on the world stage.

PIEMONTE

Considering the affinities between Pinot Noir and Nebbiolo one might think that the former would do well here, but no one yet seems to have cracked the code. A few producers are having a go, but no paid-up burgundy-lover would give them more than E for effort. These include: Marchesi **Alfieri** (San Germano), San Martino Alfieri; Ceretto (Monsordo); Poderi Colla (Campo Romano); Cordero di Montezemolo; Forteto della Luja (Le Grive); Rocche dei Manzoni (Pinònero).

VALLE D'AOSTA

A tiny amount of Pinot Nero exists here, producers being the Institut Agricole Régional (Valle d'Aosta PN) and **Les Crêtes** (Vigne la Tour), both in the town of Aosta.

LOMBARDY

Pinot Nero is the fourth most planted black variety here with about 7 per cent of vineyard area. It has long been established in the Oltrepò Pavese, principally for the making of sparkling wines but also for still reds and the occasional white vinified *in bianco*. Franciacorta is an area of small but increasing importance for table wines.

Easily the most famous Lombard version of Pinot Nero as a red table wine is the Pinero of Cà del Bosco. Despite its pedigree and correctness of bouquet (soft fruits, tomatoes), its generally fairly hefty alcoholic degree (around 13 per cent) and its even heftier price, not to mention the passion and perfectionism that has gone into every centilitre of its production from bud to bottle, it is a wine which has failed to date to deliver full satisfaction. Perhaps this is the eternal fate of Pinot Noir from sparkling wine country. It should be said, however, that if anyone is going to get over the cross-bar here it will probably be Cà del Bosco.

Other producers whose efforts merit attention include: Bellavista (Casotte); **Carlozadra** (Don Ludovico), Grumello del Monte; Doria (Querciolo); Frecciarossa (Oltrepò Pavese PN); Mazzolino (Oltrepò Pavese 'Noir'); Monsupello (Oltrepò Pavese 3309); **Monzio Compagnoni** (Rosso di Nero), Cenate Sotto; **Ruiz de Cardenas** (Brumano), Casteggio; Vercesi del Castellazzo (Oltrepò Pavese Luogo dei Monti).

VENETO

Pinot Nero has very little presence in the vineyards of the Veneto. I have only come across three rather scattered producers at good quality level, all of whom have already been mentioned in other contexts: Gini (Sorai Campo alle More); Scarpa Afra e Tobia; and Serafini & Vidotto.

FRIULI-VENEZIA GIULIA

Pinot Nero is easily the least important of Friuli's Pinots, accounting, as in Veneto, for less than 1 per cent of vineyard space. It does, however, have DOC status in most of Friuli's production zones, and a few quite good wines are produced, lacking perhaps the complexity and magic of burgundy but having reasonable varietal character. On the whole, the growers of Friuli lack the confidence to throw themselves into this admittedly difficult battle. The few who have, with some measure of success, include Dorigo (Ronc di Juri), Vigne dal Leon and **Le Due Terre** of Prepotto (DOC Colli Orientali del Friuli), and Masut da Rive of Mariano del Friuli with an Isonzo DOC.

ALTO ADIGE

Pinot Nero (Blauburgunder) is actually the third most planted black variety in Trentino-Alto Adige (separate figures for the provinces not available) although it occupies less than 4 per cent of total vineyard area. In Trentino the grapes are used mainly for sparklers, but on mountain slopes above San Michele all'Adige, around the village of Faedo, there exist conditions suitable for the production of good quality grapes – without which, obviously, no good Pinot Nero wine will ever happen.

These conditions resemble those of that small sector of Alto Adige on the slopes east of the river, around the villages of Montagna, above Ora, and Pinzon and particularly Mazzon (German speakers spell it Mazon), above Egna, from which come the best Pinot Neros of Italy. If you can call this Italy, that is; certainly no one living there would ever speak Italian except at gunpoint.

Anyway, said conditions consist of a sort of sloping shelf part way up a towering mountain, the exposure being towards the west where, because of the mass of rock immediately behind, the sun doesn't shine on the vineyards till mid-morning, remaining then till latish evening during the growing season. This may be the reverse of the situation in Burgundy's Côte d'Or, but what seems important is the fact that there is a long period of the day when the vineyards are in cool, shaded conditions, and an equal period when the sun is beating directly down upon them. No doubt the soil, rich in glacial deposits, has an effect too on grape quality.

Historically and actually, the pre-eminent producer is **Hofstätter** of Termeno. This is a private winery arising out of a marriage link-up between two growers' families – Paolo Foradori from Mazzon and Sieglinde Oberhofer (Hofstätter was her great-uncle) from Termeno. The cellars and offices, recently totally rebuilt and refurbished, are situated in downtown Termeno, on the west (thus east-facing) side of the valley, and from the surrounding vineyards they produce wines typical of the zone, in particular Gewürztraminer, to a high standard. But the most prized vineyards today are those on the eastern side, including Yngram, where the *cru* wine of that name comes from 70% Cabernet Sauvignon and a whacking 30% Petit Verdot, and especially Villa Barthenau, which incorporates the *cru* Vigna S. Urbano, to date Italy's most prestigious Pinot Nero. A tasting of past vintages of this wine, up to ten years old,

revealed that not only does Vigna S. Urbano have that enthralling Pinot Noir capacity to weave magical aromas of flowers intertwined with nobly decomposing vegetables, helped along by a whiff of woodsmoke and vanilla from barrel, but, most importantly, that the wines have the structure to improve and transform themselves, growing in complexity, with age. In particular, the 1989 is showing a brilliant mix of evolution and youthfulness, with potential to continue on an upward arc.

But there's a rival on the horizon. From a *vasca* (vat) in Hofstätter's cellars I tasted a Pinot Nero from the vineyard Crozzol, above Buchholz at Salorno. A recent acquisition, explained young Martin Foradori: old vines, still on *pergola*, but wonderful perfumes. When, towards the middle of the next century, both S. Urbano and Crozzol are entirely on *guyot* vines of mature age (the former already is, in part), they are going to give each other, and the Pinot Noir producers of the world, a run for their money.

Other producers of the Alto Adige turning out Pinot Nero of some interest include the *cantine sociali* of Caldaro, Colterenzio, Cortaccia and San Michele Appiano. C.S. Burggräfler makes a good *cru* called Tiefenthaler, and C.S. **Termeno** are experimenting with grapes from Glen, above Montagna. Among private producers, wines to look out for include the Riserva from Josef Niedermayr, Raut from Ignaz Niedrist and Mazzon Riserva from Hans Rottensteiner. The alpinist Reinhold Messner of **Castel Juval** at Stava in the Val Venosta, Luis Ochsenreiter of Haderburg (Stainhauser) and Franz Haas (Schweizer) are among private producers who are making serious efforts to unravel the mysteries of Pinot Nero.

TRENTINO

I alluded earlier to the vocation of Faedo, above San Michele all'Adige, for quality Pinot Nero production; the producers in question are the usual Pojer & Sandri and Graziano Fontana. Other people making good to respectable wine include C.S. Lavis (Ritratti), **Longariva** (Zinzele Riserva) at Rovereto, and Maso Cantanghel (Riserva Piero Zabini).

PINOT GRIGIO

Although Pinot Grigio (French Pinot Gris) is a mutation of Pinot Noir, it never caught on to any great extent in Burgundy, rather in Alsace (sometimes under the disappearing name of Tokay d'Alsace) and in areas of southern Germany and Austria, where it is known as Ruländer. Indeed it is likely, according to Mondini, that it was from Austria that it found its way into north-eastern Italy, where it remains widely planted although not so widely as you'd think from the number of bottles sold. In recent years Pinot Grigio has been the subject of much *sofisticazione*, or fiddling, the grape standing in for it very often being the similar but cheaper and more common – when grown in volume in the plain – Pinot Bianco. In this context it may be of interest to note that the area planted to Pinot Grigio in all Italy is about 1,600 hectares, around one third the area devoted to Pinot Bianco, although looking round Italy and the world one sees far more bottles with the former label than with the latter.

The wine style of Pinot Gris in Alsace can be anything from gently perfumed, medium weight, to amazingly rich, concentrated and creamy. In Germany and Austria the wines will often have a bit of residual sugar, indeed some fabulously opulent and concentrated sweet wines are made there from late-harvested grapes. In Italy it rarely if ever attains or aspires to such heights, but has been typecast as an easy-going, medium-bodied *non-impegnativo* white of broad flavour and moderate acidity capable of carrying you through the meal.

In the not so distant past, thanks to its in-between or 'grey' colour, Pinot Grigio was commonly used to make *ramato* or copper-coloured wines, especially in Friuli, and occasionally one still finds such a wine (an example comes from **Specogna** of Corno di Rosazzo in the Colli Orientali del Friuli). It doesn't take much maceration to achieve this result; rather is it often necessary to resort to charcoal fining to avoid a certain blush-colour in the finished product.

NORTH WEST AND VENETO

In the North West Pinot Grigio's presence is negligible, although there are a few knocking around in Valle d'Aosta, where it is sometimes confusingly called Malvoisie despite a total absence of relationship with Malvasia. The inevitable Institut Agricole Régional makes a Vallée d'Aoste Pinot Gris (sic) and the private producer La Crotta di Vegneron, of Chambave, makes a dry Vallée d'Aoste Nus Malvoisie and a sweet Nus Malvoisie Flétri, from *passito* grapes.

In Lombardy's Oltrepò Pavese producers of DOC Pinot Grigio include Le Fracce and C.S. **La Versa** at Santa Maria della Versa.

Despite the presence of Santa Margherita, Veneto is not particularly well-known for the excellence or abundance of its Pinot Grigios – the grape occupies less than 1 per cent of planted area.The most important production zone here is Breganze. Maculan and C.S. Beato Bartolomeo da Breganze turn out typical versions.

FRIULI-VENEZIA GIULIA

We do not begin to find serious Pinot Grigio until we arrive in Friuli, where it claims over 4 per cent of vineyard space. The style here can be likened to that of Alsace for weight and texture, though it rarely if ever succeeds in capturing quite the richness of concentration. Good producers are legion, great ones will perhaps arise in the near future but cannot in all honesty be said to exist today. One who is working towards excellence is:

Lis Neris – Pecorari, San Lorenzo Isontino. It's amazing how many people come into wine from other lines of work and, somehow, stay there, incorporating who they used to be in their new persona. Alvaro Pecorari is an architect by training, but in 1982 he took over from his father Francesco the running of this 23 hectare estate in what is today fashionable Isonzo, and he has been there ever since, designing and building liquids. He is a passionate and committed experimenter at the detailed level, yet with a clear blue-print in mind of where he wants to go and how to go about it. Although perhaps best known for his Merlot-Cabernet blend Lis Neris ('the black ladies'), white wines constitute the great bulk, and for my money the best part, of his production. He divides his Chardonnay, Sauvignon and Pinot Grigio into two lines, the lesser one being made entirely in stainless steel, the greater (qualitatively) from selected grapes rather than from particular sites. The wines of this latter line are (at least partially) fermented in wood, generally 5-hectolitre *tonneaux* of French oak, complete with *bâtonnage*, for a period of at least ten months to give wine and wood plenty of time to integrate.

Pecorari's top-of-the-range Pinot Grigio, called Gris, is a blend of oak- (40 per cent) and steel-fermented wine. Though the only one of the top line not to receive crio-maceration (to avoid colour in the wine) it has great concentration of aroma and fruit flavour balanced by fascinating hints of coffee from the oak – a risky but ultimately successful marriage. The weight and breadth in the mouth are both characteristic and impressive. I have not come across a better example in Friuli, therefore in Italy.

Gris - Pinot Grigio

LIS NERIS - PECORARI

VINO PRODOTTO CON UVE PINOT GRIGIO
MESSO IN BOTTIGLIA ALL'ORIGINE DAL VITICOLTORE ALVARO PECORARI
SAN LORENZO IS.-FRIULI

1996

Other producers of good to very good quality Friulian Pinot Grigio include: Boris and David Buzzinelli (Collio PG); Conti **Attems** (Collio PG), Lucinico; Drius (Isonzo PG); Livio Felluga (COF PG); Marco Felluga (Collio PG); Jermann; Conti **Formentini** (Collio PG), San Floriano del Collio; Polencic (Collio PG); Doro Princic (Collio PG); Puiatti (Collio PG); Ronchi di Manzano (COF PG); Ronco del Gelso (Sot Lis Rivis); Russiz Superiore (Collio PG); Schiopetto (Collio PG); Matijaz Tercic (Collio PG); Franco Toròs (Collio PG); Venica & Venica (Collio PG); Vie di Romans (Dessimis); Villa Russiz (Collio PG); Zof (COF PG).

ALTO ADIGE

Friuli and Alto Adige are certainly the most favoured zones for Pinot Grigio. While Friuli concentrates on breadth of flavour and creaminess of texture, the best wines of Alto Adige feature crispness and bouquet, although there is an increasing and perhaps unfortunate resort to fermentation in new *barrique*, which doesn't always go with the style, as in the case of the much vaunted, but to my mind frankly over-oaked, St Valentin from San Michele Appiano. Even so, while the Alto Adige style makes for good table wines, in the true sense (wines to be drunk at table), they do not normally achieve great heights. As good as any is the one from:

Elena **Walch**, Termeno. After the mighty cooperatives, the most important element in the South Tyrol wine trade has traditionally been the *commerciante* or *négociant*. In recent years their role has been diminishing due to the rise and rise of small producers who used to sell grapes and now prefer to seek the extra profit and satisfaction of selling in bottle. One of the most respected of the remaining *commercianti* is the house of W. Walch of Termeno. Current proprietor Werner Walch also owns vineyards at the medieval castle of Kastelaz in Termeno and at the seventeenth century Castel Ringberg in Caldaro, but decided in the late 1980s to divide the two aspects of the *azienda* between himself and his wife.

Elena Walch is another architect who, despite knowing nothing of wine, found herself sucked into the business and has remained happily ensconced there ever since. From the very fine vineyards of the two castles, increasingly being converted from *pergola* to *guyot* and from Schiava to the more modern likes of Merlot (French clones, of course), she produces a range of whites and reds of an impressive general quality level. In particular, she consistently scores well with her Castel Ringberg Pinot Grigio – one of the few from these parts, incidentally, with no German on the label. This is a sagacious and felicitous blend of wine fermented in *large* oak barrels, conferring an element of gentle oxidation but little wood aroma, as well as a certain softness thanks to the carrying out of the malo-lactic, and wine fermented in stainless steel with, generally, no malo-lactic fermentation. This, it seems to me, is the way to handle wood in relation to this grape whose subtle aromas are too susceptible to being knocked out by great waftings of woodsmoke and vanilla.

Other producers whose wines merit attention include: C.S. Colterenzio (Puiten); Franz Haas (AA PG); Lageder (Benefizium Porer); C.S. Terlano (Klaus); Tiefenbrunner (AA PG); **Viticoltori Alto Adige** (Unterebnerhof), Appiano; **Waldgrieshof** (AA PG), Bolzano.

TRENTINO

There is not so much here by way of really good Pinot Grigio. Probably the best in the whole of Trentino and Alto Adige is the almost voluptuous version of the Cesconi brothers at Pressoni near Lavis – a wine of almost Alsatian richness and mouth-feel. Lavis, indeed, seems to be the centre of production of good Pinot Grigio in Trentino – both Bolognani (Trentino PG) and C.S. Lavis, to whom the Cesconi used to sell their grapes (Ritratti), do a good job. The version of nearby C.S. **MezzaCorona** (Zablani) is also very acceptable.

PINOT BIANCO

The story of Pinot Bianco – its origin in Burgundy, diffusion in the Germanic lands (as Weissburgunder) and arrival in north-eastern Italy via Austria – is akin to that of Pinot Grigio.

Pinot Bianco remains today the most planted member of the Burgundians, with around 4,500 hectares nationally, practically all in the North East, although Chardonnay is rapidly catching up.

In a way this is the Cinderella of the family, although there is no good reason why it should be. Grown in a good hillside site, Pinot Bianco can be a grape of real character capable, albeit in relatively few examples, of making some excellent table wines – gentle of perfume and steely yet flavoursome of palate, with a remarkable ability to age well in favourable circumstances. All too often, alas, it is overproduced in valley sites, disappearing thence into sparkling wines or other blends, and of course it shadows for both Pinot Grigio and Chardonnay in more cases than one would perhaps care to know about. I quote one prominent South Tyrolean white winemaker: 'The best Chardonnay in Alto Adige is that made with Pinot Bianco.'

NORTH WEST AND VENETO

In the North West there are few if any winemakers who will admit to using Pinot Bianco varietally, although it does figure among the important varieties in Lombardy, where it plays a significant role in the blends of Valcalepio Bianco, of which there are no particularly noteworthy exponents that I know of, and Terre di Franciacorta Bianco. Significant producers of this latter include (although it is often difficult to know whether Pinot Bianco prevails in this denomination, which may also be 100% varietal Chardonnay): **Barone Pizzini** (Pulcina), Cortefranca; Bellavista (Convento dell'Annunciata); Cavalleri (Vigna Seradina); Tenuta **Castellino** (Solicano), Coccaglio; Monzio Compagnoni (Ronco della Seta); Uberti (Frati Priori).

In Emilia Pinot Bianco has its own sub-DOC in the Colli Bolognesi, and is produced at decent if uninspiring quality level by Vallania, Vallona and Tenuta Bonzara (Borgo di Qua; Montesevero – plus 30% Chardonnay) at Monte San Pietro.

In the Veneto the above-profiled Maculan (Prato di Canzio – with Chardonnay and Tocai) and Vignalta (Colli Euganei PB) are worthy practitioners.

FRIULI-VENEZIA GIULIA

Only when we arrive in Friuli and Alto Adige do we find producers taking the variety seriously. In the former Pinot Bianco covers over 5 per cent of vineyard area, more than any other member of the family; in the latter, while trailing Chardonnay and Pinot Grigio, it has over 6 per cent.

Doro **Princic**, Pradis di Cormons, Collio. Alessandro Princic, son of Isidoro, has earned a reputation as one of Friuli's finest white winemakers, not by pro-active self-promotion but by staying at home and doing what he does best: tending his vineyards, making sure everything is and remains all right in the cellar, and offering a genial and totally informal welcome to those wine-lovers and writers who seek him out. His particular *forte* is a Collio Pinot Bianco made without wood, a wine which somehow manages to combine perfect cleanness of aroma with subtlety and complexity of palate. It is a wine for connoisseurs, not for those who like the brash bouquet and the flashy flavours of the show trophy winners. Princic, who also makes good red from Merlot and Cabernet Franc, explains his affection for Pinot Bianco in simple economic terms. 'The reds here come good three years in ten. You need six or seven out of ten to make a good living. But even in a bad year, Pinot Bianco *si salva sempre* (always saves itself).' Fair enough, if the wine then proceeds to turn out as well as his does year after year.

Most, but by no means all, of the best Pinot Biancos of Friuli come from the Collio. Excellent versions are turned out as a matter of routine by Silvio Jermann, Russiz Superiore, Mario Schiopetto and Villa Russiz, all profiled elsewhere.

Other representative producers include: Borgo Conventi (Collio PB); **Borgo Lotessa** (Collio PB), San Floriano del Collio; Cà Ronesca (COF PB); Castello di Spessa (Santarosa); Marco Felluga (Collio PB); Edi Keber (Collio PB); Renato Keber (Grici); La Boatina (Collio PB); Livon (Collio PB); Masut da Rive (Isonzo PB); Pierpaolo Pecorari (Fara); Polencic (Collio PB); Puiatti (Collio PB): Rodaro (Bosc Romain); **Ronco delle Betulle** (COF PB), Manzano; Scubla (COF PB); Torre Rosazza (COF PB); **Vazzoler Redi** (Collio PB), Mossa; Venica & Venica (Collio PB); Vigne dal Leon (Tullio Zamò).

ALTO ADIGE

As in Friuli, so here has Pinot Bianco yielded the high ground to Chardonnay, though there are some wines of beautifully clean lines and penetrating flavour, without frills. I have in the past tasted some delicious older Weissburgunders from Hofstätter, demonstrating the variety's ability to age well, generally following *botte*-maturation as is sometimes still practised. One *cantina sociale* representing the best of the Alto Adige style is:

C.S. San Michele Appiano, Appiano. 'I believe in Pinot Bianco – it is our reality. It's the market that doesn't believe.' Thus Hans Terzer, since 1977 *cantinista* then *Kellermeister* at this large cooperative (founded 1907), described by one pundit as 'the best in Alto Adige for white wines'. From their 280 hectares of vineyard belonging to 300 members, mostly in the vicinity of the winery at varying altitudes between 250 and 700 metres, San Michele produce the usual plethora of wines divided into three lines: 'Classic' (read normal), 'Selection' (wines based on specific sites) and St Valentin, named after an actual castle on one of their domains. It is for St Valentin, created in the 1980s and dedicated to the highest quality, that they are most lauded, in particular for the *barrique*-fermented Chardonnay and Pinot Grigio and the fruit-driven Sauvignon (indisputably one of Italy's best) and Gewürztraminer.

Weissburgunder Schulthauser does not belong to the St Valentin range, rather the 'Selection' line, yet it is clearly Terzer's most beloved, the one which 'succeeds best in expressing both the essential quality of Alto Adige white wine and the production philosophy of our winery'. The grapes are produced in a 12-hectare area at around 500 metres by a small band of dedicated growers, interestingly enough all training being on *pergola*; indeed Terzer declares himself to be 'not 100 per cent convinced by *guyot* for

white wines, because what you gain in sugar you risk losing in aroma'. Vinification takes place in stainless steel except for around 20 per cent which is aged in large French oak barrels. The young wine displays a delicious balance of fruity acidity and creamy texture, but Terzer was able to demonstrate with wines up to eight years old that it has the potential to age brilliantly, taking on ripe fruit-cum-yeasty/biscuity aromas of great penetration and length.

Will he not make a Weissburgunder St Valentin? I gathered that, despite the market, he is indeed planning a higher grade version of Pinot Bianco, but it will have to be something 'quite different'. Schulthauser, now an institution, stays as it is.

Others making Alto Adige Pinot Biancos of which it is never difficult to get down a second glass after the first, or a third after the second, include: the *cantine sociali* of Colterenzio (Weisshaus), Cornaiano (Plattenriegl), Terlano (Vorberg) and Viticoltori Alto Adige (Eggerhof Plattenriegl); Baron Widman (AA PB); Hofstätter (Villa Barthenau); Lageder (Haberlehof); Niedrist (AA Terlano PB); Hans Rottensteiner (AA PB); and Tiefenbrunner (AA PB).

TRENTINO

Trentino's style is very like that of Alto Adige, good producers of Trentino Pinot Bianco DOC including: Cesconi; Conti Martini; Elisabetta Foradori (Vigneto Sgarzon); Istituto Agrario Provinciale; Maso Roveri; Simoncelli.

CHARDONNAY

The confusion earlier alluded to between Chardonnay and Pinot Bianco was not restricted to Italy. Until nearly the end of the nineteenth century the grape was known even in France as Pinot Blanc Chardonnay, and enjoyed many synonyms, including Pineau de la Bourgogne (the Loire-style spelling may be significant). According to ampelographers, while Pinot Blanc is a true native of Burgundy, being a genetic mutation of Pinot Noir, Chardonnay is descended from that Melon Musqué which originated in the Orléannais in the Middle Ages and later travelled to Champagne's Côte des Blancs and down into Burgundy, ultimately deriving its present name from the Mâconnais village of Chardonnay, itself being somewhat unpoetically named after the green-leafed vegetable known to the French as *chardon*.

It was only in 1872 that the distinction between the two varieties was officially recognized in France. Official Italian differentiation (by the Ministry of Agriculture) was not to arrive until over a century later, in 1978, although since the beginning of the century the confusion had been limited to the non-academic community, ampelographers being clear in their minds as to the differences between what were sometimes called 'Pinot Bianco Vero' (true Pinot Blanc) or 'Pinot Verde' or 'Borgogna Verde' on the one hand; and 'Pinot Giallo' or 'Borgogna Gialla' on the other (this latter being Chardonnay).

Indeed the distinction was already understood by that pioneer General Emilio di Sambuy who imported both 'Chardonnay' and 'Pinot Bianco' into his vineyards in the province of Cuneo in the 1820s.

When Chardonnay started becoming the buzz word among world white grapes in the 1970s, suddenly growers all over northeastern Italy began to realize that it was in their interests to determine exactly what it was they had growing on their *pergole*. Although the majority of it was Pinot Bianco, a lot more than expected turned out to be Chardonnay, from which point the lawmakers have been busy creating new DOCs in the wake of demand.

Today Chardonnay is produced in virtually every region of Italy. The figure of 3,154 hectares recorded by Fregoni and Schiavi (*I Primi Cento Nostri Vitigni*, Civiltà del Bere, February 1996) as being the total for the country is probably a gross underestimate, although it is still only in the North East and Lombardy that the grape is grown in large volume.

Wine styles have traditionally – where a tradition exists, that is: mainly in Alto Adige – followed Pinot Bianco lines (overcropped and unoaked), and only when Chardonnay started becoming sexy did the *barrique*-fermented, lees-stirred versions begin to emerge. Today, together with everyone else in the Chardonnay-producing world, some Italians have begun to make a positive virtue out of *not* oaking the wine.

PIEMONTE

Although Chardonnay in any commercial sense is a recent phenomenon in Piemonte, growers have taken to it with some alacrity because it allows them to use vineyard sites which are north-facing or low-lying and therefore too cool for the regular ripening of the classic red grapes. These days there are numerous versions, oaked and unoaked, among them wines of great character, balance and concentration, wines capable of standing alongside the best in the world. The only trouble is that production in most cases is very low and prices rather high. Outstanding practitioners include Gaja (Gaia e Rey; Rossi-Bass) and Aldo Conterno (Bussiador; Printanié – this latter pair an excellent example of oaked versus unoaked, respectively). Another producer of wines of real excellence is:

Luigi **Coppo**, Canelli. Situated in the heart of Moscato and Barbera country, this *cantina* has been operating as what the French would call a *négociant-éleveur* since the early years of the twentieth century. It is, however, only with the present generation of four brothers Coppo – Roberto, Gianni, Paolo and Piero – that the emphasis has been been placed on top quality as distinct from commercial production. Barbera has remained the main priority, their Pomorosso and Camp du Rouss being considered among the best of the modern *barrique*d versions, especially the former, coming as it does from older vines while being aged in newer barrels. Other categories in which they excel are champagne-style sparkling wines (Riserva Coppo and Piero Coppo Riserva del Fondatore) and – a niche market, this – serious still dry Freisa, of which their *barrique*-aged Mondaccione is consistently one of the finest examples.

But it is for their pioneering work in the development of high-quality Piemontese Chardonnay that they, along with Gaja and Pio Cesare, are perhaps most noteworthy. The difference between their two *crus*, Monteriolo and Costebianche, is (apart from grape quality) the fact that Monteriolo is entirely vinified in oak, where it completes its malo-lactic and remains on the lees for about eight months, with *bâtonnage*; while Costebianche is one-third vinified in *barrique* and two-thirds vinified in steel, half of which is then aged in *barrique*. It is interesting, but not surprising, that the wine which completes all its transformations in oak achieves the greater integration, while in the Costebianche the oak tends to stand out somewhat from the wine.

Other Piemontese capable of seriously good Chardonnay include:

Orlando Abrigo (Rocca del Borneto); Araldica (Alasia – oaked and unoaked); Bertelli (Giarone); Cisa Asinari (Chardonnay Grésy); Conterno-Fantino (Bastia); Gastaldi; Elio Grasso (Educato); La Spinetta (Lidia); La Tenaglia (Oltre); Moccagatta (Buschet); Mauro Molino (Vigna Livrot); Pio Cesare (Piodilei; l'Altro); Rivetti (Lydia); Bruno Rocca (Cadet); Rocche dei Manzoni (l'Angelica); Saracco (Prasù); Roberto Voerzio (Fossati e Roscaleto).

VALLE D'AOSTA

The Institut Agricole Régional and Les Crêtes (Cuvée Frissonière) of Aosta both produce reasonable Chardonnays.

LOMBARDY

Lombardy is second only to Trentino-Alto Adige in Chardonnay production in Italy, the grape representing some 3.5 per cent of total regional plantings. Most of it is destined for use in sparkling wines of various descriptions, but there is a growing number of classic wines along burgundian lines coming mainly out of the Franciacorta zone.

The denomination Terre di Franciacorta Bianco, created in the mid-1990s to distinguish the sparkling wine of the zone (Franciacorta DOCG) from the still stuff, has actually created new confusion. What was traditionally called Franciacorta Bianco, generally a blend of Chardonnay and Pinot Bianco in varying proportions, can now cover that blend (with Pinot Nero *in bianco*, if you like) or any of the three at 100% – *in purezza*. So with Terre di Franciacorta Bianco you're never too sure what you're getting, although if it's pure Chardonnay it will probably say so somewhere on the bottle.

The archetype for what is now called Terre di Franciacorta Chardonnay in the classic mode is indisputably that of Cà del Bosco. Others in the immediate area who are capable of wines of good to excellent character include: Bellavista (Uccellanda); Tenuta **Castellino** (Solicano), Coccaglio; Cavalleri (Rampaneto); Enrico Gatti (Gatti Bianco); Guarischi (Le Solcaie); **La Ferghettina** (Favento), Erbusco; **Mirabella** (Bianco *Barrique*), Rodengo Saiano; Monzio Compagnoni (Ronco della Seta), Cortefranca; **Principe Banfi** (Pio IX), Erbusco; Uberti (Maria dei Medici; Bianco dei Frati Priori); Villa (Riserva Marengo).

In the Valcalepio area Castello di Grumello make a good version called Aurito. Monsupello are producers of a good Oltrepò Pavese Chardonnay called Senso.

EMILIA

Both Vallania (Cuvée Giovanni Vallania) and Vallona make good Chardonnay wines, though it is not a much used grape there.

VENETO

Chardonnay has never caught on particularly in this region, possibly because of the strength of Garganega in the western section and of Prosecco towards the east. Probably the best-known version comes from the centre, being the Ferrata of Maculan in Breganze, alluded to earlier. Recently, as we have seen, there has been a bit of a surge in the Soave zone, partly because of the admittance of Chardonnay into the Soave blend. Good examples are Gini's Sorai and Inama's Campo dei Tovi. Zenato turn out a good *barrique*d Chardonnay from the Lugana area. In the Colli Berici Luigino Dal Maso makes a decent version from his Casara Roveri vineyard.

FRIULI-VENEZIA GIULIA

Considering the number of Chardonnay and Chardonnay-based wines there are in this region, it is surprising to note that the actual hectarage devoted to the grape is well below 1 per cent of total plantings. Outstanding producers include Vie di Romans (whose *crus* Vie di Romans and Ciampagnis Vieris offer an interesting insight into the oaked versus unoaked genres); Borgo del Tiglio; Lis Neris – Pecorari (St Jurosa); and Dorigo (Ronc di Juri). Two of the greatest stars in the Chardonnay context over the past few years have been Josko Gravner and the Bensa brothers of La Castellada, both of Oslavia; but despite the glory, there seems to be some doubt as to whether these producers will continue to make varietal wines.

Another major force in Friulian Chardonnay is:

Azienda Agricola **Livon**, San Giovanni al Natisone. This is a family-owned enterprise with vineyard holdings in Collio, Colli Orientali and Friuli Grave. In the past their wines have been considered good-value, reliable but unexciting, however the *crus* they have been developing over the past few years have been winning them increasing praise to the point where they are now positioned not only among the biggest (they own well over 100 hectares of vineyard) but among the best. The range is wide and embraces white and red, blend and varietal, indigenous and international. Some examples: the Bordeaux blend Tiareblù, the Verduzzo Friulano Casali Godia, the Collio Sauvignon Valbuins, all judged top of their class in recent years.

Chardonnay is an essential component of the mix, the main *cru* being Braide Mate, which scores among Friuli's best year after year. It is barrel-fermented but the oak is nicely integrated and behind the ripe fruit and custard flavours there is a firm acid backbone capable of holding the wine together for some years. The stainless steel-fermented Tre Clas is considerably less complex, clean and fresh if somewhat monolinear, but no doubt the combination of the Livon family's will and oenologist Rinaldo Stocco's skill should succeed in coming years to add dimension to this wine.

Others capable of good to excellent wines include: Abbazia di Rosazzo (COF Ch.); Borgo Conventi (Colle Russian); **Borgo San Daniele** (Isonzo Ch.), Cormons; Jermann; Edi Kante; Renato Kante (Grici); Masut da Rive (Maurus); Pierpaolo Pecorari (Soris); Primosic (Gmajne); Puiatti (Collio Ch.); **Radikon** (Collio Ch.), Oslavia; Ronco del Gelso (Isonzo Ch.); Ronco del Gnemiz (COF Ch.); Leonardo Specogna (COF Ch.); Tercic (Collio Ch.); **Vidussi** (Collio Ch.), Capriva del Friuli; Tenuta Villanova (Monte Cucco); Volpe Pasini (Zuc di Volpe).

ALTO ADIGE

Separate figures are not available for Alto Adige and Trentino, but overall Chardonnay represents nearly 20 per cent of total production in the region, making it by a wide margin the most-grown white grape. Traditionally by far the most important area for varietal Chardonnay, as distinct from *spumante* base-wine (which is also very important, especially in Trentino), quality levels in South Tyrol have risen dramatically since I first started looking nearly twenty years ago. But there's still a lot of work to do, mainly in getting the vines off *pergola* and on to *spalliera* training systems of much greater density per hectare and much less yield per plant.

Among the best producers of Alto Adige Chardonnay are the C.S. Colterenzio (Cornell – oaked; Coret – unoaked); Lageder (Löwengang); and San Michele Appiano (St Valentin). But one producer deserves to be limelit here not only for the consistently high quality of his Chardonnay but for length of service to the cause of fine wine in Alto Adige:

Tiefenbrunner – Schloss Turmhof, Cortaccia. Herbert Tiefenbrunner is probably the longest serving *cantiniere* in Italy (he would prefer the word *kellermeister*; indeed, he would prefer not to be in Italy), having celebrated his fiftieth anniversary in that role in 1993; and while, bit by bit, he is yielding ground to his son Christof, he can still be found wearing his cellar-master's blue apron whenever you turn up for a tasting. Nor has his enthusiasm dimmed in this half-century plus by a single watt – he will still, in the course of the tasting, rush down to the cellar to fish out further samples from this tank or that *barrique* for your further delectation, and his eyes will gleam and winning smile flash when you confirm your approval.

The house of Tiefenbrunner, having a thriving in-house tourist trade to cater to, in the form of busloads of Austrians and Germans, still offers the vast range of wines which cover practically all the possibilities in South Tyrolean varietal production, red, white and pink, Germanic, French and local varieties, from grapes grown in estate vineyards or from grapes bought in. You wonder how they manage to keep track of it all, but somehow they do, turning out excellent Cabernet and Pinot Nero (Linticlarus), Lagrein (Castel Turmhof), Pinots Grigio and Bianco, Sauvignon, Riesling, Goldmuskateller and, most importantly, a steely, elegantly perfumed Müller-Thurgau from a 1,000-metre high vineyard on the Fennberg mountain that looms above them, called Feldmarschall.

Perhaps the grape they have managed best in recent years is Chardonnay, which they produce *barrique*-fermented with *bâtonnage* under the Linticlarus name as well as (mainly) stainless steel-fermented under the Castel Turmhof label. Those in Italy and elsewhere whose *barrique*d wines practically knock you backwards with the rush of oak vanilla and toast to the nose could take a lesson from Linticlarus, where the wood is used to enhance the fruity, biscuity aromas, not overwhelm them. And because 25,000 bottles are produced you won't be floored either by the price, or enraged

by the non-availability of the wine two days after it has received some prestigious award.

Other noteworthy South Tyrolean Chardonnay producers include: C.S. Andriano (Tor di Lupo); C.S. Caldaro (Waldleith); C.S. Cortaccia (Eberlehof); Erste & Neue (Puntay); C.S. Termeno (Glassien Renommée); Haderburg (Stainhauser); Elena Walch (Castel Ringberg); Peter **Zemmer** (Etichetta Tradizione), Cortina.

TRENTINO

Those Chardonnay grapes which do not get poured into *spumante* go towards the making of some pretty decent Chardonnays, representative producers including: Cavit (Maso Torresella); **Ferrari** (Villa Margon), Trento; La Cadalora; C.S. Lavis (Ritratti); Longariva (Perer); Maso Cantanghel (Vigna Piccola); Pojer & Sandri (Fayé); Vallarom; **Zeni** (Sortì), San Michele all'Adige.

The best Chardonnay I have tasted from Trentino comes from a producer already mentioned several times, namely:

Cesconi, Lavis. Although a recent phenomenon on the Trentino scene, this small estate in no time has shot to the top of the charts, certainly in terms of white table wines. But the four young brothers – Alessandro, Franco, Roberto and Lorenzo, who between them share responsibility for the vineyards, the winery and the business side – are not newcomers to grape-growing, an activity which goes back in their family seven or eight generations. Until 1994 all the grapes were sold either to the nearby Cantina Sociale di Lavis, who used them for making their Ritratti wines, or to Pojer & Sandri up the mountain in Faedo, for both of which producers they retain the greatest respect and who indeed encouraged them to seek further satisfaction in wine production.

The first wines from their 6 hectares of vineyard – plus the odd hectare under rental – were of the 1995 vintage, but they were preparing the ground from a decade earlier, when they began to substitute relatively densely planted *guyot* for the traditional *pergola*. Their belief that great wines come from great raw material has certainly, to date, been justified, their partially *barrique*-conditioned Pinot Grigio, Sauvignon and Chardonnay, as well as their stainless steel-made Pinot Bianco, Traminer and Nosiola, all showing brilliant but not excessive varietal character and excellent concentration.

The Chardonnay is perhaps the star, its melon and grapefruit aromas offset by discreet oak and a house-style mouth-feel which combines velvety viscosity with firm acidity. Another lesson-wine for the over-oakers.

As a footnote, the Cesconis have planted a vineyard in a site at Ceniga di Drò ideal, they claim, for Merlot, Cabernet Sauvignon and, surprisingly, Syrah, and are cooking up some, at first view, highly interesting red wines. Which mention of Syrah brings us neatly to:

THE RHÔNE CLONES

This category includes Syrah and Grenache among reds and Viognier, Marsanne and Roussanne among whites. While all of these are to be found in northern Italy today, their presence is extremely limited.

SYRAH

According to Mondini, there was a time when Syrah was quite widespread in the north, although never in significant volume. In his time it was planted in parts of Piemonte, Lombardy, Veneto and Emilia, sometimes under the name Sirah, sometimes known as Sirah dell'Ermitage or simply Ermitage which, in dialect, became Arnitas.

So why did it not develop the following that the grapes of Bordeaux and Burgundy were to acquire? The question is not easy to answer, since Mondini mentions several factors which might have endeared it to growers. It is a hardy vine, he reports, quite disease resistant, giving a wine of good colour and sweet fruit, good for blending. Its disadvantages include low yield per plant (but the same is true of Cabernet Sauvignon) and a weakness against winter frost, which could indeed be a problem in northern Italian climes.

What little exists in northern vineyards today is more often than not recently re-introduced, with clones from France and *spalliera* training systems. It is also rare for Syrah to be recognized in a given zone as an authorized variety, which means its name cannot be mentioned on labels. Contemporary producers in Piemonte include Ceretto under the Monsordo label and Bertelli (St Marsan Rosso). Ascheri have also recently brought out a notable version in very reduced quantity. The Paradiso of La Tenaglia is another good example.

In Aosta the Institut Agricole Régional makes a Syrah called Trésor du Caveau.

In Alto Adige Lageder, at Casòn Hirschprunn, is experimenting with Syrah as well as with Mourvèdre, Viognier, Roussanne and Marsanne, some of which are finding their way into the blends Casòn (red) and Contest and Etelle (white).

In Trentino good Syrah is being produced by Elisabetta Foradori (Ailanpà) and by Pravis (Syra), while others, such as Cesconi, continue to experiment.

GRENACHE

Grenache is virtually non-existent in the north. Exceptions include the Granaccia (sic) of Innocenzo Turco at Quiliano in Liguria and possibly the Tocai Rosso of the Colli Berici in Veneto. If the latter is indeed Grenache, perhaps it might be taken as proof that Grenache has no business being grown in northern Italy.

VIOGNIER, MARSANNE AND ROUSSANE

Despite the great promise displayed by its wines in central Italy,

Viognier is grown hardly at all at present in the north. Ceretto's Monsordo Bianco is a rare exception. Matteo Ascheri has recently unveiled a version which, while pricey, is of considerable character.

To my knowledge, the only example of Roussanne and Marsanne in northern Italy is the St Marsan Bianco of Bertelli at Costigliole d'Asti in Piemonte.

THE TEUTONICS AND EASTERN EUROPEANS

Despite the lengthy presence of Austria in what is now Italy (however much that fact may be resented by some), the Austro-Germanic varieties have never really caught on to any great extent. Insofar as they have, it has of course been the white varieties that have led the way, it being in Alto Adige, obviously, and to a somewhat lesser extent in Trentino that these have had the greatest influence.

Just to run rapidly through the reds, one could mention **WILD-BACHER** in passing, and anyone desperate to try an Italian Wildbacher could seek out the versions of Lino **Ballancin** or Le Case Bianche, both of Pieve di Soligo, or of **Conte Collalto** at nearby Susegnana in the province of Treviso, Veneto, the area into which it was introduced in the nineteenth century. The vine is fairly prolific, and the wines tends to be of a bright ruby colour, having little polyphenolic structure but plenty of acidity. Mondini dismisses Wildbacher by commenting that its quality 'leaves much to be desired'.

FRANCONIA, a.k.a. Blaufränkisch, is another Eastern European (Croatian?) or possibly German (from Frankfurt-am-Main?) curiosity, occasionally encountered in Trentino and Friuli. Ronco delle Betulle, of Manzano in the Colli Orientali di Friuli, produce an interesting version.

Of the Teutonic white varieties the only one that figures in the top 100 most planted grapes is **RIESLING ITALICO**, known in Austria as Wälschriesling. This variety, which seems to have arrived in Italy in the late nineteenth century, has come in for a lot of stick from wine writers indignant that it should seem to be laying impertinent claim, by its name, to a relationship with the noble Rheinriesling. Riesling Italico may indeed be distinctly inferior in that context, but it is not so prolific nor so devoid of character as some would have us believe, being capable of good sugar levels with balancing acidity, even when grown in the plains of Veneto and Friuli. From hilly sites – in the Collio, Oltrepò Pavese, Colli Bolognesi and various parts of Veneto and Trentino – it can make a wine of some substance, good at least for use as a blender if not varietally.

Prestigious names associated with Riesling Italico production include Leonildo Pieropan of Soave and Mazzolino (Oltrepò Pavese Camarà).

RIESLING RENANO, or Rheinriesling, according to some (not me) the world's single greatest grape variety, is a grape of considerable potential in northern Italy, although no one has yet taken it beyond a discreet quality level, the style as a varietal being almost invariably dry-table-wine, comparable with basic Alsace. Increasingly, however, Riesling Renano is being used as a blend component, as we shall see in the next section.

An example of Riesling Renano from Piemonte is the Langhe Bianco of Aldo Vajra of Barolo. In Lombardy producers include C.S. La Versa (Oltrepò Pavese R.R. La Campostella) and Doria (Oltrepò Pavese R.R. Roncobianco).

In Veneto an unusually successful version is made by Le Vigne di San Pietro under the name I Balconi Bianco. In Friuli a notable example is that of Jermann (Afix). Other good producers include Puiatti, Schiopetto and Villa Russiz in the Collio and Paolo Rodaro in the Colli Orientali.

The biggest concentration of quality Riesling Renano is predictably in Italy's Germany, South Tyrol. Good producers of Alto Adige Riesling Renano DOC include Castel Juval in Val Venosta, Istituto Sperimentale Laimburg, Josef Niedrist, C.S. Santa Maddalena, C.S. San Michele Appiano (Montiggl), Schwanburg and Tiefenbrunner. In Trentino the flag is flown by the Istituto Agrario Provinciale at San Michele all'Adige and Zeni (Reré).

Riesling Renano is one partner in the cross developed at Geisenheim in the late nineteenth century by Dr Hermann **MÜLLER-THURGAU**; the other partner being Sylvaner (actually doubts have been raised as to the grape's antecedents, but we'll stick to the official line having no evidence to gainsay it). The cross was planted by its creator in Switzerland, and later became the subject of research at Klosterneuburg in Austria, from whence it travelled south to the Istituto Agrario at San Michele all'Adige in 1939. That institute being strongly influential through Trentino-Alto Adige, the variety found favour in both provinces where today it retains a modest following.

Apparently, even earlier than 1939, Müller-Thurgau was experimented with by producers in Friuli via the Istituto Sperimentale at Conegliano, but it was not considered a success, and trials were not pursued. Today it may be found in various parts of northern Italy.

From Gavi in Piemonte comes a version under the Monferrato DOC by Villa Sparina. In Valle d'Aosta La Crotta di Vegneron is a producer, as is Ronco del Gnemiz in Friuli. Pasqua in Verona bottle a Müller-Thurgau, but it's from Trentino.

It is not until we arrive in Trentino itself, and Alto Adige, that we find Müller-Thurgau produced in any volume. Tiefenbrunner, with his 1,000 metre high Fennberg vineyard, would be the most obvious candidate for a profile if he had not already been profiled for Chardonnay. Feldmarschall is a wine of steely acidity and gentle aromaticity, capable of evolving interestingly in bottle over a period of some years.

Another notable producer is the C.S. Valle **Isarco** (Kellereigenossenschaft Eisacktal) at Chiusa, which specializes in Germanic varieties: Gewürztraminer, Ruländer (Pinot Grigio), Sylvaner, Kerner and Veltliner. Their Müller-Thurgau goes under the *cru* name Aristos. Other South Tyrolean producers of note include C.S. Cortaccia and **Abbazia di Novacella** (Stift Neustift) at Varna.

In Trentino the way is led by Pojer & Sandri, who have been famous for Trentino Müller-Thurgau since their inception. Graziano Fontana is another one making the steely, ripe, slightly flowery style for which Faedo has become known. The Istituto Agrario Provinciale, needless to say, is another prominent producer. Then there is Bolognani (M.T. della Val di Cembra), C.S. Lavis and Pravis (St Thomà).

Perhaps the most successful of the Germanic grapes in Italy, probably because it, or at least its name, derives, as we have seen, from the town of Tramin (Termeno) in South Tyrol, is **TRAMINER AROMATICO** or **GEWÜRZTRAMINER**. Up to the mid-1980s, whether because of the wrong clones, or overproduction, or a distaste on the part of Italians for very scented wines, it was rare to find a Traminer with that spicy, perfumed character quite common in Alsace. On the subject of clones, see below. As for the question of taste, this is probably a red herring (one I myself have swallowed and regurgitated in the past), since Italians seem happy enough to hail scented wines now that they are beginning to produce them to a good standard. The problem, as in most cases, was probably overproduction, not that Traminer lends itself to great volumes: it can be 'overproduced' even at relatively low volume. Poor siting (the grape responds best in heavy soils, not so well in chalk) may also have had something to do with it, as indeed may training on *pergola*.

In the last few years the situation has improved dramatically, and although Italian styles rarely display that lush, heady scent of the wealthy widow anxious to compensate for wrinkles with Chanel, nevertheless varietal character is coming through quite distinctly. There is, indeed, a case to be made for the Italian style, since the toning down of the scented side makes arguably for a more drinkable wine.

The question of clones is a tricky one. There appear to exist three shades: Bianco, Rosa and Rosso, all deriving from the same root via diverse genetic mutations, as in the case of Pinot. The pigmented sub-varieties have been taken by some to be inferior, but this is not the case intrinsically – the problem being that less skin contact, and therefore less leaching of aromatic substances, is possible because of the undesirability of colour in what is supposed to be white wine.

Where this grape originated from no one seems quite sure – Alsace, the Rhine and Alto Adige itself all have their proponents. Certainly it has been in South Tyrol for centuries, and if Mondini tells us that, in his time, Traminer was not much diffused in Italy, that is explicable by the fact that neither Alto Adige nor eastern Friuli were then in Italy.

In the North West there are, to my knowledge, no notable examples of Traminer, nor is it included in any of the DOC *disciplinari* for that part of the country. The same is true for Veneto, and it is only when we arrive in Friuli that we find official recognition. Despite enjoying sub-DOC status in all the main Friulian production zones, however, there are precious few wines to show for it. Jermann's is the only one I know of.

The grape's real stamping ground, predictably, is the area around Tramin in Alto Adige. Indeed practically all of the best Traminers in Alto Adige, and therefore in Italy, come from the western side of the Adige valley between the villages of Appiano and Magrè, of which Tramin is more or less the central point.

It seems only appropriate, in this context, to feature a producer of Tramin itself, and who better than the local cooperative, C.S. **Termeno**. Of course, being in the environs of Lake Caldaro, this is also, indeed mainly, the heart of Schiava country, and a whacking 75 per cent of C.S. Termeno's production is of that grape. But let's ignore that unfortunate fact, and concentrate on the positive. In an average year the members will produce around 1,200 quintals of Traminer grapes, as I was informed by the young winemaker Wilhelm Sturz, which translates into about 750 hectolitres of wine – which is still quite a lot of Traminer. Production is divided according to provenance and quality, the best vineyards being of old vines on *pergola* or younger vines on *guyot*, subject to bunch-thinning (*diradamento*) and various other quality controls. The most important *crus* of Traminer Aromatico are Nussbaumerhof and Maratsch, the former being subject to more *diradamento* and having more vines planted to *guyot*. Both have the characteristic perfume of the variety, though certainly not in excess (rather leaning in the other direction), and good mouth-feel, Nussbaumerhof being somewhat superior in this respect.

The aforementioned Mr Sturz came to the winery in 1992, and graduated to chief winemaker in 1994. He does not pretend that everything is exactly as it should be at the moment, but feels that progress is being made. Certainly, to judge by the newest wines in tank, this appears to be the case. We look forward to the continuing revival of Traminer in the zone which gave it its name.

Other good to very good producers of Alto Adige Gewürztraminer include: Abbazia di Novacella (Valle Isarco); C.S. Caldaro (Campaner); C.S. Colterenzio (Cornell); Erste & Neue (Puntay); Hofstätter (Kolbenhof); **Kuenhof** (Valle Isarco), Bressanone; Laimburg; C.S. San Michele Appiano (St Valentin); Tiefenbrunner (Castel Turmhof); Elena Walch (Kastelaz).

Trentino Traminer Aromatico is of very little significance. Examples of some interest come from: Cesconi, Istituto Agrario di San Michele, Madonna delle Vittorie and Pojer & Sandri.

The presence of **SYLVANER** in Italy verges on the non-existent, though there are a few producers in Alto Adige's Valle Isarco who turn out good wines, these including Abbazia di Novacella, Kuenhof and C.S. Valle Isarco, who actually go to the extreme of making two separate *crus*, Aristos and Dominus.

VELTLINER is produced by all three of the above under the

Alto Adige Valle Isarco sub-DOC. This, apparently, is not the Grüner Veltliner of Austria but a Roter (red) Veltliner of obscure origin, perhaps – as the name suggests – from the Valtellina. Alas, no one really cares.

KERNER has, if anything, even less presence than Veltliner. Hofstätter have one but it will soon be walking the plank. That leaves C.S. Valle Isarco, Pravis of Lasino in Trentino, and – er . . .

IV
BLENDS

—

Obviously, in a book based on grape varieties, complex blends need to be considered apart. By 'complex blend' I mean one in which no single variety is predominant, either percentage-wise or in organoleptic terms. The purpose of the maker, in such cases, is to create a wine of disparate parts, bringing them together in a harmonic synthesis in such a way as to place the emphasis on the sum of the parts rather than on any particular constituent. One might draw an analogy with music. The solo obviously focuses the attention on the sound of a single instrument, the concerto on that of one instrument against a background of others, the string quartet or wind ensemble on the consonance of instruments of a single family, while the symphony features no sound in particular but rather the harmony of a variety of different sounds.

In wine terms, the 'solo' is the pure varietal, even if oak and/or fermentation or maturation aromas may somewhat complicate the issue. The 'concerto' – where a single grape represents a dominant component of a blend – still falls near the definition of varietal. The 'ensemble', where only grapes of a particular family – say the Bordeaux family – are used, would still, I would argue, be classifiable varietally under the heading of its lead player, since the primary aromas of all players are interrelated. Perhaps opportunistically, I have extended this category to include the likes of Nebbiolo plus Barbera (Langhe) or Corvina plus Rondinella plus Molinara (Valpolicella) – in other words blends traditional in a given zone. Such a blending I would describe as a 'marrying in', and the phenomenon is treated in this book under the heading of the major partner (so, in Valpolicella's case, under Corvina).

What we are talking about here is the fourth type, the 'symphony' – the blend of grapes of mixed, generally unrelated aromatic or structural styles. This would be 'marrying out'. Although the creative blend is by no means new on the scene, this is an increasingly interesting feature of modern Italian oenology, one which Italians are, indeed, uniquely positioned to explore and exploit; and not only thanks to the enormous range of varieties available to them, originating from places as diverse as their own back yard to other parts of Italy to ancient Greece, imperial Spain, or nineteenth/twentieth-century France, Germany, Austria and Eastern Europe; but also, if not principally, because their artistic and anarchic temperament allows them to go down roads which would be closed to that relatively ordered and traditionally hidebound Gallic mentality which still leads world wine opinion.

The French, for example, would never *dream* of putting Bordeaux grapes together with those of Burgundy, or of Alsace, still less together with those of Italy or Germany or Spain. The Italians on the other hand have no qualms at all about attempting to juxtapose Sauvignon Blanc with Chardonnay, throwing in a bit of Gewürztraminer and perhaps a drop of Nosiola or Verduzzo or Rheinriesling or Vermentino for good measure. Further experiments would involve different fermentation vessels and methods, different types of wood for fermentation and/or ageing, fractioning of the malo-lactic, blending times, etc. It's all about the intermingling of (hopefully) complementary aromas with good structure and mouth-feel – the right acidity, the right alcohol and glycerine levels, the right viscosity: the right level of aromatic maturity and vivacity.

In northern Italy the area where perhaps the most experimentation is going on is eastern Friuli, specifically Collio, Colli Orientali and Isonzo. There are producers here who would elevate the blend to the level of art form – or who already have, according to the point of view. But there is plenty of activity afoot, too, in Alto Adige, Trentino, Veneto, Piemonte and Lombardy.

And where the producers go, the law is obliged to follow, so that we are now seeing new DOCs and IGTs being created to accommodate these works within the system. Many producers, to be sure, scorn the law, considering it to be the plaything of business and political interests, having little or nothing to do with wine-as-art. But ultimately the law, however crass, will be obeyed. And arguably the categorizing of styles does give some guidance to the consumer as to what he might expect to find inside the bottle; a consideration surprisingly often lost on the 'artists', whose sole concern may be to create something unique.

PIEMONTE

In the mid-1990s two new DOCs were created, Langhe and Monferrato, each containing a Rosso and a Bianco sub-DOC of sufficiently broad definition to embrace most of the ingenious blends that producers had been coming up with over the previous couple of decades. Both Rossos can be 'made with one or more non-aromatic red varieties listed as recommended or authorized for the province of Langhe (e.g.)'. Langhe Bianco's *disciplinare* is similar except for the word 'white' for 'red', while Monferrato Bianco is allowed to go one step further and include red grapes vinified white (which virtually invariably means Barbera).

I have already referred, in the section on the North West, to the blending of Nebbiolo with Cabernet or Merlot – but this practice is often illicit and therefore clandestine, so it is difficult to cite examples. The most successful and celebrated example of the permitted sort (i.e. not masquerading as Barolo or Barbaresco) is doubtless the (Monferrato Rosso) Pin of Giorgio Rivetti of La Spinetta at Castagnole Lanze, where 50% Nebbiolo is joined by 25% Barbera and 25% Cabernet Sauvignon. A similar blend is used for the Countacc! (sic) of Michele Chiarlo of Calamandrana, while the Soleo of I Paglieri consists of a preponderance of Cabernet Sauvignon with a splash of Nebbiolo.

Much more versatile is Barbera, which takes to *barrique* like a duck to water (*barrique* treatment being almost a *sine qua non* for this style of wine) and whose high acidity, soft tannicity and straightforward fruit-character make it an ideal blender with contrasting varieties. A small handful of producers have raised the marriage of Piemonte and Bordeaux to happily-ever-after status, probably the most successful being:

La Barbatella, Nizza Monferrato. This *boutique* operation in the heart of Barbera d'Asti country owes its inspiration to a Milanese businessman, Angelo Sonvico, his friendship with the late Giacomo Bologna (see under Barbera, page 101) and the technical skills of one of Piemonte's foremost oenological consultants, Giuliano Noè. Wine, for Sonvico, may be a hobby, but his personal commitment to the highest quality is symbolized by the inclusion of one of his names in the title of each of his two famous wines, La Vigna dell'Angelo, a DOC Barbera d'Asti, and La Vigna di Sonvico. The latter, a *barrique*-aged blend of Barbera and Cabernet Sauvignon, subjected to minimal treatment for maximum concentration and retention of nature's flavours, regularly features among the highest rated wines of of all Piemonte; no mean feat. Most importantly, each of the components is giving without dominating. Doubtless we shall be seeing more of its type in years to come.

Another excellent example of Cabernet/Barbera *barricato* is the Sul Bric of Franco Martinetti at Calliano, near Turin; not surprisingly, Giuliano Noè is the brains, or the palate, behind this one too. Other worthy practitioners of the genre include Cisa Asinari at Barbaresco (Virtues) and Livio Pavese at Treville (Montarucco). **Liedholm** of Cuccaro Monferrato makes a Rosso della Boemia which combines Cabernet and Barbera with Pinot Nero, to which, in Colle Manora's Palo Alto, Merlot is also added, a mix that might cause the ordered Gallic mind to succumb to a fit of the screaming ab-dabs.

The combination of Barbera with Pinot Nero alone has also been tried, examples being Forteto della Luja's Le Grive and Braida's Braida Rosso. Results so far are less convincing.

Trinchero, of Alba, has attempted a blend of Dolcetto and Merlot in his Le Taragne, as previously mentioned.

In the white department there have, to my knowledge, been no successes so impressive as La Vigna di Sonvico, Sul Bric or Pin, but there have been some interesting experiments. Gastaldi makes a tasty non-*barrique*d Chardonnay/Sauvignon blend called Bianco Gastaldi. Piero Busso's Langhe Bianco is a similar mix, *barricato* this time. Damonte of Malvirà adds to this combination the native Arneis in his Treuve. Bava attempts the unlikely blend of Erbaluce and Chardonnay in Alteserre. Riesling Renano comes into the act too, both in Poderi Colla's Sanrocco (with Chardonnay and Pinot Nero *in bianco*) and in the I Fiori of **Serra dei Fiori** of Trezzo Tinella (with Chardonnay and local varieties).

LOMBARDY

Cross-breeds are more institutional in this region, where the DOC Terre di Franciacorta (formerly plain Franciacorta) Rosso has long thrown Barbera and Nebbiolo together with Cabernet (Sauvignon and/or Franc) and Merlot. Examples are given under Cabernet in the chapter on International Varieties, even if, by my own definition, they belong here.

Valtellina, especially in its non-Superiore version, allows the inclusion, together with Nebbiolo (Chiavennasca) and the indigenous Rossola, Pignola and Brugnola varieties, of Pinot Nero and Merlot.

Oltrepò Pavese Rosso permits a modicum of Pinot Nero in the Barbera-dominated blend which also includes Croatina, Uva Rara and Vespolina. Two significant sub-DOCs under the Oltrepò Pavese umbrella with *uvaggi* similar to that of the Rosso are Buttafuoco and Sangue di Giuda. The former is a dry, sometimes spritzy red of considerable body and presence, the latter one of those idiosyncratic, archetypal Italian jobs – intensely bitter-sweet in its most interesting versions (it may also be dry), dark and brooding yet with a characteristic sparkle delivering light at the end of the tunnel. A representative producer of both styles is **Fiamberti** at Canneto Pavese. Bruno **Verdi**, of the same town, is known for a characterful Buttafuoco.

Riviera del Garda Rosso allows the inclusion of 10 per cent other grapes in the quasi pan-Italian blend of Groppello, Sangiovese, Marzemino and Barbera. The Bianco is a curious mix of Riesling (Renano and/or Italico) with 20 per cent 'other white grapes of the zone'.

Among interesting individual efforts, to be noted are the following: Mazzolino (Corvino: Barbera and Pinot Nero); Cascina la Pertica (Bianco Le Sincette: Tocai plus Chardonnay and Sauvignon); Cà dei Frati (Pratto: Trebbiano di Lugana plus Chardonnay and Sauvignon).

Special mention must be made of my old friend Mario **Pasolini** of Mompiano, on the outskirts of the city of Brescia. The Pasolinis, fathers and sons, have been working vineyards in this site for hundreds of years, but Mario is getting on now and he and his wife Irma have no children. When he passes on the land will be inherited by nephews who couldn't care less about wine or family tradition and will doubtless allow the vines to be buried beneath tons of concrete, the property, on the city's edge, being ripe for urban 'development'.

Though a graduate of the wine school at Alba, Mario remains an enthusiastic amateur, taking endless delight in putting together wines and spirits of all sorts, including applejack and brandy (which privately he calls calvados and armagnac respectively). His occasional *passiti* are blockbusters, his *spumante*, from Pinot Bianco, Chardonnay and Pinot Nero, is one of the best in Lombardy. But the wine dearest to his heart is Ronco di Mompiano, a blend, mentioned earlier, which he perfected years ago, of Marzemino and Merlot, aged in traditional Slavonian oak *botti*. In special years he puts a red sun on the label to indicate *riserva* (which he's not allowed to say) and then you have a wine of richness of flavour and smoothness of texture unique in this part of the world. What a pity it must disappear! Anybody got any suggestions?

VENETO

In Veneto there are various DOC *disciplinari* permitting the blending of the unlikely with the improbable. Colli di Conegliano Bianco, for example, would bring Incrocio Manzoni 6.0.13 together with Pinot Bianco, Chardonnay and Sauvignon as well as Rieslings Renano and Italico. Colli Euganei Bianco combines Garganega, Prosecco (Serprina), Tocai, Sauvignon, Pinot Bianco, Chardonnay, Riesling Italico and something called Pinella (!?). The recently established Bagnoli di Sopra DOC intermingles Chardonnay, Tocai, Sauvignon and (believe it or not) Raboso vinified *in bianco*, plus 'other non-aromatic varieties'.

On the red side, apart from the increasing use of Cabernet and Merlot in the Valpolicella blend, there are oddities in the *disciplinari* of Colli di Conegliano Rosso (the Cabernets plus Marzemino, Merlot and Incrocio Manzoni 2.15), Colli Euganei Rosso (the Cabernets plus Merlot, Barbera and Raboso) and Bagnoli Rosso, similar to Colli Euganei but without the Barbera.

As far as actual wines are concerned, however, there are not many. Reds of some interest include those from the following producers: Bertani (Catullo Rosso: Corvina plus Cabernet Sauvignon); **Gregoletto** (Rosso Gregoletto: Cabernet plus Merlot plus Marzemino), Miane; Le Vigne di San Pietro (I Balconi Rosso: Cabernet plus Corvina, Rondinella, Molinara); Ottella (Campo Sireso: Cabernet, Merlot, Croatina and Barbera); **Villa Sceriman** (Colli Euganei Rosso Superiore), Vò Euganeo.

Among whites generally the following sources are worth noting: **Bepin de Eto** (Colli di Conegliano Il Greccio), San Pietro di Felletto; Guerrieri Rizzardi (Castello Guerrieri Bianco: Garganega, Sauvignon, Cortese, Marco Bona); Masi (Bianco Serego Alighieri: 70% Garganega plus 30% Sauvignon); Vignalta (Colli Euganei Bianco Marlunghe). Even Soave is permitted a significant percentage of Pinot Bianco and Chardonnay in the mix today, and while Sauvignon is not specifically mentioned in the *disciplinare* that does not prevent it from being used.

Probably the best-known of all the weirdos is Bianco di Custoza from the south-eastern shores of Lake Garda, where no less a concoction than Trebbiano Toscano, Garganega, Tocai Friulano, Cortese, Malvasia, Pinot Bianco, Chardonnay and Riesling Italico is contemplated. Indeed, the existence in this corner of Garda of quality white wines from a mixed bag of varieties goes back further than one might think, there being references in seventeenth-century literature to '*i vini bianchi di bottiglia*' from 'Garganega', 'Reno' (Rhein Riesling?) and 'Champagne' (Pinot Bianco and Nero?). It is recorded that these white wines were highly regarded in the nineteenth century, and having gone through a dip in production and popularity for most of the twentieth century they began coming back into favour towards the very end.

Probably the producers of Bianco di Custoza with the highest profile are:

Montresor, Verona. The largest vineyard proprietor in this zone, Montresor is run by brothers Paolo and Giorgio, the family name being indicative, apparently, of a French Huguenot past. Montresor's production is big, though a lot less so than it was a few years back, and the range is broad, covering the entire range that Verona has to offer, plus some. Their standard Soave and Valpolicella Classico wines are probably the best value for money around, their *cru* selections are invariably representative, their Amarones and Reciotos can be outstanding: indeed their Recioto Re Teodorico was rated by the pundit Luca Maroni as the best Italian wine (out of thousands) tasted by him in 1997.

As for Bianco di Custoza, Montresor produce a *normale* called Vigneti Cavalcaselle and a *cru* Monte Fiera. The former is a wine of fresh-fruit aromas, with a clean, lively palate. The latter is fuller, denser, with ripe almost tropical fruit perfumes and a velvety viscosity. In an area somewhat lacking in individual white wines, this is among the best.

Other reliable to very good producers include: **Arvedi d'Emilei** at Cavalcaselle; Cavalchina (Amedeo); Corte Gardoni; **Le Tende** (Oro), Lazise; Le Vigne di San Pietro (San Pietro); **Sparici Landini** at Sona; and **Zeni** of Bardolino.

FRIULI-VENEZIA GIULIA

It is in eastern Friuli that the blend, specifically the white blend, has attained the greatest heights and the greatest prestige. Collio, Colli Orientali (with its sub-zone Cialla), Friuli Grave and Friuli Isonzo DOCs all provide for a white which may be based on Ribolla Gialla, Malvasia Istriana and Tocai Friulano with addition of other grapes in specific percentages, as in the case of Collio; or may be based on Chardonnay and Pinot Bianco with possible additions, as in the case of Friuli Grave; or may embrace all 'non-aromatic white varieties', as in the case of Colli Orientali and Friuli Isonzo. In any case the door is open to just about anything the producer fancies throwing in, especially as, if it doesn't accord with the law, the producer will either simply ignore that fact and use the DOC anyway, or resort to IGT or even Vino da Tavola – the last-named manoeuvre being one, however, which the law's posse is determined to head off into a box canyon.

In the same way the various *disciplinari* provide for a red, which in Collio and Friuli Grave is liable to be based mainly if not exclusively on the Cabernets plus Merlot, with the addition of other red types, while in Colli Orientali and Friuli Isonzo there are no restrictions except on aromatic varieties. The reality of the situation is that Friulian red blends – of which there are far fewer than there are white – tend to keep the ingredients largely if not exclusively within the Bordeaux family. Such wines have been mentioned under Cabernet or Merlot (see International Varieties). The cases of 'marrying out' are few, so it is possible to list them here complete with ingredients.

Representative producers include: Cà Ronesco (Sariz: Pinot Noir, Cabernet Franc, Refosco); Dri (Il Roncat Rosso: Refosco, Schioppettino, Cabernets Franc and Sauvignon, others); Il Carpino (Rosso Carpino: Merlot, Refosco); Le Due Terre (Sacrisassi Rosso:

Refosco, Schioppettino, Pinot Nero); Miani (Miani Rosso: Refosco, Cabernet, Tazzelenghe).

In the case of whites, on the other hand, there are so many valid examples of the cross-marriage that to mention the make-up of every blend would be unnecessarily long-winded and repetitive, so I will content myself with a once-only listing of the ingredients which may be used by winemakers (exception made for profiled producers). In almost every case there will be some French input (Chardonnay and Sauvignon are the favourites, followed by Pinot Bianco and Pinot Grigio) and some indigenous material (Tocai Friulano and Ribolla Gialla make the most frequent appearances, together with Malvasia Istriana, Verduzzo and Picolit); the Germanic influence is less, being represented by Riesling Renano, Müller-Thurgau and Gewürztraminer.

The use of wood varies, certain producers fermenting all or some of the parts of the blend in oak, with malo-lactic, others avoiding wood altogether for greater fruitiness and freshness. The oak-fermentation and maturation school is best represented by the radical Josko **Gravner** of Oslavia. There are those, indeed, who consider the dense, rich, concentrated style of Gravner's white blend named Breg, a blend of Chardonnay, Sauvignon, Pinot Grigio, Riesling, Ribolla, Malvasia and the obscure Blera, involving months of oak-ageing, to epitomize the best of Friulian white wine, and certainly for weight, complexity and longevity it is remarkable. Stanislao Radikon's Slatnik and the Bianco della Castellada of the brothers Bensa of La Castellada, Gravner's neighbours (not to say disciples) in the village of Oslavia, hard by the border of Slovenia in the Collio, are of a similar ilk, requiring several years of bottle-ageing before they peak. These are wines which aim to compensate in opulence and complexity for what they lack in elegance and freshness, they are not for early drinking as Italian whites are generally 'supposed' to be but are rather for admiring almost as icons. They are not afraid of the tannins or the element of oxidation derived from extensive oak treatment, and in general they are far removed from the light, varietal, 'fruit-driven' type of wine that prevails today. Followers of the New World style may hate them, but they must admit one thing: they are wines of tremendous character and indeed courage which deserve to be taken seriously for all their sins against contemporary thinking.

A more popular, though still serious, style of blended white has been achieved by Silvio **Jermann** of Farra d'Isonzo. Jermann does not actually disdain the use of wood in the making of whites, as do his legendary neighbours Mario Schiopetto (whose Blanc des Rosis, made of Pinot Bianco, Tocai, Sauvignon and Malvasia, is one of the best in this genre) and Vittorio Puiatti, this latter scorning oak-maturation even for red wines. Indeed, some of Jermann's most successful white wines have been 'educated' in oak – examples being the much sought-after *barrique*-fermented Chardonnay called Where the Dreams Have No End (sic) and the blended Capo Martino, aged in 7.5 hectolitre Slavonian and Czech *botti*. But his most successful wine – probably the most successful in modern Friulian history – has year after year been Vintage Tunina, sometimes dubbed the Tignanello of Italian whites because it was the first one that broke the mould. While continuing in good years to turn out varietal whites (something which Gravner and Co. have threatened to discontinue, except perhaps for Ribolla), Jermann decided back in 1977 that the way to make a wine of unique character, avoiding the pitfalls of passing fashion, was to blend. Although the proportions may vary, the grapes going into Vintage Tunina are every year the same: Sauvignon, Chardonnay, Ribolla, Malvasia and Picolit. The fruit must be absolutely clean and ripe, Jermann's idea being to make a wine of complex aroma, with the accent on fruits and flowers, and luscious palate: one may detect peaches, tropical fruits, spices. Absolutely no wood. And this peculiarity: the grapes are all picked and vinified together.

Another pioneer of the blended white in Friuli is Livio **Felluga** of Cormons (*frazione* Brazzano), an estate now run mainly by the octogenarian Livio's sons Andrea (production) and Maurizio (commercialization). One of the largest vineyard owners of eastern Friuli, with some 135 hectares mostly in the Colli Orientali at Rosazzo, purchased from 1956 on, Livio Felluga has for decades now been at the top of the quality tree not only for their white varietals (perhaps somewhat less so for their reds) but especially for Terre Alte, a non-oaked blend of Tocai, Chardonnay and Sauvignon, which year after year (though it's not produced in poor vintages) receives the highest ratings from Italian and international pundits. Not that they have anything against wood – they use both *barrique* and *botte* for maturing the reds, and ferment their recently developed Chardonnay/Pinot Grigio blend, Esperto, in

barrel. But the accent, for Terre Alte, is on ripe fruit and sumptu-
ousness of palate. And as the production is large the price is not
outrageous, as it is becoming for some.

Apart from these, the list of producers making good to excellent
white blends is impressively long and includes: Abbazia di Rosazzo
(Ronco delle Acacie); **Ascevi** (Verdana; Col Martin Luwa), San
Floriano del Collio; Borgo del Tiglio (Bianco); Cà Ronesca
(Marnà); Collavini (Conte di Cuccanea); Dorigo (Ronc di Juri);
Marco Felluga (Molamatta); **Fiegl** (Leopold Cuvée Blanc), Oslavia;
Edi Keber (Collio Bianco); Renato Keber (Beli Grici); La Viarte
(Liendo); Livon (Masarotte); Miani (Miani Bianco); Pighin
(Soreli); Ronchi di Cialla (Cialla Bianco); **Ronco dei Tassi** (Fos-
arin), Cormons; Ronco del Gelso (Làtimis); Russiz Superiore (Ron-
cuz); **Subida di Monte** (Bianco Subida), Cormons; Venica &
Venica (Vignis di Venica); Vie di Romans (Flors di Uis); **Vigna del
Lauro** (Collio Bianco), San Floriano del Collio; Zamò & Zamò
(Trevigne).

There are also various sweet blends made from late-harvested
and/or *passito* grapes in Friuli. Worthy representatives include: **Dal
Fari** (Gagliano Bianco: Riesling Renano plus Chardonnay), Cividale del Friuli; and Pittaro (Apicio: Incrocio Manzoni 6.0.13 plus
Chardonnay).

ALTO ADIGE

The DOC system as it stands at the time of writing does not cater
for a red blend in the province of Bolzano, exception made for the
DOC Cabernet-Lagrein and of course for the up-to-15 per cent tol-
erance granted under the *disciplinare* of certain varietals. The same
is true for whites with the exception of Terlano Bianco DOC,
which most may use but few wish to as it might give a false impression of where their grapes come from. There exist also the DOCs
Valdadige Rosso and Bianco, which cover a range of varieties from
anywhere in the Adige valley from Merano right down to and
including northern Veneto; but this name is generally used for
cheap wines, and is avoided by quality producers for image reasons. There remains the possibility of resorting to IGT Mitterberg
or Vigneti delle Dolomiti.

Those who find no acceptable route within the system might fall
back on Vino da Tavola, using the devious ploy of printing the bot-

tling code on the label as a means of alerting the consumer to the vintage (reminder: simple Vino da Tavola status now disqualifies its user from any mention on the label of grape variety, provenance or vintage). But in general, whether it be due to the lack of compliance on the part of the law, or whether it be because of a deep-rooted preference for varietal wines, there is little production of blended wines of the 'marrying out' sort in Alto Adige. It is true that, in contrast to Friuli, there is virtually nothing on the white side that can be described as indigenous to Alto Adige, unless you allow Traminer. Among reds there are just Schiava or Lagrein. On the other hand there is great potential for the mixing of the Gallic with the Germanic, or the Gallic with the Gallic (e.g. Sauvignon-Chardonnay), and one begins to sense a movement gathering strength, led by established powers like Lageder and newer entities like Franz Haas.

To take the reds first, the following are producers at a good to very good level of the recognized Cabernet-Lagrein blend: C.S. Burggräfler; Martini & Sohn (Coldirus); Josephus Mayr (Composition Reif). Tiefenbrunner make a convincing Linticlarus Cuvée which combines Lagrein and Cabernet Sauvignon with a small percentage of Pinot Noir. Josef Niedermayr's admirable Euforius no doubt contains similar elements – they're pretty cagey as to exactly what goes into it. And while on the subject of blends and Niedermayr, one should mention their much raved-about sweet wine Aureus, a blend of Chardonnay, Pinot Bianco and Sauvignon grapes dried to the point of partial botrytization: a wine more Austrian in style than Italian, having tremendous concentration and complexity balanced by high acidity (over 9g per litre) to allow for a non-cloying finish despite fiercely high residual sugar (around 140g per litre).

Casòn, a medium-weight, nicely balanced but as yet unexceptional red from **Casòn Hirschprunn**, is mainly a Bordeaux-type blend (Merlot, Cabernet Sauvignon, Cabernet Franc and Petit Verdot) as one detects from the slightly herbaceous notes, but just about qualifies in this section thanks to splashes of Lagrein and Syrah, which, coming from young vineyards, have yet to make a decisive mark on the mix. Casòn Hirschprunn, incidentally, is an historic *azienda* at Magrè which was taken over in 1991 by Alois Lageder of the same commune (see under Cabernet, page 245). Ambitious plans for the development of the 31-hectare estate are

afoot, including a move towards bio-dynamic methods in the vineyards and a replanting programme involving various French, Germanic and local varieties. Another red blend, pure Bordeaux this
time (Merlot-dominated), is called Corolle.

It is, however, with the white Contest that Hirschprunn has
mainly scored to date. This is a truly eclectic concoction representing just about every major white wine zone of France, led by the
Pinot Grigio and Chardonnay of Burgundy (or Alsace/Champagne)
together with Sauvignon and Sémillon (Loire central vineyards/
Bordeaux), Riesling (Alsace again), Chenin Blanc (Anjou-
Touraine), Marsanne and Roussanne (Hermitage) and Viognier
(Condrieu), *barrique*-fermented and -matured, with *bâtonnage*.
The wine displays a ripe, slightly evolved nose and palate with
apple and pear primary aromas, nicely judged oak and some ter-
tiaries, particularly impressive on the back-palate where it achieves
remarkable spread and length.

Lageder, under his own name and that of Baron Dürfeld, also
produces an excellent Terlano (Chardonnay-Sauvignon) called
Tannhammer. That tireless seeker Franz Haas has meanwhile
come up with the fascinating Mitterberg Manna, a blend of Riesling Renano, Gewürztraminer, Chardonnay, Pinot Bianco and
Sauvignon, a little under half of which is fermented and aged in
barrique, while the rest remains in stainless steel until the *assemblaggio* and bottling.

TRENTINO

The Trentino DOC does make provision for a Bianco allowing up
to 20% of Sauvignon and/or Müller-Thurgau and/or Incrocio
Manzoni 6.0.13, though the bulk of the wine must be Chardonnay
or Pinot Bianco. There is also a red but it is a straight Bordeaux
blend. The DOC Valdadige is more likely to be used here than further north, although nobody to my knowledge makes anything
particularly interesting under that rubric, despite the considerable
scope offered by the *disciplinari*: Valdadige Bianco may include
Pinots Bianco and Grigio, Riesling Italico, Müller-Thurgau,
Chardonnay, Nosiola, Garganega and Trebbiano, as well as one
you wouldn't expect to find up here, Vernaccia (probably not of
San Gimignano), and another which we haven't mentioned before,
Bianchetta Trevigiana. Valdadige Rosso, for its part, may blend in

unspecified proportion the likes of Merlot, Pinot Nero, Lagrein, Teroldego and Negrara, as well as the dreaded Schiava and the local Lambrusco. And if that's not good enough, there is always IGT Vigneti delle Dolomiti to fall back on.

Nevertheless, few producers are availing themselves of the possibilities to come up with an interesting blend. The previously described Rosso Fayé of Pojer & Sandri, mainly a Bordeaux blend, does contain 10% Lagrein, it's true. Maso Solengo's Salengo Vallagarina is another Bordeaux blend, this time with a splash of Marzemino. Somewhat more adventurous on the red side is Elisabetta Foradori with her Karanar – Cabernet, Merlot and Petit Verdot for the most part but with a significant input of Syrah (or is it Petite Syrah?) and Franconia.

On the white side, as in Alto Adige, there is less happening blend-wise than one feels ought to be. Wines of interest in this category include those produced by: Balter (Clara: Sauvignon, Chardonnay, Traminer – a wine whose considerable aromatic possibilities were somewhat overwhelmed by new oak when I tasted it); Bossi Fedrigotti (Foianeghe Bianco: Chardonnay, Pinot Bianco, Gewürztraminer), Rovereto; Marco **Donati** (Terre del Noce: Sauvignon, Chardonnay, Moscato Giallo), Mezzocorona; Ferrari (Villa Margon: 80% Chardonnay plus Müller-Thurgau, Sauvignon and Nosiola); Maso Cantanghel (Forte di Mezzo: Chardonnay, Pinot Bianco, Sauvignon – one I found unconvincing despite its good reputation).

V
SPARKLING WINES OF THE
METODO CLASSICO

Northern Italy abounds in wines with bubbles. There can be no disputing that North West Italy is the leading zone in the world for sparkling wines of low pressure – between 1 and 2.5 atmospheres; what the Italians call *frizzante*. We have come across these under their various principal grape varieties: Moscato, Cortese, Chardonnay, Prosecco, Barbera, Freisa, Bonarda, etc., not forgetting the biggest of them all in volume terms, Lambrusco.

Once upon a time, not so very long ago, the generic name for wines having a pressure of 3.5 to 6 atmospheres was *spumante*. Nowadays, if you use the word *spumante* in the presence of a producer of Franciacorta or Trento he will wax *spumante* at the mouth and demand (for reasons which will presently be explained) that you use *any* word rather than that one. But if you try the French word *mousseux* they have almost the same reaction, and the English 'sparkling' is hardly satisfactory either as it fails to distinguish between semi-sparkling and fully sparkling, not to mention the distinction, which *spumante* and *mousseux* also fail to make, between wines whose sparkle has been achieved by secondary refermentation in bottle or in tank (usually called the *charmat* method), not to speak of the unspeakable 'bicycle pump' method.

It is about wines whose sparkle comes from refermentation in bottle that I write here and, to be more specific, about wines produced from the same grapes as used in a certain district in France to the north-east of Paris. These days, however, to use the words 'champagne method' or 'metodo champenois' in the European Union on anything that is not actually from that district is considered by some to constitute a crime so heinous as to merit the modern equivalent of hanging, drawing and quartering.

Instead I will use the Italian phrase *metodo classico* as a generic description, although not all wines made by the secondary-fermentation-in-bottle method are made from grapes associated with *that* district, i.e. Pinot (used for any member of the family: Bianco, Grigio, Nero, Meunier; and Chardonnay). Indeed, the earliest were not. In the 1850s in Piemonte, the Frenchman Oudart applied the method to wines made from the Cortese grape – which some, notably Soldati at La Scolca in Gavi, still do today to a high level of quality. And Carlo Gancia applied it around the same time to Moscato, a practice no longer followed.

From the 1860s various producers began making sparkling wines by the classic method, some of them also using the classic grapes. Cantine Brozzone, today known as Banfi, at Strevi in Piemonte began in 1860. Cinzano, also in Piemonte, began in 1867; Carpenè Malvolti in 1868, in Conegliano Veneto; Contratto in 1880, at Canelli in Piemonte; Ferrari in 1902, at Trento; La Versa in Oltrepò Pavese in 1905. There followed, in the 1920s, Martini & Rossi and Riccadonna of Piemonte, and in 1946 Fontanafredda, also of Piemonte. Franciacorta, today's highest-profile *metodo classico* zone, did not, on the other hand, really get going until the 1970s.

Indeed, the 1970s saw a regular boom in *metodo classico* production throughout Italy, and in the early 1980s you couldn't go to any *cantina*, it seemed, without the proprietor proudly displaying the first fruits of his sparkling production, despite the fact that it is strictly illegal in Italy to make sparkling wine in a normal winery because of the prohibition on the use of sugar (essential to the making of sparklers) in still wines. Such artisanal activity is noticeably diminished today, partly owing to a lack of reciprocal enthusiasm on the part of the market, partly thanks to a stricter policing of the legal controls. On the other hand there has, as we have seen, and will see, been quite a flurry of activity during the 1990s in respect of nomenclature and regulation.

Most producers of *metodo classico* wines in northern Italy today are subject to the regulations of a particular DOC or to those of a voluntary consortium of producers organized for purposes of quality control and/or marketing; or both. The main purpose of these organizations has been to develop an awareness on the part of the market of the distinction between what *metodo classico* makers would consider the real thing and the various pretenders. These bounders would include tank or *charmat* method wines, wines made by the classic method but not with the kosher Burgundian grapes, or wines having both credentials but lacking a specific provenance or not satisfying certain production criteria, such as amount of time on yeasts.

The most important production zones have their own DOCs, and these we will consider in their place. Before doing so, however, we should look for a moment at the influential grouping today known as the Istituto Talento Metodo Classico or ITMC.

The institute actually originated back in 1975 under the name Istituto Italiano Spumante Metodo Champenois. The present name, together with a new set of control regulations, was adopted in 1996, although the established logo – of a *pupitre de remuage* – was retained. The individual members are a mere two handfuls, out of the 200-plus *metodo classico* producers throughout Italy, but their influence is spread wide, and *cantine* coming under the aegis of the producers' associations of Alto Adige and Friuli, or covered by the DOCs Trento or Oltrepò Pavese, may all participate should they so wish.

The central aim, via the imposition of supposedly stringent production regulations (e.g. a minimum of fifteen months on the yeasts, which most in fact exceed), is gradually to establish in the mind of the consumer an association of the name Talento with the idea of high quality Italian sparkling wine on a par with the best. The only major grouping which has gone its own way is Franciacorta, whose producers with some justification consider *themselves* as 'the best' and who impose upon themselves even more stringent rules in an attempt to establish *their* name as representative of the highest quality in this sphere in the land.

Needless to say, this being Italy, there are individuals here and there who spurn membership in any club, considering themselves to be sufficiently lofty as not to need the company of lesser (or to be precise, more industrial) producers, association with whom might tarnish their *bella figura*, their good image.

I do not propose to go into detail here about the *metodo classico* as it is not essentially an Italian but a French method which can be studied in any number of books on champagne. Suffice it to say that the rules of the game are similar except, obviously, for geographic considerations.

Metodo classico wines still constitute a small segment of the market, about 15 million bottles compared with the nearly quarter-billion bottles of Italian wine produced yearly with bubbles of some sort in them. Nevertheless the quality overall is growing perceptibly, and there is a case for maintaining that, in terms of sheer finesse and character, Italian *metodo classico* is the most serious rival in the world to the original. On the whole, however, they have failed to put this message across to the rest of the wine universe, partly no doubt due to the fact that their wines at the various levels are actually as expensive if not more so than said original. In other words they are taking on the French at the level of quality rather than price, which is bold of them but which has as yet, as I say, not convinced many punters outside of Italy.

If I had to use a single word to pinpoint what the significant difference is between Italian *metodo classico* and you-know-what I would choose 'ripeness'. The grapes are just that bit riper, so the wines are just that bit riper; and yet without sacrifice – as in the case of so many New and indeed Old World sparklers whose ripeness is not in dispute – of elegance and balance. Thanks to the slight extra ripeness of the grapes the acidity is less agressive, and there is consequently less need for addition of sweeteners and therefore of sulphites, so you can drink more with less risk, the following morning, of a gut-ache. Of course, I am talking of the very best, which generally, but mercifully not invariably, means the very expensive. The majority of Italian *metodo classico* wines, like the majority of such wines from France, are still fairly dull and not very good value for money.

But let's have a look at the regions.

PIEMONTE

Since the nineteenth century Piemonte has been a major force on the Italian sparkling wine scene, and not just in respect of Moscato and Cortese, as we have seen, although historically Pinot grapes have been bought in from neighbouring regions and in particular from the Oltrepò Pavese. Producers here include those associated with Asti and/or vermouth, and while such firms operate on a massive industrial scale they have shown themselves capable of turning out some reasonably good *metodo classico* wines.

A new DOC Piemonte Spumante was introduced in 1994 to cover production of sparklers from Piemontese Pinot and

Chardonnay grapes, although without specification as to the method to be used. The grapes for these may be grown in recognized areas of the provinces of Cuneo in the west, through Asti to Alessandria in the east. In 1990 a grouping of seven major producers was formed to carry out experiments in vineyard and *cantina* in respect of *metodo classico* wines, under the name Progetto Spumante Metodo Classico Piemonte.

Early results indicate that Piemonte does have good conditions for growing Pinot and Chardonnay grapes for use in *metodo classico* wines provided you get altitude, soil/drainage, micro-climate and exposure right. Soil and drainage are no problem, there being plenty of calcareous material in the terrain and certainly no shortage of slopes. Pinot Nero requires a fairly limited band of altitude – between 300 and 450 metres – while Chardonnay can succeed up to 500 metres and as low as 150 metres. The most important aspect of micro-climate is marked alternation between daytime and night-time temperatures, which links up to some extent with exposure. And this, for growers, is the best news (although it's not very new), that in order to achieve such alternation, as well as the relatively cool mean temperatures needed for good aromas and balance in Burgundian grapes, the best slopes are north, north-east and north-west facing – the very ones which are unsuitable for the classic red grapes of the region.

Among the producers in the consortium Tradizione Spumante, as the Progetto became known in 1993, are the following (with their current *metodo classico* in brackets): Banfi of Strevi (Banfi Brut); Cinzano (Cinzano Padosé); Fontanafredda (Gatinera and Contessa Rosa); Gancia (Mon Grande Cuvée Riserva and Riserva dei Gancia); Martini & Rossi (Riserva Montelera). Banfi, Fontanafredda and Martini & Rossi are all founder members of the ITMC.

The two best *metodo classico* wines from Piemonte that I have tasted come from producers profiled earlier, namely Luigi Coppo (see page 276), whose Piero Coppo Riserva del Fondatore is 85% Pinot Nero with 15% Chardonnay, and Bruno Giacosa (see page 88), whose Extra Brut is a pure Pinot Nero vinified *in bianco*. These are wines of greater body and weight than you find in the wines of Champagne, but without the power of top Californian or the heat of the better Australian versions. And if you like oak with your sparkling wine you will love the rich but woody Valentino

Brut Zero from Rocche dei Manzoni of Monforte d'Alba.

Other Piemontese producers capable of making good to very good *metodo classico* wines include Bava (Giulio Cocchi); and Contratto (Riserva Giuseppe Contratto) of Canelli.

LOMBARDY

Undoubtedly Italy's premier production area for *metodo classico* wines, Lombardy boasts not one but two important sub-zones: Franciacorta and Oltrepò Pavese, plus a significant smattering of producers in other areas. The former, the first wine zone to achieve DOCG status for *metodo classico*, is a phenomenon of recent years, while the latter has, since the nineteenth century, been an important producer of Pinot and Chardonnay grapes and base wines for the booming sparkling wine trade of Piemonte.

Most of the bottlers of Lombardy make their *cuvées* from grapes grown on their own property. A few large ones, however, either buy in all their grapes or supplement their production by buying in grapes and musts from within and without the region. Foremost among these latter are **Villa Mazzucchelli** of Ciliverghe (Brut Carato Oro) and:

Guido **Berlucchi**, Borgonato. Berlucchi lay claim to having been the first in Franciacorta to make sparkling wine in the classic manner, co-proprietor/oenologist Franco Ziliani giving birth as early as 1961 to Cuvée Imperiale Berlucchi. The material for this lightly yeasty, easy-drinking blend is made up of Pinot Bianco from Franciacorta together with Pinot Nero from Oltrepò Pavese and Chardonnay from Trentino-Alto Adige, Ziliani having decided back in 1975 that this kind of far-flung selection more closely reflects the spirit of the orignal champagne-style *cuvée* than would a wine based on the grapes of one small growing area. Such has been its popularity that sales today are in the region of 4.5 million bottles per annum, almost all of them on the home market, making Berlucchi, by a handsome margin, the biggest producer of *metodo classico* in the land. Recently they have developed a special *cru* called Cellarius as well as a genuine Franciacorta DOCG from their Antiche Cantine Fratta at Monticelli Brusati.

Franciacorta is a hilly zone in the province of Brescia, between the city of that name to the south-east and the Lago d'Iseo to the north.

Its importance as a vinicultural area goes back centuries, even if its present identity as a sparkling-wine producer does not pre-date the activities of Berlucchi, whose success, indeed, provided the impetus for later arrivals.

It was in 1995 that Franciacorta attained DOCG status. The new *disciplinare* contains certain important stipulations, some of which have been touched upon previously. For example, the wine may only be made by the *metodo classico*, it being expressly forbidden to use the dreaded 's' word (*spumante*) or make any reference on the label to the method employed, these being implicit in the DOCG – and you'd better remember it when talking to a Franciacorta producer if you don't want your head bitten off. Production may not exceed 65 hectolitres per hectare, which is low by French standards. The minimum period for the ageing of the wine on the yeasts, i.e. in the bottle during secondary fermentation, is eighteen months for the non-vintage and thirty months for the *millesimato* (vintage), the former being high by French standards, the latter a little low.

The Franciacorta producers' consortium is staking the future marketing strategy of its members on their collective name, just as the Comité Interprofessionel du Vin de Champagne stakes all on the name champagne, which is why they battle so hard in the courts of the world to preserve it. Franciacorta producers recognize that it will take decades for the world to recognize the name with all its implications in the same way as it does that of their French rivals; but they consider that they have no recourse but to seek to occupy the high ground.

It should be noted that it was also from 1995 that the name Franciacorta no longer applied to still wines, which became known as Terre di Franciacorta DOC. This name, too, I am assured, will change to avoid confusion with the sparkling product, but the details are yet to be finalized.

There are over 50 *aziende* producing Franciacorta DOCG, but two stand out:

Cà del Bosco, Erbusco. Maurizio Zanella is one of the giants of the Italian wine scene, and I don't mean physically, although in that respect he is no midget. Since the early 1970s, when he first began developing his determination to produce Italian versions of the classic French wines, champagne, bordeaux and burgundy, he has

poured money and passion into what is indisputably one of the world's most impressive private wineries, complete with all the hi-tech equipment necessary to quality production. This without sac-rifice of those traditional principles which also contribute to quality, such as barrel fermentation for the base wines of his best *cuvées*; he even purchases the wood for his *barriques* in France, leaving it there to season for up to three years before having the barrels built by French craftsmen. To such extent, indeed, has he travelled the road of spare-no-expense that he was obliged in 1994 to sell a 60 per cent share to Santa Margherita of Pinot Grigio fame, although he is happy to report that they let him get on with business as before.

Cà del Bosco own nearly 100 hectares of vineyard in various parts of the zone, feeding a production of some 900,000 bottles of which just under half is *metodo classico*. His Franciacorta wines divide into three categories: Brut, the non-vintage blend of Chardonnay and Pinot Bianco with 15% Pinot Nero; Vintage, which sub-divides into Brut, Dosage Zero, Rosé (40% Pinot Nero) and Satèn (Francia-corta's word for *crémant*, 4.5 atmospheres pressure as against 6 for the fully sparkling wines); and Annamaria Clementi, the *tête de cuvée* wine, one-third Pinot Nero, two-thirds Chardonnay and Pinot Bianco, which after six months in *barrique* spends five and a half years in bottle on the yeasts, developing in the process an amazing complexity on the nose together with a tremendous wealth of flavour on the palate, plus a creaminess of texture, thanks to the fineness of the bubbles, remarkable for a sparkling wine.

It is important, I think, to note that the *metodo classico* wines of Cà del Bosco, while inspired by champagne, are by no means carbon-copies. I mentioned above that what differentiates them more than anything is this element of ripeness, a quality which the wines of Cà del Bosco possess in spades.

Bellavista, Erbusco. At the foundation of this remarkable estate – superbly sited on the aptly named Bellavista hill, and comprising 117 hectares of vineyard in various parts of the Franciacorta zone – are two men and a philosophy. The men are owner Vittorio Moretti, a wealthy entrepreneur who purchased the property in 1977, and Mattia Vezzola, an oenologist who joined in 1981 and has stayed with Moretti ever since through good times and better. The philosophy is quality through respect for nature and tradition, not forgetting the benefits that technology can bring. This may sound corny, being words that anyone can reel off and thousands do, but here, as at Cà del Bosco, it has a genuine ring. Vezzola, indeed, believes in a natural lifestyle in all respects, and it was he, albeit with the full agreement of Moretti, who introduced unusual aspects such as an element of bio-dynamics in the vineyard (no herbicides or organic pesticides, among other things) and the hyperoxygenation of musts in order to minimize the use of sulphur dioxide in the wines (he tries to limit the total to 55 mg/litre). Not forgetting the use of the type of basket press still used by quality producers in Reims and Epernay.

Bellavista, like Cà del Bosco, produce a range of still and sparkling wines, the former including an outstanding Chardonnay (Uccellanda) and an excellent Cabernet-Merlot blend (Solesine) as well as a tasty Terre di Franciacorta Bianco, Convento dell'Annunciata. But it is for the sparkling wines that they are justly famous, the range including the non-vintage Cuvée Brut and the vintage Gran Cuvée Brut, Gran Cuvée Brut Pas Opéré (no *liqueur d'expédition* added at *dégorgement*, only wine – see Glossary), Gran Cuvée Satèn (a pure Chardonnay, unlike the others which all contain between 20 and 35% Pinot Nero) and Gran Cuvée Brut Rosé (60% Pinot Nero). In exceptional years they make a special *cuvée* called Riserva Vittorio Moretti, which matures six years on the yeasts.

Another special *cuvée*, created to welcome in the millennium, is called just that, the name writ in glass on the very elegant bottle.

A feature of all the wines is the harmonic juxtaposition of fruit, yeast and subtle wood aromas, together with a fine *mousse* and, once again, that characteristic ripeness. Says Vezzola: 'Our wines have less of the greenness that characterizes champagne. We reckon that since we can get more ripeness, we should take advantage of it. The French have their acidity not because they want it, but because they can't avoid it.'

One of the gentlemen mentioned above under Franciacorta reckons that, at present, there are ten to twelve quality producers of Franciacorta. He hopes that, forced by the more stringent regulations of DOCG, the number will soon rise to twenty. He didn't tell me whom he had in mind but the list would probably include the following: Fratelli **Berlucchi** (Brut Millesimato), Borgonato; Cavalleri (Brut Satèn); Lorenzo **Faccoli** (Extra Brut), Coccaglio; La Ferghettina (Brut); Enrico Gatti (Brut); Guarischi (Brut Contessa Camilla Maggi); Il Mosnel (Brut millesimato); **Monte Rossa** (Brut Cabochon), Cazzago San Martino; Uberti (Magnificentia); Villa (Extra Dry Cuvette).

The Oltrepò Pavese zone, south of Milan on the border with Emilia, has, as we have seen, one of the longest histories of Pinot production in Italy. The first Pinot-based wine made by the *metodo classico* came from the Cantina Sociale La Versa in 1930, today a member of the Istituto Talento turning out 350,000 of the 600,000 bottles produced in Oltrepò every year.

In 1995 two types of *metodo classico* wine were recognized by the Oltrepò Pavese *disciplinare*: OP Spumante Metodo Classico, which must be 70% Pinot Nero vinified *in bianco*, plus Chardonnay, Pinot Bianco and Pinot Grigio; and OP Pinot Nero Metodo Classico, which must have not less than 85% Pinot Nero in it. In both cases twelve months is the minimum period on the yeasts, although members of the local consortium 'Classese' must leave the wine for eighteen months in contact with the yeasts, while the maximum yield is a mere 54 hectolitres per hectare – lower than Franciacorta. Despite which no one has yet come up with a *metodo classico* from Oltrepò Pavese that is likely to set the world, or any part of it, on fire. Apart from La Versa, reasonably good producers include Monsupello (Brut Classico) of Torricella Verzate and **Monterucco** of Cigognola.

Elsewhere in Lombardy good producers are quite spread out. Those of interest would include Cà dei Frati of Sirmione, in the Lugana area; **Carlozadra** of Grumello del Monte in the Valcalepio zone; and, last but not least, Mario Pasolini of Mompiano in Brescia, whose individualistic Brut is a personal favourite.

EMILIA

Amid the hundreds of millions of bottles of bubbly coming out of Emilia scarcely any are made either from Pinot grapes or by the *metodo classico*. In the Colli Piacentini, as in neighbouring Oltrepò Pavese, there exist several small producers having a go, no one to my knowledge at a particularly elevated quality level. The law is no great help, providing for a Pinot Spumante under the umbrella DOC, but without specification as to method of production.

If there is one producer of Pinot-based *metodo classico* wine worthy of mention in Emilia it is Giuseppe Bellei of Francesco **Bellei** at Bomporto in the province of Modena. It was in the 1980s that Bellei became fascinated by champagne, visiting France and acquainting himself with producers and techniques, and while not abandoning his bottle-fermented Lambrusco di Sorbara found himself a site in the Apennines, at 500 metres altitude, where Pinot Noir and Chardonnay could enjoy the correct mean temperature and the right type of soil. The result is to be tasted in his Extra Cuvée Brut and Brut Rosé, wines of surprising class and authenticity considering their provenance.

VENETO

Various umbrella DOCs in Veneto provide for a *spumante*, but in no case is the *metodo classico* a necessary condition. This is the region of Italy's most characteristic dry sparkling wine, Prosecco, but it is rare today that the classic method is employed, nor, obviously, are French grapes involved. A number of Prosecco producers, however, do make French-style *metodo classico* wines as an increasingly important side-line, these including Bisol of Valdobbiadene (Riserva Brut) and Carpenè Malvolti of Conegliano, the founder of which latter, Antonio Carpenè, was one of the great men of Italian wine in the nineteenth century, being the founder of Italy's first school of viticulture and oenology at Conegliano in 1873 as well as one of the first to use the *metodo classico*. Both the above are members of the ITMC.

FRIULI-VENEZIA GIULIA

The region has an abundance of Pinot Bianco and Chardonnay grapes, but little history or actuality of *metodo classico* production, as indeed is reflected in the laws which do not provide for such wines, although in a few cases there is provision for *spumante* without specification of method. There is an active consortium, called Associazione Spumante Friuli Classico, founded in 1988 for purposes of overseeing *metodo classico* production, and the producers in it account for some 300,000 of the 350,000 or so bottles of Pinot- and Chardonnay-based made in Friuli annually.

I can personally only recommend two producers, but I can recommend them highly, as I have found their sparklers excellent in terms of concentration of flavour and mouth-feel. They are Dorigo of Buttrio in the Colli Orientali (Dorigo Brut); and Puiatti of Farra d'Isonzo, the former being a member of the consortium, the latter predictably not (on the Groucho Marx principle). Puiatti actually makes two excellent wines of this type, an Extra Brut Chardonnay as well as an Extra Brut Pinot Nero, both vintage wines, usually having had several years on the yeasts.

ALTO ADIGE

Again, Alto Adige is rich in Pinot and Chardonnay grapes (indeed, considerably richer than Friuli in Pinot Nero), and yet, again, there is no great past or present in respect of Pinot-based *metodo classico* production. Instead, as in the case of Lombardy's Oltrepò Pavese, Alto Adige has served more as a source of grapes for *spumantisti* of other regions than she has for her own producers. Gradually, today, this is changing. In 1990 the Associazione Produttori Spumante Metodo Classico Alto Adige was formed at Bolzano, most of today's dozen or so producers being members. The grouping is all the more necessary as Alto Adige's DOC *disciplinari* do not provide for any classic method sparklers. Members are responsible for about two-thirds of the total *metodo classico* production (around 450,000 bottles) of the province of Bolzano.

If experience is an essential ingredient of quality then it will come as no surprise that the two best *cantine* for high-class sparkling wines in Alto Adige are the two that have been going the longest. One is **Haderburg** at Salorno, where the provinces of Bolzano and Trentino meet. Luis Ochsenreiter began as a specialist *spumantista* in 1977, giving his wines a lengthy thirty-six months in bottle on the yeasts. At first he bought in the base wines, but over the years he has acquired some 14 hectares of vineyard and extended production to still wines too, notably Sauvignon and Pinot Nero. He remains best known, however, for his sparklers, in particular for his Pas Dosé, a wine in the French style for lightness and yeasty-fruity aroma which in my view would see off many a famous name from north-eastern France.

Josef Reiterer, of **Vivaldi/Arunda** in Meltina, above Terlano, at 1,200 metres one of the highest wineries in Europe, began about the same time. Two ways in which he differs from Ochsenreiter are (1) that he continues to produce sparkling wines only; and (2) that he owns no vineyards and continues to buy in his base wines, the whites mainly from the high slopes of Terlano and lower down in Cornaiano, the Pinot Nero from the classic zone further south, around Salorno. The style reflects the region and his place in it, even if the grapes don't come from vineyards quite as high as the winery (1,200 metres would be *too* high): clean, mountain fresh, floral, fragrant, light and zesty yet penetrating rather than fat and sumptuous, as Franciacorta or Friuli can be. The lead wine is the Brut, topped by the Extra Brut, a *pas dosé* which typifies the Italian advantage in that it is completely convincing even without addition of *liqueur d'expédition* (something that the French originals can rarely do); and the Extra Brut Riserva, vintage wines both, though they don't trumpet the fact. The latter is aged on the yeasts for six years and competes with the non-vintage *barrique*-fermented Cuvée Marianna for *tête de cuvée* position.

TRENTINO

Trentino vies with Lombardy for pride of place among Italian regions producing *metodo classico* wines from Pinot/Chardonnay grapes. In fact Trentino's production exceeds that of Lombardy, with nearly 5 million bottles per annum; but most would award the prize for overall quality to Lombardy, specifically Franciacorta.

Until the late 1960s the history of *metodo classico* wine in Trento was the history of Ferrari, which we will look at shortly. The generic story doesn't really begin until 1984, when a group of producers banded together to form the Istituto Trento DOC Metodo Classico which to this day, with the help of the Istituto Agrario di San Michele all'Adige, oversees production and quality control. Out of this burgeoned, in 1993, the DOC Trento (as distinct from Trentino), indicating, in the same way as Franciacorta, wines (white or rosé) made by the *metodo classico* with Chardonnay, Pinot Nero, Pinot Bianco and in this case also Pinot Meunier grapes.

A curiosity of the denomination, which in most other ways is similar to Franciacorta, is the production of 150 quintals per hectare in the vineyard, 50 per cent more than allowed in the Lombard DOCG. This the producers of Trento conveniently if not entirely convincingly justify by saying that the local training system, called *pergola semplice*, can manage without loss of quality this kind of load for grapes destined for sparkling base wine – wine, that is, in which sugar is less important than aroma and acidity – and, indeed, practically all vineyards for such purposes in the province remain on *pergola*, even though people are gradually switching to *guyot* for still wines.

Prominent among producers of *metodo classico* wines in Trentino are the cooperatives MezzaCorona at Mezzocorona (Rotari Riserva; Rotari Brut Arte Italiana); and Cavit at Trento (Graal; Firmato), these two turning out together about half as much as the market leader (see below), though their aim is to greatly increase production. Others, smaller, but capable of good to excellent quality in a business in which a certain industrialization is necessary for success, are: **Abate Nero** (Extra Dry), Gardolo; **Cesarini Sforza** (Riserva dei Conti), Trento; Concilio Vini (Angelo Grigolli Riserva); Endrizzi (Masetto); **Equipe Trentina** (Equipe 5), Lavis; **Le Brul** (Marchesa Pallavicino); Pojer & Sandri (Cuvée Brut).

Head and shoulders above everyone else in Trentino, indeed one of the cornerstones of high quality fizz in Italy, is the Trento-based firm of:

Ferrari (no relation, although they make the most of the perceived connection with the motor car; apparently Ferrari is the third commonest name in Italy). The founder was Giulio Ferrari who, back in 1902, when Trentino was still part of the Hapsburg Empire, decided on the basis of experiences in Reims and Geisenheim that the Trentino would be an ideal location for the production of Chardonnay and Pinot for sparkling wines.

Cut to 1952, when Bruno Lunelli, *enotechista* of Trento, buys Ferrari out; the company today, in its hi-tech offices-cum-*cantina* off the *autostrada* at Ravina near Trento, is known as Ferrari Fratelli Lunelli. Said *fratelli* are in fact Bruno's sons Franco, Gino and Mauro, now being joined by *their* sons, among whom is the San Michele all'Adige-trained oenologist Marcello. With 9 million bottles in stock at any given time and 3 million being sold annually Ferrari are second after Guido Berlucchi among *metodo classico* producers in Italy and first among members of the ITMC. Grapes for the non-vintage wines are bought in from about 150 growers, many of whom have been with the firm since Ferrari's day, the *cuvées* being 95% Chardonnay, with a touch of Pinot Nero – more than a touch for the Rosé. Minimum time on yeasts is twenty-four months for the Brut and Rosé, rising to thirty for the Maximum Brut and thirty-six for the vintage Perlé, a 100% Chardonnay from the firm's own vineyards, of which they have 70 hectares at uppish altitude. Since 1987 they have been producing, also from their own vines, still Chardonnay-based wines under the *cru* names Villa Margon and Villa Gentilotti, and the empire also extends to water (Surgiva) and grappa (Segnana). Next on the agenda will be red wines, Cabernet and Merlot, and Pinot Nero, from their own vineyards adjoining those of San Leonardo at Avio.

Top of the range, however, will remain the now renowned Riserva del Fondatore Giulio Ferrari, a regular recipient of the coveted Tre Bicchieri award. This is a pure Chardonnay from fifteen (plus)-year-old vineyards which receives between seven and eight years on the lees, like a grand old *récemment dégorgé*. The wine has the light gold colour of mature, not old, Chardonnay, its sparkle being less than ebullient but none the worse for that. The aromas are intensely biscuity, with notes of vanilla and cream, and the palate is concentrated, complex yet elegant. In short, wine of a quality that it is difficult to find, and only then at great price, from Champagne itself. (Hope they don't prosecute.)

A rapid guide to Italian wines*

The purpose of the Rapid Guide, as explained earlier, is to give an overview of Italian wine in a brief space. The same issues are treated in much greater detail in the body of this book and its companion volume.

You start by dividing Italy's twenty regions into four zones: North West, North East, Central and South & Islands. In each zone you highlight the indigenous grape varieties. The 'international varieties', Cabernet and Co., come into a separate section.

Using different type, you indicate the importance of the grapes, wines and production areas mentioned. Thus the great grapes and wines get **CAPITALS IN BOLD**; as do the zones. Those of secondary, but still high rank, get CAPITALS. Third rankers get **bold lower case**. Those of minor interest get SMALL CAPITALS. The rest – those of little or no international interest – are simply omitted. (Note: this system does not relate to the use of type in the main part of the book.)

NORTH WEST

Red
The king here is the **NEBBIOLO** of Piemonte, a notoriously difficult but highly gifted variety capable of making wines of enormous complexity and longevity. Because of its difficult nature its growing area is quite restricted. The main production zones/wines are **BAROLO** and **BARBARESCO**, on either side of the town of Alba. Other wines produced from Nebbiolo are ROERO, an increasingly important zone across the Tanaro river from Alba; **Gattinara** and

*First printed in *Decanter* magazine, Italy 1997 supplement, November 1997; modified for this book.

Ghemme in the northern Piemontese provinces of Vercelli and Novara; **Carema**, on the border with the Aosta region; and **Valtellina**, in northern Lombardy, on the Swiss border.

Alba, capital of the LANGHE hills, is also home to BARBERA, hence BARBERA D'ALBA. Barbera's true home, however, is in the hills of ASTI and **Monferrato**, which give their names to varietal wines. Barbera, with its rich fruity acidity, is grown in several parts of the North West, including **Oltrepò Pavese** in Lombardy and **Colli Piacentini (Gutturnio)** in Emilia. Indeed it is grown all over Italy, but its best varietal wines come from Piemonte, increasingly *barrique*-aged in the finest examples.

Alba and Asti are also among the several growing areas of another Piemontese original, **Dolcetto**, which generally gives easy fruity wines for early drinking. And there are still more from Piemonte: **Freisa**, GRIGNOLINO, PELAVERGA, ROUCHET, and the aromatic **Brachetto**, generally made into a sparkling wine.

Original reds from the rest of the North West do exist, but are generally too obscure to be dealt with here; this is certainly the case for anything from LIGURIA or VALLE D'AOSTA. A decent, plummy red is made in the Oltrepò and Colli Piacentini from CROATINA (here mistakenly called Bonarda); and the GROPPELLO of RIVIERA DEL GARDA ORIENTALE can make a full, spicy wine. One red variety, from Emilia, does need signalling, however, if only for its volume production and its commercial importance: **Lambrusco**. Don't knock it: the serious stuff is dry and comes in several styles from pale and delicate to full and gutsy. Lambrusco can be just the thing for accompanying greasy pork dishes of the Emilian type.

White

Easily the most important white grape of the North West is **MOSCATO BIANCO**, certainly in terms of volume production. Best quality wine is **MOSCATO D'ASTI**, unique in the world for delicacy, aroma and refreshingly acidic sweetness. The fully sparkling *spumante*, today simply called ASTI, does not approach Moscato d'Asti for finesse and character. Like Barbera, Moscato Bianco is grown all over Italy, indeed quite a lot in the Oltrepò Pavese, but is nowhere so important as here. A bit of Moscato *passito*, rich dessert-wine from semi-dried grapes, is made in the Monferrato hills, in Aosta and around Bergamo in Lombardy.

Dry whites have not traditionally been where it's at in Piemontese viniculture, but several natives have risen to importance over the past few years. One thinks first of CORTESE, the grape of GAVI, increasingly produced as a varietal in other parts of south-east Piemonte. The wines may be acidic, even lime-like, in youth, but are capable of ageing surprisingly well.

Arneis is making quite a splash these days. Produced principally in the Roero, it can make a pleasantly broad, multifaceted dry white, though some doubt exists as to its ageing ability.

FAVORITA, in itself, is of lesser importance – there are few wines of real importance made from it. Actually, Favorita is a cousin of VERMENTINO, grown right along the Ligurian coast (as for example in the COLLI DI LUNI), and into Tuscany's Maremma, not to mention widely in Sardinia. Vermentino is rapidly becoming seen as one of Italy's best white varieties in potential.

Other North West whites of real character include Piemonte's ERBALUCE, which makes tasty dry whites and *passiti* from *Caluso*, north of Turin; the PIGATO of Ligure di PONENTE (west of Genoa); and the PIGNATELLO of Emilia, capable of making wines of surprising richness and character.

NORTH EAST

Red
This zone is so locked into Gallic and Germanic varieties that there is not a great deal to say about native grapes. By far the most important is **CORVINA**, chief grape, with RONDINELLA and CORVINONE of **VALPOLICELLA**, from the hills behind Verona, itself probably Italy's capital of wine. Ordinary Valpolicella can be pretty insipid, as we all know too well, but **AMARONE** (near dry) and **RECIOTO** (sweet, made from semi-dried or *passito* grapes), can be not just powerful but amazingly rich and complex – wines, again, unique in the world, and absolutely delicious now that producers have at long last learned to conquer oxidation and pack their bottles with sheer fruit. A less potent and potentially high quality table wine is made from what is called the *ripasso* method, where an ordinary finished Valpolicella wine is 'passed back over' the rich lees of the *passito*, after racking, for a refermentation. For legal reasons such wines are generally referred to as Valpolicella **CLASSICO SUPERIORE**, although this description does not guarantee a *ripasso*.

TEROLDEGO is a grape which, in Trentino, can make some very fine and dense wine, even though in most cases it doesn't. On a similar level must be considered LAGREIN, grown both in Trentino and in the German-speaking Alto Adige. Trentino's **Marzemino** is, in my view, a step down from these in terms of concentration and interest, and the prolific SCHIAVA GENTILE is a good step down from that, making wines generally overstretched and lacking substance. **Schiava Grigia**, or Grauvernatsch as the German speakers call it, has a bit more going for it.

The regions of Veneto and Friuli are scattered with lesser red grape varieties, some of which are capable of some pretty good quality, but none of which are produced in any great quantity. In Veneto there is RABOSO, in Friuli **Refosco**, **Pignolo**, **Schioppettino** and TAZZELENGHE. Worth a try when they're offered, generally not, in the language of Michelin, worth a detour.

White
Of the natives, GARGANEGA is the most important non-foreign variety of the North East, which is a measure of the lack of importance of the native white grapes of the zone. Garganega is behind SOAVE, from the hills east of Verona, and also GAMBELLARA, both of which may come in a Recioto version, that is, from semi-dried grapes.

Prosecco makes interesting, yeasty sparklers in the Valdobbiadene/Conegliano area of Veneto. Trentino's NOSIOLA, **Breganze**'s VESPAIOLA, **COLLIO** and **COLLI ORIENTALI**'s TOCAI FRIU-LANO, Ribolla, **Picolit**, **Verduzzo** and **Malvasia Istriana** are all worthy of mention, though increasingly overshadowed by the French grapes. There is some good **Moscato Giallo**, dry and sweet, from Alto Adige and Trentino.

CENTRAL ITALY

Red
One grape enjoys quasi-total domination throughout north Central Italy, east and west: **SANGIOVESE**. It goes by various names and, according to terroir, transmutes itself into a thousand clones, but it's always essentially Sangiovese. In most cases it is blended with other grapes – local reds, whites (decreasingly), French reds (increasingly) – but as clonal research improves the

stock it is more and more to be found in varietal form.

Sangiovese-based reds are legion in Tuscany. Head of the list, of course, would be **CHIANTI** in its highest manifestations **CLAS-SICO** and **RUFINA; BRUNELLO DI MONTALCINO; VINO NOBILE DI MONTEPULCIANO; CARMIGNANO**; and some **SUPERTUSCANS** of diverse origins. Lesser Tuscans would include the other Chiantis, plus **Morellino di Scansano, Parrina, Pomino, Rosso di Montalcino, Rosso di Montepulciano, Val di Cornia** and several more to boot.

TORGIANO and **Montefalco Rosso** are the more important names in Umbria. In Romagna both the very good and the bloody awful go under the name SANGIOVESE DI ROMAGNA, so it is important to look for qualifying words like 'Superiore' or 'Riserva'. In the Marche **Rosso Piceno** is the nearest thing to a good Sangiovese. From Lazio there is little Sangiovese of distinction.

MONTEPULCIANO (the grape, not the Tuscan town) is the only other red variety with a major presence in Central Italy. Its most prominent manifestation is in the form of **MONTEPUL-CIANO D'ABRUZZO**, from the eponymous region, where it produces vast quantities of mediocrity and the occasional brilliant bottle. The Marche's **Rosso Conero** is the only other DOC of note.

SAGRANTINO DI MONTEFALCO's growing zone in central Umbria may be tiny, but it makes one of Italy's most distinctive reds, powerful and concentrated, especially in the *passito* form.

There are no other Central Italian red grapes of international importance. Tuscany's CILIEGIOLO and CANAIOLO, Latium's CESANESE, the Marche's LACRIMA DI MORRO and VERNACCIA DI SERRAPETRONA can at best be described as bit players.

White

TREBBIANO TOSCANO and MALVASIA BIANCA are ubiquitous in Central Italy, but the enormity of their production is only matched by the mediocrity of their wines, whose names are legion and too inglorious to record. **Malvasia Puntinata**, of Latium, is behind what is best from **Frascati**, which ain't much. Umbria boasts **Grechetto**, Tuscany the overrated **Vernaccia di San Gimignano** and the underrated VERMENTINO. BOMBINO BIANCO, in Romagna called PAGADEBIT, has considerable presence along the east coast. The Marche's favourite son is **VERDICCHIO**, a contender for Italy's best native non-aromatic white grape, especially now that it is being taken seriously in the wake of the mercifully disappearing amphora bottle.

SOUTH & ISLANDS

Red

AGLIANICO, an ancient Greek grape, 100% varietal in Campania's famous **TAURASI** and Basilicata's potentially excellent **AGLIANICO DEL VULTURE,** is often considered the southland's finest red grape. Campania also has PIEDIROSSO which stands behind a number of easy-fruity reds including LACRIMA CHRISTI ROSSO.

Puglia's Salentino peninsula boasts two important red varieties which modern technique and technology are whipping into shape as succulent, round, fruity numbers, NEGROAMARO and PRIMITIVO (= Zinfandel). The first, of Greek origin, is the main component of COPERTINO, SALICE SALENTINO, BRINDISI ROSSO and others of lesser renown. The second attains its potent and concentrated best from the flat, bush-trained vineyards of the commune of Manduria, near Taranto. UVA DI TROIA, at home in central Puglia, notably in CASTEL DEL MONTE ROSSO, also has merit.

From Calabria there is little apart from **Gaglioppo,** but considering that grape's ability to produce Barolo look-alikes at much lower prices that's not nothing. **Cirò** is the only internationally significant production zone.

Sicily's principal home-grown red is NERO D'AVOLA, a variety of impressive levels of colour, concentration, natural sugar and, less attractively, tartaric acid, which, when harmonized, can make wines of very high calibre. FRAPPATO, behind the fragrant CERASUOLO DI VITTORIA, is another interesting grape, as can be NERELLO MASCALESE, they say, though personally I have never been turned on by any of its wines, which include ETNA ROSSO.

Sardinia's **Cannonau,** a close relative of Grenache, makes Rhône-like wines from many parts of the island. **Carignano,** akin to Spain's beefy Cariñena, is concentrated more in the south of the island. MONICA is home-grown, making wines of medium body and easy drinkability.

White

The South has a surprising range of really interesting white grapes, including Campania's FALANGHINA, **Fiano** and CODA DI VOLPE, not to mention the FORASTERA and BIANCOLELLA of the island of Ischia. GRECO is a variety of extraordinary diversity and character, found under the same general name, though from quite divergent clones, not just in Campania but also in northern Puglia and throughout Calabria.

Sicily's white heritage is as impressive as that of Campania, with GRILLO, the quality grape of MARSALA; INZOLIA, behind many of the best native white table wines of the island; GRE-CANICO, an excellent back-up grape; CATARRATTO, produced in massive profusion in the west of the island (Alcamo DOC, commercial Marsala, vermouth base), but capable of some character when from a low-yielding, high-altitude site. Sweet whites of tremendous character are made from **Malvasia** and ZIBIBBO or Moscato di Alessandria, the former mainly in the Aeolian islands north of Sicily (**Malvasia delle Lipari**), the latter in Pantelleria to the south (MOSCATO PASSITO DI PANTELLERIA).

Sardinia also specializes in full, rich whites from Malvasia, Moscato, the native NASCO (sweet) and VERNACCIA DI ORISTANO (dry aperitif). Dry white table wines of character can come from **Nuragus,** TORBATO and especialy from that VERMENTINO which brings us back in a loop to Liguria and the North West.

As for the 'international varieties': **MERLOT, CABERNET SAU-VIGNON, CABERNET FRANC** and PETIT VERDOT have been in residence in northern Italy, especially the North East, for well over a century, flourishing especially post-phylloxera. The same is true of the Burgundy family, **PINOT NOIR, PINOT GRIGIO, PINOT BIANCO** and **CHARDONNAY.** Today both the Bordeaux and the Burgundy grapes are spreading to all parts of Italy, being used both as blending or 'improving' grapes and varietally, on occasion at quality levels which rival the best in the world. The Rhône varieties, SYRAH and VIOGNIER, ROUSSANNE and MARSANNE, are making their presence felt increasingly in Central Italy. The Teutonics – **Rheinriesling, Traminer,** MÜLLER-THURGAU, SYLVANER and others – have been ensconced in the North West since the Austrian occupation, but tend at most to trickle to other parts.

Glossary

---

agronomo – agriculturist.
albese – referring to the wine zone of Alba in Piemonte.
amabile – medium sweet.
Amarone – see Recioto.
ampelography – (the study) of vines.
anthocyanins – colouring matter in the skins of grapes.
appassimento – the process of drying grapes to concentrate their sugar
    content. The grapes are either laid on cane or bamboo racks (or more
    recently in wooden fruit crates) or they are hung from wires, usually in
    a room with a non-insulated roof and plenty of windows which can be
    opened to allow for dry air to circulate or closed to keep out moisture.
    Wine made with these dried grapes is designated *passito*.
aromas (primary, secondary, tertiary) – referring to the aromatic sub-
    stances in grapes (primary), finished wines (secondary) or aged wines
    (tertiary).
assemblaggio – the putting together of different parts of a blend.
astigiano – referring to the wine-zone of Asti, as in Barbera d'Asti.
autochthonous – indigenous.
autoclave – pressurized, thermo-controllable stainless steel container for
    purposes of fermenting or storing wine, especially sparkling.
azienda – estate; *azienda agricola/agraria* – estate whose wines are made
    entirely or mostly from grapes grown at the property; *azienda leader*
    (sic) – an Italian phrase for 'leading producer' (of a given zone).
barolista – Barolo producer.
barricato – fermented and/or stored in *barrique*.
barrique – French term for a small barrel of 225 to 350 litres' capacity.
bâtonnage – French term, widely used in Italy, for the stirring up of the
    lees in barrel, with a more or less sophisticated form of *bâton* (stick).
bianco – white; *in bianco* – of red grapes vinified off the skins, as if they
    were white (what the French call *blanc de noirs*).
blocked fermentation – fermentation which stops before completion

when yeasts are no longer able to transform sugars into alcohol.

botrytis (cinerea) – a grey mould that forms on ripe grapes at harvest-time; negative in cases where skins are split, it can be positive for the making of sweet wines where skins are only punctured by tiny holes, in which case it is called 'noble rot' (in Italian, *'muffa nobile'*).

bricco, bric – in Piemonte, a hilltop.

botte – wooden barrel of wide-ranging capacity – anything from around 10 to 100 hectolitres or more; traditionally of chestnut or, more recently, of oak from Slavonia, more recently still of oak from France.

campanilistic – from *campanilismo*, an attitude of mind which concerns itself only with events happening within sight or sound of the village bell-tower (*campanile*).

cantina – winery.

cantina sociale – cooperative winery; *c.s. di secondo grado* – cooperative which bottles wines vinified by producing cooperatives.

cantiniere – cellar master.

cascade – when a wine which might qualify for a higher DOC is down-graded, for reasons of quality, image or commerce, to one of less stringent requirements, the process is called 'cascade'.

cascina – farmhouse, sometimes designating an estate, especially in the north-west.

chaptalization – the adding of cane or beet sugar to wine musts before fermentation in order to increase alcohol; illegal in Italy, widely practised in France and Germany.

charmat – a method, named after its French originator, of inducing secondary fermentation in sparkling wines in large volumes (see *autoclave*).

ciabot – Piemontese word for a small shepherd's shelter, today used to indicate a particular vineyard or part of a vineyard.

classico – the historic section of a long-established wine zone, as distinct from the part tacked on, generally in the twentieth century. (Also means 'classic' in the normal sense.)

colle/colli – hill/hills.

collina/colline – smaller hill/hills.

commerciante – dealer in bought-in grapes or wines; French equivalent is *négociant*.

commune – Italian *comune,* the smallest administrative unit, comprising one or several towns or villages (see also *frazione*).

conca – literally 'shell'; refers to hills in the shape of a shell, concave and heat-retaining.

cordone speronato – (English 'cordon spur'); a vine-shaping method whereby a mature branch, as distinct from a new cane (*guyot*), is trained horizontally along a wire; with *guyot* one of the two methods referred to by the term *spalliera* (see below).

crio-maceration – refers to the retention of juice on skins at low temperature for purposes of extracting aromatic substances (in respect of whites), or colour (reds) with minimum leaching of tannins.

cru – French term for a particular plot, or its wine. Italians have borrowed the term but interpreted it more broadly to indicate anything from a growth (in the French sense) to a marketing name.

cutting-wine – cheap wine, generally of deep colour or high alcohol, or both, used to improve wines that are deficient.

damigiana – large, often raffia-wrapped bottle containing around fifty litres, used for selling wine in bulk to individuals or for storage of excess or topping-up wines.

dégorgement – French term, often preferred by Italians to their own '*sboccatura*', referring to that process in the making of bottle-fermented sparkling wines when the inverted bottle, the *remuage* (q.v.) process completed, is opened and the sediment trapped in the neck ejected. See also *liqueur d'exédition* and *metodo classico*.

denominazione(i) – wine name(s), equivalent to French *appellation*.

diradamento – the cutting away of already formed bunches in order to increase concentration of extract in those remaining.

disciplinare – rules governing a particular DOC.

DOC(G) – *Denominazione di Origine Controllata* (*e Garantita*); the Italian quality designation. DOC guarantees origin, grape type(s), aspects of production, but not necessarily quality. DOCG is supposed also to guarantee a minimum level of quality. See also multi-DOC.

enologo – winemaker or expert; *enotecnico* – qualified wine technician.

enoteca/enoteche – wine-shop(s); can be a wine bar, even a restaurant.

fattoria – largish farm, not to be confused with English 'factory'.

frazione – part of a *comune*.

frizzante – semi-sparkling.

fusto – barrel of 5 to 7.5 hectolitres' capacity; the French equivalent is *tonneau*.

Geneva Double Curtain (GDC) – a system of training vines, developed by Professor Nelson Shaulis at Geneva in New York State, which encourages production by dividing the canopy of each plant into two sections.

giro a poggio – the planting of a vineyard in rows which follow a hill's contours horizontally.

governo all'uso toscano – a slight refermentation caused by pouring a finished wine over partially dried grapes.

graticci – cane or bamboo mats on which bunches intended for *passito* wines are laid to dry (see *appassimento*).

grigio – grey; in grape terms, between black and white.

guyot – see *cordone speronato.*

IGT – Indicazione Geografica Tipica; the higher form of Vino da Tavola (q.v.), equivalent to French Vin de Pays.

imbottigliato (a) – bottled (at).

in bianco – see *bianco.*

in purezza – at 100 per cent.

kellermeister – German for *cantiniere* (q.v.), cellar master; term employed in South Tyrol.

layering – the propagation of new vines by working branches of existing vines into the soil; no longer practised because the danger of phylloxera forces planting on American rootstock.

liqueur d'expédition – referring to bottle-fermented sparkling wines, after *dégorgement* (French) or *sboccatura* (Italian), when the deposit is removed, a liquid, usually of sugar dissolved in brandy, is added by way of replacement.

liquoroso – wine of high alcoholic degree, generally over 15 per cent, generally fortified.

lotta guidata ed integrata – an ecological approach to viticulture, not always synonymous with organic viticulture.

malo-lactic fermentation – the transformation, these days induced in most red wines immediately following the alcoholic fermentation, of the grape's natural malic, or appley, acid into the much milder lactic, or milky, acid.

millesimato – vintage, as in 'vintage champagne'.

metodo classico – refers to the method, used in Champagne, of inducing an alcoholic refermentation in bottle (as distinct from in tank) by adding yeasts and sugars to the made wine prior to bottling; the process is completed by *remuage* (see *pupitre*) and *dégorgement* (q.v.).

mosto – must, unfermented grape juice.

mosto concentrato rettificato (mcr) – rectified concentrated must, a neutral sugary liquid made from grape juice(generally excess southern Italian production), used for increasing sugar levels in a must (alcohol levels in a wine) in a situation where the use of cane sugar is forbidden, as it is throughout Italy for still wines.

multi-DOC – neologism (invented by myself) for an 'umbrella' DOC, such as Collio, which has many sub-DOCs (e.g. Collio Pinot Bianco, Collio Merlot, Collio Chardonnay, etc.). A sub-multi-DOC would be a multi-DOC under a wider multi-DOC, e.g. Valle Isarco, which comes under the multi-DOC Alto Adige, but which itself stands as an umbrella for various varietal DOCs.

normale – a non-official term widely used to designate the basic wine of a given type, e.g. Valpolicella *normale* as distinct from Classico Superiore or *cru.*

oenology – the study or science of wine; oenologist – winemaker.

organoleptic – pertaining to or perceived by a sensory organ; commonly used in wine-tasting parlance.

oidium – powdery mildew, which attacks leaves, stalks and grapes, capable of ruining wine and, ultimately, destroying the vine; dealt with by sulphur, generally mixed in powder form with the copper sulphate spray used against peronospera (q.v.).

paese – means both country, as in nation, and village.

pas dosé – not given any *liqueur d'expédition* (q.v.).

passito – a wine made by the process of *appassimento* (q.v.).

patrimonio – the inheritance handed down by previous generations.

pergola – high-training method enabling a single vine to produce multiple bunches; gradually being replaced as a training system as quality becomes increasingly an imperative. *Pergola trentina* involves a cordon trained at an upward angle on the trellis; on the *pergola veronese* the cordon is trained at a right angle to the trunk.

peronospera – commonly known as mildew; controlled by copper sulphate sprays.

phylloxera – aphid of American origin which destroys European *Vitis vinifera* vines by gnawing at their roots, the solution being to graft European plants on to American rootstock.

pianura – the plain.

podere – a small farm.

poggio – hill, mainly in central Italy.

polyphenols – substances present in grapeskins, including anthocyanins (q.v.) and tannins.

privati – private individuals.

profumato – scented.

province – see region.

pupitre de remuage – riddling desk, in the champagne method; the bottles, upon completion of the secondary fermentation, are placed in holes at a downward angle and are shaken and turned periodically in order to work the sediment down the bottle on to the upturned cork.

quintal, *quintale* – still widely used term for 100 kilos of grapes or 100 litres of wine; now replaced in official parlance by *tonnellata* (1000 kilos).

Recioto – sweet *passito* (q.v.) wine made from dried grapes in Verona; dry equivalent is called Amarone (from *amaro* = bitter + *one* = big). See also *appassimento*.

region – specifically, a region in Italy is like a state in the USA. There are twenty of them, and they are divided into provinces, named after their principal city. In this book the word 'region' is also sometimes used in the normal sense.

Ricasolian – after Baron Ricasoli, a nineteenth-century Tuscan statesman who found time while not politicking to lay down the code of practice (including an *uvaggio* which included Trebbiano and Malvasia as well as Sangiovese and Canaiolo) for the making of Chianti.

Rinascimento – Italian for renaissance or rebirth. As I have said elsewhere, I fail to understand why English-speaking people have to use a French word for an Italian phenomenon.

ripasso – a process, mainly used in Valpolicella, whereby a finished wine is 'passed back over' the sugar-rich lees of Recioto after racking of the latter for a further small fermentation.

riserva – principally used in an official capacity to indicate a wine which has been aged longer than the equivalent *normale* (q.v.).

ritocchino – the planting of a vineyard in rows which follow a hill's descent.

rosato – pink, rosé.

rosso – red.

selvatico – wild

serbatoio – large wine container, tank.

sfuso – in bulk.

socio/soci – member(s).

sofisticazione – fraud.

sorì – Piemontese dialect word indicating a vineyard with southern exposure.

sottozona – with particular reference to wine law 164 of 1992, an officially recognized sub-zone or 'geographical sub-denomination' (see Barolo or Barbaresco: The Best Sites).

spalliera – see *cordone speronato*.

specializzazione – the practice of planting vines as an exclusive crop in a given terrain.

spumante – sparkling; *spumantista* – producer of sparkling wines.

sub-DOC – see multi-DOC.

sub-multi-DOC – see multi-DOC

sub-zone – used in this book in two ways: (1) loosely, to indicate a geographical area within one of the four 'zones' of Italy; (2) precisely, as translation of the official term '*sottozona*' (q.v.).

superiore – an official term indicating a wine with a little more alcohol, perhaps a little extra age, compared with the *normale* of the same.

SuperPiemontese – neologism derived from 'SuperTuscan', meaning a Tuscan wine of high quality which does not conform to local or traditional norms.

tendone – literally 'big tent'; high-producing, high training system adopted in hot areas, using leaf canopy to shade the grapes.

terra bianca – terrain which is white due to a high chalk content.

terroir – a combination of factors involved in grape and therefore wine quality, relating particularly to soil and climate but also sometimes to viticultural practices and tradition generally.

tino/tini – vat(s); often used specifically to refer to the sort of upright oaken container making an increasing comeback as a fermentation vessel for red wines.

tipicità– sometimes translated as 'typicity', this refers to a given wine's level of conformity to a norm or type.

titolare – the person after whom, for example, an estate is named.

toar – a mineral-rich volcanic soil, very friable, found in Valpolicella.

tonneau(x) – see *fusto*.

Tre Bicchieri – top award in the annual Gambero Rosso/Slow Food guide to Italian wines, *Vini d'Italia*.

tunnel – a recent invention designed to achieve the first 10 per cent or so of the *appassimento* (q.v.) process under synthetic conditions, thus practically eliminating any subsequent risk of rot.

umbrella-DOC – see multi-DOC.

uvaggio – mix of grapes in a given blend; *uvaggio di vigneto* – where the said mix of grapes exists in the vineyard itself.

V.A. – see volatile acidity

vasca – vat

vendemmia – vintage, harvest; *vendemmia tardiva* – late harvest.

vigna, vigneto – vineyard.

vigniaolo – grape grower.

viniculture – the culture of wine.

vino da meditazione – 'meditation wine', i.e. a wine of such concentration and richness that it lends itself to being sipped on its own, meditatively.

vino da tavola – table wine, in ordinary sense.

Vino da Tavola – in the legal sense, refers to what is supposedly the lower grade of wine (but which in Italy has often been the highest); Vino da Tavola con Indicazione Geografica – pre-mid-1990s way of describing on labels a table wine of a particular provenance.

viticoltore – grape grower; both a *vignaiolo* and a *viticoltore* may also make wine.

viticulture – the growing of grapes.

volatile acidity – acetic or vinagary acid, present in tiny doses in all wines but negative in larger doses; 'volatile' because it comes out on the nose. Abbreviated as V.A.

Key to Italian Pronunciation

Italian is almost entirely phonetic and follows simple rules of pronunciation, unlike French and especially English. A few minutes studying those rules will be found to be deeply rewarding in respect of the study of Italian wines and is strongly recommended.

a – as in 'pat'

b – as English

c – **always** pronounced 'k' except before 'e' or 'i' when it is like English 'ch' ('chop'); conversely 'h' hardens 'c' before 'e' or 'i'. So *Ciampi* = **champ**-ee, *Chianti* = **kyan**-tee

d – as English

e – as in 'pet'

f – as English

g – **always** pronounced 'g' ('got') except before 'e' or 'i' when it is like English 'j' ('jot'); 'h' hardens 'g' before 'e' or 'i'. Consider *Giotto* (= **jot**-to), *spaghetti*. Also see *gl*, *gn*, below

h – silent as in cockney; but see 'c' and 'g'

i – as 'ee' ('feet') when dominant in a syllable, e.g. *trattoria* (= trat-to-**ree**-a); as 'y' when subordinate to a following vowel, e.g. **kyan**-tee; or just as a softener (*Ciampi*, *Giotto*)

j – as 'y' ('yet'), rarely occurs

k – as English, rarely occurs

l – as English; but see *gl* below

m – as English

n – as English; but see *gn* below

o – as in 'pot'

p – as English

qu – always pronounced 'kw' (e.g. *questo* = **kwes**-to)

r – pronounced using tip of tongue, as in Scottish

s – as English, though sometimes pronounced as 'z' alone in middle of word. Compare *spesso* (= **spes**-so; often) and *speso* (= **spe**-zo, spent).

t – as English
u – as 'oo' ('boot')
v – as English
w – as 'v', rarely occurs
x – as English, rarely occurs
y – occurs extremely rarely
z – 'ts' or 'dz'

ANOMALIES

gl – as 'ly', e.g. *Aglianico* = a-**lya**-nee-ko
gn – as 'ny', e.g. *agnello* = a-**nyel**-lo
sc – before 'e' or 'i', pronounced as English 'sh' as in 'show'. Thus *scelto*
(= **shel**-to, selected)
double consonants: both are pronounced. Compare *cane* (= **ka**-ne; dog)
and *canne* (= **kan**-ne; canes); *latte* (= **lat**-te; milk) and *lato* (= **la**-to; side)

STRESS

Usually falls on penultimate syllable, e.g. *Barolo* (= ba-**ro**-lo), *Barbaresco*
(= bar-bar-**es**-co). If on final syllable, it is written with a grave accent, e.g.
Cirò (= chee-**ro**), *Prapò* (= pra-**po**). Sometimes occurs on third syllable
from last, in which case there is no orthographic clue, e.g. *Garganega* (=
gar-**ga**-ne-ga), *Aglianico* (= a-**lya**-nee-ko); you just have to know.

Bibliography

Anderson, Burton, *Wine Atlas of Italy*, London, Mitchell Beazley, 1990.
Belfrage, Nicolas, *Life Beyond Lambrusco*, London, Sidgwick & Jackson, 1985.
Bertini, Luigi, *Terre & vini di Gavi*, Gavi, 1990.
Busso, Mario and Minetti, Giovanni, *Roero Arneis*, Torino, Barisone.
Consorzio Barbera d'Asti e Barbera del Monferrato, *Barbera*, Asti, Sagittario, 1994.
Di Lello, Luciano, *Viaggio nel nuovo vino italiano*, Roma, Lithos, 1997.
Enoteca Italiana, *Il paese del vino/The Wine Country – Guide to the DOC and DOCG Wines* (in English and Italian); compiled and regularly updated by the Enoteca Italiana, Siena.
Fezzi, Elisabetta and Penna, Fabrizio, *Bollicine di classe – Guida ai migliori vini italiani prodotti con il metodo classico*, Milano, Mondadori, 1996.
Filiputti, Walter, *Terre, vigne e vini del Friuli V.G.*, Udine, Gianfranco Angelico Benvenuto, 1983.
Fregoni and Schiavi, *I primi cento nostri vitigni*, Civiltà del Bere, 1996.
Gambero Rosso/Slow Food, *Vini d'Italia* or, in English-language version, *Italian Wines*; highly useful annual guide to the wines of Italy, with evaluations of wines and brief discussion on developments in featured wineries over the past 12 months; use also for locating wineries in communes and for telephone numbers.
Garner, Michael and Merritt, Paul, *Barolo, Tar and Roses – A Study of the Wines of Alba*, London, Random Century, 1990.
Mannini, Schneider, Gerbi and Credi, *Cloni selezionati dal Centro di Studio per il miglioramento genetico della vite*, Torino, Consiglio Nazionale delle Ricerche, 1989.
Maroni, Luca, *Annuario dei Migliori Vini Italiani* (annual); also *Guide to Italian Wines* (English edition, annual); also *The Taste of Wine*, quarterly review, Roma, Lm s.r.l. edizioni.
Martinelli, Massimo, *Il Barolo come lo vedo io*, Asti, Sagittario, 1993.

Masneghetti, Alessandro, *Enogea* (bi-monthly review of mainly Italian wines, very useful for keeping up to date and getting unbiased, intelligent view); by subscription only, available from fax (0039) 039 2302601.

Ministero dell Risorse Agricole, Alimentari e Forestali, *Riepilogo delle produzioni provinciali di vini DOC e DOCG* (updated annually).

Ministero dell'Agricoltura e delle Foreste, *Principali vitigni da vino coltivati in Italia* (4 vols); Roma, 1952–1965.

Molon, G., *Ampelografia*, Milano, 1906.

Mondini, Salvatore, *I vitigni stranieri da vino coltivati in Italia*, Firenze, 1903.

O'Toole, Tom, *South Tyrol Wine Guide*, Chamber of Commerce, Bolzano.

Paolini, Davide, *Guida alle città del vino d'Italia*, Milano, Sterling & Kupfer, 1996

Paronetto, Lamberto, *Viti e vini di Verona*, Verona, INTEC, 1991.

Pittaro, Piero and Plozner, Lisio, *L'uva e il vino*, Udine, Magnus, 1982.

Silvestri, Giuseppe, *La Valpolicella*, Verona, 1983.

Steinberg, Edward, *The Vines of San Lorenzo*, Hopewell, NJ, Ecco Press, 1992.

Supp, Eckhard, *Enciclopedia del vino italiano/Enzyklopadie des Italienischen Weins* (invaluable for facts and profiles on wineries throughout Italy; useful for facts on Italian wine generally; in Italian and German); Offenbach, Enotria News, 1995.

Veronelli, Luigi, et al., *I vini di Veronelli* (useful for evaluating wines of Italy and for determining grape mix of wines if not official; also for locating wineries in communes and for telephone and fax numbers); Bergamo, Veronelli Editore, annual.

Index